# Be Your Own
# Financial Adviser

**FT** Prentice Hall
FINANCIAL TIMES

In an increasingly competitive world, we believe it's quality of thinking that gives you the edge – an idea that opens new doors, a technique that solves a problem, or an insight that simply makes sense of it all. The more you know, the smarter and faster you can go.

That's why we work with the best minds in business and finance to bring cutting-edge thinking and best learning practice to a global market.

Under a range of leading imprints, including *Financial Times Prentice Hall*, we create world-class print publications and electronic products bringing our readers knowledge, skills and understanding, which can be applied whether studying or at work.

To find out more about Pearson Education publications, or tell us about the books you'd like to find, you can visit us at **www.pearsoned.co.uk**

# Be Your Own Financial Adviser

## The comprehensive guide to wealth and financial planning

Jonquil Lowe

**Financial Times
Prentice Hall
is an imprint of**

Harlow, England • London • New York • Boston • San Francisco • Toronto • Sydney • Singapore • Hong Kong
Tokyo • Seoul • Taipei • New Delhi • Cape Town • Madrid • Mexico City • Amsterdam • Munich • Paris • Milan

PEARSON EDUCATION LIMITED

Edinburgh Gate
Harlow CM20 2JE
Tel: +44 (0)1279 623623
Fax: +44 (0)1279 431059
Website: www.pearsoned.co.uk

First published in Great Britain in 2010

© Pearson Education Limited 2010

The right of Jonquil Lowe to be identified as author of this work has been asserted by her in accordance with the Copyright, Designs and Patents Act 1988.

Pearson Education is not responsible for the content of third party internet sites.

ISBN: 978-0-273-72779-8

*British Library Cataloguing-in-Publication Data*
A catalogue record for this book is available from the British Library

*Library of Congress Cataloging-in-Publication Data*
Lowe, Jonquil.
  Be your own financial adviser : the comprehensive guide to wealth and financial planning / Jonquil Lowe.
    p. cm.
  Includes index.
  ISBN 978-0-273-72779-8 (pbk.)
  1. Finance, Personal. I. Title.
  HG179.L688 2010
  332.024--dc22
                        2010002465

10 9 8 7 6 5 4 3 2
14 13 12

Typeset in 9pt Stone Serif by 30
Printed and bound in Great Britain by Ashford Colour Press, Gosport

The publisher's policy is to use paper manufactured from sustainable forests.

# Contents

# Introduction

When I first started to write about financial planning, I likened making personal financial decisions without any plan to setting out on a long journey without a map. Since then, GPS (global positioning system) has become standard equipment in vehicles, enabling motorists to successfully reach a destination without advance planning – though the route may be less than ideal. There is no GPS for financial planning. In most cases, there is no last minute detour or short-cut that can save your finances if you have set out on completely the wrong track. Especially when it comes to long-term goals such as having a comfortable retirement, paying for education or leaving an inheritance. Without a plan you put yourself at high risk of failing to reach your destination at all. Even with shorter-term financial goals, the lack of a plan can mean you pay over the odds, get caught out by the small print or have the wrong products altogether. To avoid joining the one in five pensioners who live in poverty[1] or the 3,000 people who take a complaint to the Financial Ombudsman every day[2], or the countless others who silently put up with shoddy products, poor service and bad outcomes, planning ahead is essential.

Financial planning means systematically working out and prioritising your goals, appraising your resources, identifying generic solutions (in other words, the broad systems and schemes that would work for you), tracking down the most suitable products and providers, and regularly reviewing progress to keep your plan on track. Chapter 1 describes this process in detail. There is a further element which should be added to any financial plan whether for a large banking institution, an international company, a small business, or your own household: that is stress testing. (We have all learned from the global financial crisis that hit the world in 2007.) We seem to live in an ever more volatile world and ordinary people like you

[1] House of Commons Work and Pensions Select Committee, *Tackling pensioner poverty*, July 2009.

[2] Financial Ombudsman Service, *Annual review 2008/09*.

and me are increasingly forced to engage with it as the State puts greater pressure on individuals and households to provide financially for themselves. Any financial plan must be robust in the face of this volatility. You can't know what the future holds, but you can pre-test your plan to see how it would be affected if a range of possible changes and events were to occur. The UK regulators have stress tested the big banks to see how robust they are; households need to do the same. Therefore, as each chapter of this book looks at a key area of financial planning – protecting your income (Chapter 3), providing for your family (Chapter 4), planning for health and care (Chapter 5), organising where you live (Chapter 6), building a pension (Chapter 7), making decisions at retirement (Chapter 8), saving and investing (Chapter 9), managing your wealth (Chapter 10) and planning inheritance (Chapter 11) – it will also suggest ways to stress test the plans you create.

Hopefully, you are convinced of the need for financial planning. But why be your own adviser? Why not rely on a professional? Financial advice has had, and is still experiencing, a long and painful evolution from glorified selling to the status of a profession. There have always been good, highly professional advisers but picking them out from the mass of the mediocre and downright bad has been no easy task. Financial advice has been regulated for over two decades, so you might wonder why there are still questions over the quality and professionalism of advisers. Part of the answer lies in the strength of insurance companies, banks and other big financial providers which have, for example, resisted the abolition of the 'commission system' that has rewarded advisers according to what and how much they sell rather than the quality of the advice they give. The distorting effect of payment by commission has been at the root of many scandals over the years, such as endowment mis-selling (see Chapter 6) and pensions mis-selling (Chapter 7). At last, the regulators have grasped the nettle and payment for investment advice by commission is due to be abolished from 2012 onwards (see Chapter 2). This may signal the start of financial advisers becoming part of a proper profession, in the same way as solicitors and accountants.

Even now, not all financial advisers are paid by commission. Advisers whom you pay by fee have no incentive to sell you unwanted or unsuitable products. But consumers often baulk at paying £75 to £250 an hour for advice[3]. In some cases, the nature of your financial planning issue may

---

[3]  http://www.unbiased.co.uk/independent-financial-advice/how-to-pay-for-advice.
Accessed 14 August 2009.

be too small to warrant such an outlay. In other cases, you may be unsure that the cost of the advice really will be reflected in a superior plan. This book, by showing you what is involved in creating good financial plans, will help you decide whether the tasks involved are ones you want to take on yourself or whether using an adviser would be money well spent. It will also guide you through the process of selecting an adviser and ensure that you have the background knowledge to appraise and make the most of the adviser's skills and resources. In practice, you are likely to mix-and-match, using an adviser where issues are complex or finding information would be hard or time-consuming, but in many areas fully able to be your own financial adviser.

## Note

This book was written in late 2009 and takes into account tax measures implemented in the Finance Act 2009 and proposals announced in the Pre-Budget Report on 9 December 2009.

# Acknowledgements

I liken writing a book to giving birth: in the joy of publication, one forgets the preceding pain which is inevitably shared by family and close friends. I would like to thank them – particularly Tom and Michael – for their great tolerance and support. Most especially, my thanks go to my daughter, Natasha, who braved my handwriting to type some of the early drafts, written on trains and trips away. Finally, I must thank the editors and team at Pearson who encouraged me in this project in difficult circumstances and whose care, attention and careful editing I cannot praise enough.

## Publisher's acknowledgements

We are grateful to the following for permission to reproduce copyright material:

**Figures**

Figure 1.7 from http://www.fsa.gov.uk/tables, accessed 20 August 2009, © Copyright of the Financial Services Authority 2009; Figure 3.2 from www.direct.gov.uk/redundancy.dsb. Crown Copyright material is reproduced with the permission of the Controller, Office of Public Sector Information (OPSI); Figure 6.4 from Financial Services Authority, 2009, Trademark No 3866688, The Key Facts Logo; Figure 10.2 from www.advfn.com/index/StockMarketIndices.asp.

**Tables**

Table 1.1 from Energy Saving Trust; Table 2.2 from FSA Handbook, *Rule PRIN 2.1.1*, http/fsahandbook.info/FSA/html/handbook/PRIN/2/1, accessed 24 August 2009, © Copyright of the Financial Services Authority 2009; Tables 3.3, 4.2, 8.4 after *Investment, Life & Pensions Moneyfacts* (Moneyfacts August 2009); Table 5.2 from www.spirehealthcare.com; Table 7.1 after *Family Spending*, November (Office for National Statistics 2008), Crown Copyright material is reproduced with the permission of the

Controller, Office of Public Sector Information (OPSI); Table 9.1 from Barclays 2009 Equity Gilt Study, Barclays Capital; Table 9.10 from Debt Management Office, 2009, Purchase and Sale Service. Terms and Conditions. http://www-uk. computershare.com; Table 10.2 from Association of Private Client Investment Managers and Stockbrokers, 2009, http://www.apcims.co.uk/investors/private_ investor_indicies.php.

**Text**

The following case studies have been used with kind permission of Financial Ombudsman Service:  Case Study on page 59 from Financial Ombudsman Service, *Ombudsman News*, January/February (2006),  Case Study on page 83 from Financial Ombudsman Service, *Ombudsman News*, January (2002), Case Study (1) on page 294 from Financial Ombudsman Service, *Ombudsman News*, August (2001), Case Study (2) on page 294 from Financial Ombudsman Service, *Ombudsman News*, March (2003), Case Study on page 319 from Financial Ombudsman Service, *Ombudsman News*, May (2002) – The illustrative case studies in 'Ombudsman News' are based broadly on real-life cases but are not precedents. Individual cases are decided on their own facts; Extract on page 245 adapted from *Shaping the Future Together* (Department of Health, July 2009); Extract on page 245 adapted from *A New Pension Settlement for the Twenty-First Century. The Second Report of the Pensions Commission*, 'Second Turner Report', The Stationery Office (Pensions Commission 2005), Crown Copyright material is reproduced with permission under the terms of the Click-Use License.

**The Financial Times**

Table 5.3 after *Money Management* (September 2008); Table 10.1 after *Money Management* (January 1998–December 2009).

In some instances we have been unable to trace the owners of copyright material, and we would appreciate any information that would enable us to do so.

part

1

# Planning and advice

# 1

# Financial planning

## Introduction

Talk to people from older generations and they often have an attitude of 'make do' and may be grateful for whatever help the State provides. They remember years of rationing, poor standards of housing, and parents or grandparents who could not retire because they had no pension. As the UK has become wealthier, our aspirations have changed. We don't want to just 'make do': we want to live life to the full.

Although state safety nets for periods of illness, unemployment, bereavement and retirement still exist – and in value equal around a quarter of the UK's total national income – they have become inadequate to support the lifestyle that most people want. To contain the cost, some state support – such as NHS dentistry – has been eroded virtually to nothing. Typically, cash state benefits have become more difficult to qualify for and less generous, as shown in Figure 1.1 which demonstrates how key state benefits have fallen over the past 20 years relative to the earnings they replace.

There is an emphasis on self help, which started with the Thatcher governments of 1979–90 and is continuing today, for example, through the debates about who should pay for long-term care as a large proportion of the population enter older age (see Chapter 5). Government support now often takes the form of schemes to encourage you to build up your own savings and pensions as an alternative to catching you in a state safety net. As a result, everyone increasingly needs to engage with financial products and services and take decisions to ensure their own financial well-being.

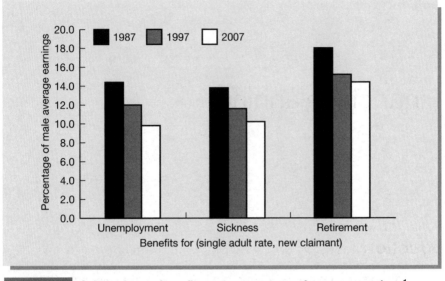

Figure 1.1    Selected state benefits as a percentage of average earnings[1]

[1] Unemployment benefit or jobseeker's allowance, sickness benefit or incapacity benefit and state basic pension for a single adult as a percentage of male full-time earnings.

*Sources*: Central Statistical Office, *Annual Abstract*, 1989 edition; Office for National Statistics, *Annual Abstract*, 2000 and 2009 editions.

# How financial planning works

Simply accessing financial products and services is not difficult – there is no shortage of commercials, advertisements, direct mail, email and marketing calls to entice you to take out loans, buy insurance and invest your money. But taking out products as a knee-jerk reaction to a sales pitch – or even worse a scam – is a hit and miss approach to ensuring your financial health. Financial planning is a systematic approach that starts with you and arrives at well-thought-out decisions about the courses of action and financial products that are most suitable for you personally, given your own particular circumstances, attitudes, beliefs and timescale.

Financial planning is a framework that you can use to make any financial decision. There is no single, hard and fast method. The framework presented in this book is a six-stage model, as shown in Figure 1.2, but you can adapt this. In particular, some financial decisions – such as buying car insurance – are very familiar and usually straightforward, so using such a model may seem overkill. But, with more complicated and/or infrequent decisions, you may find it helpful to work through all six stages.

As you can see from Figure 1.2, financial planning is a continuous process. In the context of a single goal, it ends only when that goal is achieved which may be many years or decades away. In the context of a lifetime of goals, financial planning is not a one-off exercise but a lifetime habit – less like a crash diet, more like a permanent change in eating habits.

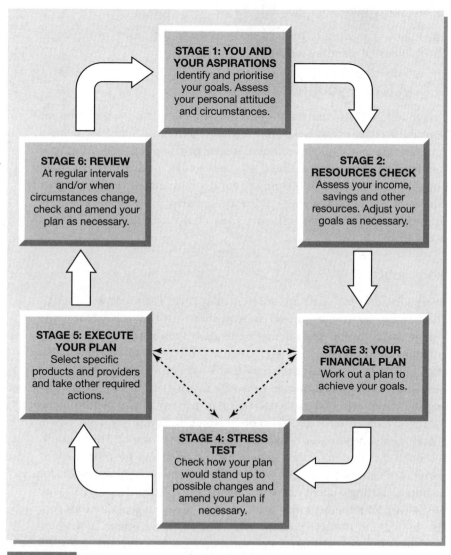

**Figure 1.2**    A six-stage financial planning framework

Although Figure 1.2 presents financial planning as six discrete stages, in practice one stage often runs into the next. This is particularly so when working through Stages 3 to 5. For example, working out a suitable financial plan (Stage 3) may well depend on finding out the charges, minimum price and other features of the specific products available (Stage 5). Similarly, stress testing (Stage 4) depends both on the generic plan you have identified (Stage 3) and the particular features of the products you might use (Stage 5). This inter-relationship between the stages is indicated by the dashed arrows in Figure 1.2.

The following sections of this chapter consider in detail each of the stages of this financial planning model.

## Stage 1: you and your aspirations

Everyone has goals. Some are aspirations and ambitions you choose for yourself, such as, taking a year out to travel, going to university, buying a boat, leaving an inheritance. Others are less of an option – ensuring your family will be financially secure if you were to die, making sure you could cope if you lost your job, helping to fund your children through higher education and putting savings aside for retirement. Most people also have attitudes and beliefs that influence their choice of goals and decisions about them.

### Your goals

Everyone's detailed goals are different. But there is a broad set of goals that tend to be similar for everyone, as shown in Figure 1.3. Not many people will have enough money to pursue all their goals at once, so it is useful to think about which goals are most important to you and which you could defer or at least scale back if you have to. Figure 1.3 sets out the basic goals as steps on a hillside path with the highest priority goals forming the lower steps and goals decreasing in priority as you climb higher. The precise order of the goals – in other words, the priority you give them – may vary depending on whatever stage of life you are at. For example, although it is undoubtedly a good idea to start saving for retirement as early as possible, in your 20s you are likely to be preoccupied with, for example, clearing student debts and buying a home. But if you are in your 50s, saving for retirement may have become the urgent goal that tops your list. In addition to these priority goals, you may have others, and where you place these on the steps is a personal decision. So everyone's goals will be a bit different, while falling into the general pattern suggested by Figure

1.3. If you arrange your own goals in a similar way to Figure 1.3, you can think of yourself as climbing higher up the hill as you achieve more of your goals – the view from the top is magnificent!

Whatever your life stage or personal goals, clearing debts should always be the first step of your way up the goal path. This is because, with a

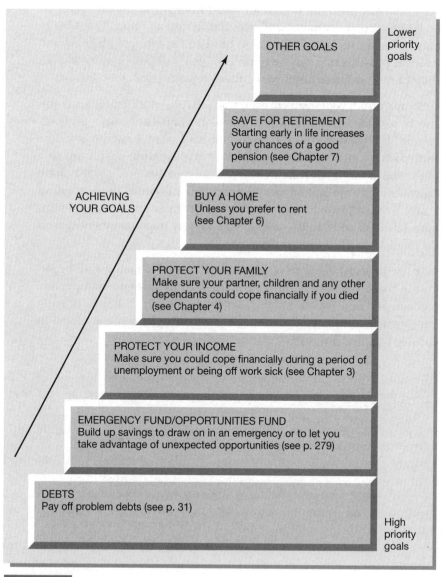

**Figure 1.3**    A financial goal path

few exceptions, it is very hard to make progress with any other financial planning if you are hampered by debts. The last section of this chapter (starting on p. 31) considers this important issue in detail.

## Your attitudes, beliefs and circumstances

One of the most important self-attributes that will affect all aspects of your financial planning is your attitude towards risk. For example, you might be cautious by nature and reluctant to take any risks. This will not only influence the goals you choose but also the types of planning and financial products that may be suitable for you. The box below contains a simple test to help you assess your attitude towards risk.

Quite apart from your instinctive approach to risk, your circumstances will also be relevant. For example, when you are young and single, generally no-one else relies on you, you might not have many possessions to lose and you have plenty of time to earn and save later on, so this can be a good time to take high risks. By contrast, in your 40s, say, you may have dependent children and be worrying about your eventual pension and so it may be appropriate to take a more cautious approach to financial planning. Life stage and family commitments are very important influences on the financial decisions you make.

Very few financial decisions do not involve at least some risk and the following chapters will consider the risk inherent in different strategies and products and how this affects their suitability for you. Risk is particularly important in the context of saving and investing and is considered in detail in Chapters 9 and 10.

### Are you risk averse?

The questions below are loosely based on theories developed to explain how people react when faced with choices involving risk. Note down your answers and then check the feedback at the end of this chapter (p. 36).

**Q1** You win a draw and have a choice of prizes. Either (a) £1,000 in cash, or (b) a lottery ticket which gives you an 80 per cent chance of winning £1,500 or a 20 per cent chance of getting nothing. Which option do you take?

**Q2** As a birthday present, you are given a lottery ticket with an 80 per cent chance of winning £1,500 or a 20 per cent chance of getting nothing. Your friend wants to buy the ticket from you. How much money would persuade you to sell?

Other personal attributes, apart from attitude towards risk, will influence your financial planning. You may have religious or ethical beliefs that affect your choices. For example, if you are a Muslim you may want to avoid savings and investments that involve *riba* (interest) or involve investment directly or indirectly in prohibited products and services, such as pork, alcohol, gambling and sexual entertainment. Throughout this book, various Shariah-compliant alternatives are considered.

Whatever your religious convictions, you might have a dislike for investing in companies involved in, say, the arms trade or that have poor labour policies or a bad pollution track record. You might want to actively support firms engaged in protecting the environment or fighting global poverty. In either case, 'ethical investments' may be the answer for you (see pp. 284 and 323).

A further important factor in your financial decisions is your tax situation. Your personal tax position will be determined by, for the example, the amount and type of income you have and your age (which may influence the tax-free allowances you get). Different financial products – particularly savings and investments – are taxed in different ways that make them more or less suitable given your particular tax status. While tax concerns should not normally be the sole reason for choosing one course of action over another, dovetailing your personal tax situation and the tax treatment of the various options available is an important element in building an effective and efficient financial plan. Throughout the chapters that follow, tax is discussed wherever relevant. For details of the UK tax system and how it determines your personal tax position, see Appendix A (p. 357).

In some situations your state of health will also be an important personal factor. It may influence the time horizon you want to consider and the deal you can get from some products, particularly life and health insurances – though perversely, when it comes to pensions, poor physical health can actually be *good* for your financial health.

## Case study

Callum is a higher-rate taxpayer in 2009–10, so his top slice of income is taxed at 40 per cent. From 2010–11, his top slce of income is taxed at the new additional rate of 50 per cent. He looks for investments that give him tax relief, such as stocks-and-shares individual savings accounts (ISAs) and also those which provide capital gains rather than income, since gains are taxed at just 18 per cent in 2009–10. (See Chapter 9 for information about investments.)

## Stage 2: resources check

With a few goals, any outlay is minimal – such as writing a will to achieve your inheritance aims or transferring assets to your partner to improve tax efficiency. But most involve some financial outlay – paying off debts, buying insurance, saving regularly or investing a lump sum. So part of the resources check is assessing what income and existing assets you can put towards the goals you identified in Stage 1. Broadly, the more resources you have, the higher you will be able to climb up the hillside of goals (see Figure 1.3). If your resources fall – say, your income drops or you lose money on the stock market – you may have to climb back down a few steps or narrow the size and scope of your goals.

A resources check – or more correctly a resources estimate – is also an essential part of the goals that aim to ensure you or your family have adequate income in the case of either a certain future event – such as retirement or a period spent studying – or a contingent event – for example, being unable to work because of redundancy or illness.

Whether you are taking a snapshot today or trying to estimate the future, the basic tools of the resources check are the household budget and the household balance sheet.

### The household budget

Figure 1.4 presents a basic budget template which you can use for a variety of purposes as you draw up your financial plan, for example, assessing how much surplus income you have today, estimating how much income your family might have if you were to die and forecasting how much income you might have in retirement.

Use the template to record or forecast regular spending but not what you pay for one-off capital items (such as buying a house or a car) – though if you borrow to buy such items, the loan repayments should be included as part of your regular expenditure.

You can use the template to work out your budget on a weekly, monthly or yearly basis, provided you are consistent throughout. If you are estimating a future budget, enter the figures in today's money – don't try to adjust them here for inflation. The impact of rising prices (see p. 28 for an indication of how severe this can be) will be taken into account in the later stages of the planning process, and the chapters of this book, as applicable, will suggest how to protect your plan against inflation.

You can complete this template with weekly, monthly or annual amounts, provided you are consistent throughout. All income should be in today's money and after tax, National Insurance and any other deductions – i.e. record the amount you have available to spend.

| INCOME | | Current budget | Estimated future budget |
|---|---|---|---|
| Earnings from a job or self-employment | | | |
| State benefits and tax credits | | | |
| Pensions | | | |
| Maintenance from former partner | | | |
| Interest from savings accounts | | | |
| Income from investments | | | |
| Student loans/other student finance | | | |
| Other income | | | |
| TOTAL INCOME | A | | |

| EXPENDITURE | Current budget | Estimated future budget |
|---|---|---|
| Mortgage payments or rent | | |
| Council tax | | |
| Regular household bills (water, gas, electricity, other) | | |
| Phone, internet and TV | | |
| Home insurance (contents, buildings) | | |
| Home maintenance | | |
| Household goods | | |
| Food and non-alcoholic drinks and other 'supermarket shop' items | | |
| Alcohol | | |
| Tobacco | | |
| Clothing and footwear | | |

**Figure 1.4**  Budget template

| | | | |
|---|---|---|---|
| Motoring costs (tax, insurance, fuel, etc.), fares, other travel | | | |
| Going out, holidays, other leisure | | | |
| Maintenance payments to former partner | | | |
| Birthday presents, charitable donations, other gifts | | | |
| Life insurance, medical insurance, other insurance | | | |
| Regular saving and investing, pension contributions | | | |
| Loan repayments (excluding credit card) | | | |
| Other expenditure | | | |
| TOTAL EXPENDITURE | B | | |
| Spending above paid for by credit card | C | | |
| Credit card repayments | D | | |
| DEBT-ADJUSTED EXPENDITURE = B − C + D | E | | |

| SURPLUS/SHORTFALL | Current budget | Estimated future budget |
|---|---|---|
| Surplus (positive answer) or shortfall (negative answer) = A − B | | |
| Debt-adjusted surplus or deficit = A − E | | |

If you have shortfall or a debt-adjusted shortfall, you are either running down your savings or building up debt. This is not sustainable in the long run.

| CREDIT MANAGEMENT | Current budget | Estimated future budget |
|---|---|---|
| Credit increasing (positive answer) or decreasing (negative answer) = C − D | | |

If C − D is positive, you are building up new card debt faster than you are paying it off. This may indicate that you have a debt problem – see p. 31

**Figure 1.4**    **Budget template** *continued*

The categories in the budget are largely self-explanatory and you can aggregate them or break them down into smaller groups if you wish. The only slightly complex area is how you treat purchases paid for by borrowing – for example, those bought with a credit card. As a general rule, it is not sustainable to finance your everyday spending through borrowing and, if you are doing this, it normally suggests you are heading for debt problems. However, there are a couple of exceptions:

■ **Planned debt.** You may have borrowed specifically to support your-self during a period out of work. For example, you may be taking out student loans to finance a period of studying. Provided you have a robust plan for paying off these debts, they need not be treated as a problem. The budget template treats student finance as an item of income rather than debt. Once you start to repay the loans, they would either reduce your 'Earnings from a job or self-employment' in the Income section or be recorded as part of your normal expenditure under 'Loan repayments'.

■ **Transaction-only debt.** You might be using very short-term credit simply as a convenient form of payment. The most common situation is where you pay by credit card and pay off the bill in full when you get your monthly statement. To avoid counting the same expenditure twice (once in the item categories and again when you pay off part or all of your credit card balance), the budget template makes an adjust-ment to your expenditure.

The surplus/shortfall and credit management calculations at the end of the template provide a guide to whether your spending and credit arrangements are sustainable, but you need to take into account all the cir-cumstances to get the full picture – see Figure 1.5 for some examples. The basic surplus/shortfall indicates whether you are buying more each month than you are getting in income. A shortfall suggests you are running down your savings or building up debts, so needs further investigation to see whether this is stoking up future problems. The debt-adjusted surplus/shortfall gives an indication of whether you are managing your credit card repayments, as well as everyday spending, out of your current income. To be in a position to pursue your financial goals, a debt-adjusted surplus is essential. However a surplus does not necessarily indicate a healthy finan-cial position because you might be fuelling your current spending out of credit. To check this, also look at the credit management figure which shows whether your credit card debts are on the increase or being reduced. If they are increasing, this should ring alarm bells. The household balance sheet (see p. 17) provides further indicators of your debt position and the overall health of your finances.

## Improving your budget

If you have a budget shortfall or you have a surplus but it is not enough to finance your goals, you have two strategies available to improve the posi-tion: boost your income and/or cut your spending.

### Scenario 1: controlled credit

During the month, Jamal has £1,000 income and spends exactly £1,000, using his credit card to pay for all items. His budget position looks like this:

| A | Total income | £1,000 |
|---|---|---|
| B | Total expenditure | £1,000 |
| C | Spending above paid for by credit card | £1,000 |
| D | Credit card repayments | £1,000 |

| Surplus/shortfall | £0 |
|---|---|
| Debt-adjusted surplus/shortfall | £0 |
| Credit increase/decrease | £0 |

Jamal is not running down savings or increasing borrowing and his credit management is stable, so his budget looks sustainable.

### Scenario 3: problem debt

During the month, Jane has an income of £800 but she spends £1,100 using her credit and store cards to pay for £300 worth of spending. She pays off the minimum, £20, on her cards each month. Her budget position looks like this:

| A | Total income | £800 |
|---|---|---|
| B | Total expenditure | £1,100 |
| C | Spending above paid for by credit card | £300 |
| D | Credit card repayments | £20 |

| Surplus/shortfall | −£300 |
|---|---|
| Debt-adjusted surplus/shortfall | −£20 |
| Credit increase/decrease | £280 |

Jane has a large shortfall and debt-adjusted shortfall, as well as increasing credit card debt. It looks as if she has budgeting and debt problems and needs to take action fast. See p. 33 for organisations that can help with problem debts.

### Scenario 2: future problems?

During the month, Julie has £1,000 income and spends exactly £1,000, using her credit card to pay for all the items. She pays off half her credit card bill. Her budget position looks like:

| A | Total income | £1,000 |
|---|---|---|
| B | Total expenditure | £1,000 |
| C | Spending above paid for by credit card | £1,000 |
| D | Credit card repayments | £500 |

| Surplus/shortfall | £0 |
|---|---|
| Debt-adjusted surplus/shortfall | £500 |
| Credit increase/decrease | £500 |

Julie has not used all her income to pay off her credit card bill so she has left a debt-adjusted surplus for the month. However, the outstanding card debt is increasing, so this position may not be sustainable in future.

### Scenario 4: student loan

During the month, Jack lives on £600 income from his student loan and student overdraft and spends it all. His budget position looks like this:

| A | Total income | £600 |
|---|---|---|
| B | Total expenditure | £600 |
| C | Spending above paid for by credit card | £0 |
| D | Credit card repayments | £0 |

| Surplus/shortfall | £0 |
|---|---|
| Debt-adjusted surplus/shortfall | £0 |
| Credit increase/decrease | £0 |

Jack is borrowing in a sustainable way to provide himself with income and is living within his budget. Repayment of the loan and overdraft are due to be managed in a structured way once he has finished his course.

**Figure 1.5**  Budgeting and borrowing

If you are working, you may be able to boost your income by doing overtime or, if you are self-employed, taking on extra contracts. Could you take on a second job, say in the evenings or at weekends? Or perhaps you have a hobby that could generate some extra money, such as making garden items or cooking speciality cakes.

Another possibility, if you have space, might be to take in a lodger. There is a special tax scheme, called Rent-a-Room-Relief, that allows you to have up to £4,250 a year income in rent from a lodger tax-free (to get details, see Appendix B). You will need permission from your landlord or mortgage lender before you rent out a room, otherwise you may invalidate your contract. You should also let your buildings and contents insurers know about the changed circumstances.

Especially if your income is low, check whether you are claiming all the state benefits to which you are entitled, such as council tax benefit (to meet part or all of your council tax bill), housing benefit (to pay your rent), pension credit (if you are over the qualifying age which is 60 2009–10 but due to increase from April 2010 in line with women's state pension age – see Chapter 7), working tax credit (if you are in work but your earnings are low) and child tax credit (if you have children). Some state benefits are payable even if your income is very high or regardless of your income – these include child tax credit (in 2009–10) and, if you need the help of a carer or have poor mobility, disability living allowance and attendance allowance. For details of state benefits, contact Jobcentre Plus if you are of working age or the Pension Service if you are retired. See p. 53 for where to go for advice about benefits.

Looking at the other side of your budget, there are three main ways to cut your spending: check that you are not paying over the odds; strip out or cut back on non-essentials; and cut the amount you use and spend on essentials.

There is huge competition between service providers, so to get, and continue getting, the best deals for gas, electricity, phone and the internet, you need to shop around regularly and switch if necessary. The easiest way to do this is to use an internet comparison site, such as uswitch or money-supermarket.com. To find fuel comparison sites, contact Consumer Focus (see Appendix B for contact details).

What you count as essential and non-essential spending is personal to you. Obvious candidates for saving money are alcohol, tobacco, going out, holidays, other leisure, and maybe charitable donations. But you must decide what you can live without or manage with less of.

It is much harder to cut essential spending but with, for example, fuel bills and travel, there are numerous ways to reduce the amount you use – and you'll be helping the environment as well as your wallet. Table 1.1 gives just a few suggestions, you can get many more and a personalised home energy check by contacting the Energy Saving Trust (see Appendix B). If you are a small household paying water rates, check whether you might save by switching to a water meter – contact your water company for advice or visit its website which may have an interactive tool to help you compare metered bills and rates.

**Table 1.1  Some ways to save energy[1]**

| *What you can do* | *What it might cost* | *Amount you might save each year* |
|---|---|---|
| Draught-proofing | £100 DIY | £25 |
| Turn appliances off rather than to standby | No cost | £33 |
| Buy energy-saving appliances | Varies | £12–£36 |
| Top-up loft insulation | From £250[2] | £45 |
| Energy-saving lightbulbs | £45 | £37 |
| Double-glazing | Varies | £135 |
| Cavity wall insulation | Around £250[2] | £115 |
| Hot water tank jacket | £12 | £35 |

[1] All costs and savings are estimated for a gas heated three bed semi-detached home.

[2] You might qualify for a grant.

*Source*: Energy Saving Trust, www.energysavingtrust.org.uk

## Household balance sheet

The household balance sheet is a snapshot of everything you own (your assets) less everything you owe (your liabilities) at a set point in time. The difference between your assets and liabilities is called your 'net worth'. Usually you draw up a balance sheet to show your position now, which can be particularly helpful in highlighting strengths and weaknesses in your financial position. But you might also want to estimate a future balance sheet to help you plan ahead to meet your various goals. Figure 1.6 sets out a balance sheet template that you can use for either purpose.

If you are familiar with business balance sheets, you'll appreciate that a household balance sheet is directly analogous to the balance sheet of a company with the household's net worth being equivalent to shareholders' funds. So a household with negative net worth (liabilities exceeding assets) is technically bankrupt. The higher the net worth, the richer and more financially sound the household is. However, the value of assets, such as property, shares and collectibles can fall as well as rise and it may be hard to value some assets, such as shares in a family business or loans to family members, which might in fact never be repaid, so net worth varies from one balance sheet snapshot to another.

Many assets first enter the balance sheet through the household current account(s). Surplus funds are then invested, for example, in savings accounts or on the stock market (either directly or more likely through investment funds of one type or another – see Chapter 10). Other assets enter the balance sheet directly, for example, because they are inherited or their purchase is funded through borrowing (as is typically the case with the family home). Assets may grow as new savings are added, as income from existing assets is reinvested and as assets appreciate in value. Liabilities may reduce as they are paid off out of income or through the sale of assets.

To achieve a financial goal, you may need to build up your assets. Alternatively, you may have existing assets which can be redirected towards a new goal or sold to fund it. So, in general, high net worth is likely to make it easier for you to achieve your goals.

The balance sheet separates out current assets and current liabilities, so you can judge the short-term position of your household as well as its overall strength. Current assets are items which can quickly and reliably be converted to cash. Assets such as shares can usually easily be sold on the stock market but you can't be sure what price you will get, so they are

| ASSETS | | £ |
|---|---|---|
| **Current assets** | | |
| Current account | | |
| Savings account: instant access and notice periods of less than a year | | |
| National Savings & Investments products,[1] including premium bonds | | |
| Other short-term assets[2] | | |
| TOTAL CURRENT ASSETS | F | |
| **Other assets** | | |
| Government and corporate bonds, including funds invested in them | | |
| Shares and share-based investment funds | | |
| Property-based investment funds | | |
| Second home, buy-to-let property | | |
| Main or only home | | |
| Antiques, paintings, classic cars and other collectables | | |
| Personal possessions with a resale value | | |
| Pension funds | | |
| Value of defined benefit and state pension[3] | | |
| Other assets | | |
| TOTAL ASSETS | G | |

[1] Although some NS&I products have terms greater than one year, most can be cashed in at short notice with some loss of interest but no loss of capital.
[2] For example, money you have lent to family and friends that could be recalled at short notice.
[3] As a rough guide, multiply the pension due from age 65 by 20.

| LIABILITIES | £ |
|---|---|
| **Current liabilities** | |
| Overdraft | |
| Bills paid in arrears[4] and bills due within one year | |

[4] For example, quarterly fuel and phone bills and tax paid through self-assessment (see Appendix A).

| | | |
|---|---|---|
| Credit and store card debts | | |
| Other debts repayable within one year[5] | | |
| TOTAL CURRENT LIABILITIES | H | |
| **Other liabilities** | | |
| Personal loans | | |
| Amount outstanding on hire-purchase agreements | | |
| Mortgage | | |
| Other secured loans | | |
| Student loans | | |
| Other liabilities | | |
| TOTAL LIABILITIES | I | . |

[5] For example, money you have borrowed from family and friends that could be called in at short notice.

| BALANCE SHEET RATIOS | |
|---|---|
| Net worth = G – I | |
| Current ratio = F/H | |
| Leverage = I/(G – I) | |

**Net worth** (in £s) measures the total wealth of the household. If it is positive, the household's total assets exceed its liabilities.

**Current ratio**, which is expressed as a number, compares short-term debts to the assets which the household could quickly realise to meet those debts. A ratio of less than 1 suggests the household cannot meet its immediate debts and so is vulnerable to any shocks, such as job loss.

**Leverage** compares total liabilities to net worth and is expressed as a percentage. A low value suggests financial strength but could mean the household is missing out on opportunities to acquire assets through borrowing (such as buying a home with a mortgage). A high value may indicate over-indebtedness and could mean the household budget is vulnerable to increases in the cost of borrowing.

**Figure 1.6**  Household balance sheet template

not a reliable way to raise money at short notice and are therefore excluded from current assets. Current liabilities are debts you may have to pay fairly soon, typically meaning within one year. The current ratio divides current assets by current liabilities. If they were exactly equal, the ratio would be 1. A ratio of less than 1 indicates that short-term debts exceed liquid assets, so your household would not be in a position to clear its immediate debts if you wanted to. This makes your household vulnerable to any shocks, such as losing income because of redundancy or illness or a rise in tax rates or interest rates that might affect your household's ability to carry on meeting its debt repayments. Therefore the current ratio is an important figure to bear in mind when stress testing your financial plan: a low current ratio makes it more likely your plan will be blown off course. The main ways to increase the current ratio are to pay off debts and build up extra emergency funds (the first two steps of the goal path in Figure 1.3). There are no strict rules, but a current ratio of at least 1.5 to 2 would be a prudent minimum.

The final ratio, leverage, looks at the overall liabilities of your household as a percentage of net worth, so it is a measure of total indebtedness: the lower the percentage, the less indebted the household. Low levels of debt may indicate financial strength but equally may indicate a household with a low credit rating and so poor access to borrowing, which may hold back its ability to build up assets, such as housing. For many households, leverage is likely to be highest in the earlier half of working life and diminish as retirement approaches.

High leverage may suggest a household that is vulnerable to falling asset prices that could turn net worth negative. The consequences of this are most easily understood in the context of housing: if you have a high mortgage relative to the market price of your home, a fall in house prices can tip you into 'negative equity' (where your mortgage exceeds the value of your home). Negative equity is not a problem, provided you do not need to sell the home. Similarly negative net worth is not an immediate problem, but becomes one if you have to sell assets, which then turns paper losses into real losses. High leverage may also mean the household is vulnerable to factors such as increases in interest rates which will push up the amount it spends each month servicing its loans (unless they have been taken out at a fixed rate). Strain on the budget is just the circumstance that may trigger the sale of assets. So high leverage increases overall risk for the household.

Leverage is not necessarily bad. Borrowing to pay for everyday spending or consumer items, such as holidays, does nothing to strengthen your balance sheet. But leverage to buy assets can have positive as well as negative effects. Table 1.2 compares the situation of buying an asset – say, a home – with and without borrowing. In Scenario 1, you buy the asset outright. If the price of the asset rises by £10,000 you make a profit equal to the rise in the asset price of 4.5 per cent. But, if you borrow as in Scenario 2, the modest £10,000 price increase gives you a profit of 50 per cent on your outlay of £20,000. Leverage has increased your profits dramatically. However, as Scenario 4 shows, leverage also magnifies your losses. So leverage is a double-edged sword: it increases the chance of big gains but also increases the risk of large losses.

In building your financial plan, you should check the impact that any strategy may have on your balance sheet. If it pushes up the level of leverage, it tends to indicate that the strategy is relatively high risk.

### Table 1.2 The effect of leverage

*The table shows the profit or loss you would make buying an asset, such as a home, for £220,000 and selling it one year later (ignoring buying and selling costs).*

| | Scenario 1: buy outright, make a profit | Scenario 2: borrow to buy, make a profit | Scenario 3: buy outright, make a loss | Scenario 4: borrow to buy, make a loss |
|---|---|---|---|---|
| Purchase price of asset | £220,000 | £220,000 | £220,000 | £220,000 |
| Amount you borrow | £0 | £200,000 | £0 | £200,000 |
| Balance you pay | £220,000 | £20,000 | £220,000 | £20,000 |
| Sale price of asset... | £230,000 | £230,000 | £210,000 | £210,000 |
| ...of which, loan repayment and your capital | £220,000 | £220,000 | £220,000 | £220,000 |
| Profit/loss | £10,000 | £10,000 | –£10,000 | –£10,000 |
| Profit/loss as percentage of your capital | £10,000 ÷ £220,000 = 4.5% | £10,000 ÷ £20,000 = 50.0% | –£10,000 ÷ £220,000 = –4.5% | –£10,000 ÷ £20,000 = –50.0% |

## Stage 3: your financial plan

Having identified and prioritised your goals and assessed your resources, you are ready to move on to building a suitable financial plan. The specific plan will depend on the goal in question. Chapters 3 to 11 of this book look at different plans for the main goals you are likely to pursue at various stages of your life. The chapters discuss the options available, which ones are most likely to be suitable for you, and the opportunities and pitfalls involved.

An important part of creating a financial plan is understanding the range and nature of financial products available and Chapters 3 to 11 explain these. However, be aware that products may change their character over time and so does the context within which they are used, so a strategy that worked well some years ago may not be appropriate now. Endowment mortgages are a classic example, where the successive removal of tax reliefs and the changing performance of the economy and financial markets transformed the product from a good choice to a very poor one (see Chapter 6 for details). A more recent example, has been the way some 'money market' investment funds thought to be investing in very safe investments similar to bank deposits in fact started to use more complex investments to boost returns and lost money when financial conditions changed (see Chapter 10). Therefore it is important, even if you think you know a product, to check whether its essential features have altered and exactly what characteristics lie underneath the familiar exterior.

Be aware that there is seldom a single, correct financial plan. For any set of circumstances, there may be several viable plans each with their own pros and cons. One may clearly be more suitable than the others, but sometimes that's not the case and, given the information available at the time, several plans may do. With hindsight, it might turn out that one plan would have been better than the others, but you cannot know that at the time you had to make your decision. The future is always unknown – you can make educated guesses and build assumptions into your plan, but you will never be able to plan for the future with absolute certainty, hence the importance of stress testing (Stage 4) and review (Stage 6).

## Stage 4: stress test

Following the global financial crisis that hit in 2007, the idea of stress testing became very topical. Banks have had their balance sheets stress tested to see how they would cope with various adverse scenarios. But stress testing is important for individuals and households too. Any financial plan you make needs to be robust in the face of changing external forces outside your control – for example, a rise or fall in interest rates or an increase

in inflation – and as far as possible changes in your personal circumstances, such as job loss. Of course, you can only test against events that
you predict and there is always the possibility of some completely unfore-
seen event. In addition, there will often be a cost to protecting yourself
against risks, so you need to weigh up how far it is worth going down the
protection route. There may be some events that could happen but seem
so unlikely that you deem the cost of protection is not warranted.

Stress testing is about being aware of the risks inherent in any strategy
– and, crucially, it is about accepting that even small risks can actually
happen. Don't make the mistake of assuming that low risk means no
risk (see the box). In fact, there is no such thing as a completely risk-free
investment or strategy. Having identified possible risks, it's up to you to
decide whether you want to take steps to protect yourself or just bank on
the risks not materialising. Which option you choose comes back to your
attitude towards risk (discussed on p. 8) and your ability to withstand risk
– for example, whether you have other resources to fall back on. Chapters
3 to 11, in considering the different financial goals, suggest stress tests for
each of the strategies identified and protective measures you might build
into your plan.

### Life savings lost in 'low-risk' investments

According to the Financial Services Authority (FSA), the UK's financial regulator,
5,620 UK investors lost an average of £14,500 each (£107 million in total) when the
investment bank, Lehman Brothers, collapsed in September 2008. One man 'had
invested £200,000 that he had made from the sale of his business… others have
lost their nest eggs, redundancy payments and lump sums from their pensions. It
is a personal catastrophe for many thousands of individuals'.[1] They had invested
in 'structured products', which offer a return linked to the performance of the stock
market but in any event guarantee to return the original capital (see Chapter 9 for
details). These investments are typically marketed to risk-averse, often elderly investors, seeking a better return than savings accounts but without any capital risk.

In fact, the guarantee to return the original capital is only as sound as the organisation providing it, usually a big bank and, in this case, Lehman Brothers. In the
aftermath of the bank's collapse, debate raged over whether the products had been
marketed in a misleading way which downplayed the risks and UK investors waited
to find out if they would be eligible to claim compensation. However, right up to the
day that Lehman went bankrupt, credit rating agencies (organisations that specialise
in assessing risk) were rating the bank as safe and past experience suggested that
large investment banks, such as Lehman, would not be allowed to collapse. This
meant that generally the risk of structured products failing appeared to be small.
But small is not the same as impossible and both marketing literature and advisers
should make this clear to investors.

---

[1] Commons Hansard, *Structured products marketing*, 7 July 2009, Column 238WH.

## Stage 5: execute your plan

Once your plan is stress tested and, if necessary, adapted to reduce the risks you have identified, the next stage is to buy the products or take the actions that make up the plan. As noted earlier, not all strategies involve buying products – for example, your plan might involve cutting spending to free up income for debt repayment or writing a will to ensure your family would be provided for in the event of your death. But often strategies will involve, say, buying insurance, choosing a savings product or taking out an investment. The crucial part of this stage is shopping around to ensure that you get the most suitable product at the best price or offering the best return. Avoid the temptation to be driven solely by price or return – sometimes that's a good tactic, but usually the terms and conditions on offer or quality of service will be just as important. And always be aware that, if an offer sounds too good to be true, then it probably is just that: in other words, a scam to be avoided.

The opportunity to shop around has been enhanced enormously by the development of the internet. Most providers have their own websites, where you can download product details, including where relevant 'key facts documents' which set out the most important information in a standardised form required by the FSA and which aid the comparison of one provider's product with another's. In addition, there are also a number of internet comparison sites.

Internet comparison sites are extremely useful as a way of quickly finding out what's available and making basic comparisons. However, most internet comparison sites do not cover the whole market. Some have marketing arrangements so they earn commission if you click through to specific providers: this tends to compromise the site's independence. Therefore, it's a good idea to check out two or three sites and separately contact direct any key providers that are missing. Often comparison sites focus unduly on price. Make sure you search out all the further information you need, for example, the terms and conditions including exclusions, before you commit yourself to buying or investing, especially if your circumstances are unusual, for example, you have health problems that could be relevant.

The FSA runs its own comparison websites (at www.fsa.gov.uk/tables) covering a limited range of products and providing impartial, reasonably comprehensive information (see Figure 1.7).

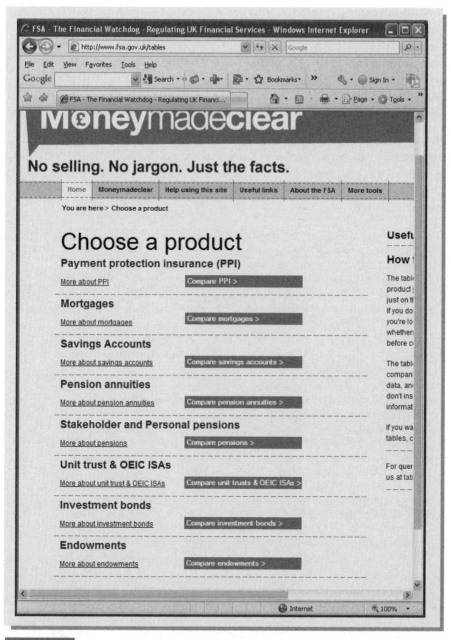

**Figure 1.7**  Product comparisons available on the FSA website

*Source*: www.fsa.gov.uk/tables. Accessed 20 August 2009. © Copyright of the Financial Services Authority 2009.

If you don't have access to the internet at home, you could use your local library or an internet café, but make sure you take the precautions suggested in the box below. If you are not comfortable using the internet, you can still shop around for yourself but it will be a little more laborious and perhaps not quite so up-to-date. For example, you can ring around for quotes or use comparison tables published in the money pages of newspapers and personal finance magazines (see Appendix B).

However, this may be the part of financial planning where you prefer to delegate the task to an adviser or broker, who will normally have access to specialised 'platforms' – professional websites that compare products and provide specific quotes. Chapter 2 describes the various types of adviser available.

### Using the internet safely

- If you are using a computer in a public place, make sure that the screen and keyboard are not overlooked either by people or security cameras.
- When using a computer shared with others, always log off fully at the end of a session, so that the next user cannot access the screens you have visited.
- On your own computer, install a firewall and virus software with an updating service.
- If you use a wireless connection to the internet, install a password so that strangers cannot access your service.
- Be selective about the websites you rely on for information. For example, government sites and voluntary organisations, such as Citizens Advice are a better source of impartial information than trade bodies and individual providers.
- Never respond to spam email or click through to any addresses included in such mail. They will be bogus sites designed to extract confidential information from you and/or install malicious software on your computer. Forward suspect emails to reports@banksafeonline.org.uk and then delete them from your machine.
- Before buying or investing over the internet, check that the firm is authorised by the FSA (see Chapter 2 for why this is important) by looking up the firm's entry on the FSA Register (www.fsa.gov.uk/register/home.do). Make sure the website includes a real-world address and phone number and cross-check (for example, against a phone book or the FSA Register) that the contact details are genuine.
- Do not go ahead if anything seems a bit odd about the website – it might be a bogus site.
- Only key in personal information if you are on a secure website – look for 'https' in the website address and a locked padlock or similar security symbol in the toolbar.
- Choose passwords that are difficult to guess or break. For example, include a mix of letters, numbers, upper case and lower case. Try to avoid real words, for example, use instead the initials of the opening words of a book or poem.
- Use a different password for each account and change your passwords regularly.
- Do not share your account security details with anyone. Try to memorise passwords and other security information. If you write them down, disguise them.
- If a deal sounds too good to be true, it probably is. Avoid it.

## Stage 6: review

Wouldn't it be nice if, having set up your financial plan, you could just sit back and wait for it to deliver? Unfortunately, life is not so straightforward. However good your stress testing, it's impossible to predict or protect against every future event. Moreover, decisions about long-term planning are necessarily based on assumptions about the future, for example, about inflation and investment growth. Only by luck would your assumptions turn out to be correct, so periodically you need to check and adjust your plan to take into account these deviations from what you had expected.

In general, you should aim to check your financial plan once a year. If you are on track or only slightly adrift, there may be no need for any action. If the review shows that you are not currently on track, you'll need to take a view about whether the situation might self-correct (for example, if the stock market has fallen recently, you might weigh up the chance of recovery over the term of your plan) or whether you need to take action now. Action might take the form of, say, saving extra, or switching to different products or investments.

There will be other occasions when a review is needed, for example, when insurance policies come up for renewal, you should check whether your need for cover has changed and shop around again for the best policy. Most importantly, you should review your plan whenever you face a major life event – such as redundancy, expecting a child, bereavement, inheritance or relationship breakdown. This will be a major review that includes reassessing your goals in the light of the new situation and may trigger the need for a full revision of your plan. This will not necessarily imply abandoning all your previous strategies and financial products, but might involve, say, reassigning existing assets to new goals.

## Case study

Kim and Lee are in their 30s. They both have established careers and their financial planning has focused mainly on protecting their incomes and buying and renovating a Georgian property in London. Out of the blue, Kim has learned she is expecting a baby. The couple urgently need to revise their planning. They need to make decisions about work and childcare which will affect their budget, life cover will be important, and they need to assess whether their current home is suitable.

Harriet and John had been married for 32 years when John announced that he wanted a divorce. As a couple, they had a stable financial plan that included a good income, generous emergency fund, a home with only a small mortgage to meet and pension savings on target for a comfortable old age. Harriet needs to assess what income she will have in her newly separated situation and plan how to use it most effectively, in particular to meet her housing and pension saving needs.

# The impact of inflation

A risk that needs to be addressed in all medium- to long-term financial planning is inflation. Inflation is a sustained increase in prices and even low rates can play havoc with the buying power of your money, throwing your financial plan off course.

In the UK, inflation is usually measured by looking at changes in either the Retail Prices Index (RPI) or Consumer Price Index (CPI). Both indices measure changes in the prices of a basket of goods and services that reflect average household spending. The main difference between the indices is that the CPI excludes housing costs, such as mortgage repayments, while the RPI includes them. The CPI is the inflation measure used for economic policy purposes. But the RPI is important because it is the basis for the return from some investments (see Chapter 9), increases in state benefits including state pensions (see Chapter 7) and wage bargaining.

Which measure of inflation is most relevant to you personally depends on your circumstances. If you do not have a mortgage, the CPI may better reflect the inflation that you are experiencing. But, unless your spending patterns happen to correspond exactly to the average for all UK households, neither the CPI nor the RPI will be a particularly good estimate for you. However, you can check out your own personal inflation rate using an online tool from the Office for National Statistics (www.statistics. gov.uk/pic). You key in the proportion you spend each month of different categories of goods and services and the tool gives you a personalised inflation rate. Although this is a bit of fun, it can also be useful in helping you to plan your household budget more effectively.

Rising prices reduce the amount that a fixed sum of money can buy. For example, if you spend £100 on your weekly supermarket shop and prices double over the next ten years, in ten years' time, your £100 will only buy half as much, in other words, only the same as £50 today. Table 1.3 shows how different rates of inflation erode the buying power of your money over time.

To maintain buying power, a future sum of money needs to be larger in cash terms than an equivalent sum today. Consider the goal of retiring on a comfortable income. If you decide you will need £20,000 a year income, presumably you mean you want to be able to buy the same in retirement as £20,000 can buy today. The actual cash amount you will need will be much higher if prices rise over the next 30 years. If price increases average 2 per cent a year over the next 30 years, you would need £36,220 a year. If inflation averages 6 per cent a year, you would need £114,870 a year to buy the same as £20,000 today. As you can see, even quite modest rates of inflation have a big impact. Table 1.4 shows how much you would need in future to compensate for the effects of different rates of inflation.

**Table 1.3 How inflation erodes buying power**

*The table shows the buying power (called the 'real value') of £1,000 in cash after the number of years shown if inflation averages the rate shown.*

| | *Average inflation rate (% pa)* | | | | | | | | | | |
|---|---|---|---|---|---|---|---|---|---|---|---|
| *Term (years)* | *–2* | *–1* | *1* | *2* | *3* | *4* | *5* | *7.5* | *10* | *12.5* | *15* |
| 1 | £1,020 | £1,010 | £990 | £980 | £971 | £962 | £952 | £930 | £909 | £889 | £870 |
| 2 | £1,041 | £1,020 | £980 | £961 | £943 | £925 | £907 | £865 | £826 | £790 | £756 |
| 3 | £1,062 | £1,031 | £971 | £942 | £915 | £889 | £864 | £805 | £751 | £702 | £658 |
| 4 | £1,084 | £1,041 | £961 | £924 | £888 | £855 | £823 | £749 | £683 | £624 | £572 |
| 5 | £1,106 | £1,052 | £951 | £906 | £863 | £822 | £784 | £697 | £621 | £555 | £497 |
| 10 | £1,224 | £1,106 | £905 | £820 | £744 | £676 | £614 | £485 | £386 | £308 | £247 |
| 15 | £1,354 | £1,163 | £861 | £743 | £642 | £555 | £481 | £338 | £239 | £171 | £123 |
| 20 | £1,498 | £1,223 | £820 | £673 | £554 | £456 | £377 | £235 | £149 | £95 | £61 |
| 30 | £1,833 | £1,352 | £742 | £552 | £412 | £308 | £231 | £114 | £57 | £29 | £15 |
| 35 | £2,028 | £1,422 | £706 | £500 | £355 | £253 | £181 | £80 | £36 | £16 | £8 |
| 40 | £2,244 | £1,495 | £672 | £453 | £307 | £208 | £142 | £55 | £22 | £9 | £4 |

Inflation has a number of important implications for financial planning:

- If you are saving, investing or insuring to provide a target lump sum or target income many years ahead, the target needs to be adjusted to take account of inflation during the intervening years.
- If you are saving, investing or insuring to provide an income either now or starting some time in the future, you need to consider how inflation will affect the buying power of the income over the years it is being paid out.
- If you expect prices to rise, it may be better to bring forward your decisions to buy goods and services today rather than waiting. So inflation can provide an incentive to consume and borrow more today.

■ Just as inflation reduces the future buying power of investments, so too it reduces the future value of a fixed sum of borrowing. If you are a borrower, inflation is good news – see the case study on p. 31.

### Table 1.4 Future amounts needed to compensate for inflation

*The table shows the cash sum you would need after the number of years shown to have the same value as £1,000 today if inflation averaged the amount shown.*

| | | | | | | | | | | | | |
|---|---|---|---|---|---|---|---|---|---|---|---|---|
| | Average inflation rate (% pa) | | | | | | | | | | | |
| Term (years) | −2 | −1 | 1 | 2 | 3 | 4 | 5 | 7.5 | 10 | 12.5 | 15 |
| 1 | £980 | £990 | £1,010 | £1,020 | £1,030 | £1,040 | £1,050 | £1,075 | £1,100 | £1,125 | £1,150 |
| 2 | £960 | £980 | £1,020 | £1,040 | £1,061 | £1,082 | £1,103 | £1,156 | £1,210 | £1,266 | £1,323 |
| 3 | £941 | £970 | £1,030 | £1,061 | £1,093 | £1,125 | £1,158 | £1,242 | £1,331 | £1,424 | £1,521 |
| 4 | £922 | £961 | £1,041 | £1,082 | £1,126 | £1,170 | £1,216 | £1,335 | £1,464 | £1,602 | £1,749 |
| 5 | £904 | £951 | £1,051 | £1,104 | £1,159 | £1,217 | £1,276 | £1,436 | £1,611 | £1,802 | £2,011 |
| 10 | £817 | £904 | £1,105 | £1,219 | £1,344 | £1,480 | £1,629 | £2,061 | £2,594 | £3,247 | £4,046 |
| 15 | £739 | £860 | £1,161 | £1,346 | £1,558 | £1,801 | £2,079 | £2,959 | £4,177 | £5,852 | £8,137 |
| 20 | £668 | £818 | £1,220 | £1,486 | £1,806 | £2,191 | £2,653 | £4,248 | £6,727 | £10,545 | £16,367 |
| 30 | £545 | £740 | £1,348 | £1,811 | £2,427 | £3,243 | £4,322 | £8,755 | £17,449 | £34,243 | £66,212 |
| 35 | £493 | £703 | £1,417 | £2,000 | £2,814 | £3,946 | £5,516 | £12,569 | £28,102 | £61,708 | £133,176 |
| 40 | £446 | £669 | £1,489 | £2,208 | £3,262 | £4,801 | £7,040 | £18,044 | £45,259 | £111,199 | £267,864 |

The reverse implications hold if prices are falling – deflation. Falling prices benefit savers and investors because the buying power of their money automatically increases over time, as shown in the first two columns of Table 1.3. (However, offsetting this beneficial effect, when inflation is low, the return paid on savings and investments is likely to fall close to zero.) If you expect prices to fall, it makes sense to hold off buying goods and services because they are likely to be cheaper if you wait. If you borrow, the amount you owe automatically increases in terms of what you could buy with the money you owe. Over the past hundred years or so, periods of deflation have been rare and short-lived but, before then, periods of deflation and broadly stable prices were common. Over the 40 years to

2009, annual inflation peaked at 26.9 per cent in August 1975 and reached a low of –1.6 per cent in June 2009. So, if you are creating a financial plan looking ahead over the next 40 years (quite possible if you are planning for retirement), it is very hard to predict how inflation might affect you – another reason for regularly reviewing your financial plan.

## Case study

Five years ago, Emma lent her son George £10,000 to help him study abroad. Emma has said she would like the money back eventually but will not charge George any interest. George now has a job and is ready to pay the £10,000 back. Over the past five years, prices have increased by around 11 per cent, so £10,000 now buys only around the same as £9,000 would have done five years ago. This means Emma gets back less in real terms than she originally lent, and correspondingly George gives up less in real terms through the repayment than he gained from the original loan.

# Borrowing and debt

Before you can embark on any serious financial planning, you need to put your day-to-day finances on a sound basis by clearing away any problem debts and making sure that you are not paying more than you need to for other borrowing.

Debt can arise in many ways – taking out a student loan, taking out a mortgage to buy a home, borrowing on credit cards, a car loan. Not all debts are problems. For example, student loans are a relatively cheap form of debt (with the interest rate set to match inflation, while more usually loan interest is a margin above inflation) and designed to be paid off in an affordable way with repayments kicking in only when your income exceeds a set level – see the box. Other debts are not a problem provided you have a clear plan for repaying them and the plan is not disrupted.

### Reasons for keeping your student loans

It's estimated that students starting university in 2009 will owe £23,500 by the time they graduate.[2] This is a large debt burden to carry at the start of a working life. Not surprisingly young people – or perhaps generous parents and grandparents – would like to clear these student debts. But there are some good reasons repayment should be low down your list of priorities:

[2] Credit Action. http://www.creditaction.org.uk/credit-action-and-student-loan-repayment.html. Accessed 21 August 2009.

■ You may be able to earn more by putting a lump sum in a savings account than you would save by paying off student debt. For example, if inflation is running at 2 per cent a year, each £1,000 of student loan outstanding increases by £20 over the space of a year. If you can earn, say 3 per cent a year after tax from your savings, £1,000 in a savings account would grow by £30 over one year. So you would be £10 better off saving your money rather than repaying the loan.

■ Similarly, there is no point making extra student loan repayments if you would then borrow more in some other, more expensive way. For example, you are likely to be worse off using your savings to pay off your student loan, if you then take out a larger mortgage than you would have done had you still had the savings available as extra deposit for a home purchase.

■ If, say, you lost your job so that your income fell below a set limit (£15,000 in 2009–10), your student loan repayments would stop. The balance of your loan is written off if you become permanently disabled and unable to work. So, unlike other forms of borrowing, there is no need to plan how you would keep up the repayments in adverse situations.

■ Under current rules, after 25 years any unpaid balance on your student loan account is cancelled. So, if you will be a low earner for most of your working life – for example, pursuing an artistic or musical career or combining part-time work with having children – paying off your student loan could be wasted money.

Whenever you intend to borrow to buy something, it is worth running through a quick checklist in your head:

■ **Do you really need this item?** It's easy to run up debts buying things that seem desirable at the time but which you then seldom use or wear.

■ **Do you need it straight away?** You will nearly always pay more if you borrow to buy something than if you save up and buy it later. The exception is where you expect the price to have risen later on.

■ **Are you borrowing in the best way?** Try to avoid expensive forms of borrowing, such as store cards, catalogue shopping (where you pay in instalments) and unauthorised overdrafts. Credit cards can be a reasonably cheap way to borrow for short periods because of their flexibility and lack of arrangement fees but are generally costly for longer-term borrowing. Shop around for personal loans – you don't have to borrow from your existing bank or the store where you are buying goods. Internet comparison sites can help you find best buy credit cards and loans. To weigh up the cost of different options, compare their annual percentage rate (APR) – see the box.

### Annual percentage rate

The annual percentage rate (APR) is a way of expressing the cost of borrowing in a standardised form so you can compare one deal with another. The APR takes into account not just the interest you'll be charged but also any fees and other costs you must pay (such as insurance that is a compulsory part of the deal). It also takes into account the timing of the repayments and charges. For example, if you borrow £100 and have to pay it back in ten monthly instalments of £12, the APR will show how this is more expensive than a loan of £100 that you pay back in one single instalment of £120 at the end of ten months. You do not need to be able to work out the APR for yourself. You just need to know that the higher the APR is, the greater the cost of the loan.

As well as the APR, you need to look at the loan repayments to make sure that you can afford them. It is possible to have a loan that is cheap overall (low APR) but that you have to pay back quite quickly in a few large payments. Conversely, it is very common to find loans where you pay back just a few pounds a week or month but over a very long period, so that the overall cost is very high (high APR). You might decide that the high cost is worth paying for the convenience of smaller repayments that you can afford.

Debts become a problem if you cannot afford to keep up the repayments. In 2008, around a third of those who contacted Citizens Advice Bureaux (CAB) for help did so because of debt problems. The most common reasons they gave for falling into debt were low income (31 per cent of CAB clients), over-commitment (20 per cent), illness (24 per cent), job loss (19 per cent) and relationship breakdown (16 per cent). On average, the clients owed around £17,000 each.[3] Once debt problems start, they tend to snowball, so it is important to admit that you have a problem and tackle it as soon as possible. You don't have do this alone: there are a variety of agencies that will give you free, independent advice and help, including Citizens Advice, National Debtline, the Consumer Credit Counselling Service and Payplan (see Appendix B for contact details). Do not confuse commercial debt management companies (DMCs) with these agencies. DMCs' main income is from the fees they charge for running debt repayment plans. This means DMCs have an interest in putting you into their own plans rather than exploring the best solutions for you. Moreover, you can get the same sort of planning free from the independent advice agencies. The fees you pay unnecessarily to a DMC just eat into the money you could otherwise be putting towards clearing your debts.

---

[3] Citizens Advice, *A life in debt*, February 2009.

The advice agencies will help you work through a fairly standard procedure. First you need to draw up a budget (for example, using the budget template on pp. 11–12) excluding your debt repayments. From this, you can see what income, if any, you have available to put towards your debts and what scope you have for cutting back your spending. The advice agency will also check that you are getting all the income you can: for example, are there state benefits or tax credits (see Appendix A) that you could claim, and are you due a tax rebate? The advice agency will also check whether you have any assets that could be used to pay off debts.

Whatever income and assets you have available should be used first to settle any 'priority debts'. These are debts where the consequences of non-payment are that you may be imprisoned, lose your home or lose essential services (such as gas and electricity) or goods (such as your car). The box below lists the most common priority debts. Other debts are 'non-priority' because there is only a limited range of action that creditors can take against you. You need to negotiate with your creditors and the advice agency can help you to do this. The aim is to agree a plan for gradually reducing your outstanding debt by steadily paying whatever amount you can afford. Ideally, the creditor will agree to freeze any interest while you do this. If you have several creditors, the advice agency may be able to organise a free debt management plan for you where you make one centralised payment each month which is then distributed to your creditors in the proportions previously agreed.

### Priority and non-priority debts

If you have debt problems, you should focus first on sorting out priority debts because the consequences of non-payment are severe. The main priority debts are:

- **Mortgage or rent arrears**. You could lose your home.
- **Other loans secured on your home**. You could lose your home.
- **Council tax**. You could be imprisoned.
- **TV licence**. You could be imprisoned.
- **Gas and electricity**. You could be cut off.
- **Hire purchase for essential goods** (such as a car you need for work). The goods can be repossessed.
- **Income tax and National insurance**. You could be forced into bankruptcy.

Most other debts are 'non-priority debts'. The creditor can take you to court but a judge would probably then make an order (a county court judgment or CCJ) for you to repay the debts in a similar way to a debt repayment plan that you negotiate voluntarily. Non-priority debts include overdrafts, credit cards and mail order catalogues.

If it is not possible to clear your debts with an informal repayment plan, there are three more formal options administered by the Insolvency Service (a government agency) and for which you have to pay a fee:

■ **Debt relief orders**. This could be an option if you have debts of less than £15,000 and you have a low income (less than £50 a month available to pay off debts) and very low savings (less than £300). For a period, usually 12 months, the creditors named in the order may not take any action against you and you do not have to make any repayments of these debts. At the end of the year, any remaining amount of these debts is written off. You agree to restart repayments if your circumstances change within the 12 months. The order can only cover certain types of unsecured debts. It can't, for example, cover your mortgage. You will have to keep on making payments for any debts not covered by the order. You can apply through the free debt advice agencies.

■ **Individual voluntary arrangement (IVA)**. This is a formal arrangement with your creditors to pay off a proportion of your debts over a period of five years. Interest and charges on the debts are frozen during this period. You must stick to the agreed payments and you must also declare all of your assets which creditors can ask to be put towards the settlement of the debts. At the end of five years, any remaining debts are written off.

■ **Bankruptcy**. On being declared bankrupt, you cease to be liable for your debts, but your assets – including your home – are taken over and sold to pay off as much as possible of what you owe. While bankrupt, you cannot be a director of a company or work in certain occupations, such as the police, Armed Forces and local government, and may be restricted from working as a solicitor or accountant, so going bankrupt could mean losing your job. Usually you will be discharged after one year.

The details above apply in England and Wales, but similar arrangements apply in Scotland and Northern Ireland.

Debt arrears and orders and arrangements to pay them off affect your credit record and usually continue to do so for up to six years after the debts have been cleared or written off. So you are likely to have difficulty for some time getting a mortgage or taking out other loans.

## Feedback to *Are you risk averse?* (on p. 8)

In the first question, if you could play the lottery many times, the average win under option (b) would be (80% × £1,500) + (20% × £0) = £1,200 – in other words, £200 more than the fixed sum available from option (a). So the expected value of the outcome from (b) is better than from (a). If you chose (a), you are deemed to be risk averse.

In the second question, the expected value from the lottery is again (80% × £1,500) + (20% × £0) = £1,200. If you would need more than £1,200 to persuade you to sell the ticket, you are deemed to be a risk lover. If you would accept less than £1,200, you are risk averse.

If these tests seem a bit abstract, consider how they compare to the following real-life choices:

■ You win a prize draw and can choose between a large cash lump sum or an income for the rest of your life. It seems reasonable to assume that the company offering the draw has set the amounts so that, on average, the cost to the company of either option is the same. If you choose the income, you are in effect gambling that you will live longer than average and get more in the total than you would have had from the lump sum. Choosing the lump sum suggests you are risk averse.

■ You reach retirement age and have to decide whether to take a tax-free cash lump sum from your pension scheme, but this means giving up some of your pension. As you will discover in Chapter 8, this is a very common option at retirement and presents a similar choice to the prize-draw scenarios discussed above. If you are willing to take cash that is worth less than the value of the pension given up (assuming average life expectancy), you are risk-averse.

# 2

# Do you need an adviser?

## Introduction

The framework described in Chapter 1 is a standard method of financial planning used in one form or another by most professional advisers either implicitly or explicitly. In theory there is no reason why you cannot apply this framework yourself to your own financial decisions – and in fact, you have a major advantage over a professional adviser. Financial planning is a process of marrying up, on one side, your own personal data and, on the other, the financial strategies and options available. A crucial stage for a professional adviser is gathering enough data about you – called a 'fact find' – to put the adviser in the position of being able to select suitable advice. You have the advantage of already being an expert about yourself. On the other hand, a professional should have greater expertise than you in knowing what financial tools and strategies are available. This suggests four distinct approaches you might take to financial planning:

■ **Complete DIY (do-it-yourself).** If you want to construct your own plan yourself without any help from professional advisers, you have to set aside time for research so that you can acquire the knowledge that a good adviser would have. This book will help you find out about the strategies and products available, when they may be suitable and pitfalls to watch out for. It will also signpost you to sources of up-to-date information about prices, product details, charges and features for specific products. You will need to allow time for gathering this data, executing your plan and making regular reviews. Therefore, the complete DIY approach is unlikely to be feasible if you are a workaholic or have little free time.

■ **In-the-driving-seat**. A more realistic approach for many people is to learn enough to construct a financial plan but seek the help of an adviser when it comes to the stage of choosing specific products and companies. Another possibility is to organise the main elements of your financial plan for yourself but use an adviser for unusual events – such as investing a lump sum from redundancy or inheritance. Either way, essentially you control your financial plan and can cherry pick help from advisers to supplement your growing knowledge and expertise.

■ **Collaboration**. You might prefer to use a professional for the bulk of your financial planning, especially if you lack time or do not feel entirely confident making financial decisions on your own. Even so, a knowledge of the planning process, strategies and products available will help you to make the most of an adviser's services. You should look on your relationship with the adviser as a partnership with each of you bringing your expertise to the table to jointly create the most suitable plan. Using this book as your financial planning 'homework' will help you to understand what the adviser is trying to do at each stage and to strengthen the process. It will also mean you are able to assess the advice you are given, to ask questions when a recommendation seems unusual and to guard yourself against being sold unsuitable products.

■ **Delegation**. The opposite extreme from DIY planning is to delegate your planning completely to a professional, for example, choosing a discretionary investment management service. Your job is to tell the adviser your goals, attitude toward risk and other salient facts about yourself and your circumstances. The adviser then constructs a plan based on these, implementing it without referring back to you at each stage.

Except where you opt for the full DIY approach, you will at some stage interact with one or more advisers, so you need to know what types are available and the services they offer.

## What to expect from an adviser

Understanding what an adviser will do and the nature of the advice they can give will help you to prepare in advance and get the best from an adviser, whether you use one for just part of your financial planning or the whole process.

There are different types of adviser specialising in different areas of advice. You have already seen how debt advisers can help (in Chapter 1). This chapter considers overall financial planning and generic advice, insurance and mortgage advice, equity release, various types of investment advice, and estate planning and tax advice. A quick overview of who to consult is given in Table 2.1.

**Table 2.1 Types of advice**

| *Area of financial planning (where to find information in this book)* | *Type of adviser* | *For advice/to find an adviser (see Appendix B for contact details)* |
| --- | --- | --- |
| Debt (Chapter 1) | Debt adviser/ money adviser | Citizens Advice Consumer Credit Counselling Service National Debtline Payplan Community Legal Advice Money Advice Scotland Advice NI |
| Overall financial planning (all chapters) | Independent financial adviser | IFA Promotion Institute of Financial Planning Personal Finance Society |
| Generic financial advice (all chapters) | Money guidance service | Moneymadeclear |
| Insurance (Chapters 3 to 5) | Insurance broker Independent financial adviser Insurance providers | British Insurance Brokers Association IFA Promotion Institute of Financial Planning Personal Finance Society |
| Mortgage (Chapter 6) | Mortgage broker Mortgage providers | IFA Promotion |
| Equity release | Independent financial adviser Equity release providers | IFA Promotion Institute of Financial Planning Personal Finance Society Safe Home Income Plans (SHIP) |

▶

**Table 2.1 Types of advice** *continued*

| *Area of financial planning (where to find information in this book)* | *Type of adviser* | *For advice/to find an adviser (see Appendix B for contact details)* |
| --- | --- | --- |
| State pensions (Chapters 7 and 8) | Government<br>Independent advice organisation | The Pension Service<br>The Pensions Advisory Service |
| Occupational pensions (Chapters 7 and 8) | Pension scheme trustees/pensions administrator<br>Independent advice organisation<br>Independent financial adviser | Pension scheme trustees<br>Your HR department at work<br>The Pensions Advisory Service<br>IFA Promotion<br>Institute of Financial Planning<br>Personal Finance Society |
| Personal pensions (Chapters 7 and 8) | Independent financial adviser<br>Independent advice organisation<br>Personal pension providers | IFA Promotion<br>Institute of Financial Planning<br>Personal Finance Society<br>The Pensions Advisory Service |
| Pension transfers | Independent financial adviser<br>Consulting actuary | IFA Promotion<br>Institute of Financial Planning<br>Personal Finance Society<br>Association of Consulting Actuaries<br>Society of Pension Consultants |
| Stock-market investments (e.g. shares and bonds) (Chapters 9 and 10) | Stockbroker | London Stock Exchange<br>Association of Private Client Investment Managers and Stockbrokers (APCIMS) |
| Other investments (Chapters 9 and 10) | Independent financial adviser<br>Investment providers | IFA Promotion<br>Institute of Financial Planning<br>Personal Finance Society |

**Table 2.1 Types of advice *continued***

| Area of financial planning (where to find information in this book) | Type of adviser | For advice/to find an adviser (see Appendix B for contact details) |
| --- | --- | --- |
| Estate planning (Chapter 11) | Tax adviser<br>Independent financial adviser | Chartered Institute of Taxation<br>Society of Trust and Estate Practitioners<br>IFA Promotion<br>Institute of Financial Planning<br>Personal Finance Society |
| Tax (all chapters and Appendix A) | Tax advisers<br>Independent advice organisation | Chartered Institute of Taxation<br>Accountants<br>Tax Aid<br>Tax Help for Older People |
| State benefits (all chapters and Appendix A) | Government<br>Money advisers | Jobcentre Plus<br>The Pension Service<br>Citizens Advice<br>Community Legal Advice<br>Money Advice Scotland |

## Overall financial planning

Independent financial advisers (IFAs) can either help you with specific aspects of financial planning (as described below) or take a holistic
approach that aims to sort out all aspects of your finances in an integrated
way, often developing a life-long relationship with you in much the same
way as you might choose one firm to act as your family solicitor. Members
of the Institute of Financial Planning, who are IFAs and all have qualifications that entitle them to use the designation 'Certified Financial Planner',
specialise in particular in this overall approach to financial planning.

Overall financial planning advice is likely to include many or all of the elements described below, for example, life and health insurances, mortgages,
equity release, pensions and investments. To give advice on these areas,
advisers must be authorised by the UK's financial regulator, the Financial

Services Authority (FSA). (See p. 54 for more information about authorisation and how the regulations protect you when you use an adviser).

You may pay for advice from an IFA either by a fee direct to the adviser or by commission (see the box). To describe themselves as 'independent', advisers must offer you the option of paying by fee if you want to. Some IFAs only accept fees and off-set any commissions received against the fee you pay.

### Payment by commission

There are basically two ways to pay for advice: a fee paid direct to the adviser or by commission. With commission, the adviser receives payment from the provider of the product you buy. Although you might think you are getting free advice, in fact you are paying the adviser's commission indirectly through the charges built into the product. If you cancel the product in the early years, the adviser may have to repay some of the commission he or she received. In addition, you may have to pay a surrender charge, which in effect pays the balance of the costs of selling you the product that due to the cancellation can now no longer be fully recouped through the regular charges.

Payment by commission may tempt advisers to sell you products (even if none is needed), persuade you to replace old products with new ones (a process called churning), recommend products and providers who pay high commission over those that pay less or no commission (for example, life insurance bonds rather than unit trusts), and encourage you to take out more insurance or to invest more than you really need to. Where products are sold by commission, the salespeople, agents, brokers and advisers involved might use 'hard sell' tactics to persuade you to buy. You need to be doubly careful to ensure that any product you're being offered really is suitable for you.

The FSA is proposing to abolish payment by commission for investment advice from 2012 onwards (see p. 50). But there are no plans to ban commission for other types of advice.

## Money Guidance

Money Guidance, under the brand name Moneymadeclear, is an advice service, which has been trialled by the FSA and is due to be rolled out nationwide during 2010.

Although the FSA is primarily a financial regulator, it was given an unusual additional role, set out in legislation, of 'promoting public understanding of the financial system'.[1] As part of this remit, the FSA has used

---

[1] Financial Service and Markets Act 200, section 4(1).

a range of initiatives, including, for example: free information leaflets and booklets; a consumer website; working with employers; financial information packs for people facing major life events, such as becoming new parents; and resources for use with young people and in schools. Most recently, it has been testing the new Money Guidance service. During 2010, the FSA's role of promoting public financial understanding is due to be transferred to a separate, independent body.

The aim of the Money Guidance service is to make free 'generic advice' available to everyone. Unlike the advice from an IFA which will be tailored to you personally and will result in concrete recommendations about what you should do, generic advice is not specific to your particular situation and instead indicates what people in your sort of situation might do. Money Guidance will not direct you to specific strategies or companies, but it will signpost you to appropriate organisations for any specific advice you might need – for example, a money adviser if you need debt advice or to The Pensions Advisory Service or an IFA if you need pensions advice. This book you are reading now also gives generic advice, though in more detail than you are likely to receive from the Money Guidance service. The FSA describes Money Guidance as:

> *the guidance and information people need on the money matters that shape everyday life. It covers areas like:*
>
> ■ *budgeting their weekly or monthly spending;*
>
> ■ *saving and borrowing, and insuring and protecting themselves and their families;*
>
> ■ *retirement planning;*
>
> ■ *understanding tax and welfare benefits;*
>
> ■ *jargon-busting – explaining the technical language we use in the financial services industry; and*
>
> ■ *money guidance is also completely sales-free.*[2]

The Money Guidance service is being set up particularly to offer guidance to people on opting out of a new national pension scheme (called the National Employment Savings Trust or NEST), which is due to start being phased in from 2012 and is described in Chapter 7.

---

[2] Financial Services Authority, http://www.fsa.gov.uk/financial_capability/our-work/money_guidance.shtml. Accessed 23 August 2009.

In 2009, Money Guidance was being piloted as a face-to-face service in two areas (the North West and North East of England), online through the FSA's Moneymadeclear website and by phone on the Moneymadeclear Helpline (see Appendix B for contact details). Because Money Guidance offers only generic advice and not strategies tailored to you or specific recommendations, you are not in the position where the guidance offered could be deemed to be unsuitable and so the advisers do not need to be authorised by the FSA.

## Insurance advice

There are three broad types of insurance: life insurance and health insurances, which tend to be the domain of IFAs; and general insurance, which is usually sold by brokers and insurance agents. 'General insurance' is a catch-all term that usually means the types of policy that run for just a year at a time, such as car, home, travel and pet insurance.

Brokers specialise in helping you shop around for a suitable policy. IFAs tend to deal with more complex needs and are likely to spend time helping you work out your insurance needs as well as finding a suitable policy. Brokers and IFAs may be able to select policies from the whole of the market or a panel of insurers. (Different rules apply where IFAs are giving investment advice – see p. 47.) Agents – who take many forms, such as shops selling extended warrantees, lenders selling payment protection insurance (PPI), mortgage lenders selling buildings insurance, and so on – often sell the products of a single insurance company.

You might also buy insurance direct from the provider on either an advised or non-advised basis. In this case, you will just get information and advice about that particular firm's products.

Insurance advisers must find out enough about your needs in order to recommend a suitable policy for you. They must also draw to your attention any unusual or particularly onerous conditions of the policy.

Typically, advisers receive commission from the provider for each policy they sell – often a substantial amount. A recent survey by the UK's competition regulator, the Competition Commission, found that lenders selling PPI typically receive £68 in commission and profit-sharing out of every £100 you paid in premiums.[3] On income protection insurance or life

---

[3] Competition Commission, *Market investigation into payment protection insurance*, January 2009.

insurance, an adviser might receive a lump-sum commission equal to, say, 130 per cent of your first year's premiums[4] (but would have to pay some of this back if you stopped the policy within the first few years).

Intermediaries must tell you how much you will pay if there is a direct fee for their advice. But, if they are selling you protection insurance, they do not currently have to tell you that they are being paid commission or how much. However, in late 2009, the FSA was consulting on introducing commission disclosure for life and health insurances sold alongside investments. For advice about insurance with an investment element, see p. 47.

## Case study

Mick takes out £100,000 of life cover, paying a premium of £30 a month (£360 a year). Under the particular insurance company's payment terms, the adviser who sells Mick the policy receives an immediate initial commission payment of £468. This is calculated as 25 per cent of Mick's premiums for the first four years (sometimes referred to as 'LAUTRO' because this commission calculation is still based on a scale used in the 1980s and set by a former financial regulator called LAUTRO), increased by an extra 30 per cent. If Mick cancels the policy within the first four years, the adviser will have to pay back some of the initial commission (called 'clawback'). Provided Mick keeps the policy going, from the fifth year the adviser will receive further commission (called 'renewal' or 'trail commission') equal to 2.5 per cent of each premium (so £9 a year). Mick's £30 a month premium has been set at that level in order to pay for the life cover, meet the company's costs and provide it with profit, and also cover the cost of paying commission to the adviser.

## Mortgage advice

If you want a mortgage, you could go direct to a lender who may offer just information about its products or also advice – it must tell you which. Alternatively, you might use a mortgage adviser (sometimes called a broker), covering either the whole of the market or a selection of firms, or acting as an agent selling the mortgage products of a single lender. A mortgage adviser can describe its advice as 'independent' only if its recommendations are based on a review of the whole market. In practice, this condition can be satisfied if the adviser identifies selections of products suitable for particular types of customer and keeps those selections up-to-date through regular reviews of the market.

---

[4] HM Revenue & Customs, *Business economic note 20. Insurance brokers and agents, undated;* *Moneyfacts, Investment, life & pensions moneyfacts,* August 2009.

Mortgage advisers must find out enough about you to recommend a suitable loan. In particular, they must check that any mortgage they recommend is affordable given your income and other resources. In the past, affordability checks have been rather crude, for example, basing the amount you can borrow on a multiple of your income. Following the global financial crisis that started in 2007 which resulted at least in part from the heavy selling of mortgages to low-income households (mainly in the USA but also in the UK), affordability checks are likely to become more realistic, taking into account your income and also your existing expenditure commitments.

As with insurance, mortgage advisers and agents usually receive commission for each loan they sell, so you need to be alert to how this might colour the advice you get. An independent mortgage adviser must offer you the option of paying for the advice by fee rather than commission. The adviser must make clear at the start of doing business with you what you will have to pay in fees or the basis on which the adviser will receive commission or any other form of payment.

## Equity release

Equity release schemes (which let you raise an income or lump sum against the value of your home) are considered complex products, so advisers have to observe a number of special rules. For example, in assessing the suitability of a scheme, advisers must satisfy themselves that the benefits to you of the scheme outweigh any drawbacks, such as loss of state benefits or an increase in your income tax bill. See Chapter 6 for details about the pros and cons of equity release schemes.

Advice about equity release schemes is available direct from the providers or from an IFA. You may pay for advice from IFAs through fees or commission. Most equity release providers belong to a trade body, Safe Home Income Plans (SHIP), which can provide you with a list of its members.

## Pensions advice

For advice about state pensions, either contact The Pensions Service (the government department responsible for state pensions) or The Pensions Advisory Service, an independent voluntary organisation, partly funded by the government, which has a remit of both giving general advice and also helping to resolve disputes about occupational and personal pensions (see p. 61) but not the state scheme. In either case, the organisation can give you detailed information and guidance about the state scheme and, through The Pension Service, you can find out about your personal entitlement to the state pension. There is no charge for the advice.

With occupational pension schemes, the scheme officials should normally be your first port of call. These will be the trustees of the scheme – the people or a company with overall responsibility for looking after and operating the scheme on behalf of the members – or the pensions scheme administrator – a paid official who looks after the day-to-day running of the scheme. You should be able to find the contact details in literature you have received about the scheme, the scheme website or from your employer's HR department. The trustees and administrator can give you information and guidance about the scheme but not any advice on choosing between the scheme and other possible pension arrangements. There is no charge for the advice.

Personal pensions are classified as investments for the purpose of regulation and so the information about investment advice below applies. Some IFAs specialise in particular areas of pensions advice, such as annuity purchase – see Chapter 8 for details.

If you want advice about whether to take out a personal pension rather than join an occupational scheme or whether to transfer the rights you've built up in an occupational scheme to a personal pension, consult an IFA who holds additional qualifications required to give this type of advice. (See p. 61 for how to check that an adviser has the expertise you need.) If you need advice about transferring a pension from an old employer's scheme to that of a new employer, there is no product involved on which an IFA can earn commission, so you should be prepared to pay a fee for this type of advice. If your transfer involves a large sum, you might consider getting advice from a consulting actuary: however, most specialise in advising companies rather than personal investors and the fees tend to be steep.

## Investment advice

At the time of writing, different rules apply to investment advice, depending on the type of investment involved. However, this is due to change (see p. 50). This section explains the rules that applied in 2009 and were expected to continue until 2012.

If you are buying and selling investments that are traded on a market, such as shares and bonds, you are most likely to go to a stockbroker. Brokers offer a range of services:

■ **Execution-only**. The broker merely carries out your orders to buy and sell without giving any advice. Usually you deal by phone or internet, though postal dealing services are also available. The broker is required to get you the best available price unless you give some other instruction. Typically, you pay commission or a flat fee per transaction and sometimes a monthly or quarterly administration fee as well. An administration fee might entitle you to one or two free transactions.

■ **Advisory**. In addition to carrying out your orders, the broker typically provides you with reports by the firm's analysts, offers recommendations, reviews your investments, say, every six months, and may on request give an opinion on trades you are thinking of making. The broker must ensure that any recommendations are suitable for you given your knowledge and experience of investments, your financial situation and your investment objectives. You pay extra for an advisory service, for example a higher rate of commission per transaction and/ or a fee which may be flat-rate or set as a proportion of your portfolio. Usually, the advisory service is available only if your portfolio is a minimum size, for example, at least £50,000.

■ **Discretionary management**. With this service, you hand your portfolio to the broker to run for you. The broker, based on its knowledge of you, including your attitude towards risk and your investment objectives, takes investment decisions on your behalf. To qualify for this type of service, your portfolio must be at least, say, £150,000 in size. (The precise limit varies from one firm to another.) In addition to dealing charges, you normally pay an annual fee set at a percentage of your portfolio.

If you want to buy and sell the more complex investments, such as options, futures and spread betting (see Chapter 10), the broker or other firm involved must ask you to provide information about your knowledge and experience of the investments in order to assess whether you understand the risks involved. The firm can provide training to ensure that its customers do have the necessary knowledge.

The vast majority of ordinary investors do not buy shares, bonds or complex investments direct, but invest indirectly through investment funds, such as investment-type life insurance, unit trusts (or the very similar open-ended investment companies) and pension arrangements. Along with investment trust savings schemes and annuities, these are collectively known as 'packaged products'. (See Chapters 7, 8 and 10 for details of these investment funds and products.) Special rules apply when you are sold or given advice about packaged products.

Until 2005, packaged products used to be sold through a regime called 'polarisation' under which a firm that sold or gave advice was either independent or tied to a single product provider. When the polarisation rule was abolished, a much more complicated system was introduced. Now an investment adviser may be any of the following:

▪ **Independent**. To describe the advice as 'independent', the adviser must recommend a suitable product from the full range of what's available across the whole market. In practice, this can mean the adviser selects panels of products that are suitable for different types of customer, provided the whole market is reviewed regularly and the selections are up to date. Independent advisers must offer you the option to pay for the advice by fee rather than commission. Some independent advisers give only fee-based advice. Paying a fee is relatively straightforward. Many advisers will give you the first half hour or hour of their time free. After that you pay, for example, by the hour just as you would if you hired a solicitor or accountant. The amount you pay varies from firm to firm and depends on the seniority of the person considering your case. For example, you might pay £200 an hour for fully-fledged advice but £50 an hour for behind-the-scenes work done by an assistant.

▪ **Multi-tied**. This is a firm, or its representatives, that offer the products of several different providers. The products keep the brand name of each provider but the firm you deal with is responsible for the advice it gives about them. The firm must recommend the most suitable product for you from its range or make no recommendation if it does not have anything suitable. Usually, this will be commission-based advice.

▪ **Tied**. This adviser is the subsidiary or representative of a product provider and can recommend only that provider's products. The adviser must recommend the most suitable product from its range or tell you if it has nothing suitable. Again, this is usually commission-based advice. Most high street banks offer tied advice, selling just the products of the companies within the banking group.

Firms giving advice about packaged products must make their status clear to you before starting to do business, telling you if they are independent, multi-tied or tied. They must also have a list of the firms whose products they can offer, ready to give you if you ask.

Finally, a different type of advice may be offered if a firm offers stakeholder products. These are intended to be straightforward, good value products which should be easy to understand: for example, there is a stakeholder pension (see Chapter 7) and a stakeholder child trust fund (see

Chapter 9). Firms may sell most stakeholder products using a 'basic advice' regime, governed by simpler rules than normally apply to investment advice. Under the basic advice regime, firms may offer just one stakeholder product of each type and the advice consists of taking you through a set of pre-scripted questions (sometimes called a decision tree) to determine whether a product is suitable for you.

Investment advisers must tell you at the start of doing business what fees, commissions or other charges you will pay or, if it is not possible to give you a firm figure, the basis on which the charges will be worked out. With packaged investments, you must be given a Key Facts document, setting out the main features of the investment in a standardised way. The Key Facts document includes the amount (if any) that your adviser will receive in commission if you take up the product.

### Tied versus independent advice

If you want the chance of finding the best product for you, choose independent advice. Only independent advisers will recommend a product drawn from the whole market. A tied adviser – such as your local bank – can only recommend a product from its own limited range. While this might not be the worst product available, it is also unlikely to be the best. It may be tempting to seek advice from a familiar provider, such as your own bank, but you should be aware that the compromise is a product that is likely to be less than the best you could have had.

## Changes on the way: the Retail Distribution Review

Independent, multi-tied, tied and basic investment advice create a confusing mosaic of choice. Combined with the widespread practice of advisers being paid by commission from providers whose products they sell, there is a real risk that you may end up being given unsuitable advice (see the box on p. 51). In mid-2007, the FSA launched a review (called the Retail Distribution Review) to address these and other issues.

As a result, the FSA is proposing to introduce a new regime, from 2012, which will apply to all investment advice, not just advice about packaged products. The new regime has four main aims:

■ **Improve clarity of service**. Advisers will have to describe their services as either 'independent advice' or 'restricted advice'. To be 'independent' the firm must 'make their recommendations based on a comprehensive and fair analysis and provide unbiased, unrestricted advice'.[5] Restricted advice can be based on a narrower product range and so corresponds to multi-tied or tied advice.

▪ **Address the potential for remuneration bias.** Payment for advice by commission will be banned. Advisers will have to set their own charges, which can be negotiated with customers. However, as an alternative to paying a lump sum fee up-front, you may be able to arrange to pay the advice charges through deductions from the product you buy or the investment you take out and the provider will be asked to administer this arrangement. Although that sounds like commission by the back door, the key difference is that the adviser – not the product provider – sets the charge. Providers do not have to agree to deduct charges through their products, so this form of payment will not always be available. These changes to the way you pay for advice should have a knock-on effect on the way product charges are structured.

▪ **Increase the professional standards of advisers.** To practise at all, advisers and salespeople will have to have new minimum-standard qualifications that are higher than the current level (and will be equivalent to first-year degree level). They will also have to keep their knowledge up to date through more rigorous continuous professional development requirements and abide by a newly introduced Code of Ethics.

## Mis-selling of investments

### Pensions mis-selling

Between 1988 and 1994, many people who would have been better off at retirement saving through their employer's occupational pension schemes were advised to transfer to, or take out, a personal pension instead. Following a lengthy investigation, over 1.1 million people were paid over £10 billion in compensation.[6] Over 90 per cent of the cases involved advice given by pension providers and banks.[7]

### Endowment mis-selling

During the 1980s and early 1990s, endowment mortgages accounted for the majority of new mortgages taken out. However, many consumers said their advisers had not pointed out that their mortgage was linked to stock market performance. This became apparent only when market conditions changed and the consumers realised they were no longer on track to repay their mortgages in full by the end of the term. Nearly 700,000 customers complained and received around £1.1 billion in redress.[8]

---

[5] FSA Consultation Paper CP09/18, *Distribution of retail investments: Delivering the RDR*, June 2009.

[6] Financial Services Authority, *Annual report* 2003/04.

[7] Financial Services Authority, *FSA on track to bring the pensions mis-selling review to a close*, Press notice, 28 January 2002.

[8] Financial Services Authority, *Mortgage endowments: Progress report and next steps*, July 2005.

**Free-standing additional voluntary contribution (AVC) schemes**

In 2000, the FSA launched a review of the sales between 1998 and 1999 of these schemes (designed to top up pension savings – see Chapter 7) to people who could have joined better AVC schemes through their workplace or who were advised to switch from personal pensions to these schemes. Nearly 100,000 people received £250 million in compensation.[9]

**Precipice bonds**

From 1999 to the early 2000s, around 250,000 people took out these bonds.[10] They are examples of 'structured products' (which work in a variety of fairly complex ways – see Chapter 9) that, in this case, were designed to provide a high income and guaranteed return of capital and were typically marketed to the over-60s. However, the capital guarantee held only as long as the stock market did not fall by more that a set amount. In some cases, advisers did not draw this adequately to their customers' attention. When the stock market fell over the period 2000 to 2003, many of these bonds matured with a loss. Around £159 million was paid out in compensation to customers, three large providers were fined and an IFA banned from trading.[11]

# Estate planning and tax advice

Tax advice is not regulated by the FSA or by any other statutory regulator. In fact, anyone can set themselves up and call themselves a tax adviser. But many advisers belong to professional bodies that require their members to have qualifications, keep their knowledge up to date through continuous professional development and to behave ethically and professionally in their dealings with clients. If you need tax advice, it makes sense to deal with a member of one of these bodies. For help, say, drawing up a tax return, consider a member of the Association of Tax Technicians. For advice on how to organise your tax affairs or help dealing with the tax authorities, a member of the Chartered Institute of Taxation would be appropriate. Accountants also deal with tax. Members of all these bodies give independent advice and you pay a fee direct for the adviser's services. If your income is low (in the range £15,000 to £17,000 in 2009) and you can't afford to hire one of these firms, you may qualify for free tax help and advice from Tax Aid or, if you are close to 60 or over, Tax Help for Older People. (See Appendix B for contact details.)

---

[9] Financial Services Authority, *Annual report 2003/04*.

[10] Financial Services Authority, *Regulator calls for better consumer information on precipice bonds*, Press notice, 19 February 2003.

[11] Financial Services Authority, *Summary of the SCARPS project: Detailed findings*, November 2005.

Estate planning may typically involve tax planning, investments, insurance and legal issues such as setting up trusts. Some IFAs and some tax professionals specialise in this area. They will often have arrangements with other firms so that, for example, if you go to an IFA, he or she will recommend a solicitor to handle the legal side. Similarly, tax professionals may recommend a particular IFA to advise on and handle any product purchases. Some firms combine a range of different professionals under one roof. If your estate is large enough (say, at least £1 million) to warrant the higher cost, consider using a member of the Society of Trust and Estate Practitioners (STEP).

## Benefits advice

The main sources of information and guidance about state benefits are the government departments responsible for administering them: Jobcentre Plus if you are of working age, or The Pension Service if you are retired or you need to know about state pensions. However, some benefits are administered by your local authority, including council tax benefit, housing benefit and help through social services if you have a disability. HM Revenue & Customs deals with tax credits and a few other benefits, such as the health in pregnancy grant and child benefit.

The other main source is independent voluntary bodies, such as Citizens Advice, which can give you benefits advice direct, or Community Legal Advice, Money Advice Scotland and Advice NI which can direct you to a local benefits adviser. Benefits advice is normally free. There are also online tools at www.entitledto.org.uk and www.direct.gov.uk (Benefits advisor) which you can use to estimate the benefits you may be eligible to claim.

The UK benefits system is notoriously complicated with a vast array of rules on, for example, eligibility, the calculation of income for means testing and restrictions through overlapping benefit regulations. The 14 volumes of the specialist guide used by benefits staff (*The Decision Maker's Guide*), along with other resources, is accessible through the Department for Work and Pensions website (see Appendix B). But this is an area where you really do benefit from getting expert advice.

## The DIY adviser and price

As you have seen in the previous pages, for now at least, it is common for many types of adviser to be paid by commission, rather than a fee, for their advice and their commission payment to be built into the charges for the products that you might buy. If, you are being your own financial adviser, you need to avoid buying products whose charging structure allows for this commission, otherwise you will in effect be paying for an advice service you haven't had.

With packaged investments, buy through fund supermarkets or discount brokers. Typically, the charges – in particular the 'front-end' or 'initial charge' – are reduced. With mortgages, some lenders offer more competitive interest rate deals or lower charges if you go direct to the lender rather than through an intermediary. There are no hard and fast rules, so check any product's charges carefully, look at the Key Facts document or illustration to see if any commission is available to an adviser, ask the provider if it has better deals available on a no-advice basis and, if not, see if you can negotiate to have the adviser commission rebated to you or invested on your behalf.

If you cannot get a no-advice deal, either shop around elsewhere or, if you really want that product, use an adviser after all – that way, you will have an extra layer of consumer protection (see below).

## How you are protected

With the exception of tax and benefits – and also occupational pension schemes which are covered by different arrangements (see p. 61) – most firms and organisations giving financial advice or offering financial products and services must be authorised by the FSA. Authorised firms must satisfy the FSA that they are solvent, prudently run, operated by fit and proper people and comply with the FSA's rules. The latter include high-level principles and, in some areas, detailed rules about how firms conduct their business. However good the rules, there will always be some firms that flout them, but, provided you deal with an authorised firm, you will have access to proper complaints procedures and, if necessary, a compensation scheme.

Authorised firms may be UK-based organisations or the UK-based subsidiaries of foreign parent companies. Firms established elsewhere in the European Economic Area (EEA) – Austria, Belgium, Bulgaria, Cyprus, Czech Republic, Denmark, Estonia, Finland, France, Germany, Greece, Hungary, Iceland, Ireland, Italy, Latvia, Liechtenstein, Lithuania, Luxembourg, Malta, Netherlands, Norway, Poland, Portugal, Romania, Slovakia, Slovenia, Spain, Sweden – are able to do business in the UK without being authorised by the FSA. Instead they are authorised by the equivalent regulator in their home country. This means that if you have problems, you will need to deal with the complaints and compensation systems there (possibly grappling with the added complication of a foreign language), so you should make sure that you are happy with the arrangements (see the box for UK investors' experience with Icelandic banks).

If you do business with firms based outside the UK or EEA, or firms trading in the UK without being authorised, you may have no consumer protection at all. To check whether a firm is authorised and safe to do business with, consult the FSA Register (see Appendix B for contact details).

## Saving with foreign banks

### Iceland

In 2007, Icelandic banks were growing aggressively, targeting customers in the UK. Savings accounts and bonds from the brands Icesave, Heritable and Kaupthing Edge regularly appeared near the top of the best-buy tables. In October 2008, these banks came crashing down, unable to withstand the effects of the global financial crisis. The Heritable accounts and most of those from Kaupthing Edge were taken over by the Dutch Bank, ING Direct, but Icesave account holders had to turn to the compensation arrangements. The first port of call was the Icelandic compensation scheme which covered the first €20,887 (around £16,200 at the time). Icesave was also voluntarily part of the UK compensation scheme which ensured that the total compensation would be topped up to the UK maximum of £50,000 per account holder. This would still have left some savers out of pocket. Anxious not to damage the already very fragile confidence in the banking system, the UK government stepped in to guarantee that no UK savers would lose any of their money.

### Ireland

Many accounts and other products for savers available through the UK Post Office® are provided by Bank of Ireland, authorised by the Irish Financial Regulator. Normally, savers with Bank of Ireland would have access to the Irish Deposit Guarantee Scheme, where the maximum compensation limit was increased from €20,000 to €100,00 in September 2008. However, at the same time, to improve confidence in its banking system, the Irish government announced that, until September 2010, deposits with certain banks, including the Bank of Ireland, would be guaranteed without limit under a special government arrangement.

### India

Another bank with savings products often in the best buy lists is ICICI. This brand is offered in the UK through ICIC UK plc, a UK-registered subsidiary of the Indian parent bank, ICICI Bank Ltd. Because the subsidiary is UK-based, it is authorised by the FSA and covered by the UK compensation scheme which would protect the first £50,000 per person of deposits (in 2009).

## FSA rules

All authorised firms must observe the FSA's high-level principles, which are reproduced in Table 2.2.

**Table 2.2 The FSA's principles**

| | |
|---|---|
| **1** Integrity | A *firm* must conduct its business with integrity. |
| **2** Skill, care and diligence | A *firm* must conduct its business with due skill, care and diligence. |
| **3** Management and control | A *firm* must take reasonable care to organise and control its affairs responsibly and effectively, with adequate risk management systems. |
| **4** Financial prudence | A *firm* must maintain adequate financial resources. |
| **5** Market conduct | A *firm* must observe proper standards of market conduct. |
| **6** Customers' interests | A *firm* must pay due regard to the interests of its *customers* and treat them fairly. |
| **7** Communications with clients | A *firm* must pay due regard to the information needs of its *clients*, and communicate information to them in a way which is clear, fair and not misleading. |
| **8** Conflicts of interest | A *firm* must manage conflicts of interest fairly, both between itself and its *customers* and between a *customer* and another *client*. |
| **9** Customers: relationships of trust | A *firm* must take reasonable care to ensure the suitability of its advice and discretionary decisions for any *customer* who is entitled to rely upon its judgement. |
| **10** Clients' assets | A *firm* must arrange adequate protection for *clients'* assets when it is responsible for them. |
| **11** Relations with regulators | A *firm* must deal with its regulators in an open and cooperative way, and must disclose to the *FSA* appropriately anything relating to the *firm* of which the *FSA* would reasonably expect notice. |

*Source*: FSA Handbook, *Rule PRIN 2.1.1*, http://fsahandbook.info/FSA/html/handbook/ PRIN/2/1. Accessed 24 August 2009. © Copyright of the Financial Services Authority 2009.

In addition, when selling investments, insurance, mortgages, equity release and, from November 2009, banking products, authorised firms must also abide by the conduct of business rules. Some of these rules, which have been described earlier in this chapter, require firms to disclose the nature of their services and the fees they may get. Another key rule requires firms to give you suitable advice which requires gathering sufficient information from you to make a judgement about suitability. Usually this information is collected through a fact find – a detailed paper-based or computer-based questionnaire asking about your age, family, goals, attitude towards risk, income, spending, existing financial products, and so on. In many areas, the rules require providers to give you product information in standardised formats (labelled 'Key Facts') to help you understand and compare what's on offer.

Although still detailed, the FSA rules are less prescriptive than in the past, because the FSA now expects firms to follow more principles-based regulation. This means firms should build the spirit of the high-level principle into their firm's ethos and management systems. When it comes to Principle 6 (see Table 2.2) which requires firms to treat customers fairly, in 2006 the FSA published six outcomes that should be delivered when firms treat their customers fairly[12]. The first outcome requires firms to embed the fair treatment of customers at the centre of their culture, so that you should not have to question whether or not you will be treated fairly. The second requires that, where firms have developed products or services that are designed to meet the needs of specific types of customer, then those products and services should only be marketed to and targeted at those customers. This might apply, in particular with complex products, such as hedge funds (see Chapter 10), that may have initially been designed for sophisticated investors – firms should be very wary of extending these to a mass market. The third outcome requires firms to provide you with clear information throughout the sales process and afterwards. If you seek advice, under the fourth outcome, this must be suitable given your personal circumstances. The final two outcomes require that products and services perform as you should be able to expect from the information and any advice previously provided, meet acceptable standards, and that no unreasonable barriers are put in your way if later on you want to switch product or provider, or make a complaint.

---

[12] FSA, *Treating customers fairly – towards fair outcomes for consumers*, July 2006.

## Complaints

All authorised firms must have proper complaints procedures. If you are unhappy with the service or products you've received, first you should complain to the firm concerned. An informal approach might be enough to sort out the issue but, if not, say that you wish to complain using the formal procedure. It is best to make your complaint in writing. Include all the necessary detail – what happened, what date, who you spoke to, and so on – but try to be succinct and to the point. If you talk to the firm by phone or in person, make a record of the date, time, who you spoke to and what was said.

The firm should give you a response within eight weeks. If it doesn't or you are unhappy with its reply, you can take your case to the Financial Ombudsman Service. This is a free complaints procedure. It is less formal than going to court. Usually the Ombudsman will decide a case on written evidence, without you having to attend any meeting or hearing, and the Ombudsman can take into account best practice in the industry as well as the strict letter of the law. If your complaint is upheld, the Ombudsman will recommend a course of action. This might be financial compensation from the firm (up to a maximum of £100,000 in 2009) but could be, for example, reinstating an insurance policy or whatever other remedy is appropriate to the circumstances. The Ombudsman's judgement is binding on the firm but not on you. This means, if you are still unhappy, you could take your case to court. But bear in mind that court action tends to be slow and expensive and might simply come to the same conclusion as the Ombudsman.

To succeed, a complaint must be valid. Many financial products involve risk and you will not have ground for complaint simply because, say, an investment performed poorly. However, if you followed the recommendations of an adviser who had not made clear the risks inherent in a strategy, then you could have a valid complaint that you were given bad advice. This highlights a key advantage of taking professional advice over being your own adviser: if you get it wrong, you have no-one to blame but yourself and no source of redress. If an adviser gets it wrong, you can expect to be compensated – as the case study from the Ombudsman opposite shows.

# Case study

Mr J contacted an independent financial adviser, mentioning a high-income bond (sometimes known as a 'precipice' bond) that he had seen advertised in the press. Mr J and his wife wanted to invest a capital sum of approximately £300,000. The income they got from this capital would form their main source of future income, as they had little pension provision. The adviser offered a positive opinion of the bond and forwarded Mr J an application form to complete. The adviser subsequently sent Mr J a letter saying the transaction had been carried out on a 'limited advice' basis.

Not long afterwards, Mr J approached the adviser again, saying he was seeking a way to invest the proceeds of a maturing investment. The adviser suggested four possibilities, including another high-income bond – which Mr J subsequently invested in. Again, the firm sent him a letter saying the transaction had been carried out on a 'limited advice' basis. The following year, concerned about poor returns from both of his bonds, Mr J complained to the adviser's firm. He said he had received poor advice and had never been warned of any risk attached to his investments. When the firm rejected the complaint, Mr J came to us.

**Complaint upheld**

The firm argued that it was not responsible for the appropriateness (or otherwise) of either of these bonds, as it had made it clear that it had given only 'limited' advice. It said that in the first transaction it had given only a general opinion of the product Mr J had selected for himself. And for the subsequent transaction, it had 'simply offered a few suggestions for Mr J to research for himself'.

As we have noted, in our view there is no category of 'limited' financial advice as far as sales to private clients are concerned. And it was clear to us that the firm had not carried out either of these transactions on an execution-only basis. The firm had made recommendations that had guided Mr J in his investment decisions. So it was responsible for the sale. We were concerned not only about the suitability of the firm's recommendations, but also about its failure to provide any risk warnings. We concluded it was unlikely that Mr J would have proceeded with the investments if the firm had given him appropriate risk warnings, even if the bonds had been suitable for him. And on the facts of the case we did not think they were suitable. We therefore upheld the complaint.

*Source*: Financial Ombudsman Service, *Ombudsman News*, January/February 2006

# Compensation

If you make a loss because of the negligence or dishonesty of a firm, you have a legal claim against the firm and can pursue it as described above using the firm's complaints procedure and, if necessary, the Ombudsman and/or the courts. However, this route is no use if the firm has gone out of business – you might win the case, but what would be the point if the firm is not in a position to pay what it owes you? In this situation, the Financial Services Compensation Scheme (FSCS) may step in.

Where a UK-authorised firm has ceased trading or looks unlikely to be able to meet claims against it, the FSCS will declare the firm 'in default' and invite customers who are owed money to submit their claims to the compensation scheme. There is no charge for using the compensation scheme service. You will not necessarily get all your money back – the maximum limits are set out in Table 2.3.

**Table 2.3   Financial Services Compensation Scheme: maximum pay-outs**

| *Financial product or service* | *Level of compensation cover* | *Maximum pay-out* |
|---|---|---|
| Deposits (e.g. bank and building society accounts) | 100% of the first £50,000[1] | £50,000 |
| Investments (e.g. unit trusts, shares) | 100% of the first £50,000 | £50,000 |
| Long-term insurance (e.g. life insurance) | 90% of the claim (including future benefits already declared) | Unlimited |
| Mortgages and equity release schemes: arranging and advice | 100% of the first £50,000 | £50,000 |
| General insurance (e.g. car insurance, home insurance) | Compulsory insurance (e.g. third party motor insurance, employer's liability insurance): 100% of claim | Unlimited |
| | Non-compulsory insurance: 90% of the claim | Unlimited |

[1] The FSA has proposed that from a future date (possibly late 2010) the limit should be extended to £500,000 for a maximum of six months for temporarily higher balances as a result of receiving a lump sum from the sale of a home, a pension scheme, inheritance, divorce settlement, redundancy, protection insurance pay-out or personal injury settlement.

## Occupational pension complaints and compensation

If you have a complaint against the scheme administrator or trustees of an occupational scheme, first take up the matter through the scheme's internal dispute resolution procedure (IDRP). You can get help doing this from The Pensions Advisory Service, which can resolve misunderstandings and, if necessary, offer mediation and arbitration services. If this fails, you can take your case to the Pensions Ombudsman, a free, independent complaints body that can order the scheme to make appropriate redress. Decisions of the Ombudsman are binding on you as well as the scheme.

In general, the employer is responsible for ensuring that an occupational scheme can meet its obligations to its members. But where the employer is insolvent and there is a shortfall in the fund because of dishonesty, a Fraud Compensation Fund may step in to replace lost benefits. See Chapter 7 for details of other occupational scheme compensation arrangements.

See Appendix B for contact details. (See under Pension Protection Fund for the Fraud Compensation Fund.)

### Finding and using an adviser

- Decide what type of advice you want.
- Search for advisers conveniently located for your home or workplace – see Table 2.1 on p. 40.
- If there is a choice, decide whether you want to pay for the advice by fee or commission.
- Pick two or three advisers. Check they are authorised to give the type of advice you need by consulting the FSA Register. If a firm is not authorised, report it to the FSA or police and do not do business.
- Phone each adviser to find out if they offer the advice you want, what they will charge and to gain a general impression of whether you would feel comfortable with this firm. If you are happy, make an appointment.
- Gather together information the adviser will need to complete a Fact-Find, including details of your income, spending and existing financial products.
- Use this book or other sources to find out something about the area on which you are seeking advice. This will help you to understand and evaluate the advice.
- If any recommendations seem too good to be true, be suspicious. Unless you can verify the information against a reputable source, report the firm to the FSA and do not do business.
- Very few advisers are authorised to handle client money – you can check this at the adviser's entry on the FSA Register. Make payments direct to providers whose products are recommended, not the adviser.

part

2

# Planning for protection

# 3

# Protecting your income

## Introduction

While you are of working age, your income is both the bedrock of your current financial security and the key to funding your financial plans. Therefore, maintaining your income should be a high priority goal. Given that a prolonged spell off work is more likely than dying – just over two out of every 1,000 people of working age die before retirement[1] but around 56 out of every 1,000 have been off work sick for more than three months[2] – protecting your income should arguably be even higher priority than taking out life insurance. However, income protection is a neglected area of financial planning with few people making much private provision. This could be logical if adequate protection were available from the State or through your employer, but as this chapter explores, that is rarely the case.

There are two main threats to your income: unemployment and health failure. Because of its prolonged nature and your relative lack of control over the situation, long-term illness or disability is the most serious of these threats. Figure 3.1 summarises a possible financial plan to protect your income, drawing on the resources and products explained in this chapter.

If you live in a dual-income household, you might be tempted to rely on just one income if you or your partner lose your job or become ill. This may be a realistic plan in the event of unemployment. But bear in mind that,

---

[1] Office for National Statistics, *Population Trends*, Summer 2009.

[2] Department for Work and Pensions, *Incapacity benefit caseload*, http://research.dwp.gov.uk/asd/tabtool.asp Accessed 15 August 2009; Office for National Statistics, *Social Trends*, 2009 edition.

if one of you became disabled, the other might have to take on the role of carer which could further damage the household income, so this is not a robust approach for dealing with the financial impact of long-term illness.

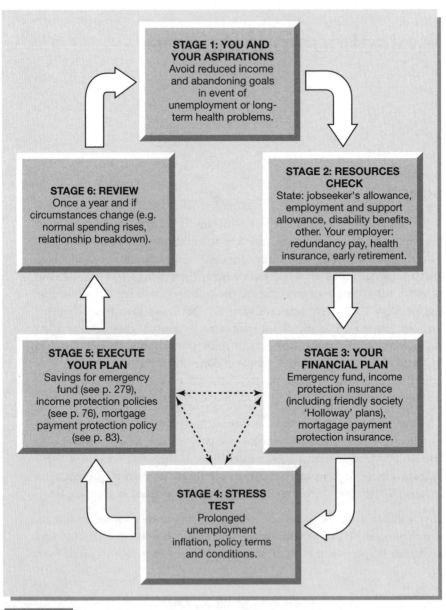

 **Figure 3.1**    A possible financial plan for protecting your income

# Protection from the effects of unemployment

It is very difficult to assess your likelihood of becoming unemployed and the duration of any spell out of work. It will depend on a myriad of factors, for example, your skills and qualifications, your ability to transfer and adapt to different areas of work, and the size and strength of the firm you work for. But crucially it also depends on the overall state of the economy: in a recession the chances of being made redundant or failing to find work are much higher than when the economy is booming. So, while it makes sense to build into your financial planning some protection against the problems of unemployment, it is impossible to quantify realistically the extent of the protection you might need. In general, the most feasible approach is to assume that any period of unemployment is likely to be relatively short term.

As with all financial planning, you should consider what resources you would have available in the event of unemployment and you may find the budget template in Chapter 1 (Figure 1.4) useful. The assessment of your possible resources should include state benefits and any help you might get from your employer. This will enable you to identify any financial gap and consider what steps you might take to plug the gap.

## Help from the State

The main state benefit in the event of becoming unemployed is jobseeker's allowance (JSA). It is payable if you are out of work or working less than 16 hours a week provided you are seeking work. JSA is a tax-free benefit. It comes in two versions: if you have been working for some time, you are likely to qualify for contributions-based JSA; if you can't get contribution-based JSA but your income and savings are low, you can claim income-based JSA.

Only employees can claim contribution-based JSA; you are not eligible if you are self-employed. Contribution-based JSA is based on the record of National Insurance contributions you have paid or been credited with (see Appendix A for information about National Insurance and other taxes). It is paid at a flat-rate of £65.45 a week in 2010–11 (or £51.85 for anyone under age 25). In general, you get this benefit regardless of any other income or savings that you have, but it may be reduced if you are already drawing a pension. You don't get any extra if you have a partner, but equally any earnings your partner might have will not affect your claim. Contribution-based JSA is paid for a maximum of 26 weeks, so it could help to give you a breathing space of up to six months in which to find a new job. Longer than that, you either switch to income-based JSA or will have to rely on your savings or other resources. If you qualify for contribution-based JSA but your income and savings are low, you might also get some income-based JSA – for example, to help you with your mortgage (see *Help from the State* below).

You can qualify for income-based JSA even if you have not paid or been credited with National Insurance contributions and even if you count as self-employed. This is a means-tested benefit, so entitlement depends on your having low income and savings. If you have a partner, their income and savings are taken into account as well. The basic amount is again £65.45 a week in 2010–11 but you may get extra for your partner or if, say, you have a disability. The amount you get is reduced if you have any income from part-time work or other sources and if you have savings of more than £6,000. You can't get income-based JSA at all if you have savings over £16,000 or your partner (if you have one) works for 24 hours a week or more. Income-based JSA can be paid indefinitely and, if you qualify for it, the amount you get may be increased to help you meet your mortgage costs, although this does not kick in until the 13th week of your claim (see *Support for mortgage interest* in Chapter 6), and/or you might also be able to claim other means-tested benefits, such as council tax benefit and housing benefit to meet your rent (see Chapter 6).

The amounts of JSA for 2010–11 are summarised in Table 3.1. To claim JSA, contact your local Jobcentre Plus (see Appendix B). When you claim, you will also be offered free help finding a new job.

**Table 3.1  Main state unemployment benefits in 2010–11**

| Benefit/component | Amount per week |
|---|---|
| Contribution-based JSA (aged 25 and over) | £65.45 |
| Income-based JSA: | |
| Personal allowance (aged 25 and over or lone parent 18 and over) | £65.45 |
| Couple (both 18 or over) | £102.75 |
| Disability premium (single person) | £28.00[1] |

[1] Plus extra for more severe disabilities.

## Help from your employer

If you are made redundant and have been working for your current employer for two or more years, you will at the very least qualify for statutory redundancy pay. The amount you can get depends on your age, how long you have been with your employer and your before-tax pay at the time you leave, but is capped at a maximum of £11,400 (for the year from 1 October 2009). The government website, Direct.gov, has a calculator you can use to work out how much you might get (see Figure 3.2). In practice, your employer may offer a more generous redundancy package. Genuine compensation for loss of your job up to £30,000 is normally tax-free, but any payments due, or customary, under your contract of employment are taxed in the same way as ordinary pay. Your employer should sort out the correct tax treatment for you.

Some employers offer staff who are being made redundant free sessions with recruitment consultants to help you search for a new job.

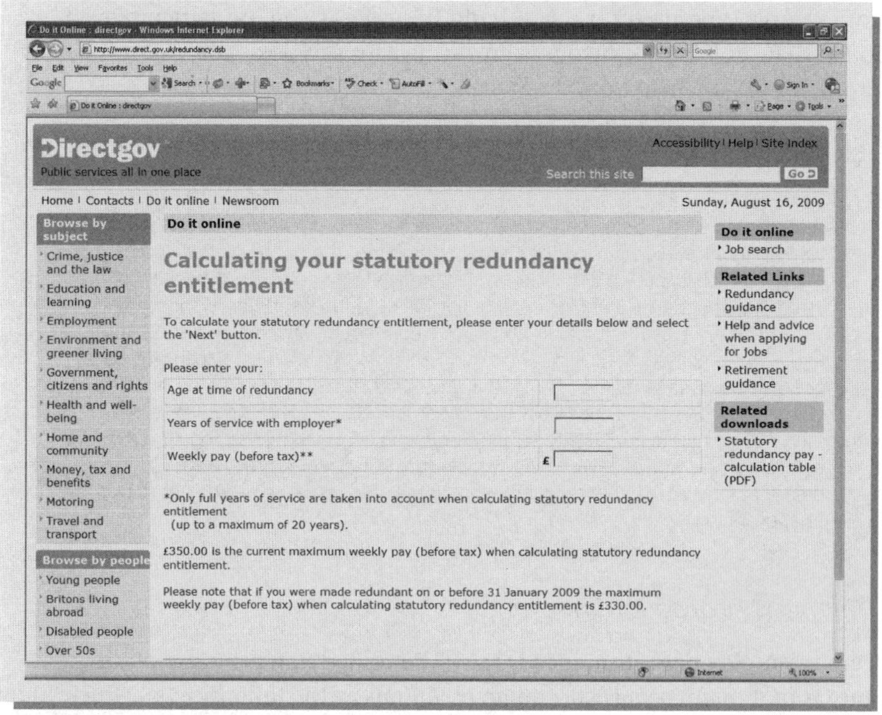

**Figure 3.2**  Statutory redundancy pay calculator

*Source*: www.direct.gov.uk/redundancy.dsb. Accessed 15 August 2009.

If you lose your job for reasons other than redundancy, you generally have no rights to any special help from your employer. Your final pay packet might be larger than usual if it includes, say, unused holiday pay.

# Building a plan for unemployment

Unless you have build up resources of your own, becoming unemployed is likely to mean a severe drop in income. There are two main elements in a financial plan for unemployment: savings to replace your income and insurance to meet key expenses.

## Savings

Being able to draw on savings in the event of unemployment is a key reason for having an emergency fund – see Chapter 9 for guidance on suitable types of saving for this purpose. Advisers tend to suggest that you build up enough savings to cover three to six months' normal spending. However, the amount that is right for you depends on your circumstances: for example, you might want to build up more if you are self-employed given that, unless your income and savings are very low, you will not be able to claim any help from the State.

## Case study

Rasheed and Diana both work, though a large slice of Diana's earnings pay for childcare. However, if either of them lost their job, the one out of work would take over the childcare and so save on these costs. They have both paid enough National Insurance to qualify for contribution-based jobseeker's allowance (JSA), which in 2010–11, would provide £65.45 a week, equivalent to just over £280 a month. This, together with the one remaining income, would be tight financially but they could manage for up to six months. After that, the JSA would stop, so they decide to save extra now to boost their emergency fund. They could then draw around £300 a month from this to top up their income for a further six months or so. They think a year would be more than ample to find a new job. They also think it is unlikely that they would both be out of work at the same time, so decide not to plan for that event.

## Payment protection insurance

Pure unemployment insurance is rare. The underlying principle of insurance is that many people contribute premiums to the insurance pot which is used to meet the claims of the few. The problem with unemployment is that, during an economic downturn, many people may need to claim all at the same time. Therefore, unemployment is a risk which insurers generally claim can only be adequately covered by a state scheme (such as jobseeker's allowance). However, unemployment cover is combined with other types of insurance.

Payment protection insurance (PPI), mortgage payment protection insurance (MPPI) and loan protection insurance are all names for accident, sickness and unemployment (ASU) policies, which are often used to cover the cost of repaying a specific loan if you can't because of illness or unemployment. This type of insurance has in the past typically been sold by personal loan and mortgage providers at the time you start to borrow, but can also be bought as free-standing insurance. Typically, following a claim, it pays out a regular monthly sum for up to 12 or 24 months to meet the loan repayments or, in other cases, for you to use as you choose.

In theory, ASU insurance seems a useful product that directly matches your need to keep up, say, your mortgage payments following redundancy. In practice, there are many exclusions which mean your claim might fail and which may not be made clear at the time you take out the policy. For example, some policies do not cover the self-employed, people on short-term contracts or part-timers. Unemployment cover may not start until two or three months into the policy term and, once you claim, there might be a 'deferred period' of one or two months before the pay-out starts. In addition, these policies usually last for a year at a time and, during a recession when the risk of unemployment increases and you need the cover most, you may find the insurer sharply increases the renewal premium or even withdraws cover.

These policies have been mis-sold in the past and, as a result, the authorities have proposed special regulations to reduce the risk of ending up with an unsuitable policy. For full details and information on choosing and buying, see p. 83, where the health aspects of PPI and MPPI are also discussed.

## Stress testing and review

There are two key elements in stress testing a financial plan for unemployment. The first is to consider your position if unemployment were to last longer than just a few months. To cover this possibility, consider whether you have additional savings currently earmarked for another purpose which would be accessible and could be drawn on if really necessary. This would mean reviewing and re-prioritising the goals in your overall financial plan in the face of the changed circumstance of medium-term unemployment. The additional savings could extend the period during which you search for a job, but might also fund retraining or help you to relocate to another area where job prospects are better.

The second area of stress testing is to make sure you fully understand the terms and conditions of any insurance policy you take out so that you can be confident that it will pay out as you expect.

Review your plan, say, once a year to ensure that the amount of your emergency fund is still in line with your normal spending and that any insurance policies are still required and offer a reasonable deal compared with competing products available. You should also review your plan if your circumstances change, for example, your normal spending increases on the purchase of a new home or birth of a child, or relationship breakdown.

# Protection if your health fails

The most common reason for men of working age being 'economically inactive' (in other words, neither employed nor unemployed and seeking work) is long-term sickness or disability. For women it is the third most common reason (after looking after a family or home and studying).[3] Being off work sick for a prolonged period can quickly erode your standard of living and make achieving your financial goals impossible. Working age people who either have a disability themselves or live with a disabled partner account for three out of ten people living below the poverty line.[4]

These grim statistics provide a strong incentive to include in your financial plan the goal of protecting yourself and your family against the financial effects of health failure. Your starting point is to estimate what resources you might have available in the event of illness or disability and you might find it helpful to use the budget template in Chapter 1 (Figure 1.4). In assessing what resources you would have available, consider what the State or your employer might provide. You can then measure any gap you need to fill.

## Help from the State

The main benefit if you are unable to work because of illness is employment and support allowance (ESA) which replaced incapacity benefit for new claimants from 27 October 2008 onwards. The introduction of the ESA marked an ongoing shift in the emphasis of state benefits from cash for inability to work towards support to get you back into work.

---

[3] Office for National Statistics, *Social Trends*, 2009 edition.

[4] Department for Work and Pensions, *Households below average income*, 2009. The 'poverty line' is defined as 60 per cent of median income.

Employees normally get statutory sick pay for the first 28 weeks of illness (see *Help from your employer* below) before moving on to ESA; self-employed people get ESA from the start.

You cannot get any state help for the first three days of illness and after seven days you require a note from your doctor. For the first 13 weeks, you are in the assessment phase of your ESA claim. Around the eighth week, you will be invited to undergo a work capabilities assessment. This will involve filling in a questionnaire, an interview with a health professional and possibly a medical examination. The aims of the assessment are to check whether you qualify for ESA, what needs to be done to get you back to work, what type of work you can do if your health problems are long-term and what support you might need at work. There are three possible outcomes to the assessment: your claim is rejected (in which case you have the right to appeal); you are assigned to a work-related activity group; or, if your health problems are so severe that you cannot work, you are assigned to a support group but can voluntarily opt to take part in work-related activities. From the 14th week, you move into what is called the 'main phase' of ESA and the amount of cash and type of support you get depends on the group to which you have been assigned.

There are two forms of ESA: contributory (which is taxable) and income-based (which is tax-free). If you have been working, you will usually have paid or been credited with enough National Insurance contributions to qualify for contribution-based ESA. In 2010–11, during the assessment phase, you get £65.45 a week (or £51.85 for claimants under 25). Once you move into the main phase, you get an additional £25.95 a week if you are in the work-related activities group or an extra £31.40 a week if you are in the support group. There is also some cash support to help you during your first year back in work and, if your earnings from work are low, you might qualify for tax credits (see Appendix A). Contribution-based ESA is personal to you and not affected by any work or income of your partner (if you have one), but equally you do not get any extra to help you support a partner. Contribution-based ESA can be paid indefinitely but, if your income and savings are low, you might also qualify for income-based ESA to, say, help with your mortgage costs.

Income-based ESA is a means-tested benefit that you can get only if your income and savings are low. (The first £6,000 of savings is disregarded, savings up to £16,000 usually reduce the amount of ESA you get and you are unlikely to qualify if you have savings of more than £16,000.) In 2010–11, during the assessment phase, the standard ESA is £65.45 a week (£51.85 for under-25s) but you get extra if you are a couple, according to the severity of your disability or if you are a carer. If you have a mortgage, ESA may also include extra to help you pay this (see Chapter 6). In the main phase, you also get the same supplements and help moving back into work that apply to contribution-based ESA (see above). Your entitlement to income-based ESA depends on your household rather than personal circumstances, so any income and savings of your partner affect the amount you can get. If you get income-based ESA, you are also likely to qualify for other means-tested benefits, such as council tax benefit and housing benefit (see Chapter 6).

If your health problems are such that you need help with your personal care or your mobility is restricted, you may qualify for a range of disability benefits which may be paid in addition to ESA – see Chapter 5 for information about these.

The main benefits available are summarised in Table 3.2. To claim ESA, contact your local Jobcentre Plus (see Appendix B).

**Table 3.2  Main state and statutory sickness benefits in 2010–11**

| Benefit/component | Amount per week |
| --- | --- |
| Statutory sick pay | £79.15 |
| *ESA: assessment phase (first 13 weeks)* | |
| Contribution-based ESA (aged 25 and over) | £65.45 |
| Income-based ESA:[1] | |
| Personal allowance (aged 25 and over or lone parent 18 and over) | £65.45 |
| Couple (both 18 or over) | £102.75 |
| Enhanced disability premium (single person) | £13.65 |
| Severe disability premium | £53.65 |
| *ESA: main phase (week 14 onwards)* | |
| Amounts as above plus: | |
| Work-related activity component | £25.95 |
| Support component | £31.40 |

[1]  Plus extra for more severe disabilities.

## Help from your employer

By law, if you are off work sick for more than three days, your employer must usually pay you statutory sick pay (SSP). In 2010–11, it is paid at a standard rate of £79.15 a week (or 90 per cent of your earnings if less) for a maximum of 28 weeks. SSP is paid by your employer in the same way as your normal pay with tax and National Insurance deducted if your earnings are high enough. If you earn less than a set amount, called the low earnings limit (£97 a week in 2010–11), your employer does not have to give you SSP and you should claim ESA instead (see *Help from the State* above). Similarly, if you are still unable to work after 28 weeks, you move on to claiming ESA instead.

Statutory sick pay is the minimum that your employer must pay and, in practice, larger employers in particular tend to have more generous sick pay schemes, but even this is unlikely to pay out for more than a few months and you might be on full pay only for the first few weeks. Some employers have group insurance policies which pay out a replacement income to any employee unable to work for longer periods. You need to check your contract of employment or with your HR department at work to see what sickness and disability benefits apply in your case.

If your health problems are so severe that you cannot return to work, then taking early retirement, so that you start your pension early, might be an option – see Chapter 7.

## Building a plan for health problems

Sick pay from your employer usually lasts only a few months and state benefits are low, so it is likely that a prolonged spell off work would leave you with a considerable shortfall in your household budget. Realistically, you cannot build up savings to cover the risk of a whole working life out of work. So the main way to plug this gap is to take out insurance – but make sure you choose a type that is appropriate for your needs.

# Case study

Frances works as a course manager at a university. It has a generous sick pay scheme which would top up SSP to her full normal wage for up to 28 weeks. After that, she would have to rely on employment and support allowance (ESA) from the State. Frances draws up a household budget statement. She identifies spending that she could cut (such as holidays, meals out) and estimates her ongoing expenses if she were off sick – these would be largely unchanged from now but there would be some savings in travel to work, though probably an increase in heating bills if she were at home all day. Her food, mortgage, household bills, and so on would come to around £1,100 a month. She also estimates her income after 28 weeks. She assumes she would get ESA of £65.45 + £25.95 = £91.40 a week, which is just under £400 a month. She also has some savings which could provide around £100 a month. This would still leave her with a shortfall of £600 a month.

## Income protection insurance

Income protection (IP) insurance most directly targets the need to replace income if you cannot work because of illness. Despite this, IP insurance is often overlooked, mainly because it is perceived to be complex. While this is a valid observation, it should not be a reason for rejecting IP insurance out of hand.

Insurance is all about risk. A typical insurance company aims to set its premiums at a level which will produce enough money to meet claims and leave a bit over to cover costs and provide a profit. To do this, the insurer needs a way of measuring the risk of claims and limiting its exposure to any risks that it deems unacceptable. There are broadly two approaches that companies use to achieve this:

- Make the process of taking out insurance simple and rely on the policy terms, particularly the exclusions, to limit claims. When a claim is made, the company will check carefully to see whether it must pay out. This is the normal approach with, say, travel insurance. It's easy to take out a travel policy but up to you to check whether any of the exclusions apply and, if they do, you may find a claim is refused.

- Fully underwrite each application. The insurance company asks for a lot of information at the time you apply for insurance so that it can assess what risk you pose. If it seems there is a high risk you might claim, you may have to pay a higher premium, accept some exclusions to your cover or even be refused altogether. This is the approach typically used for IP insurance. While it makes the process of taking out a policy complex, it should increase the likelihood that a claim will be met.

A less complex process is available if you take out IP insurance through a friendly society – see *Holloway plans* on p. 79.

The central concept of IP insurance is straightforward: you pay a regular premium for a policy which will pay out a tax-free income if you are unable to work because of illness or an accident. So that you will not be better off sick than working, there is usually an upper limit on the income you can have which takes into account the tax and National Insurance you save, the state benefits you can claim and any pensions you are drawing. Typically, there is an overall limit of, say, 50 to 60 per cent of your after-tax income.

Different policies use different definitions of being unable to work and the premium reflects this. The most expensive policies pay out if you are unable to pursue your own occupation. Less expensive are policies which pay out if you cannot pursue any occupation for which you are suited given your qualifications, experience and so on. The least expensive are policies that pay out only if you cannot do any work at all. Alternatively, policies may define being unable to work by looking at your ability to carry out 'activities of daily living' (such as washing and feeding yourself) or 'activities of daily working' (such as walking and communicating). You need to check any policy carefully so that you are clear about the circumstances in which it will and will not pay out.

All policies have some exclusions. For example, commonly IP does not cover claims that arise from flying except as a fare-paying passenger on a commercial airline, drug or alcohol abuse, self-inflicted injury and HIV/AIDS.

Because IP insurance is fully underwritten, the premium you pay is closely linked to your personal circumstances. The insurer is concerned about the risk of your falling ill or having an accident, so will want to know about your age (the incidence of illness tends to increase with age), sex (women tend to have more health problems than men), the medical history of close relatives (since some health conditions are genetic, but see box on p. 79), your work (the risk of, say, back injuries and accidents is higher with manual work), your habits (such as smoking and drinking which might damage your health), and risky pursuits (that might put you at greater risk of accident). The greater the risk of a claim, the higher the premium you pay.

However, there are a variety of options you can choose from which can reduce your premium, in particular:

■ **Deferred period.** There is always a delay between making a claim and the policy starting to pay out. The minimum is four weeks but can be 13, 26, 52 or even 104 weeks. Normally you can choose how long this deferred period will be and the longer it is, the lower the premium. It usually makes sense to select the period so that the insurance pay-outs kick in as your sick pay or savings run out.

■ **Length of pay-out.** Once you claim, traditional IP policies pay out until you can return to work or reach retirement age, whichever comes first. But you can buy cheaper policies that pay out for a maximum period of, say, five years. Government figures show that around half of the people claiming incapacity benefit (the forerunner of employment and support allowance) had been claiming for more than five years. Weighing up how much you want to pay against leaving yourself exposed to the risk of very long-term illness is therefore a personal decision.

■ **Level or increasing pay-out.** Rising prices reduce the buying power of income over time (see Chapter 1). Some insurers offer policies where the income that would be paid out if you claim increases year-by-year and/or increases once the pay-out starts. If you choose this type of policy, your premiums will also increase each year with the cover.

■ **Fixed or changing premiums**. With some policies, the premium you pay is fixed at the outside and does not change as the years go by (except in line with the cover if you have chosen an increasing pay-out). With other policies, the premium is reviewable – say every five years – in the light of the insurer's overall business experience (but not affected by any claims you personally make). Alternatively, the premium may be renewable, in which case it is fixed for a set period – say, five years – after which you have the option to renew the policy but paying a higher premium based on your age at renewal. Reviewable and renewable premiums tend to be lower in the early years of the policy than guaranteed premiums.

IP insurance is also available to provide cover for unpaid work. If you look after the home and/or family, you are performing a range of tasks, such as housekeeper, cook, cleaner, gardener and childminder, which would be costly to replace if you were too ill to work. However, not all long-term illnesses and disabilities would prevent you from carrying out all domestic tasks, so the need for this cover is less clear cut than the need to replace earnings.

## Genetic tests

Insurers have, for a long time, used questions about family health conditions as part of the basis for determining the risk of your claiming against life and health insurances. In recent years, another source of this type of information has become available: the results of genetic tests. These tests can be very valuable medically in helping to diagnose conditions and indicate treatment. But few of these tests are reliable as definite predictors of the incidence of later disease. Fears that insurers might prematurely use the results of such tests to increase premiums or even bar some people from getting insurance at all prompted an agreement between the government and the insurance industry, which is periodically reviewed and has so far been extended to 2014. Under the agreement, insurers can ask you to disclose adverse results from a predictive genetic test only if you are applying for insurance in excess of specified limits. The limit for IP insurance is £30,000 a year of replacement income and, for critical illness cover, £300,000.

## Case study

If Frances, who works in a university, were off work sick for longer than six months, her income would fall short of the amount she needs to meet her expenses by around £600 a month. She considers taking out an IP insurance policy with a deferred period of 26 weeks to provide the £600 a month she needs. In 2009, Frances, who is aged 40 and a non-smoker, would have to pay around £20 a month for a level £600 a month payable up to age 60 (but more if she wanted the pay-out to increase to protect its buying power against inflation).

### Holloway plans

Income protection originated in the eighteenth century. Before the advent of the welfare state, communities or groups of people sharing the same work banded together to form mutual self-help organisations, often called friendly societies. Members paid in regular small sums and, in return, received help if misfortune struck. Some of these organisations still exist today and a handful offer IP insurance that, in contrast to the policies of the commercial insurers, continue to follow the mutual support model. These are known as 'Holloway plans' (named after George Holloway, an MP in the 1870s, credited with inventing the first such plan). The main differences between Holloway plans and commercial IP policies are as follows:

■ **The mutual principle**. In general, all members pay the same premium for the same benefit, so typically premiums do not vary with sex, occupation or smoking. However premiums are still age-related. Depending on your circumstances, then, you might pay more or less than for a comparable IP policy.

■ **Immediate pay-out.** You can still choose from a range of deferred periods, but one of the options is for the pay-out to start immediately. This can be useful if, say, you are self-employed and so have no employer sick pay scheme to draw on.

■ **Reducing pay-out.** Commonly the pay-out is level for the first year or two only. After that it reduces to, say, half of the full benefit.

■ **Investment element.** Because these plans are run on a mutual basis, any excess of premiums over claims belongs to the members and is paid out as a tax-free cash lump sum at retirement. (Not all Holloway plans have this investment element.)

### Islamic insurance (Takaful)

Strict Moslems avoid mainstream insurance policies because they contravene the tenets of Shariah law. Insurance companies normally invest the premiums they receive and this usually involves receiving interest (*riba*) which is prohibited under Shariah law. They may also invest in companies trading in forbidden products and activities, such as pork, alcohol and gambling. But a further problem with mainstream insurance is that it involves *gharar* (uncertainty). Under Shariah law, a contract must give all parties reasonable certainty over what they pay and what they get in return. This does not prohibit the uncertainty that arises from the parties to the contract sharing investment risk, but it does outlaw what is deemed to be the excessive uncertainty of insurance where any pay-out is contingent on a complex set of circumstances being met. The debates among Islamic scholars are complex, but a central concern is that the buyer of insurance does not have the information needed to determine whether the quality of the contract is good or bad and so exploited for the profit of others. Therefore, the Islamic finance industry has developed alternatives to mainstream insurance, called Takaful.

Takaful, like the Holloway plans described on p. 79, is based on the principles of cooperation and mutual help. A group of people join together and each subscribes to the Takaful fund. Members of the group (or their families) then all have the right to receive financial help from the pool if they suffer a loss. The amount of the subscription may vary from person to person in line with the amount they might need to draw from the fund. For example, Takaful insurance is available to pay off debts in case of disability and the amount of the subscription is related to the size of the debts. The members employ a manager or trustee to invest the Takaful fund for them in a Shariah-compliant way. The manager or trustee may receive a fee or a share of the profits from the investment. Any remaining profit belongs collectively to the members and there may be conditions on how the profit should be used.

## Critical illness insurance

Far more widely sold than IP insurance is critical illness cover (CIC). This pays out a large tax-free cash sum if you are diagnosed with a life-threatening condition. This type of insurance is very poorly targeted if your main goal is to replace income in the event of being unable to work because:

- by far the most common reasons for being off work sick for a prolonged period are mental health problems and musculoskeletal disorders (including back pain),[5] but neither of these would trigger a CIC pay-out;
- the amount of lump sum cover you choose might not in fact be enough to support you financially if you survive a life-threatening condition for many years but cannot return to work.

There are seven core conditions which all CIC policies cover – cancer, coronary artery bypass, heart attack, kidney failure, major organ transplant, multiple sclerosis and stroke – but many others that may be included as well. However, a long list of conditions does not necessarily indicate a more comprehensive policy, since one insurer may spell out many health problems separately, while another may use a collective term that covers several.

The premium you pay depends largely on your age (older people are more likely to develop these conditions so pay more), sex (women are less likely than men to claim, so pay less), the medical history of you and your close family (but see the box on p. 79 regarding genetic tests) and your lifestyle (such as drinking and smoking habits). Premiums, which you typically pay monthly, may be fixed from the outset or reviewable at regular intervals, say, every five years. Premiums vary greatly from one policy to another and, for example, in 2009 ranged from around £25 to £60 a month for a man aged 30, non-smoker, for £100,000 of cover. There is a maximum age after which you cannot start a CIC policy but this varies from one insurer to another and ranges from 55 to 75. There is also a maximum age after which cover stops and again this varies across insurers from as low as 65 up to age 85.

When it was first introduced, CIC seemed very straightforward and easier to sell than the more complex IP insurance. However, as time has gone by, there have been many medical advances so that conditions that were once life-threatening now have improved survival rates. As a result the definitions of the health problems that trigger a pay-out have become increasingly complicated and subject to exclusions, so that for example less advanced cancers do not trigger any claim. In addition, problems have arisen because of the relatively simple way that CIC is sold. Typically, the insurer asks questions on the proposal form but does not usually check your medical records or require you to have a medical. This puts a heavy burden on you to recall medical information about yourself and your family and to realise that it

[5] Department for Work and Pensions, *Working for a healthier tomorrow*, 2008.

might be significant. Only when you make a claim, does the insurer delve into your medical records. According to research by the magazine, *Money Management,*[6] around one-fifth of CIC claims are rejected, about half of these because of non-disclosure of 'material facts' (see box).

Stand-alone CIC policies are available but account for only around 5 per cent of sales. More often CIC is often combined with life insurance, in which case you need to know whether the CIC is 'accelerated cover' – in other words, the policy pays out on the earlier of diagnosis of a life-threatening condition or death – or extra cover – in which case, there would be a payment on diagnosis and a further payment on death. Accelerated cover is the most common type and suitable where the life cover/CIC is linked to a mortgage. Watch out if your goal is protecting your family (see Chapter 4). If you add CIC to the policy and opt for accelerated cover, bear in mind that if you fall ill and trigger the CIC claim, that money may be used up coping with your illness and there will be no life cover pay-out for your family if you subsequently die.

---

### Disclosure of material facts

All insurance policies are contracts of 'utmost good faith'. This means that both you and the insurer are required to volunteer to each other everything that could be a 'material fact' affecting the contract, such as information about your past health, previous insurance claims, and so on. However, unless you are an expert in insurance, you cannot necessarily know what facts will be relevant. Therefore, it is now considered good and fair practice when you apply for cover for insurers to ask for specific information and not to rely on very open general questions. Strictly in law, if you fail to disclose any material fact, the contract is void and the insurer can refuse any claim. But the Association of British Insurers (ABI), the insurers' trade body has set out guidance for its members (and most insurers are members) so that, in the case of IP insurance, CIC and similar policies, failing to disclose a material fact that would have affected the insurer's decisions about the cover offered, should be treated as follows:

■ innocent failure – pay the claim in full;

■ negligent failure – pay a proportion of the claim;

■ deliberate or careless failure – refuse the claim.

If you are unhappy with the outcome of a claim, complain first to the insurance company concerned and, if still not satisfied, you can take your case to the Financial Ombudsman Service (see Chapter 2 for details). In December 2009, it was announced that the Law Commission (a body that works with the government to improve the law and ensure it is fair) was recommending that the insurance disclosure rules be overhauled so that consumers would no longer be in the position of having to second guess the information insurers might consider to be relevant.

---

[6] *Money Management,* January 2009.

# Case study

Mrs C applied for life assurance and critical illness insurance in May 1999. One of the questions she was asked was whether she had a 'lump, growth or tumour of any kind' – she answered 'No'. She was also asked whether she had 'consulted, or been prescribed treatment by a doctor during the last 5 years'. She answered 'Yes' and listed what she and her GP considered relevant information from her medical records.

In July 2000, Mrs C claimed benefit under her critical illness policy as she had been diagnosed with a malignant melanoma. The insurer sought information from her GP and discovered that, in March 1999, Mrs C had asked her GP to look at a mole that had been on her left thigh since birth, and was starting to bother her. The insurer accepted that Mrs C's failure to tell it about this incident was innocent, but it cancelled both her policies. It considered that she should have disclosed this particular GP 'consultation' in response to its direct question about 'growths' and that by failing to do so, Mrs C had prejudiced its position.

Mrs C disputed this decision. She said her GP had told her the mole was nothing to worry about and she had not sought further advice or treatment for it until May 2000. Her GP's notes confirmed that the mole was only mentioned casually at the end of a consultation for an unrelated matter, and that Mrs C was told it was benign and had no sinister features.

**Complaint upheld**

A brief mention of a minor problem was not a 'consultation' and we did not consider that Mrs C had provided an incorrect answer to the question about consultations. The GP had not organised any further investigation of the mole or made any recommendation about it. It seemed only to have been included in the GP's notes in case a problem occurred in future. As to the question about lumps, growths or tumours, Mrs C had acted reasonably in answering 'No'. She had to answer the insurer's questions only 'to the best of her knowledge' – and – to the best of her knowledge, she did not have any condition that she needed to tell the insurer about. Her GP had told her the mole was inconsequential and since it had been present all her life, and was apparently not a matter of any concern, she could not have been expected to mention it. We did not consider the insurer had sufficient grounds for cancelling the policies and we said it should reinstate them and assess the claim. We also awarded Mrs C £400 for distress and inconvenience.

*Source*: Financial Ombudsman Service, *Ombudsman News*, January 2002.

## Payment protection insurance

Payment protection insurance (PPI) is a type of accident, sickness and unemployment (ASU) insurance linked to a particular expense, usually borrowing, such as a mortgage, personal loan or credit card. If you are unable to work because of illness, accident or redundancy, the policy pays out enough to meet your monthly repayments. The pay-out typically continues for one or two years.

There is a real need to plan how you would keep up loan repayments where the consequences of not doing so would be severe – for example, failing to keep up your mortgage payments could result in losing your home. This type of planning is less essential with lower priority debts, such as personal loans. (See Chapter 1 for a description of priority and non-priority debts and the consequences of non-payment.) Therefore mortgage payment protection (MPPI) could be useful, but it is not the only solution. Before opting for MPPI, you should consider what other resources you have or could build up:

■ **State benefits**. If your income and savings are low, you may qualify for means-tested state benefits to meet your mortgage payments (see Chapter 6 for details). However, this kicks in only from the 13th week of your claim, so you need to consider how you could maintain the repayments until then: your employer's sick pay scheme might offer full pay for a limited period; maybe you have enough savings to manage for three months; or perhaps family would help you out.

■ **Your emergency fund**. You might have or be able to build up enough savings to meet your expenses, including mortgage payments, for a fairly prolonged period.

■ **IP insurance or Holloway plan**. Taking out IP insurance (see p. 76) or a Holloway plan (see p. 79) to provide a replacement income to meet all your needs, including mortgage repayments, is a more effective solution that would protect you in the event of long-term as well as relatively short-term periods off work sick. However, unlike MPPI, IP insurance does not pay out if you lose your job (unless you are also too ill to work).

Although PPI, in particular MPPI, does meet a genuine need, the policy exclusions mean that claims are often refused. Moreover, in recent years, these policies have been over-priced and mis-sold to such an extent that a formal enquiry was launched and the Competition Commission (the UK's competition regulator) recommended the introduction of special regulations to protect consumers.

PPI, including MPPI policies, are often suitable only if you are in permanent, full-time employment. You need to check carefully whether a policy would pay out if you are self-employed, work on temporary contracts or work part-time. Most policies exclude claims arising from pre-existing health conditions, so will not pay out if a claim can be linked to any health problem you have had in the five years or so before taking out the insurance. The Competition Commission calculated the claims ratio for

PPI. The claims ratio is the amount paid out by the insurer in claims as a percentage of the money policyholders pay in premiums. The higher the ratio, the better value the insurance is for consumers. The claims ratio for, say, car insurance is 78 per cent. By contrast, the claims ratio for PPI averaged just 14 per cent. Out of each £100 paid in premiums, the Commission estimated that £18 went to the insurer to cover expenses and profit and a massive £68 went in commission and profit-sharing to the lender or other intermediary who sold the insurance.[7]

The Competition Commission also found that consumers were typically being given the impression that taking out PPI was compulsory and a condition of getting a personal loan. In fact, this is not the case: you nearly always have a choice about whether to take out PPI and, even if you do want this cover, you do not have to buy it from the provider offering the loan. You can shop around and buy freestanding PPI, including MPPI, if you want to. Moreover, by bundling PPI into the loan deal, consumers could not see the true cost of the PPI policy. Single premium PPI policies came out as particularly expensive because you are deemed to borrow the full cost of the insurance so that it is added to the loan and interest charged on it.

As a result of the Competition Commission investigation, the sale of single premium insurance has already been banned and the following new rules apply from April 2010:

- marketing material about PPI must clearly state the monthly cost for each £100 of cover;
- if you ask, the PPI provider must tell you the claims ratio: this will help you to judge whether the policy offers good value for money;
- you must be given a personal quote detailing the main terms of the cover and the cost.

In addition, the Competition Commission proposed a ban on selling you PPI at the time you take out a loan or within the following seven days. The idea was to give you a breathing space to consider whether you wanted cover and, if so, to shop around. However, the proposed ban was successfully challenged in the courts by one of the banks that sells PPI (Barclays) and, at the time of writing, it was unclear what further changes might be made.

---

[7] Competition Commission, *Market investigation into payment protection insurance*, January 2009.

## Stress testing and review

A key threat to your income protection plan is inflation (see Chapter 1 for the impact this may have on your planning). If you have chosen IP insurance or a Holloway plan that offers a level pay-out, the cover will fail to keep pace with your earnings as they rise over the years. Moreover, the pay-out itself will buy less and less each year. Over a long period of time even low rates of inflation can cut the buying power substantially (see Chapter 1). Strategies for making your plan more robust could be:

■ Consider IP insurance where the cover increases each year (some but not all Holloway plans offer this option). However, this will cost you more.

■ Review your cover regularly, say every five years and increase it as necessary. Bear in mind that taking out additional cover later on will be charged at higher premiums to reflect your increased age.

■ Put aside extra savings which can be used, if necessary, to top up the pay-out. If you never need to use these during your working life, they could provide a useful extra fund for use when you reach retirement.

Inflation is not an issue where you take out PPI or MPPI to cover a specific loan, since the pay-out is directly linked to the repayments.

Unless you opt for an IP policy or Holloway plan with premiums that are guaranteed not to change, you need to be prepared for your payments to rise each time the premiums come up for review or you renew the policy. This may not be a problem if you expect your earnings also to increase over time giving you scope to afford the extra premiums.

During a period of illness, you normally still have to keep paying the premiums for IP insurance or a Holloway plan to keep the insurance going. You could ensure that the amount of cover you choose is large enough to allow for paying the premiums. Alternatively, you can usually pay a bit extra to include 'waiver of premium benefit' which means you do not have to pay the premiums while you are claiming but the cover continues.

Aim to review your financial plan for protecting your income, say, once every five years to make sure that any products you have selected are still appropriate and the amount of cover is still in line with your earnings. You should also review your plan whenever you change job, in particular checking what help a new employer provides and whether this affects the amount and type of cover you need to provide for yourself. Finally, also conduct a review if there is a major change in your expenses – for example, you take on a bigger mortgage, pay off a large chunk of your mortgage or, say, form a new relationship or your existing relationship breaks down. These can all affect the amount of pay-out you would need.

## Choosing and buying insurance

Internet comparison sites can be useful shopping-around tools for all sorts of insurance, but not income protection or stand-alone critical illness cover. For IP insurance especially, the wide variation in cover and the way premiums are tailored to your own very specific circumstances mean this is one area where it is hard to give meaningful simplified quotes. Table 3.3 gives some examples of IP premiums in mid-2009, but because this insurance is fully underwritten the premium you personally might pay could be very different depending on your particular circumstances. However, the table does illustrate how different circumstances and policy choices have a big impact on the premium and also how the premiums vary enormously from one provider to another, in large part reflecting the different terms on offer. So you really need to check out the market in detail.

**Table 3.3  Examples of the cost of IP insurance in 2009**

| Personal circumstances | Monthly premium for a level pay-out of £250 a week (range for different providers) | | | |
| | Man | | Woman | |
| | Admin. clerk | Self-employed decorator | Admin. clerk | Self-employed decorator |
| --- | --- | --- | --- | --- |
| Non-smoker, aged 30, retire at 60, 13-week deferred period | £11.68–£26.61 | £11.68–£52.20 | £13.50–£44.31 | £13.50–£87.59 |
| Non-smoker, aged 30, retire at 60, 26-week deferred period | £10.65–£23.46 | £10.65–£45.89 | £11.76–£38.97 | £11.76–£90.09 |
| Non-smoker, aged 40, retire at 60, 26-week deferred period | £14.07–£35.18 | £14.07–£92.93 | £15.12–£56.81 | £15.12–£157.92 |
| Non-smoker, aged 50, retire at 60, 26-week deferred period | £19.41–£48.87 | £19.41–£120.02 | £22.82–£72.66 | £22.82–£205.28 |
| Smoker, aged 50, retire at 60, 26-week deferred period | £24.42–£57.44 | £24.42–£159.81 | £28.56–£95.87 | £28.56–£275.00 |
| Smoker, aged 50, retire at 60, 52-week deferred period | £23.54–£53.76 | £23.96–£148.79 | £25.20–£89.36 | £25.20–£255.57 |

*Source*: Data taken from Moneyfacts, *Investment, Life & Pensions Moneyfacts*, August 2009.

In 2009, there were around 20 IP and Holloway plan providers and you can get a broad overview of the policies on offer by looking at the specialist magazine *Investment, Life & Pensions Moneyfacts* from Moneyfacts or occasional reports in more mainstream magazines, such as *Money Management*. Alternatively, this is an aspect of your financial plan where you might want to seek out the help of an independent financial adviser or insurance broker. (See Appendix B for contact details for all magazines, firms and organisations mentioned in this section.)

There is less variation with PPI (including MPPI) and internet comparison sites (see Appendix B) can be a good starting point. For a completely independent comparison, use the FSAs Moneymadeclear Compare Products tables.

# Providing for your family

## Introduction

The risk of dying during your working years is small (around two out of every 1,000 people of working age die before retirement[1]) but the impact on your survivors is potentially so severe that protecting your family in the event of this risk is a central area of financial planning. This need does not disappear with retirement but the solutions you employ may change (see p. 100). As with all financial planning, the starting point is an assessment of whether you have a need to protect any family or other dependants and of the existing resources that may be available to you, which could include help from the State and an employer. You are then in a position to assess whether you have a protection gap and to evaluate the financial products and strategies that you could use to fill it. The process is summarised in Figure 4.1.

## Assessing the need

Not everyone needs a plan for coping with death. If you have no financial dependants, you are unlikely to need life cover. This will most likely be the case when you are young and single. It could also apply if you are part of a couple but you and your partner are financially self-sufficient. However, take care assessing this position: even in double-income households, couples are often financially co-dependent because they share major expenses, such as a mortgage. If that applies in your case, the death of your partner could cause you financial hardship and vice versa. Also

[1] Office for National Statistics, *Population Trends*, Summer 2009.

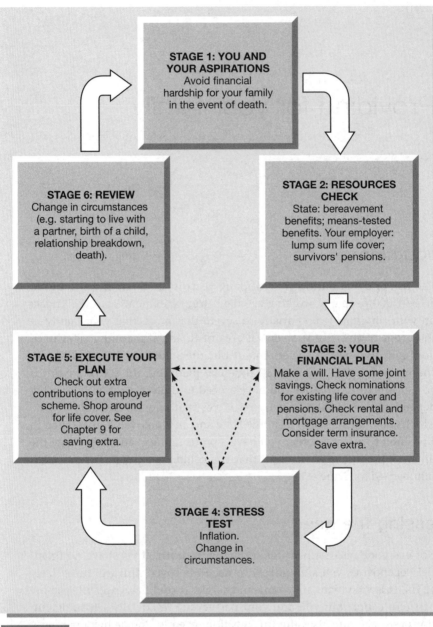

**Figure 4.1**   A possible financial plan for protecting your family

bear in mind that the death of a partner who was doing unpaid work, such as childcare and maintaining the home, can create a financial loss if survivors would have to pay to replace the unpaid work.

You are most likely to have protection needs if you have a partner and/ or children. But, the need could arise in other situations too, for example, if an elderly relative depends on you. If you are divorced and receiving maintenance from a former partner, you might want to ensure that your own financial security would not be jeopardised if your 'ex' were to die (see p. 111).

## The protection period

The greatest need for protection for your family is while children are growing up. In that case, it is common to look at the period until they reach age 18 or, if you expect they will go to university, age 21. Once children are grown up, or if you have no children, it may be possible for a surviving partner to work and so the need for protection may be less. However, this might not apply at older ages and, if your partner has had time out of work or is working part-time, for example, to raise a family, bear in mind that they may not be able to earn the same as someone who has had an unbroken career or work record.

Protection may be related to a specific expense, for example, if you are looking at a mortgage, the period to consider is the remaining mortgage term.

## How much protection?

Many professional advisers use a rule of thumb and suggest you take out lump sum life insurance equal to ten times your annual salary: for example, if you earn £60,000 a year, take out £600,000 of cover. More effective planning aims to measure the financial gap that a death may create. This helps to avoid either having too little cover or paying for more cover than you need. It also broadens the scope of planning rather than assuming life insurance is the only strategy.

The main threats to your survivors if you were to die are a loss of household income and an increase in expenditure. To assess the possible impact, it is helpful to draw up a budget, estimating how the household resources would change in the event of death. If you are a couple, you should go through this exercise twice – once for each of you – since the loss on death is seldom symmetrical. A budget template, adapted for this purpose, is set out in Figure 4.2 and this feeds into the protection calculator in Figure 4.3.

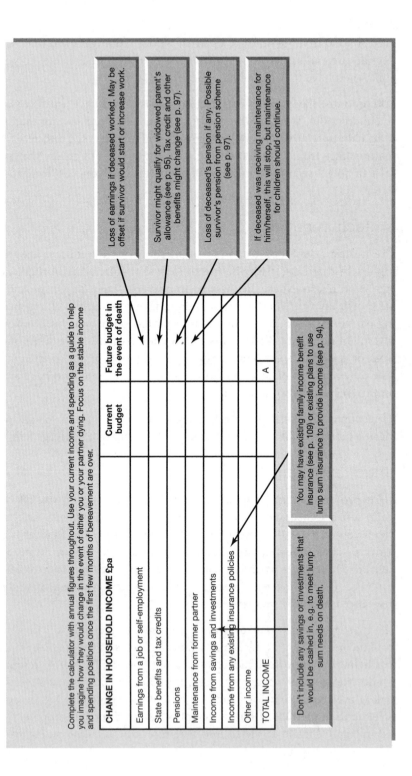

Complete the calculator with annual figures throughout. Use your current income and spending as a guide to help you imagine how they would change in the event of either you or your partner dying. Focus on the stable income and spending positions once the first few months of bereavement are over.

| CHANGE IN HOUSEHOLD INCOME £pa | Current budget | Future budget in the event of death |
|---|---|---|
| Earnings from a job or self-employment | | |
| State benefits and tax credits | | |
| Pensions | | |
| Maintenance from former partner | | |
| Income from savings and investments | | |
| Income from any existing insurance policies | | |
| Other income | | |
| TOTAL INCOME | | A |

Loss of earnings if deceased worked. May be offset if survivor would start or increase work.

Survivor might qualify for widowed parent's allowance (see p. 95). Tax credit and other benefits might change (see p. 97).

Loss of deceased's pension if any. Possible survivor's pension from pension scheme (see p. 97).

If deceased was receiving maintenance for him/herself, this will stop, but maintenance for children should continue.

You may have existing family income benefit insurance (see p. 109) or existing plans to use lump sum insurance to provide income (see p. 94).

Don't include any savings or investments that would be cashed in, e.g. to meet lump sum needs on death.

| CHANGE IN HOUSEHOLD SPENDING £pa | Current budget | Future budget in the event of death |
|---|---|---|
| Mortgage payments or rent | | |
| Council tax | | |
| Home maintenance and household goods | | |
| Household bills (water, fuel, phone, TV, internet, and so on) | | |
| Food, alcohol, tobacco, toiletries, and so on | | |
| Clothing and footwear | | |
| Motoring costs and other travel | | |
| Home insurance (contents, buildings) | | |
| Life insurance, health insurances, pension contributions, savings, loan repayments | | |
| Maintenance payments to former partner and/or children | | |
| Other spending | | |
| TOTAL SPENDING | | B |

Mortgage payments stop if you have existing insurance to pay off the mortgage. You might decide to rent somewhere smaller.

If you will be the only adult in the household, you qualify for a 25 per cent reduction in council tax.

Spending on maintenance, etc. might rise if the deceased did these jobs.

Bills and spending might fall with one less adult in the household.

Contents insurance might fall if you dispose of deceased's possessions.

If deceased was making insurance payments, pension contributions, repayments for loans and credit (not held jointly with you) these stop.

This may increase if the deceased did unpaid work, such as childcare that you would need to replace.

If deceased paid maintenance to a former partner or for children, these payments cease.

| HOUSEHOLD SURPLUS OR SHORTFALL £pa | Future budget in the event of death |
|---|---|
| SURPLUS/SHORTFALL = A – B | B |

**Figure 4.2**  Budget change calculator

| INCOME NEEDS | | |
|---|---|---|
| Budget shortfall if any. Amount C from Figure 4.2 | C | |
| Number of years you would need to cover this shortfall | D | |
| Conversion factor from table below | E | |
| Income need converted to a lump sum = C × E | F | |

## CONVERTING INCOME TO A LUMP SUM

You have a choice: you may be able to arrange insurance that would pay out an income to directly meet your income need (amount C above) – see p. 109. Alternatively, you could take out insurance that would pay out a lump sum which your survivors would invest to provide income. To convert the income need into a lump sum, use this table. The lump sum shown in column 2 is the amount you would need to invest today to produce a level income of £100 each year if the policy started to pay out today and continued for the number of years shown, running down the lump sum to zero by the end of the term. The figures assume that the invested lump sum grows at 5 per cent a year net of changes. See the discussion on p. 113 regarding inflation.

| Number of years for which you will have this need (amount D above) | Lump sum required | Factor (amount E) |
|---|---|---|
| 5 | £454.60 | 4.5 |
| 10 | £810.78 | 8.1 |
| 15 | £1,089.86 | 10.9 |
| 20 | £1,308.53 | 13.1 |
| 25 | £1,479.86 | 14.8 |
| 30 | £1,614.11 | 16.1 |

| LUMP SUM NEEDS | | |
|---|---|---|
| Lump sum to provide income (unless you choose insurance that would pay out an income – see p. 109)<br>Amount F from section above | F | |
| Funeral expenses (allow, say, £2,000) | | |
| Living expenses for, say, first two months following death | | |
| Amount needed to pay off joint debts | | |
| Other immediate expenses | | |
| TOTAL OUTLAY | G | |
| Bereavement payment (see p. 96) | | |

| | | |
|---|---|---|
| Emergency fund that can be drawn on now | | |
| Pay-out from funeral pre-payment plan/insurance | | |
| Pay-out from life insurance linked to debts (e.g. mortgage) | | |
| Pay-out from employer's life insurance scheme | | |
| Pay-out from other existing lump sum life insurance | | |
| Any amount you inherit from the deceased net of any inheritance tax (see p. 103 and Chapter 11) | | |
| Other lump sums | | |
| TOTAL LUMP SUMS AVAILABLE | H | |
| LUMP SUM SHORTFALL = F + G – H | I | |

Value I is the lump-sum protection gap you need to fill, for example, by taking out life insurance (see p. 106).

**Figure 4.3** **Protection calculator**

However before you can complete all the entries in these calculators, you need to consider what help might be available to your survivors from the State (see below), from any employer (see p. 99) and also any existing savings, pensions and insurances that you have (see p. 103).

## Help from the State

There are two strands of protection from the State: bereavement benefits which address the particular situation of a partner dying; and means-tested benefits, such as income support and tax credits which could help your survivors if they are left on a low income. A successful financial plan should generally avoid the need for your family to fall back on means-tested help. However, tax credits will be relevant to most families with children, because (in 2009–10) they continue to be paid even at relatively high income levels (over £50,000 a year). For an outline of the tax credits system see Appendix A, but be aware that the death of a partner is a change of circumstance that would have to be notified to the Tax Credits Office and would in many cases affect the amount of credits paid.

### Bereavement benefits before retirement

Bereavement benefits provide a lump sum and possibly an income to your surviving wife, husband or civil partner, provided you paid or were credited with sufficient National Insurance contributions while you were alive. Unmarried partners cannot get bereavement benefits.

Bereavement payment is a tax-free lump sum of £2,000 (in 2010–11 but unchanged for many years). For your surviving partner to qualify, you must have paid (rather than have been credited with) National Insurance contributions for at least 25 weeks during a tax year before death. Your spouse or civil partner must be under the state pension age for women (60 in 2009–10 but gradually increasing from April 2010 onwards) or, if older, you must not have been getting state retirement pension.

Widowed parent's allowance is an income payable to your partner if they are caring for one or more children for whom they get child benefit. In 2010–11, the allowance is paid at a full rate of £97.65 a week and is taxable. For your partner to qualify, you must have paid or been credited with National Insurance for at least a quarter of your working life and, if less than nine-tenths of your working life, they will get less than the full rate. Working life runs from the tax year in which you reached age 16 up to the last complete tax year before death (or state pension age). For example, if you died at age 30, your working life would be 14 years and you would need to have paid or been credited with 12 years of contributions for your partner to get the full amount. The allowance continues to be paid until your last child ceases to be dependent (usually on finishing full-time education at either age 16 or 19).

Bereavement allowance is an income, lasting just one year, payable to a surviving partner without children and aged between 45 and 65 at the time of your death. The full rate is £97.65 a week but this is reduced if your partner is under age 55. To get the full amount, you must also have met the contribution conditions described for widowed parent's allowance – see above. If not, your partner gets a reduced amount.

Both widowed parents allowance and bereavement allowance stop if your partner remarries and are suspended if they start to live with someone.

With both allowances, your partner may also be entitled to receive extra income equal to half any entitlement to state additional pension (see Chapter 7) that you had built up (but reduced in the case of bereavement allowance where your partner is under age 55 at the time of death).

## State help on bereavement after retirement

If, at the time of death, you are already drawing a state retirement pension and your partner is over state pension age (see Chapter 7), your partner does not get bereavement benefits. However, they may get an increase in their state pension based on your state pension position.

If your partner has been getting less than the full rate of state basic pension (£97.65 a week in 2010–11), this may now be topped up to the full rate, provided you had paid or been credited with sufficient National Insurance contributions during your working life (which in this case runs from the year in which you reached age 16 to the last complete tax year before you reached state pension age).

You may have received some state additional pension (see Chapter 7). In that case, your partner can inherit half this pension to be added to their own. But the inherited pension plus any state additional pension of their own is capped at the maximum a person could get based on their own National Insurance record, which is around £150 a week in 2010–11. In practice, most people's additional pensions fall far short of this maximum.

## Case study

In 2010–11, Matt gets the full state basic pension of £97.65 a week and an additonal pension of £35.60 a week. His wife, Gill, has a state pension based on her own contributions of £62.60 a week basic and £5.70 additional. If Matt were to die, Gill's basic pension would be made up to the full amount of £97.65 using Matt's contribution record to fill gaps in her own. She would also inherit half his additional pension: ½ × £35.60 = 17.80. In total, Gill's state pension would be £97.65 + £5.70 + £17.80 = £121.15 a week.

### Tax credits

Tax credits are a means-tested state benefit designed to help families with children and people who work and earn a low income. There are two types – child tax credit (CTC) and working tax credit (WTC) which includes help with childcare costs – but they are integrated, so you make a single claim for both types. Eligibility depends on your family situation and/or working hours; the amount you get depends on your income. Since all of these are likely to change in the event of death, a surviving partner will need to report your death to the Tax Credits Office (see Appendix B) and their tax credits will be reviewed. If household income would fall, the amount paid in tax credits is likely either to rise or remain unchanged. However an increase in taxable income as a result of, say, investing the lump sum proceeds of a life insurance pay-out could reduce tax credits. The pay-out from family income benefit policies (see p. 109) counts as a stream of tax-free lump sums rather than income, so should not affect a tax credit claim. For more information about tax credits, see Appendix A.

# Case study

Mel and Jim have one child, Jessie, aged eight and their household income is £38,000 a year. Jim works full-time; Mel splits her time between work and looking after Jessie. In 2010–11, they get tax credits of £545 a year. If Jim were to die, they work out that the tax credits might increase to nearly £4,400 a year. This would be due to a reduced household income of, say, £25,000 that Mel reckons she could earn by switching to full-time work and after-school care costs of £100 a week. If, as a result of their financial planning, they take out life cover, any income generated as a result would affect the tax credits claim, unless they chose a family income benefit policy.

## *Other means-tested benefits*

If your partner were left on a low income, they could be eligible to claim some of the following benefits:

■ **Housing benefit**. If you live in rented accommodation, this would cover all or some of the rent.

■ **Help with other housing costs**. If your partner claimed income support, jobseeker's allowance or pension credit, this could include help with paying mortgage interest and some other housing costs, such as service charges.

■ **Council tax benefit**. This would meet part or all of your partner's council tax bill.

■ **Income support**. If your partner would be unable to work, or would work less than 16 hours a week, because of caring for a child under age 12 (reducing to age 7 from October 2010), they could be eligible for income support.

■ **Income-based jobseeker's allowance**. While your partner is seeking work, they might be able to claim this benefit.

■ **Pension credit**. If your partner (whether a man or a woman) would be over the state pension age for women (60 in 2009–10 but gradually increasing from April 2010 onwards), they might be eligible for pension credit to top up their income to a minimum level.

■ **Social Fund grants and loans**. People getting means-tested benefits, such as income support, jobseeker's allowance or pension credit, can also apply for grants and loans from the Social Fund for certain purposes, such as paying funeral costs and interest-free budgeting loans to help meet a large expense.

For information and to make a claim contact Jobcentre Plus if you are of working age or The Pension Service if over state pension age (see Appendix B).

# Help from employers

You may belong to a pension scheme at work, in which case it will almost certainly provide some benefits for your survivors if you were to die. These may comprise a lump sum and/or pension. Even if there is no pension scheme, your employer may still operate a life insurance scheme as part of your overall pay package.

## Lump sum payments – death in service

Many employers offer a death-in-service lump sum. This might equal, say, two or four times your salary. Normally, this is arranged through a life insurance scheme and the pay-out is tax-free. In a defined benefit scheme (see the box), the only lump sum payable on death in service is this life insurance lump sum. In a defined contribution scheme, your survivors might also – or instead of a life insurance lump sum – receive the value of your pension fund at the time of death. Unlike the life insurance sum, the payment of the fund is subject to a tax deduction (at 35 per cent in 2009–10).

Whatever the source of the lump sum, it can usually be paid to anyone, not necessarily people who were financially dependent on you. You can nominate that the sum be paid direct to one or more people, for example, your partner, your children, parents, brothers or sisters. The organisers of the scheme do not have to follow your wishes, but usually will do so. The main situation where they might not is if someone you have not nominated – maybe an ex-husband or ex-wife – comes forward claiming they were financially dependent on you. The organisers would then have to make a judgement and would normally make at least some provision for someone who was genuinely dependent on you or co-dependent with you. Make sure you do complete a nomination form, otherwise the lump sum will be paid to your estate (where it may be subject to inheritance tax – see Chapter 11).

---

### Types of pension scheme

There are two types of pension scheme available through the workplace. In a 'defined benefits' scheme, you are promised a pension which is worked out according to a formula, typically linked to your pay and the number of years you have been in the scheme. Public sector schemes (covering for example, National Health Service employees, teachers and local government workers) are normally defined benefit schemes. In the private sector, larger employers may offer this type of scheme.

All other schemes available through the workplace and all personal pensions are 'defined contribution' (also called 'money purchase') schemes. These build up your own personal pension fund which is used at retirement to buy a pension. You can find more details about the different types of scheme in Chapter 7.

## Lump sum payments after retirement

Defined benefit schemes do not usually make any lump sum payments if you die after you have started your retirement.

With defined contribution schemes, at retirement you normally convert your pension fund into pension by buying a lifetime annuity. This is an investment where you exchange your pension fund for an income that will be paid out for the rest of your life. Usually you cannot get back any of your pension fund as a lump sum. However, you could choose a 'capital protected annuity' which guarantees to pay out at least as much as the pension fund you invested. If you died early in retirement and the sum of the income paid out came to less than the pension fund you invested, the balance would be paid out to your heirs as a lump sum after deduction of tax (at 35 per cent in 2009–10). You have to decide what type of annuity to have at the outset and, if you opt for a capital protected annuity, the amount of income you got each year would be lower than for an annuity without capital protection.

Another possibility with defined contribution schemes is to opt for income drawdown. Instead of buying an annuity, you leave your pension fund invested and draw your pension direct from the fund. If you die before age 75, the balance of your pension fund can be paid as a lump sum to your heirs after deduction of tax (at 35 per cent in 2009–10). If you die on or after age 75, the remaining fund can still be paid to your heirs but the tax rate is much higher (70 per cent in 2009–10) and the remaining fund automatically passes to your estate where it may be subject to inheritance tax (at 40 per cent in 2009–10). The combination of these taxes produces a potential tax charge of up to 82 per cent in 2009–10: for example, out of £100,000 of remaining pension fund, your heirs would receive a lump sum of just £18,000. These punative tax charges do not apply if the remaining fund is used to provide a survivor's pension (see below) or donated to charity (in which case the donation is tax-free).

For more information about annuities and income drawdown, see Chapter 8.

## Survivor pensions

A defined benefit scheme provides a package of benefits which usually include a pension for your partner and any dependent children if you die either before or after retirement. The maximum pension for a surviving partner is usually half or two-thirds of the amount of retirement pension you were entitled to or were receiving, but it could be less. The pension is taxable, with tax based on your survivor's personal tax position. (See Appendix A for an outline of how income is taxed.)

In a private sector occupational scheme, the pension can be paid to your husband, wife or civil partner automatically. It can also be paid to an unmarried partner provided they were financially dependent on you or co-dependent with you – often a condition will be that you had lived together for at least two years. Public sector schemes tend nowadays also to offer survivor pensions on these same terms, but until a few years ago did not pay such pensions to unmarried partners. Although unmarried partners are now included, the pension is typically based only on your service since this change was introduced. You may have the option to pay extra contributions to the scheme to improve the survivor's pension.

In a defined contribution scheme, if you die before reaching retirement, the pension fund you have built up so far is available for your heirs. It may be paid out as a lump sum (see above) or alternatively could be used to buy a pension for your survivor. Normally, your survivor would buy an annuity to provide the pension but could alternatively choose income drawdown (see Chapter 8 for details of these options). The size of the fund will determine the amount of the pensions. Depending on the choices made, the income could be level or could increase each year, which would help in coping with rising prices. The income will be taxable.

Whether or not a defined contribution scheme pays out a survivor's pension on your death after retirement depends on the choices you made at the time you retired:

■ **Single-life annuity**. This pays out an income for as long as you live and then stops. This could leave a partner who outlives you with serious financial problems unless they have enough of their own independent retirement income.

■ **Annuity with guarantee**. This pays out an income for a guaranteed period – say, five or ten years, even if you die before the period is up. So you could specify the income continues to be paid to your partner. But this is not an adequate way to protect them. If you die after the guarantee period, your partner gets nothing. Even if you die within the guarantee period, your partner may not be in a position to cope longer term when the pension payments stop.

■ **Joint-life-last-survivor annuity**. This pays out an income until both you and your partner have died and is a good option for protecting your partner. You can choose whether, on the first death, the income continues unchanged or reduces. Your own pension will be lower if you choose this option (see Table 4.1). For example, the table shows that for a couple both aged 60, the man could buy a single-life annuity for himself paying £600 a year for each £10,000 invested. Adding cover for his partner would reduce the income to £552 a year at the lowest level of protection or £516 a year at the highest level.

■ **Income drawdown.** Your remaining fund can be used to buy a pension for your survivor or they can opt for continued income drawdown. This is another good option for protecting your partner.

**Table 4.1  Examples of joint-life annuities to protect your partner**

*Level annuity rates[1]*

| Level of protection for partner | Type of annuity[1] | Your age (man)/your partner's age (woman) when you buy the annuity | | |
|---|---|---|---|---|
| | | *60/60* | *65/63* | *70/65* |
| Lowest | Single-life (for comparison) | £600 | £672 | £768 |
| ↑ | Joint-life, half reduction | £552 | £600 | £660 |
| ↓ | Joint-life, one-third reduction | £540 | £588 | £636 |
| Highest | Joint life, no reduction in income | £516 | £552 | £588 |

*RPI-linked annuity rates[2]*

| Level of protection for partner | Type of annuity | Your age (man)/your partner's age (woman) when you buy the annuity | | |
|---|---|---|---|---|
| | | *60/60* | *65/63* | *70/65* |
| Lowest | Single-life (for comparison) | £348 | £420 | £528 |
| ↑ | Joint-life, half reduction | £312 | £360 | £420 |
| ↓ | Joint-life, one-third reduction | £300 | £336 | £384 |
| Highest | Joint life, no reduction in income | £276 | £312 | £348 |

[1] Rates show yearly income for each £10,000 invested. Rates for non-smoker, annuity without guarantee. Rates shown applied in September 2009 and change continuously.
[2] Rates show the yearly starting income for each £10,000 invested. The income increases each year in line with inflation as measured by changes in the Retail Prices Index (RPI). Rates for non-smoker, annuity without guarantee.

*Source*: Based on annuity rates from the Financial Services Authority, www.fsa.gov.uk/tables. Accessed 19 September 2009.

## Existing savings, pensions and insurances

You may already have accumulated a variety of financial products which could be available to your survivors if you were to die. Commonly, these might include: savings in an emergency fund; other savings and investments; life insurance to pay off a mortgage; other life insurance policies you have taken out in the past; and personal pension schemes. Personal pensions work on a money purchase basis (see p. 99) and the fund built up can be used as described for occupational money purchase schemes.

Do not assume that your savings and investments will automatically pass to the survivors you intend or who would be in greatest need. To make sure they do, you need to be aware of the legal position:

■ **Joint ownership**. Your share of any assets that you own jointly as 'joint tenants' – see the box – pass automatically to the surviving owner or owners. This means that although your share counts as part of your estate for inheritance tax (see Chapter 11), it does not get caught up in the administration of your estate but passes immediately and directly to your co-owner(s). Holding at least some savings in joint names can be a good way of ensuring that your partner would have immediate access to at least some funds. Not all savings and investments can be held jointly – for example, individual savings accounts (see Chapter 9) can only be held individually.

■ **Insurance policies and pension funds**. Make sure these are held in trust, so that pay-outs do not form part of your estate where they could be subject to inheritance tax. Complete an 'expression of wish' form, nominating who you would like to receive the pay-out. The trustees do not have to follow your wishes, but normally will do so.

■ **Other assets**. In the absence of a will, these would be passed on in accordance with the intestacy laws (see Chapter 11). This means that an unmarried partner and step-children would not get anything at all and even a spouse or civil partner might get less than you had intended. To avoid these sorts of problems, make a will – see Chapter 11.

### Joint ownership

There are two ways you can hold assets jointly with someone else: as 'joint tenants' or as 'tenants in common'. (Despite the use of the word 'tenant' this does not just apply to land and buildings, but any type of asset.) As joint tenants, you each own the whole asset 'jointly and severally'. So you each have an equal legal share but also have the right to use or enjoy the whole asset. You are also equally liable if the asset becomes a loss or debt, such as a current account going overdrawn. When one of you dies, the other owners automatically inherit your share.

> As tenants in common, you and every other owner can have unequal shares and you can leave your share when you die to anyone you specify in your will (or, where there is no will, in accordance with the intestacy rules). For example, if you buy a home with a partner, you might put in more money and take a 60 per cent share, with your partner taking a 40 per cent share. In your will, you might leave your share to the children from your previous marriage, say, rather than your partner.

## Housing security

A major consideration for most households is ensuring that survivors would be able to remain in the family home if they want to.

### A home you own

The calculators in Figures 4.2 and 4.3 take into account the position if you own your home outright or you are buying with a mortgage. In most cases, if you have dependants when you took out a mortgage, you will also have taken out life insurance to pay off the mortgage in the event of your dying.

Make sure you write a will leaving the home or your share of it to your survivors. Check whether there would be any inheritance tax to pay on your estate (see Chapter 11). If you leave the home (or your share of it) to your husband, wife or civil partner, this is a tax-free gift for inheritance tax purposes. If you leave the home to anyone else – for example, an unmarried partner, your children, a brother or sister, a carer – and your estate is large enough, there could be an inheritance tax bill. If there are few other assets in your estate, this could mean the home has to be sold to pay the inheritance tax bill.

### Tax burden threatens home

Joyce and Sybil Burden are unmarried sisters, born in 1918 and 1925, who have lived together all their lives, for the past 30 years or so in a home built on land inherited from their parents. They own the house, valued in 2006 at £425,000, jointly. When either of them dies, there is expected to be a substantial inheritance tax bill and their home might have to be sold to pay it. In 2006, the sisters started a legal challenge to the UK inheritance tax laws which allow assets on death to pass tax-free between spouses and civil partners, but not between siblings who have lived in equally committed and supporting relationships. The sisters claimed that this discrepancy contravened their rights under the European Convention on Human Rights, in particular, articles 1 and 14 which state: 'No one shall be deprived of his possessions except in the public interest...' and 'The enjoyments of the rights and freedoms set forth in [the] Convention shall be secured without discrimination...'. The case finally failed before the European Court of Human Rights in April 2008. The Court concluded that discrimination could apply only where people in a similar situation are treated differently and that the required similarity did not exist because the bond between siblings is fundamentally different to the bond between married people and those in civil partnerships.

## A home you rent privately

If you rent your home from a private landlord or housing association and the tenancy agreement is in your name, your spouse, civil partner or unmarried partner who shares the home with you would normally have a 'right of succession' if you died. This means they could take over the tenancy. Other people sharing the home would not have this right and might have to move out, but could ask the landlord to transfer the tenancy to them.

If you share private rented accommodation and the tenancy agreement is in joint names, the other joint tenant(s) automatically have the right to stay on and take over your share of the tenancy if you die. They would also take over responsibility for paying any rent arrears.

However, most private accommodation is rented under an agreement called an 'assured shorthold tenancy'. Usually, the lease runs for six months at a time and, provided the landlord gives two months' notice, does not have to be renewed at the end of a six-month term. So the right of succession would not give your partner any greater rights to stay on than you have.

## A home rented from a council

If the tenancy agreement is in your name alone, your spouse, civil partner, unmarried partner and other family members who had lived in the home for at least 12 months would normally have the right to take over the tenancy if you died. Other people sharing the home would not have this right and might have to move out, but should discuss this with the council concerned.

If the tenancy agreement is in joint names, your joint tenant(s) can automatically take over the whole tenancy. They would also take over responsibility for paying any rent arrears.

If your survivors did not want to stay in the home, they could ask to be transferred. If you have a disability and the property has been adpated for your use, the council would probably suggest that your partner or other survivors moved to another council property so that your home could be let to someone else with a disability who would benefit from the adapted home.

# Assessing the protection gap

Now you should have enough information to complete the calculator in Figure 4.3 on pp. 94–5. This will tell you, firstly, whether your household would have an income shortfall in the event of your dying and, secondly, if there is a need for a lump sum.

The main way to fill a gap is to use life insurance – though you might consider building up additional savings instead or as well (see Chapters 9 and 10 for guidance on this route). The different life insurance options are described on p. 107 onwards. They include 'family income benefit' policies which can provide an income. However, another way to ensure that an income shortfall is plugged would be to buy lump sum life insurance that your survivors could invest to provide an income. The calculator in Figure 4.3 includes guidance on the lump sum you would need to provide the income required. See Chapters 9 and 10 for ideas on the investments to use.

If you and your partner have each worked through the calculator, it is likely that you have come up with different protection needs. This feeds through to any decision to buy insurance. For some purposes, such as cover to pay off a joint mortgage, joint-life insurance (a single policy to pay out an identical sum when one of you dies) is appropriate. For more general protection, it makes better sense to take out two separate single-life policies tailored to the amount of cover you each need.

## Implementing your plan

Life insurance comes in two forms: protection-only and investment-type. A protection-only plan, also called term insurance, pays out an agreed sum if you die within a specified period but nothing at all if you do not die. In the past, consumers sometimes considered term insurance to be a poor deal because – expecting not to die – it seemed like paying money for nothing. Today, consumers are more aware that essentially what you are buying is peace of mind and, reflecting the fact that you get nothing back if you survive, term insurance is the cheapest way to buy substantial life cover – see Table 4.2.

Investment-type life insurance pays out if you die but also builds up a cash-in value. This enables life insurance to be used as a basis for investment (see Chapter 10). Investment-type life insurance policies are either endowment policies, which run for a specified term, or whole-of-life policies, which as the name suggests are designed to run indefinitely and pay out on death whenever it happens (or be cashed in early for an investment return). Sometimes endowment policies and whole-of-life policies are sold as a means of providing protection, but generally this is suitable only in special cases, such as protecting an endowment mortgage (see Chapter 6) or covering an expected inheritance tax bill on an estate (see Chapter 11). In the vast majority of cases, if your need is for protection, term insurance is the best option.

**Table 4.2  Examples of 20-year term insurance premiums**

*The table shows the average monthly premium for level lump sum cover of £100,000.*

| Your age when you take out the policy | Man | | Woman | |
|---|---|---|---|---|
| | *Non-smoker* | *Smoker* | *Non-smoker* | *Smoker* |
| 20 | £6.91 | £9.58 | £6.22 | £6.85 |
| 30 | £7.40 | £11.30 | £6.53 | £8.41 |
| 40 | £12.56 | £23.72 | £10.30 | £18.76 |
| 50 | £30.86 | £66.78 | £23.60 | £52.01 |

*Source*: Data taken from Moneyfacts, *Life Pensions & Investments Moneyfacts*, August 2009.

## Different types of term insurance

The most basic type of term insurance provides a level pay-out – for example, you might buy £100,000 of cover for an 18-year term. The policy will then pay out exactly the same nominal sum of £100,000 whether you die in the first year or the last. These days, most policies also usually include terminal illness benefit. This means that, if you are diagnosed with an illness and expected to live less than 12 months, the policy will pay out early. This gives you the opportunity to sort out your affairs while you are still alive.

The premiums you pay for term insurance are based on the insurer's assessment of the probability of a claim, in other words, the probability of your dying during the term. Therefore, the premiums depend on the following:

▪ **Age**. The older you are when you take out the policy, the more you will pay.

▪ **Sex**. Men pay more than women.

▪ **Health and lifestyle**. Smokers pay more than non-smokers. Low levels of cover may be offered without any checks on your health and lifestyle, but for larger sums, you will have to answer questions about your health and that of close family members, and other factors that could put your life at risk. You may have to undergo a medical examination.

▪ **Amount of cover and policy term**. The larger the cover and longer the term, the higher the premium.

Premiums may be guaranteed, in other words, they stay at the same level throughout the whole policy term. Alternatively, they may be reviewable, in which case the provider may increase the premiums. When AIDS/HIV was first recognised, many insurers revised their policies to allow for reviewable premiums. This gave insurers the option of making increases if AIDS turned out to be an epidemic that pushed up claim rates significantly. In the event, AIDS has not had this effect and, in general, the option to review term insurance premiums on these grounds has not been exercised.

---

**Genetic tests**

As discussed in Chapter 3, genetic tests are potentially a source of information that could be very useful for insurers in estimating the risk of life and health insurance claims. However, under an agreement between the government and the insurance industry, which is periodically reviewed and has so far been extended to 2014, insurers can ask you to disclose adverse results from a predictive genetic test only if you are applying for insurance in excess of specified limits. The limit for life insurance is £500,000 and, for critical illness cover, £300,000.

---

Although the buying power of the amount paid out by level term insurance will tend to fall over time as prices rise, the need for the lump sum may diminish over time as well – for example, if the lump sum will be invested to provide income, the period for which the income is required may decrease if, say, the aim is to provide cover until children cease to be dependent. Because of this trade off, buying a set amount of cover can be a reasonable way of plugging an income protection gap. Set against this basic type of cover there are a number of alternative options you could choose.

## Combined with critical illness cover

Term insurance is sometimes sold as a package with critical illness cover (CIC). This pays out a tax-free lump sum if you are diagnosed with a life-threatening condition, such as cancer, stroke or heart attack. Do not confuse CIC with terminal illness benefit. The pay-out from CIC does not depend on having a terminal condition.

The CIC element of the package may provide 'accelerated cover', in which case the combined policy pays out on the earlier of diagnosis of a life-threatening condition or death. Alternatively, it may provide extra cover, so that there would be a payment on diagnosis and a further payment on death. Accelerated cover is the most common type and suitable where the life cover/CIC is intended to clear a debt, such as a mortgage. Accelerated cover is more problematic if you want generally to provide for your family. There is a danger that if a critical illness triggers the pay-out, you may spend the money, for example, on treatment and recuperation. This would then leave your family without any life cover protection. For more information about CIC, see Chapter 3.

### Family income benefit

Instead of paying out a single lump sum, this type of term insurance pays out a series of lump sums that your survivors can use as an income. The income is paid out only for the remainder of the term. For example, if you had an 18-year policy and you died in the first year, the income would be paid out for the full 18 years. If you died in the 15th year, the income would be paid out only for the last four years. Since, unlike level term insurance, the pay-out with family income benefit decreases over time, this type of cover should normally be cheaper than level cover.

It is more important with family income benefit cover to consider what impact inflation may have on the income as time goes by. The level of income you select at the outset may seem more than adequate but could buy too little when it is paid out many years in the future. Therefore, you may want to choose a policy where the income increases both in the period before any pay-out starts and once it is being paid – this would cost more than a policy paying out a level income. On the other hand, your survivor partner might need a higher income in the early years when they might have to take time out of work to care for young children, with a reducing need for income as time goes by and they can go out to work. In that case, the fall in buying power of a level income could be quite manageable.

Since the pay-out from family income benefit policies is a stream of lump sum payments, rather than genuine income, the pay-outs are tax-free and also do not affect claims for tax credits (see Appendix A).

## Case study

Mick, age 25, takes out a family income benefit policy for a term of 25 years to pay out a level income of £20,000 a year if he were to die. The premium is fixed at £18 a month. If he were to die ten years after taking out the policy and, in the meantime, inflation had averaged 2.5 per cent a year, his wife Carol would receive £20,000 a year but this would buy only the same as £15,600 in today's money.

## Decreasing term insurance

A decreasing term insurance policy – as the name suggests – pays out a lump which falls as the term progresses. It is ideal for covering a debt, such as a repayment mortgage (see Chapter 6) or personal loan, where the balance to be paid off falls over time. It can also be useful for covering the potential inheritance tax bill on a lifetime gift (see Chapter 11).

## Increasing term insurance

This variant pays out a lump sum on death within the term but the amount to be paid out increases each year. If you need to protect the pay-out against the effects of inflation, this could be an option. Your premiums increase in line with the cover.

## Increasable term insurance

Increasable term insurance pays out a level lump sum on death within the term. However, you have the option to increase the amount. The option either comes up at regular intervals – say, on each policy anniversary – or when specified events occur, such as the birth of a child. Whenever you increase the cover, your monthly premiums rise. The premium increase is based on your age at the time of the increase but – and here is the advantage – on your state of health at the time you originally started the policy even if your actual health is now worse.

## Renewable term insurance

This variation allows you to take out term insurance for a set period and at the end gives you the option to take out a further policy for a new term. The premium for the further policy is based on your age at that time but on your health at the time you started the original policy even if your actual health is now worse.

In theory, renewable term insurance could be useful if your budget is currently tight. For example, if you wanted a 20-year term policy but could not afford the premium, you might instead take out a ten-year renewable term policy for now at a lower premium and then extend the cover later on. In practice, the difference between the premium for longer and shorter terms is often quite small, especially when you are in your 20s and 30s.

## Case study

Ghada's grandchildren have come to live with her permanently and ideally she would like to take out a 20-year term insurance policy for £200,000 to protect them. But Ghada is 40 and smokes and would find it hard to pay the £38 a month premium being quoted for cover. A solution could be to take out a ten-year renewable policy which would cost her £29 a month and then look at taking out a further policy when this one expires.

### Life-of-another insurance

To take out life cover, you must have an 'insurable interest', meaning that you must stand to suffer some financial loss in the event of death. The law assumes you have an unlimited insurable interest in your own life and in that of your husband, wife or civil partner, so you can take out insurance up to any sum based on your own or their lives.

There is no automatic insurable interest in anyone else's life, not even your children, parents or unmarried partner (though there have been proposals to change the law on this). Therefore to take out insurance based on somebody else's life, you must have a specific, measurable interest. Examples include:

- taking out insurance on the life of your former partner to cover maintenance they pay you;
- taking out insurance on the life of a partner to cover their share of a mortgage on your home;
- taking out insurance on the life of your adult child to cover care-home fees they pay for you;
- taking out insurance on the life of a parent to cover education fees they pay.

Provided you have an insurable interest, you do not need the permission of the person whose life is insured to take out life-of-another insurance.

## Maximum protection policy

Whole-of-life insurance is sold in many forms, one of which is the 'maximum protection policy'. It can be used to meet your protection needs, but in a more complex and less certain way than term insurance. Instead of buying life cover direct, your monthly premiums (after the deduction of any administration fee) are invested in a fund. Part of the fund is cashed in each month to buy life cover and the rest is left invested.

You can choose to vary the balance between life cover and investment. For example, if you choose the highest, possible level of cover, very little of your money is invested and this is the maximum protection route. Alternatively, you could choose a lower level of cover and then more of your money is left in the investment fund to provide a potential cash-in value.

The level of life cover you choose is guaranteed for an initial period of five or ten years. At that stage, your plan is reviewed. If the investment fund has grown well enough, you can continue with the same or an increased level of life cover while paying the same monthly premiums. If the investment fund has not performed so well, your cover will be reduced, your premium increased or both. Reviews typically continue to take place every five years.

A maximum protection policy can be very flexible, enabling you to increase and reduce cover as your circumstances change without the need to take out additional policies. But whether you can maintain your chosen level of cover at the initial price depends on the investment performance of the fund.

## Buying life insurance

If you are an employee, you may be able to pay extra contributions to your pension scheme at work in order to boost the level of life cover you get through your employer's scheme. Because these contributions qualify for tax relief (see Chapter 7), this is likely to be the cheapest way to buy extra life insurance.

Since December 2006, it has no longer been possible to buy life cover through a personal pension (though you can continue any life insurance policy bought this way before that date).

If you feel confident sorting out and buying your own term insurance, you can do this online or by contacting companies direct. There are many online brokers who will compare quotes for you and you can download policy documents to check the detail of the cover. Usually the brokers check a panel of insurers, not the whole market, so check out two or three websites before making a choice. If you prefer to shop around offline, specialist magazines, such as those from Moneyfacts which publishes comparison tables, are a useful starting point (see Appendix B for contact details).

If you want help choosing your life cover, contact an independent financial adviser (see Appendix B).

# Stress testing and review

The main potential upset to your life cover planning is that the cover turns out to be insufficient. In general, there are two reasons why this might happen: inflation and a change in circumstances. If you choose a maximum protection policy, you are also subject to investment risk.

You can specifically build in protection against inflation by choosing increasing term insurance and/or increasing family income benefit. However, if your survivors' needs will reduce over time (for example, as children become less dependent) level term insurance might provide enough 'excess' pay-out in cash terms to offset the reduction in buying power due to inflation. But there can be no certainty that this trade-off will work. If inflation ran at very high levels, the pay-out could seriously undershoot the amount your survivors need. To provide against this eventuality, you might also want to build up extra savings. (Chapters 9 and 10 look at savings strategies that aim to protect against inflation.)

If your survivors' protection needs increase in future, it would be easy enough to take out an additional term insurance policy. However, the premiums would be based on your state of health at that time so, if your health had deteriorated, the cost could be higher than you had anticipated. You can avoid this problem by taking out increasable term insurance that gives you the option to add to your cover later on. A maximum protection policy offers the flexibility to increase and reduce the cover in line with your survivors' needs, but the amount you must pay is uncertain and could increase significantly when your policy comes up for review if investment performance has been poor.

# 5

# Health and care

## Introduction

In 2009, debate raged in the USA over whether a UK-style national health-care scheme or privately insured healthcare was the better and fairer system. Whichever side of the debate you favour, the fact is that since 1948 the tax-funded, largely free-at-point-of-use National Health Service (NHS) has been the main source of healthcare for UK citizens. That is not to say that the UK lacks private healthcare and private insurance to pay for it. These options are available and may form part of your financial plan, but – with a few exceptions – they are not an essential element.

One exception is dental treatment. Changes to NHS contracts for dentists in 2006 caused a big decline in the availability of dentists willing to take on NHS patients. As a result, in many areas of the country, you now have little option but to pay for private dental treatment either on a self-pay (pay-as-you-go) basis or through a dental plan or insurance.

While the NHS provides healthcare, there is at present no comprehensive state long-term care system for older people as they become more frail and need support. What state help there is targets people with limited means. The rest of the population must pay for care out of their own resources until these are run down to a low enough level for state support to kick in. This means your financial planning cannot just look at long-term care in isolation but is firmly connected to your goals around inheritance as well (see Chapter 11). In 2009, the government launched a review of long-term care and the prospect of changes in the years ahead needs to be taken into account as part of your planning in this area.

# Private healthcare

The availability of treatment on the NHS means that private healthcare is not an essential for UK citizens. A key reason for opting for private treatment in the past was the length of NHS waiting lists. However, these have improved considerably in recent years (see Table 5.1). Nonetheless, 7.3 million (around 12 per cent of the population) in the UK are covered by private medical insurance[1] and plans and Britons spend a further £500 million or so direct on private treatment (the 'self-pay' route).[2] Main reasons for choosing private treatment are:

- **Reduced waiting times**. Despite the fall in NHS waiting times and the option to shop around for NHS treatment at hospitals with shorter waiting lists, you could still have wait several months for treatment. Apart from the pain and discomfort, waiting could have severe financial implications if you are unable to work. This could be especially problematic if you run your own business.

- **Convenient treatment times**. You have greater freedom to fit treatment around your other commitments.

- **Choice of consultant and hospital**. Going private may give you greater choice, but not necessarily. These days, you have greater choice under the NHS about which hospital to go to. Moreover, consultants often work for both the NHS and privately, so you may in fact be seen by the same expert. And some private medical insurance policies keep down the cost by choosing your consultant and hospital for you.

- **Privacy and comfort**. A private hospital offers hotel-style facilities, for example, your own en-suite room, television, better food and less restricted visiting times.

- **Cleanliness**. A survey by a major private healthcare provider found that people worry about the incidence of infection and lack of cleanliness in NHS hospitals and perceive private hospitals to be cleaner.[3] There is no proven difference, but the perception is a driver towards the private treatment route.

---

[1] Association of British Insurers (ABI), 2009, *Private medical insurance rises despite recession*, Press release, London, ABI.

[2] Laing & Buission, 2008, *Self-pay private healthcare falls as economic slowdown bites but NHS spending supports growth for private hospitals*, Press release, London, Laing & Buisson.

[3] BUPA, 2009, *BUPA response to ABI figures showing that more people have private*, London, BUPA.

**Table 5.1  NHS waiting times**

| | Country | | | |
|---|---|---|---|---|
| | England | Wales | Scotland | Northern Ireland |
| Target waiting time from GP referral to seeing consultant | 13 weeks | 10 weeks | 15 weeks | 9 weeks |
| Percentage of patients seen within this time | 100% | 95.1% | 99.9% | 98.5% |
| Target waiting time from GP referral to admission to hospital | 18 weeks | 14 weeks | 15 weeks | 13 weeks |
| Percentage of patients admitted within this time | 98.2% | 92.1% | 99.8% | 96.5% |

*Sources*: Department of Health, *Commissioner-based waiting times*, July 2009; Statistics for Wales, *NHS Wales waiting times*, August 2009; ISD Scotland, *Waiting times and waiting lists*, August 2009; Northern Ireland Executive, *Publication of the June 2009 Northern Ireland waiting lists statistics bulletin*, September 2009.

## Case study

> Pawel is a chiropractor who runs a practice on his own, employing just a receptionist/secretary. If Pawel was unable to work for several weeks or months, this would be a disaster for his business. He would lose income and his patients might decide to go elsewhere. To help guard against this, Pawel has taken out private medical insurance. He has the peace of mind of knowing that, if he had to go into hospital for any reason, he should be able to get treatment quickly and so minimise the time he would be away from work.

Private hospital treatment is not cheap: Table 5.2 on p. 120 gives some examples of prices. Therefore, if you do decide to include this in your financial plan, you need to consider how to pay for treatment. There are two basic options: self-pay or insurance. Figure 5.1 summarises a possible financial plan for private healthcare.

This chapter focuses on using private health services in the UK. However, note that if you travel abroad, you will normally need private medical cover to use medical services abroad. When travelling or living in countries which are part of the European Economic Area (EEA) – see the box

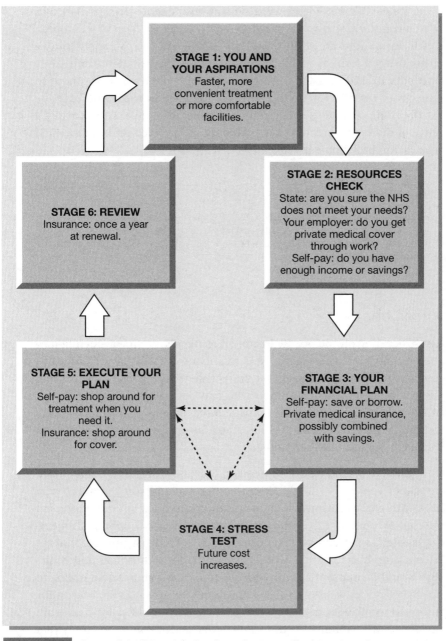

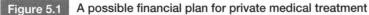

**Figure 5.1**    A possible financial plan for private medical treatment

– you are eligible for emergency treatment on the same terms as nationals of that country (usually free or reduced cost) on production of a European Health Insurance Card (EHIC). An EHIC is free and you can apply for one either using a form available from post offices, by phone or online (see Appendix B). EHICs last for five years at a time, after which you need to renew your card. To top up this cover for full medical treatment, or if you are travelling outside the EEA, you need travel insurance. This provides a range of different types of cover, including private medical insurance and repatriation back home if you are taken ill abroad.

> **European Economic Area countries**
>
> Austria, Belgium, Bulgaria, Cyprus, Czech Republic, Denmark, Estonia, Finland, France, Germany, Greece, Hungary, Iceland, Ireland, Italy, Latvia, Liechtenstein, Lithuania, Luxembourg, Malta, Netherlands, Norway, Poland, Portugal, Romania, Slovakia, Slovenia, Spain, Sweden, Switzerland.

## Resources check

Before deciding on the private treatment route, it's worth considering how the NHS operates these days. NHS treatment options have changed in recent years. A typical course of treatment starts with a visit to a GP. Your GP may refer you to a consultant who may suggest diagnostic tests and/ or treatment in hospital as an outpatient, daypatient or inpatient. A stay in hospital may be followed by outpatient check-ups and other outpatient treatment, for example, physiotherapy.

In England, a system called Choose and Book now operates. If you prefer, instead of your GP writing a letter to a hospital and you waiting to hear back with an appointment time, you can opt to book your appointment yourself by phone or over the internet. Your GP prints an appointment-request letter for you to take away which includes a unique booking reference number. Your GP will recommend a list of hospitals and clinics that would be appropriate for your treatment and you can go online to the NHS Choices website to check these out (see Appendix B). The online information includes details such as average waiting times for treatment, incidence of hospital infections and other performance measures that you can take into account in making your choice. You will be offered a range of appointment dates and times and are guaranteed an appointment within the target waiting time (see Table 5.1). By choosing a different hospital from the one nearest to your home, you may be seen more quickly.

The NHS can commission services from private hospitals and clinics, so you may find that the list your GP suggests includes some private treatment centres as well as NHS facilities.

## The self-pay route

If a visit to your GP reveals the need for hospital treatment, you should tell your GP if you want to be treated privately. They can then recommend private consultants and hospitals that are suitable for the treatment you need. If you do not have medical insurance (see overleaf), you need to check out what the treatment will cost and consider how you will pay.

Table 5.2 gives a guide to the cost of some common treatments. Cost generally relates to the complexity of the treatment and the length of hospital stay required. You may be able to negotiate a fixed price for your treatment. Check carefully what is included in the package and whether there could be extra costs. Typically, the package for surgical treatment will include: the surgeon's and anaesthetist's fees, theatre time, dressings and drugs, accommodation and meals, and nursing care. It may also include aftercare and physiotherapy. Consultations and diagnostic tests before treatment are usually charged separately.

It is for you to decide how you will pay for the treatment. If you do not have sufficient income or savings, you might decide to borrow. Check whether the hospital operates its own credit scheme. Only borrow if you are sure you can afford the repayments.

If you have critical illness cover (see Chapter 3) and your need for treatment happens to arise because you have been diagnosed with one of the conditions covered by this insurance (for example, heart attack or cancer), you could use the cash pay-out to pay for private treatment. However, because this type of insurance covers only a limited range of health problems, it is not a good choice if your main goal is to pay for private treatment whenever the need arises.

### Table 5.2 Examples of private treatment costs

| Type of treatment | Cost range |
| --- | --- |
| Carpal tunnel release | £900–£2,100 |
| Cataract removal | £1,700–£3,250 |
| Coronary angioplasty | £8,800–£14,175 |
| Coronary artery bypass graft | £13,650–£17,000 |
| Ganglion removal | £1,300–£1,750 |
| Haemorrhoids removal | £1,575–£3,075 |
| Hernia repair | £1,650–£3,800 |
| Hip replacement | £8,200–£10,300 |
| Hysterectomy | £5,000–£6,700 |
| Knee replacement | £9,300–£14,600 |
| Squint correction | £2,000–£3,075 |
| Varicose vein surgery (both legs) | £2,300–£3,300 |
| Wisdom teeth extraction | £1,425–£1,700 |

*Source*: www.spirehealthcare.com. Accessed 20 September 2009.

## Private medical insurance

Instead of using the self-pay route to pay for private treatment in a single lump sum, you could take out private medical insurance (PMI) that will pay out at the time you need treatment. In effect, insurance is a way of spreading the cost – though, of course, you will not necessarily ever need to claim. Thought of in that way, an alternative to insurance would be to put the amount you would otherwise pay in premiums into a savings account that could be used to fund self-pay treatment. There are two advantages of insurance over saving: you might need treatment before you have had time to build up adequate savings; and you might be unlucky enough to need very costly treatment that would exceed your savings. However, of the 7.3 million UK citizens covered by private medical insurance, you could be one of the 4.6 million covered through a scheme provided by your own or your partner's employer.

## What PMI covers

PMI covers private hospital treatment for 'acute' medical conditions. These are health problems that can be cured or substantially relieved by treatment, such as cataracts, hernias, heart bypass and hip replacements.

This insurance does not cover chronic health conditions, for example diabetes, needing kidney dialysis, rheumatism or dementia. It also usually excludes normal pregnancy, HIV/AIDS, regular dental treatment, organ transplant, infertility, cosmetic surgery, drug abuse, self-inflicted injury, and a variety of other health threats. PMI does not cover emergency treatment (which is not offered by private hospitals).

Importantly, PMI does not normally cover pre-existing health conditions you have. Insurers take one of two approaches:

- **Full underwriting**. The insurer asks for detailed information about your medical history and may ask to check the medical notes held by your GP. On the basis of this, the insurer decides whether to offer you cover, at what price and whether to exclude certain types of claim. Usually, claims related to any existing condition will be excluded permanently.

- **Moratorium underwriting**. You do not have to provide detailed medical information when you take out the policy. Instead, the terms and conditions will automatically exclude claims related to any health problems you have had during the past few years (usually five). The exclusion continues until you have gone two full years without the problem recurring or asking your GP for advice about it. When you make a claim, the insurer will, at that stage, make detailed medical checks to see what health conditions if any are caught by the moratorium clause.

With all PMI policies, it is essential to check with your insurer before booking any treatment, otherwise your claim might be refused.

## How PMI works

PMI is very much a case of 'you get what you pay for'. Standard policies typically cover the full cost of inpatient or daypatient treatment and related outpatient care, giving you a wide choice of private hospitals and private wards in NHS hospitals, but excluding some types of condition or treatment such as psychiatric care and the more costly cancer treatments.

Comprehensive policies are the deluxe versions, which typically add in cover for psychiatric treatment, a wider range of cancer treatments, alternative medicine, private ambulances, after-care nursing in your own home, and so on. Comprehensive policies may also have a range of frills such as cover for foreign travel, eye-care and dental treatment.

Budget policies use a variety of devices to make the cost more manageable (see below) and/or limit the cover. For example, you may pay less if you agree to choose from a shorter list of hospitals or to let the insurer specify which consultants and hospitals you use. There may be cash limits on the amount you can claim, for example, a maximum of £600 a year for out-patient treatment. Some types of cover may not be included at all, such as outpatient treatment that is unrelated to being an inpatient or day-patient, private ambulances and home nursing. Another variation will pay for private treatment only if the waiting list for NHS treatment is longer than six weeks.

A standard feature of all policies is a cash payment for each night (for example, £100 to £250) that you receive treatment as an inpatient on the NHS rather than going private.

There is a great deal of variation between individual policies, so it is important to check the detail to see if a policy offers the package of cover you want at the hospitals and clinics that would be most convenient for you.

### The cost of PMI

With nearly all PMI, the premium you pay is based on the likely cost of your claims and varies, in particular, with your age and sex. Health problems tend to increase as you get older, so someone in their 60s will pay a lot more than someone in their 30s. Pay-outs to women in middle age are much higher than for men of a similar age,[4] so in mid-life women tend to pay more than men for the same cover. But at older ages, the differences even out and premiums become similar. Most providers set a maximum age (for example, 70) after which you cannot newly take out cover.

Table 5.3 below gives some examples of the variation in premiums in 2008 for men and women of different ages. You can also take out policies as a couple or to cover a whole family.

PMI policies are annual. Normally at each renewal your premium will increase reflecting your increased age and changes in private treatment costs, which tend to rise at a faster rate than ordinary price inflation.

---

[4] Association of British Insurers (ABI), 2009, *Private medical insurance by age and gender*, Data Bulletin, London, ABI.

**Table 5.3 Examples of private medical insurance premiums**

| Your age and sex | Range of monthly premiums for: | | |
| --- | --- | --- | --- |
| | Budget plan | Standard plan | Comprehensive plan |
| Man aged 30 | £11–£49 | £19–£62 | £20–£77 |
| Woman aged 30 | £11–£54 | £19–£68 | £20–£85 |
| Man aged 60 | £27–£137 | £47–£169 | £50–£207 |
| Woman aged 60 | £27–£133 | £47–£164 | £50–£202 |

*Source*: Data taken from *Money Management*, September 2008.

One provider, National Friendly Society, is unusual in offering PMI on a different payment basis. At the outset, you choose the amount you want to pay each month and this is fixed for as long as you have the insurance with no increases at renewal (unless you choose to increase your level of cover). But you have to make a contribution towards the cost of treatment if you claim and the proportion you must pay increases as you get older. Half of your premium is paid into a deposit account with National Friendly and is used to fund your payment towards any claim. But the money in the deposit account remains yours, so, if you don't make any claims, you can get back the money in the account.

As you can see from Table 5.3, PMI can be expensive, especially as you become older when the cost can easily rise to over £1,000 per person per year. Apart from limiting your cover, most providers offer at least some of the following options which enable you to reduce your premium:

∎ **Frequency of payment.** There may be a discount of, say 5 per cent, if you pay a single annual premium up-front rather than paying monthly.

∎ **Method of payment.** You may get a discount of, say, 5 per cent if you agree to pay by direct debit. Some providers offer a discount if you pay online. Conversely, you may have to pay extra (1.5 per cent is common) if you pay by credit card.

∎ **No claims discount.** It is now fairly standard for providers to offer you a discount at renewal if you have not made any claims in the previous year. However, if you needed treatment, you would have to weigh up whether opting for self-pay in order to protect your premiums was worthwhile – after all, the whole point of having the insurance is to claim if the need arises.

■ **Adjustable excess**. Many providers offer a discount if you agree to pay the first part of any claim yourself up to a given limit which you can choose. For example, opting for a £500 excess might get you a 5 to 10 per cent discount, while opting for a £2,500 excess could cut your premium in half.

■ **Co-payment**. You agree to pay a percentage of any claim with the maximum you have to pay capped at a set limit. The insurer then pays the rest. For example, you might agree to pay 10 per cent up to a maximum of £2,000 or 25 per cent up to a maximum of £5,000. The larger the percentage you agree to, the lower your premium.

■ **Health discounts**. You may get a discount of, say, 10 per cent if you are a non-smoker or your weight is in a healthy range. Some providers have also been experimenting with giving discounts on health-related products, such as gym membership, and awarding points that earn discounts if you take up exercise or other steps to improve your lifestyle.

■ **Group discounts**. PMI is normally cheaper when taken out for a group of people than for a single individual (because the group provides a spread of risk for the insurer). This is why your employer can take out a work-based policy more cheaply than you can. You may also be able to get cheaper cover if you buy through your trade union, a professional association or any other group to which you are affiliated.

## Shopping around for PMI

Check whether you are eligible for cover through your job, your union, professional association or any other groups that you belong to. Compare against policies you can take out for yourself to see which offers the better deal on price and cover.

Some internet comparison sites, such as www.moneysupermarket.com, include comparative tables for PMI. These can be a useful starting point but make sure you check the cover matches your needs – don't just go for the cheapest price.

If you do not feel confident selecting your own policy, get help from an independent financial adviser (see Appendix B).

### Switching policies

Despite the annual nature of PMI policies, if you renew with the same provider, your policy continues to cover any health conditions that have first arisen during the time you have had a policy with that provider.

If you want to switch to another provider, it might agree to offer cover on the same basis, in which case you will need a letter from your old insurer confirming the cover you currently have. This may also apply when you have been covered through a PMI scheme at work but decide to switch to an individual policy with the same provider on leaving the job or retiring. However, in most cases, when you switch provider, your application will be assessed on a totally new basis, so any health problems you have developed since taking out your original PMI cover are likely now to be treated as pre-existing conditions which may now be excluded at least for the first couple of years (see p. 121).

---

### Hospital and health cash plans |

With hospital cash plans, you pay a regular sum (often only £10 or £20 a month) and the plan pays out a relatively small cash sum (say, £50 a night) if you have to go into hospital, whether NHS or private. Some health cash plans also pay out in relation to a range of other ordinary health-related events, such as visits to the dentist and optician, chiropody or having a baby. These plans aim to help you with the expenses associated with health issues, for example, paying for phone calls and extras while you are an inpatient, travel for relatives to-and-from the hospital, and helping with childcare costs, or to make a contribution towards the cost of, say, dental charges. They do not pay enough to cover the cost of private hospital treatment and are not intended to be a substitute for PMI.

---

## Stress test and review

The main stress test for your financial plan if you opt for the insurance route is: will you be able to afford the premiums as time goes by? PMI stops immediately if you no longer pay the premiums and few providers offer a 'waiver of premium benefit'. Waiver of premium is an optional extra with some insurance policies that makes the premium payments for you if you are off work because of illness. If your budget will be stretched to pay for PMI, the likelihood is that it may become unaffordable a few years ahead. In that case, you may want to look at ways of reducing the cost (such as choosing a budget policy rather than standard) or even reconsidering whether you need PMI at all.

Opting to build up your own savings to use for self-pay offers greater flexibility in that you can choose at the time you need treatment whether to go private or fall back on the NHS. The key risk here is that you will not have built up sufficient savings to cover the cost of major treatment.

Adjustable excesses and co-payment (which includes the approach adopted by National Friendly Society) offer a half-way house, because they enable you to reduce the cost of PMI to a possibly more manageable level while also capping the amount you will need to find from your own savings.

It makes sense to review your PMI each year when it comes up for renewal. However, if you shop around for a cheaper policy bear in mind that health problems developed since starting your old policy may not be covered by a new one. As you reach older age, you should look especially closely at whether PMI continues to offer value for money, since many health problems in older age are chronic conditions that will not be covered by PMI.

# Dental treatment

Children up to age 18 (19 if still in full-time education), women who are pregnant or have recently given birth and people on a low income can get free dental treatment on the NHS. In addition, dental check-ups are free for all in Scotland and for people aged under 25 or over 60 in Wales. Everyone else must pay, though NHS charges are capped at a maximum amount (£198 in 2009–10). However, a survey by the health plan provider, Simplyhealth, found that, in 2009, 35 per cent of people had struggled to find an NHS dentist and 21 per cent had not even tried to find NHS care.[5]

If NHS dentistry is not available in your area, you will have little choice but to pay for private treatment (or go without dental care, which is not recommended and could turn out to be costly in the long run). You might opt for private treatment for more positive reasons – for example, a private practice may be able to afford better to keep up with advances in dental treatment and may be able to spend more time with patients, focusing on prevention rather than just treatment.

You have a choice of ways to pay for private dental care: self-pay, capitation plans and insurance.

## Check your resources

Before going down the private route, you may want to check whether there are any NHS dentists in your area accepting new patients. You can find NHS dentists in England by using the search facility on the NHS Choices website or by calling NHS Direct or your local Primary Care Trust – see Appendix B for contact details – and equivalent organisations in the rest of the UK.

---

[5] Simplyhealth, 2009, *Annual dental survey*, Andover, Simplyhealth.

In England and Wales, there are three charging bands for NHS treatment as shown in Table 5.4. The charges apply to a course of treatment rather than individual elements of your care and regardless of the number of visits you need to complete the course. In Scotland and Northern Ireland, you pay for 80 per cent of the cost on an item-by-item basis.

**Table 5.4 NHS dental treatment charges in England and Wales 2009–10**

| Treatment band | Charge for course of treatment |
|---|---|
| *Band 1*<br>Examination, diagnosis (such as x-rays), scale and polish, advice. | £16.50 |
| *Band 2*<br>Band 1 treatment plus fillings, root canal work and extractions | £45.60 |
| *Band 3*<br>Bands 1 and 2 treatment plus crowns, dentures or bridges. | £198.00 |

*Source*: Based on www.nhs.uk. Accessed 21 September 2009.

## The self-pay route

If your dental health is generally good, you might opt to pay for treatment on a self-pay (pay-as-you-go) basis. The cost of each visit will depend on what treatment you receive and what your particular dental practice charges. There is no standardised set of charges. Table 5.5 gives some examples, but you might have to pay more or less than the amounts shown. You must normally pay at the end of each visit or stage of treatment.

Given that you should aim to have regular check-ups, it makes sense to budget for check-ups and scale-and-polish out of your income. You might meet the cost of larger work from savings or by borrowing. Some dentists offer their own credit schemes. Only borrow, if you are sure you can meet the repayments.

**Table 5.5 Examples of the cost of private dental treatment**

| Type of treatment | Charge |
| --- | --- |
| New patient detailed examination and assessment | £26–£66 |
| Check-up | £21–£28 |
| Scale and polish | £16–£41 |
| Filling | £31–£165 |
| Extraction | £47–£126 |
| Dentures | £210–£825 |
| Root filling | £100–£250 |
| Crown | £305–£441 |
| Out-of-hours emergency | £83–£183 |

*Sources*: Online price lists, various sources, September 2009.

## Capitation schemes

Of patients who take out some kind of plan to pay for dental care, 84 per cent opt for capitation schemes.[6] These essentially spread the cost of treatment through monthly payments instead of your having to pay in a single lump sum. Typically you pay by direct debit and there is often a 5 or 10 per cent discount if you agree to pay annually in advance.

Capitation schemes are often run by big companies, but you join through a particular dentist and the charges are specific to that dentist. Before being accepted onto a capitation plan, the dentist will assess your dental health. From this, the dentist can estimate the level of treatment you are likely to need. This will determine the level of your fixed monthly payment. Implicit in the payment may be a discount of, say, 10 per cent on the normal rates charged by that dentist. You will have a relatively low monthly payment if your dental health is good (for example, under £10 a month) and a higher payment (maybe £20 a month or more) if your dental health is not so good. If your dental health is very poor, you may need to have extensive work done before you can be accepted onto the capitation scheme.

---

[6]  Laing & Buisson, 2007, *Rise in PMI demand signals optimism: dental care cover is booming*, London, Laing & Buisson.

The scheme will cover most of the dental treatment you subsequently receive without further charge. But you will have to pay extra if you need very expensive treatment or your teeth are damaged through an accident. In that case you may be able to spread the cost through a temporary increase in your monthly payment or you might be able to claim on dental insurance (see below).

## Dental insurance

You may take out a policy as your main way of paying for dental care or, where you normally use self-pay or a capitation scheme, just to protect you against high bills for unexpected treatment. Dental insurance need not be linked to a particular dentist.

There is a choice of cover: emergency treatment only, emergencies and accidents, and comprehensive cover which includes routine treatment and may also cover serious problems, such as oral cancer. You might be covered for the full cost of treatment but more usually limits will apply, for example, £1,000 a year for routine maintenance and treatment, a further £1,000 for accidents, and so on. Insurance can cover the cost of NHS or private treatment, and emergency cover may apply both in the UK and if you are on a trip abroad. There may be a waiting period of, say, three or six months before you can start to claim on the policy. Pre-existing dental problems are not covered.

Cost depends on the level of cover you choose, but in 2009 could be around £15 a month. You can take out cover through your dentist, in which case you will be directed towards whichever provider your dentist has an arrangement with. Alternatively, you can shop around for your own cover, for example, using internet comparison sites (see Appendix B). Some employers run group dental insurance schemes for employees and comprehensive PMI policies (see p. 122) may include dental cover.

## Stress test and review

The Simplyhealth survey found that 13 per cent of people have no dentist at all and 43 per cent of respondents said they had put off dental visits because of worry over the cost.[7] Dental capitation schemes and dental insurance can help to make the cost more manageable, but may still be among the first items you think about cutting back on if, say, you are made redundant or can't work because of illness. The ideal solution would

[7] Simplyhealth, 2009, *Annual dental survey*, Andover, Simplyhealth.

be to look at your overall protection for income in these eventualities (see Chapter 3) and ensure that your income protection planning takes into account your regular spending on items such as dental care.

Not having regular check-ups could be costly in the long run if it leads to expensive emergency treatment. The cheapest option is to find an NHS practice. If there is no NHS treatment available in your area, you could put pressure on your local Primary Care Trust to address the problem. Even with the NHS, you will normally have to pay for your check-ups and treatment, but if your savings and income fell to low levels you would become eligible for free NHS treatment.

If you use a capitation scheme, you are locked into that for as long as you remain with the same dentist (unless you decide to switch to self-pay). If you use dental insurance, it makes sense to shop around when your policy comes up for renewal to see if you can get a better deal elsewhere. However, bear in mind that a new insurer will normally exclude any existing dental problems which your current insurer may be covering.

# Long-term care

One of the most difficult areas of your financial planning is preparing for the possibility of long-term care needs in the years ahead. The difficulties arise from the potentially very large cost of care and uncertainty about whether you will have care needs.

Government research found that half the population think long-term care will be free and paid for by the State.[8] Under the current system, this is true only once your wealth has been run down to a low level; otherwise you are mainly expected to pay for your own care. Two-thirds of women and one-third of men are likely to develop care needs in retirement and the average 65-year old will have to pay £30,000 for care during their lifetime, at today's prices, though individual experience could range from nothing to well over £100,000.[9]

Long-term care is not just an issue for you as an individual; as the number of older people relative to the working population is rising, how to pay for care is a social problem too. In 2009, the government launched a debate over the options for society and was proposing a partnership system under

---

[8] Secretary of State for Health, 2009, *Shaping the future of care together*, Cm 7673, London, The Stationery Office.

[9] Ibid.

which everyone would contribute towards the cost of the care system (see p. 136). You need to take these proposals into account when shaping this part of your financial plan.

Paying for long-term care is inevitably bound up with your inheritance planning (discussed in Chapter 11). Long-term care is costly and, however you fund it, needing care is likely to make a large dent in your wealth. An aspect of long-term care planning is about bringing some certainty and limit to that dent. This in turn creates more certainty about the wealth you may have left to pass on to your heirs. The other important side to long-term care planning is about giving you choice and comfort in the way your care needs are met. Figure 5.2 on p. 132 sets out a possible financial plan for long-term care.

The information in this section will also be relevant if you are helping someone else (for example, a parent) cope with care needs that they already have. Although there may no longer be an opportunity to plan ahead, they may have savings or a home which can be used to fund care and build on the help available from the State.

## What the State provides

Before you can work out what private provision you may want to make, you need to understand what support the State provides. Proposals to change the state system are discussed on p. 136. First, this section looks at current provision.

### Care in your own home

The state system aims to keep you living independently in your own home for as long as possible and currently supports you in two main ways: cash through the national disability benefits system; and provision of social services through your local authority (or your local Health and Social Care Trust in Northern Ireland). Increasingly, the latter are no longer being provided direct as services and, instead, you will be offered cash so that you can shop around yourself to buy in the services that you need. The national and local authority systems currently work separately.

Assuming you are over 65 when you start to need care, you may be able to claim attendance allowance. This is a tax-free weekly sum with eligibility based purely on the degree of your disability, regardless of your income and savings and with no need to have paid National Insurance contributions (as is the case with most non-means-tested benefits). It is payable at a lower rate if you need help during the day or the night and at a higher rate if you need support all the time. In 2010–11, the rates are £47.80 a week and £71.40 a

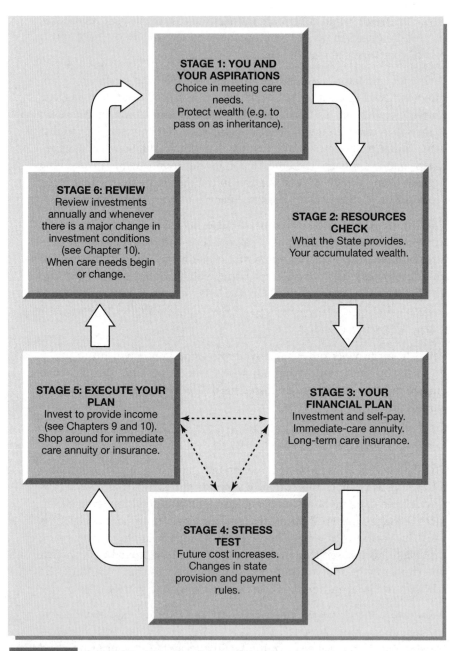

**Figure 5.2** A possible financial plan for long-term care

week. The allowance is designed to help you meet the extra costs of disability, but you are free to spend the cash in any way you like.

## Case study

Len has had Parkinson's disease for many years and the condition has slowly worsened. His wife, Joan, is his main carer, though until recently she has not really thought of herself as having that role. Now 68, Len needs help day and night with tasks such as taking his medication on time, getting dressed, getting out of chairs, going to the toilet and travelling anywhere. In 2010, their children persuaded Len to apply for attendance allowance and the couple were pleased and surprised when he was awarded the higher rate of £71.40 a week (giving the couple an extra £3,713 of income a year). They are using the money to buy in help with cleaning, taxis to a day-care centre and someone to sit with Len while Joan spends a couple of hours a week on her own activities.

People with a disability and carers are both entitled to a free assessment of needs carried out by their local authority. This identifies equipment, changes to your home and services that will help you to carry on living independently or, if necessary, recommends that you move into residential care (see below). For example, the care plan might suggest you need ramps and grab rails in your home, a downstairs bathroom, help from a personal carer in the mornings and evenings, a place in a day centre, a telephone-alert system if you are prone to falling, and so on.

If you have a reasonable income and/or savings, you will normally be expected to pay for whatever equipment, adaptations and services you need yourself, though charging practices vary from one local authority to another and Scotland has a different approach to paying for personal care services (see the box). See p. 137 for changes due in England in 2010. If your income and savings are low, your local authority may pay some or all of the cost. You must normally be offered the option of cash (called 'direct payment') so that you can choose and buy for yourself the services you need. From 2008–11, a system of 'personal accounts' is due to be introduced, under which the cash will be put into an account for you and you will have the choice of spending it yourself on services or getting your local authority to commission the services for you. Increasingly, local authorities no longer provide their own services and you will be buying in help from private firms. Local authorities can supply lists of providers in your area.

The cost of personal care services varies from provider to provider. As a rough guide, in 2009, a personal carer coming in for a short period to help with specific tasks might cost around £10 to £15 an hour, while a full-time live-in carer could be about £550 to £650 a week plus free bed and board. Government research suggests that around one-fifth of retired people needing care spend less than £1,000 a year.[10]

If you need medical care in your own home (for example, regular visits from a nurse to give you injections or change dressings) this is covered by the NHS and is free.

> ### Personal care in Scotland
>
> Anyone aged 65 or over who has been assessed by their local authority as needing it is entitled to free personal care up to £153 a week. This is paid direct to the care provider(s). It can be used for help with, for example, personal hygiene, continence management, food and diet, coping with immobility, counselling and support, assisting with medication, and other forms of personal assistance. If you live in a care home and accept the free personal care allowance, you lose your entitlement to attendance allowance. Information is available from your local authority or the Scottish Government website or enquiry line (see Appendix B).

## Care in a residential home

If your care needs are substantial, you may be better off moving permanently into a residential or nursing home (collectively referred to as 'care homes'). Residential homes provide general support and personal care services. Nursing homes additionally have a registered nurse on the premises to provide health care.

Most care homes are privately rather than state run. The cost of care in a home varies enormously depending on type of home, geography and the circumstances of care:

■ **Residential home.** Fees vary from home to home and region to region. For example, in 2009, in Somerset, you might pay around £400 a week for a place in a residential home but £500 or £600 in a smart area of London. If you need medical care, while you are in a residential home, this is provided free through the NHS just as it would be if you were living in your own home.

■ **Nursing home.** Nursing homes are more expensive than residential homes. For example, outside London, you could pay £700 a week; in London, fees could be £800 to £1,000 a week, and even more where the level of care needed is high. These fees are despite the fact that nursing care is funded by the NHS up to a set limit (in 2009–10, £101 a

---

[10] Ibid.

week in England, £119.66 in Wales, £69 a week in Scotland and £100 a week in Northern Ireland).

■ **NHS continuing care**. If moving to a nursing home or hospice is part of the plan for treating an illness for which you have been getting NHS treatment, the cost should be borne completely by the NHS. Often it is not clear whether care is a continuation of NHS treatment and you may have to fight to get care classified this way.

If you do not qualify for NHS continuing care, you can still ask for a financial assessment by your local authority to find out if it will help towards paying your care home fees. If you have savings and other capital above a set threshold, you will have to pay the full cost of the fees yourself. These upper capital limits for 2009–10 are shown in Table 5.6. If your capital is less than the upper limit, your local authority may help with the fees but only up to a set maximum which varies from one local authority to another. To find out how much help your local authority will give, your means are assessed *broadly* as set out below. The rules are complicated and this is just a broad outline:

■ Your capital up to the lower limit set out in Table 5.6 is disregarded.

■ For each £250 of capital between the lower and upper limit, you are assumed to receive £1 a week in income. The actual income you get from your savings and investments is ignored.

■ Your capital does not include the value of your home if your partner, other close relative over 60 or dependent child still lives there. Your local authority has discretion to consider the position of other people who live with you, such as a carer. But, if you are single, the value of your home does count as part of your capital.

■ You are expected to contribute most of your income – including the £1 a week you are deemed to get from each £250 of capital – towards the cost of the fees. But you are allowed to keep a personal expenses allowance (see Table 5.6) and also a small part of any savings credit (part of pension credit) that you get (see Chapter 7).

■ If you live with your partner, only your share of any jointly held assets or joint income counts towards the means test and there is an automatic presumption that pensions, other than your state pension, are shared equally between you.

■ If your local authority is paying for your care in a home, you cease to be eligible for attendance allowance.

**Table 5.6 Capital limits for state help with care home fees and personal expenses allowance in 2009–10**

| Country | Lower capital limit | Upper capital limit | Personal expenses allowance £ a week |
|---|---|---|---|
| England | £14,000 | £23,000 | £21.90 |
| Wales | £20,750 | £22,000 | £22.00 |
| Scotland | £13,750 | £22,500 | £21.90 |
| Northern Ireland | £14,000 | £23,000 | £21.90 |

There are various implications from these complex funding rules. Firstly, even if you qualify for the maximum help, your local authority will only pay fees up to a set limit. If you want to live in a home that costs more, someone else (for example, your partner or your children) will have to make up the difference. Secondly, if your capital is above the upper limit, you may have to run down your savings and investments to pay the care home fees. Even where your capital is below the upper limit, the income you are deemed to get from the amount above the lower limit (£1 a week for each £250 or over 20 per cent a year) is likely to be much more than the actual income your capital is earning. This means you are expected to run down your savings further to pay your share of the care. Finally, if you are single and your home is included as part of your capital, you may have to sell your home to pay for care, though your local authority may agree to the sale being deferred in return for a share of the eventual sale proceeds, and you might consider putting rental income from letting your home towards the fees as an alternative to sale. These are the issues that your financial planning needs to address.

## Proposals for change

In 2009, the government published a 'green paper' (a discussion document) setting out the need for increased funding for long-term care and ways in which these extra funds might be raised.[11] The proposals apply to England, though, if implemented, it is likely that the other countries of the UK would make some changes too. The government has considered three main options:

[11] Ibid.

■ **Partnership**. Everyone who qualifies for state care and support, regardless of wealth, would get at least a minimum proportion of their care costs met – say a quarter or a third. People who are less well off would get more help and those with very restricted means would have the full cost met by the State. You would no longer be able to claim attendance allowance as well. In its most basic form, the state help provided through the partnership scheme would be funded from general taxation. This would leave you to find the remaining cost (for example, using the value of your home) and could leave some people who are unlucky enough to need many years of care worse off than others who have low or no care needs.

■ **Partnership with insurance**. This would work as described above but people would be helped to fund their share of the cost through insurance. The government could either introduce measures to encourage the growth of the private long-term care insurance market (see p. 139) or provide some form of state insurance.

■ **Comprehensive**. Under this approach, long-term care would be free at the point of use and everyone over 65, who could afford to, would contribute to the system, whether they turned out to need care or not. There could be a choice of ways to pay your contribution, for example, a lump sum when you reach retirement – the government has suggested one way to meet this cost could be to use the lump sum available from deferring your state pension (see Chapter 7) – or an extra tax on your estate after you have died. In the longer term, there would be scope to build up your contribution while you were working.

These proposals address paying for care. On top of that, you would still need to pay for accommodation and food if you went into a care home (just as you do if you stay in your own home). The government has said relatively little about how people would meet this cost, but mentioned that homeowners might use the value of their homes with payment being deferred until the home is eventually sold.

Whatever proposals are taken forward, it seems you still have a need to plan ahead for long-term care, using savings, insurance or your home either to pay for the care yourself or to pay your contribution to a state-funded scheme.

In early 2010, legislation was rushed through Parliament to enable free personal care for people in England (regardless of means) with high care needs, for example due to dementia or Parkinson's disease. The measure was due to take effect from October 2010 but could change following the General Election due in mid-2010.

## The self-pay route

If you are still some way from retiring, you may decide to build up wealth that could be used, if necessary, to pay for long-term care. Chapters 9 and 10 looks at strategies for building up a lump sum.

The advantage of the self-pay route is that, if you do not need care (or need to contribute to any new state system for funding care), the wealth you have built up remains intact and can be passed on to your heirs. In theory, the downside is that, if you do need care, there is no cap on the costs you might have to meet. Care costs could use the whole sum you have set aside for care and eat into any other wealth as well. In practice, you can escape this problem by buying an immediate-care plan if and when the need for care arises (see below).

## Immediate-care plan

An immediate-care plan is a type of lifetime annuity. An annuity is an investment where you give up a lump sum and in return receive an income for life. One of the main determinants of the amount of income you get from any lifetime annuity is your life expectancy which depends on factors, such as your age, sex and health. The longer you are expected to live, the lower the yearly income you get in exchange for a given lump sum. With an immediate-care plan, the fact of your needing care suggests your health is frail or failing, so you are likely to have a reduced life expectancy and therefore qualify for an 'enhanced annuity' (also called an 'impaired life annuity'). This pays a higher income than would be normal for an average person of your age and sex.

To qualify, you must have care needs. You normally have to undergo a medical assessment and typically must be found to have problems with at least a specified number of 'activities of daily living' (ADLs). The definitions of ADLs used vary slightly from one provider to another, but are abilities such as feeding yourself, dressing, washing, going to the toilet, and transferring for example from your bed to a chair. You may need to fail, say one or two of these ADLs to be eligible, depending on the terms of the particular plan.

The income may be paid out monthly or yearly. It may be a level sum or increase each year either by a set percentage or in line with price inflation. It can be used to pay for care in your own home or to meet care-home fees. If the income is paid direct to your care provider, the whole of each payment is tax free. If the income is paid to you, a small part of each payment is taxable (but the remainder counts as the return of your original investment and is tax-free). The income continues to be paid until you die.

Most people do not take out an immediate care plan to cover the whole cost of their care. More often, you will take out a plan to pay, say, £1,000 a month and top this up from your own income to meet the full cost of the care.

You may buy the plan using money from any source, for example, savings you have accumulated during your working life, a lump sum from a pension, the proceeds from selling your home or money raised through an equity release scheme (see Chapter 8). Once you have bought an immediate care plan, you cannot get your money back as a lump sum and your estate is reduced by the amount you have paid, leaving less for your heirs to inherit. But the plan keeps on paying out for as long as you live, so provided the income continues to be enough, you have capped the cost of your care at the amount you paid for the plan. The remainder of your wealth is protected to pass on to your heirs or use for other purposes. The income from the plan may also help you to afford the type of care you want in a setting of your own choosing.

## Deferred care plans

If you can afford to pay for care out of your own resources for the time being but want to protect yourself against the cost of care going on for longer than you had anticipated, you could take out a deferred care plan. This is similar to an immediate-care plan in that you pay a lump sum and in return receive an income for life, but the income does not start immediately. Instead it starts a few months or years into the future. Deferred care plans are cheaper than immediate care plans.

## Long-term care insurance

Long-term care insurance is a way of funding for care in advance. You take out insurance in, say, your 50s or 60s, paying either a lump sum or monthly premiums. The policy then pays out a tax-free income if later on you need care. The income can be used to pay for care in your own home or care-home fees.

Long-term care insurance first became available in the UK in 1991, but has not been a successful product and, in fact, most providers have currently withdrawn from the market. The Association of British Insurers has suggested that the low take-up of long-term care insurance has been due to a common public misconception that long-term care will be provided by the State in the same way that NHS treatment is, underestimations of the likely need for care, expectations that children will provide informal care and the potentially large cost of care which feeds through to unattractively high premiums.[12] In its suggestions for reforming long-term care (see p. 136), the government has acknowledged that measures may be needed to encourage the private long-term care insurance market or that some form of state insurance scheme may be required.

As with immediate-care plans, the pay-out from long-term care insurance is triggered if you fail a given number of activities of daily living (ADLs). The pay-out can be paid to you or direct to your care provider. The premium you pay depends on the following:

■ **Age**. The older you are at the time you start the plan, the higher the premium.

■ **Sex**. Women pay more than men because they are more likely to need care.

■ **Number of ADLs you must fail**. You pay more for a policy that pays out on failing, say, two ADLs than one that requires you to fail three.

■ **Waiting period**. There may be a delay between claiming and the income starting. If you have a choice, the shorter the waiting period, the higher the premium.

■ **Type of income**. You pay less for a level income than one which increases each year.

■ **How long the income lasts**. With the most comprehensive versions, the income is paid out for life. But you may be able to reduce the cost by choosing payments that last only, say, three, five or ten years. The risk is that your care needs outlive the income.

Like immediate-care plans, long-term care insurance is not cheap, but – assuming the pay-out is adequate – puts a ceiling on the cost of care, which allows you to preserve the rest of your wealth. It may also help you to afford the care you want in a home of your choice.

## Case study

Harry is 65 and worries that he may need care later on. He is thinking about taking out long-term care insurance. He has been given a quote of £50,000 in a single lump sum premium for a policy that would pay out £1,000 a month level income.

---

[12] Association of British Insurers (ABI), 1995, *Risk, Insurance and Welfare*, London, ABI.

## Shopping around for long-term care products

The state system of funding care, the long-term care products available and the interaction between care and inheritance make this a complex area of financial planning and one where it is a good idea to get independent financial advice (see Appendix B).

## Stress test and review

The simplest way to plan for long-term care is to build up what wealth you can and then decide, at the point of needing care, whether to buy an immediate-care plan (or possibly a deferred-care plan). The main risk with this type of plan is that the income paid out will fail to keep pace with increases in care fees. You could opt for a plan where the income increases year by year but the starting income is likely to be lower. If you can afford it, consider choosing an income level which is slightly higher than you really need given your other income and any other resources, so that you have some headroom to manage care-fee increases.

Inflation is more of a problem if you take out long-term care insurance because there may be many years between the time you take out the policy and any pay-out starting. Over that period, the level of cover you chose may fall far behind the amount you need. The safest course is to choose cover that increases with inflation. Be wary of choosing a policy that limits the length of time for which the income will be paid out. Although your premium will be less, you are taking a gamble. If you survive beyond the term of the policy, you may need to fall back on state support and possibly move if the amount the State will pay falls short of the fees for your chosen home.

Try to keep track of government proposals to change the way long-term care is funded and be prepared to adapt your planning if necessary. The proposals are being spearheaded by the Department of Health and you should be able to track their progress through the Department's website (see Appendix B).

Once you have bought a long-term care product, you are generally locked into it. However, if you have bought long-term care insurance, it is worth checking every couple of years whether your planned pay-out still looks sufficient given the level of care-home fees in your chosen area. If not, consider taking out additional cover or setting aside extra savings. If you have cover and start to have health or care problems, make sure you claim as soon as you are eligible.

# Building and managing your wealth

# 6

# Somewhere to live

## Introduction

Around 70 per cent of UK households own their own home – just under half of these own their homes outright and the rest are buying with a mortgage.[1] Although owning a home is widespread in the UK, it is less popular in some other countries, such as France and Germany, and should not be treated as an automatic goal in life – there are pros and cons as examined below.

If homeownership *is* one of your goals, taking out a mortgage is likely to be essential when you are in the earlier stages of life and later on if you want to trade up to a larger property. Choosing the right loan is not just a matter of looking for the cheapest deal but, crucially, thinking about affordability both at the time you first take up the loan and in the face of possible changes in your own circumstances or general economic conditions.

Having bought a home, this opens up additional planning options later in life, for example, the possibility of releasing equity to boost income, raise a lump sum or pay for care. This is considered in Chapters 5 and 8.

### Mortgages and secured loans

A mortgage is a loan secured against the value of your home. 'Secured' means that, if you fail to keep up the agreed loan repayments, the lender has the right to sell your home in order to get back the money they lent you. Any other loan secured on your home (such as a secured personal loan) works in the same way. The interest rate charged for a secured loan is normally lower than for an unsecured loan. The lower rate reflects the lower risk for the lender.

---

[1] Department for Work and Pensions, *Family Resources Survey 2007–8*, 2009.

# Rent or buy?

The decision to rent or buy is not simply a matter of cost. In fact, government data show that households in private rented accommodation spend 28 per cent of their disposable income (take-home pay after tax and other deductions) on housing, which is very similar to the average 29 per cent spent by homeowners buying with a mortgage.[2] However, ask British people about renting and many are likely to say that rent is 'dead money'. Embedded in this answer is the idea that the alternative – taking out a mortgage to buy a property – is not just about paying for somewhere to live but also a way of acquiring a valuable asset.

Prolonged periods of house price rises (see Figure 6.1) have encouraged the UK population to think of their home as an investment and periodic downturns, as in 1982, 1992 and 2009, have so far been neither sufficiently large nor prolonged to dampen this view. Chapter 1 (see Table 1.2 on p. 21) looked at how leverage – borrowing to buy an asset, such as taking out a mortgage to buy a home – magnifies both the gains and losses from investing. Figure 6.1 vividly demonstrates how house price gains have outstripped losses in recent decades not just in incidence but also magnitude. So not only has the chance of a loss been much smaller than the chance of making a gain, for most people the size of the leveraged gains has also been much greater than the size of the leveraged losses. Little wonder that Britons have come to see home ownership as the easiest way to build up some wealth. And this view has been endorsed by the Government, for example, in statements such as:

> homes are not just places to live. They are also assets – assets which now account for over 40% of wealth, compared to just over 20% in 1971. But this increase in wealth is unevenly spread. Support for home ownership will enable more people on lower incomes to benefit from any further increases in the value of housing assets.[3]

The UK tax system also encourages investing in this way because, unlike most other large investments, any gains you make from selling your own home at a profit are tax-free. The message seems to be that, if you rent, you are missing out on the asset of a lifetime.

---

[2] Department for Communities and Local Government. *Housing statistics: live tables*, http://www.communities.gov.uk/housing/housingresearch/housingstatistics/. Accessed 27 August 2009.

[3] Office of the Deputy Prime Minister, *Homebuy – expanding the opportunity to own*, April 2005.

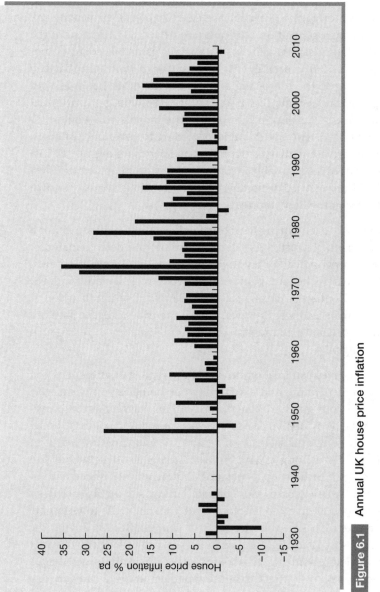

**Figure 6.1** Annual UK house price inflation

*Source:* Based on average house price data from Department for Communities and Local Government, *Housing statistics: live tables,* www.communities.gov.uk/housing/housingresearch/housingstatistics/livetables/. Accessed 26 August 2009.

There is a tension in a property being simultaneously a home and also an investment. However valuable your home becomes, you still need somewhere to live. Therefore, the return on the capital you have invested can only be realised in a limited number of ways, such as trading down, extending your mortgage, equity release (see Chapter 8) or passing the home on to the next generation on death (see Chapter 11). And until the value is realised, any capital gain is just a paper gain that could evaporate if house prices fall, especially if it turns out with hindsight that you bought at or close to the top of the market. On the other hand, as your mortgage payments become less and finally cease, you get a notional return from home-ownership in the form of the income you would otherwise be spending in rent. For example, according to government figures, a household in private rented accommodation spends on average £123 a week (28 per cent of its disposable income) on housing compared with just £39 a week (11 per cent of disposable income) for households that own their homes outright with no mortgage.[4]

Bear in mind that, even when the mortgage is paid off, a home is not a cost-free investment. To realise its full capital value, you need to maintain the home which periodically may involve paying thousands of pounds, for example, to renew the roof, paint exterior woodwork, replace windows, and so on. An advantage of renting is that the landlord, rather than you, is responsible for maintenance. However, the failure of a negligent landlord to carry out maintenance and repairs could cause you extra expense, such as higher heating bills.

Your own home gives you freedom to create the type of environment you want to live in, decorating and extending your home as you wish, with you rather than your landlord benefiting from any permanent improvements you make. Provided you keep up your mortgage payments, home ownership also gives you security of tenure, so you can stay living in the same home for as long as you choose. This is also true where you rent from a council or housing association, but, in private rented accommodation, you are less secure. Most private lettings are on six month or annual contracts that give the landlord (and you) the right to terminate the agreement at each renewal. Moreover, if your landlord is buying the rental property with a mortgage and defaults, you can be evicted with very little notice. Unlike a homeowner who defaults on their mortgage, tenants – who do not have any contract with the mortgage lender – had very few

---

[4] Department for Communities and Local Government. *Housing statistics: live tables*, http://www.communities.gov.uk/housing/housingresearch/housingstatistics/. Accessed 27 August 2009.

rights as the law stood in mid-2009. However, the government was consulting on changes to the law that would give tenants in this situation the right to at least two months' notice to leave and urging lenders to allow the rental to continue as an alternative to repossession.

A major advantage of renting is mobility – the ability to move easily and cheaply for work and other reasons. This can be especially important in the younger stages of life or during an economic recession, when you may need to move to secure a job. But mobility can also be useful in later life when being able to move easily to a smaller home, more sociable environment or closer to children could be a boon.

Table 6.1 sets out the main advantages and disadvantages of renting and buying.

**Table 6.1  Renting v buying**

|  | *Renting* | *Buying* |
| --- | --- | --- |
| Pros | Relatively small deposit needed | Benefit from rising house prices |
|  | Maintenance costs borne by landlord | Leveraged investment magnifies gains |
|  | Landlord responsible for buildings insurance | Ability to borrow against your equity in the home |
|  | Rent may be subsidised if rent from a council or housing association | Sense of achievement owning a valuable asset |
|  | Housing benefit available if income too low to afford rent |  |
|  | Easy to move (e.g. for a job) |  |
|  | You can invest any spare income in more flexible investments than property |  |
| Cons | Don't benefit from rising house prices | May need a large deposit |
|  | Can't borrow against home. | Costs of buying (stamp duty, valuation and legal fees) can be high |
|  | May be restrictions on what you can do to home | Ongoing costs of maintenance may be unaffordable |
|  | May be restrictions on how you live (e.g. no pets) | Cost of buildings insurance |
|  | Landlord might not carry out necessary repairs and maintenance | Mortgage costs may become unaffordable |
|  | Might be evicted if landlord does not pay the mortgage | Less state support if you can't manage your mortgage payments (compared with rents) |
|  | Might be evicted (e.g. for non-payment of rent or anti-social behaviour) | May lose home, if can't keep up mortgage payments |
|  |  | May be hard to sell if you need to relocate (e.g. for work) |

# Buying with a mortgage

If you decide to buy your own home – or to trade up to a larger home – the key issue in Stage 2 of your financial plan, the resources check, is affordability (see Figure 6.2). There are two aspects to this: the capital outlay you need at the time of purchase; and the ongoing monthly mortgage payments and related costs.

## The capital outlay

Before the global financial crisis that started in 2007, it was possible to get 100 per cent mortgages – in other words, a loan to cover the full cost of the home you were buying – and even some loans of more than 100 per cent. But, since the crisis, the general availability of mortgages has shrunk and 100 per cent mortgages, at least temporarily, disappeared from the market (though, in mid-2009, one lender had started to re-offer loans at this level). Lenders have become wary, preferring only to make low-risk loans to borrowers with big deposits and secure incomes. This means you typically need a deposit of at least 10 per cent of the value of the home you want to buy and, to get the best mortgage deals, 20 per cent or more. Note that the deposit required by the lender is a percentage of the valuation – if the lender's surveyor puts a lower value on the property than the market price the seller is asking (which is likely because surveyors tend to err on the side of caution), you will either have to find the difference or negotiate with the seller for a cut in the asking price. Government figures show that in 2008, the average deposit put down by first-time buyers was 21.8 per cent of the purchase price; for existing homeowners, the figure was much higher at 36.6 per cent.[5]

Another major cost is stamp duty land tax (SDLT) – usually just referred to as 'stamp duty' This is a tax you pay to the government when you buy a property, but not when you sell. Table 6.2 shows the rates of stamp duty in 2009–10. The relevant rate is applied to the whole property price, as shown in the examples. Further costs are the cost of the valuation/survey and legal fees, including search fees.

The mortgage lender requires a valuation to make sure the property will provide adequate security for the loan and you can usually pay a modest

---

[5] Department for Communities and Local Government. *Housing statistics: live tables*, http://www.communities.gov.uk/housing/housingresearch/housingstatistics/. Accessed 27 August 2009.

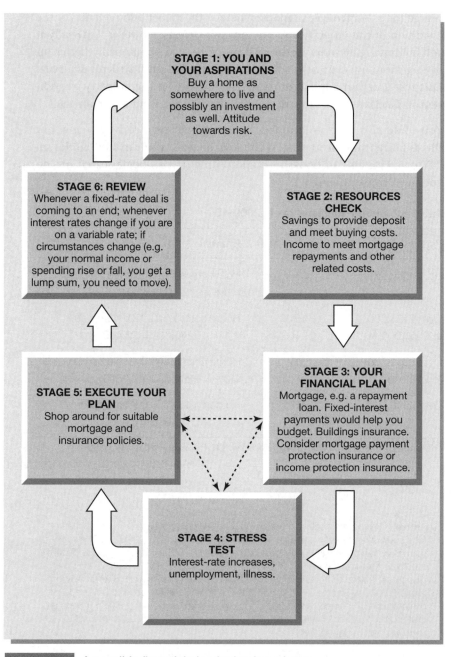

**Figure 6.2**    A possible financial plan for buying a home

charge for a 'homebuyer's report', whereby the valuer also remarks on the condition of the property and any obvious defects. However, especially if you are buying an older or unusual property, you are probably better off paying more for your own surveyor to carry out a full structural survey. This will give you a much more detailed report on the property's condition and a clearer idea of work you may have to carry out as the owner.

You could also save on legal fees by doing your own conveyancing, but this is fairly time-consuming. If the idea appeals, you can find guides on DIY conveyancing in bookshops and online (try a Google search on 'do your own conveyancing').

**Table 6.2  Stamp duty land tax in 2009–10**

| Purchase price | Stamp duty rate | Example |
|---|---|---|
| Up to £125,000[1] | 0% | Home costs £120,000: stamp duty = 0% × £120,000 = £0 |
| Over £125,000[1] to £250,000 | 1% | Home costs £240,000: stamp duty = 1% × £240,000 = £2,400 |
| Over £250,000 to £500,000 | 3% | Home costs £260,000: stamp duty = 3% × £260,000 = £7,800 |
| Over £500,000 | 4% | Home costs £550,000: stamp duty = 4% × £550,000 = £22,000 |

[1]  Until 31 December 2009 this threshold was temporarily set at £175,000.

## Case study

Amit and Shivani are hoping to buy a Victorian terraced house that is on the market for £260,000. However, the valuation puts its worth at only £240,000. The maximum they can borrow is 90 per cent of the valuation: 90% × £240,000 = £216,000 and they must find the difference £260,000 – £216,000 = £44,000 out of their own resources, unless they can persuade the seller to drop the price. Stamp duty on the £260,000 would be £7,800 (see Table 6.2), the survey fee is £500 and legal costs are likely to come to £1,250. In total, Amit and Shivani need to find a deposit and buying costs of £44,000 + £7,800 + £500 + £1,250 = £53,550 and will have removal costs to pay as well.

If Amit and Shivani can persuade the seller to drop the price to £240,000, not only would they save £20,000 of deposit but they would also drop down into the 1 per cent bracket for stamp duty (see Table 6.2), saving them another £7,800 – £2,400 = £5,400. This would reduce the cash they need to a more manageable £24,000 + £2,400 + £500 + £1,250 = £28,150 plus removal costs.

Increasingly, unless you opt for the most basic type of mortgage, you will have to pay an arrangement fee (sometimes called a booking fee). This will be anything from several hundred pounds to well over £1,000. You can usually add the fee to the sum you are borrowing if you do not want to pay it as a lump sum at the time of purchase.

If your mortgage is a high percentage of the valuation (called the loan-to-valuation or LTV), you may also have to pay a high-lending charge (also called a mortgage indemnity guarantee, MIG). A high-lending charge is usually levied only where the LTV is 90 or 95 per cent, but this varies from lender to lender. The charge is expressed as a percentage of the amount by which the mortgage exceeds a threshold LTV (usually 75 per cent). For example a lender might state its high-lending charge as: 75 per cent to 90 per cent LTV, charge 0 per cent; 75 per cent to 95 per cent LTV, charge 7.5 per cent. Instead of paying the high-lending charge upfront, you can usually add it to your mortgage loan and pay it gradually through your monthly repayments. That helps you to bear the cost, but increases the overall charge because you will be paying interest on the outstanding balance. The purpose of the high-lending fee is to protect the lender – not you – from the effect of a fall in house prices. See the case study below for how this works in practice.

The final major expense is the cost of hiring removers. This might be, say, £1,000. You could cut this by hiring a van and moving your furniture, etc. yourself, if feasible.

## Case study

Ben applied for a 95 per cent mortgage of £152,000 to buy a property valued at £160,000. The lender charged a high-lending fee of 7.5 per cent on the excess of the loan over 75 per cent LTV. 75 per cent LTV came to 75% × £160,000 = £120,000. So the charge was 7.5% × (£152,000 – £120,000) = £2,400, which Ben added to the mortgage.

A year after buying, the price of the home has fallen to £145,000, which is lower than the outstanding mortgage (a situation called 'negative equity'). This is not a problem provided Ben keeps up the mortgage payments, but, if he runs into problems and can't pay, the lender might take action to repossess his home. In that situation the lender would probably try to sell the property as quickly as possible perhaps at a knock-down price. If it were sold for £140,000, this would fall short of the outstanding mortgage by £152,000 – £140,000 = £12,000 (ignoring any capital Ben has paid off which would be a very small sum after only one year). The high-lending fee has paid for insurance, so the lender can claim the shortfall of £12,000 from the insurer. However, Ben is not protected because the insurer can then take steps to recover the £12,000 it paid out from Ben. See p. 169 for steps lenders should take before resorting to repossession.

## Monthly outlay

The type of mortgage you might choose (see p. 158) will have a major impact on the monthly expenses you face. You'll need to allow for other costs too, including buildings insurance. Because the property is the security for the loan, the lender will insist that you do have insurance. Even if you own a property outright, this is not an expense to skimp. Although you might be able to bear the cost of a broken window or a bit of storm damage, if your whole home were damaged by, say, fire or flood, it is unlikely you could afford to replace your home or pay for months of alternative accommodation while it was repaired, so this is one type of insurance you should treat as an essential.

Although repairs and maintenance will come around infrequently, it makes sense to budget a regular monthly sum for them. If you are buying a flat, you may have to pay a regular service charge. This might include the cost of buildings insurance and will also include a contribution towards maintaining the property, keeping common parts clean and possibly the upkeep of any garden.

There are various types of insurance, you might need or want to consider. If you are buying the home jointly with someone else or family members will live in the home with you, life insurance is essential so that, if you died, the mortgage would be paid off enabling your co-dependant and dependants to carry on living in the home – see Chapter 4 for information about life insurance. Often, bundled in with life insurance will be critical illness cover – this is a non-essential insurance that is not well matched to needs (see Chapter 3), but if it does not cost any extra then you might as well have it. You might decide to pay for mortgage payment protection insurance (MPPI) and this is definitely worth considering unless you have followed the better strategy of taking out income protection insurance (see Chapter 3 for a detailed discussion about this).

There will also be a regular outlay on expenses, such as council tax and contents insurance, which you would in any case have been paying as tenants in a rental property. However, the cost may change – for example, if the home you buy is in a different council tax band, if you buy extra furniture for your new home or move to an area where insurance is more or less expensive.

Often, you will work back from your available budget to decide how big a mortgage you might be able to afford. Table 6.3 shows the monthly cost for each £1,000 you borrow given the mortgage rate and term. The figures are shown for a repayment mortgage, where your monthly payments pay off both interest and the sum you borrowed, and an interest-only

**Table 6.3 The monthly cost of each £1,000 of mortgage**

*Repayment mortgage*

| Interest rate % pa | | | Term (years) | | | | Interest-only mortgage[1] |
|---|---|---|---|---|---|---|---|
| | 5 | 10 | 15 | 20 | 25 | 30 | |
| 1 | £17.09 | £8.76 | £5.98 | £4.60 | £3.77 | £3.22 | £0.83 |
| 2 | £17.51 | £9.19 | £6.43 | £5.06 | £4.24 | £3.69 | £1.67 |
| 3 | £17.95 | £9.65 | £6.90 | £5.54 | £4.74 | £4.21 | £2.50 |
| 4 | £18.39 | £10.11 | £7.39 | £6.05 | £5.27 | £4.77 | £3.33 |
| 5 | £18.84 | £10.59 | £7.90 | £6.59 | £5.84 | £5.36 | £4.17 |
| 6 | £19.29 | £11.08 | £8.43 | £7.16 | £6.44 | £5.99 | £5.00 |
| 7 | £19.75 | £11.59 | £8.97 | £7.74 | £7.06 | £6.65 | £5.83 |
| 8 | £20.22 | £12.11 | £9.54 | £8.35 | £7.71 | £7.33 | £6.67 |
| 9 | £20.70 | £12.64 | £10.13 | £8.99 | £8.38 | £8.04 | £7.50 |
| 10 | £21.18 | £13.18 | £10.73 | £9.64 | £9.08 | £8.77 | £8.33 |
| 11 | £21.67 | £13.74 | £11.35 | £10.31 | £9.79 | £9.52 | £9.17 |
| 12 | £22.17 | £14.31 | £11.98 | £11.00 | £10.52 | £10.28 | £10.00 |
| 13 | £22.67 | £14.89 | £12.63 | £11.70 | £11.27 | £11.06 | £10.83 |
| 14 | £23.18 | £15.49 | £13.30 | £12.42 | £12.03 | £11.84 | £11.67 |
| 15 | £23.69 | £16.09 | £13.97 | £13.16 | £12.80 | £12.64 | £12.50 |
| 16 | £24.22 | £16.71 | £14.66 | £13.90 | £13.58 | £13.44 | £13.33 |
| 17 | £24.75 | £17.33 | £15.37 | £14.66 | £14.37 | £14.25 | £14.17 |
| 18 | £25.28 | £17.97 | £16.08 | £15.42 | £15.17 | £15.07 | £15.00 |
| 19 | £25.82 | £18.62 | £16.81 | £16.20 | £15.97 | £15.89 | £15.83 |
| 20 | £26.37 | £19.28 | £17.54 | £16.98 | £16.78 | £16.71 | £16.67 |

[1] In addition to these interest payments, you will normally need to pay into a savings product to build up a lump sum to repay the loan at the end of the term (see p. 158).

mortgage, where you pay off the loan in a single lump sum at the end of the term and, in the meantime, your monthly payments meet just the interest. See p. 158 for more information about these two types of mortgage.

## Case study

Natasha and Chris have a joint income of £1,600 a month. Currently they pay rent of £420 a month and have other regular bills and expenses of £1,000. If they buy they will save the rent and they spend around £180 a month on non-essentials that they could instead put towards a mortgage. They reckon, in total, they can afford to pay around £600 a month towards owning a home. £10 a month is the probable cost of buildings insurance, leaving a maximum of £590 a month for the mortgage. They think they can probably get a 25-year repayment mortgage at a rate of 6 per cent a year. Checking the row for 6 per cent and column for 25 years in Table 6.3, they find that each £1,000 of repayment mortgage would cost £6.44 a month. Therefore, they could afford to borrow £590/£6.44 × £1,000 = £91,600 (rounded to the nearest £100). If they can put down a 10 per cent deposit, they could afford a property costing around £102,000.

## Resources checklist

As you can see from the previous sections, buying a home is an expensive business and you will need to find more than just the price of the home. You may find it helpful to complete the resources checklist in Figure 6.3 to see whether you have enough savings and income to fund your goal. If not, see Chapter 9 for guidance on building up extra savings and Chapter 1 for ideas on improving your budget. Consider also what other resources might be available to you, for example, raising cash by selling a valuable item you could manage without or help from parents. Analysis by the Council of Mortgage Lenders, a trade body, suggests that in mid-2009, 80 per cent of first-time buyers under the age of 30 were receiving help from their parents in finding a deposit.[6]

The alternative to finding extra resources could be to scale back your goal, for example, by looking at smaller properties or in a cheaper area.

## Choosing a mortgage

At Stage 3 of the financial planning process, you need to consider what sort of mortgage to take out. This inevitably involves Stage 4 (stress testing) since one way to deal with the risks you identify is to modify your choice of products. Stage 5 (selecting specific loans and lenders) is also

---

[6] Council of Mortgage Lenders, *Tightening in lending criteria abates*, Press Release, July 2009.

| DO YOU HAVE ENOUGH SAVINGS? | | £ |
|---|---|---|
| Available savings *from Chapter 1, Figure 1.6* | A | |
| **Capital outlay:** | | |
| Deposit | | |
| Stamp duty | | |
| Valuation charge | | |
| Legal fees | | |
| Mortgage fees | | |
| Removal costs | | |
| Total outlay | B | |
| EXTRA YOU NEED TO SAVE<br>*If A – B is a negative number, you need to save extra*<br>*If A – B is positive, you already have enough savings* | A – B | |

| DO YOU HAVE ENOUGH INCOME? | | £ |
|---|---|---|
| Available income *from Chapter 1, Figure 1.4* | C | |
| **Monthly outlay:** | | |
| Mortgage payments | | |
| Buildings insurance | | |
| Service charge, maintenance costs, other | | |
| Life insurance/critical illness cover | | |
| Other insurance | | |
| Change in council tax and contents insurance<br>*If the cost goes down, record this as a negative figure* | | |
| Total outlay | D | |
| EXTRA YOU NEED TO SAVE<br>*If C – D is a negative number, you need extra income*<br>*If C – D is positive, you already have enough income* | C – D | |

**Figure 6.3**   Resources checklist

relevant here since the availability and cost of the products will also affect your choice. Mortgages have a variety of characteristics, from the broad type (see below) to the interest rate deal (p. 160) on offer. There are also some more unusual products which are considered on p. 165.

## Type of mortgage

There are two basic types of mortgage. Which one you choose depends on both cost and your attitude towards risk:

■ **Repayment mortgage**. Your monthly payments pay the interest and also pay off part of the capital. It is what is technically called a 'reducing balance loan' and provided you make all the repayments, the whole loan is paid off by the end of the term. With a reducing balance loan, at the start you have a big outstanding balance and so the total interest charge is high; as you pay off the loan, the outstanding balance falls and the interest charge becomes less. However, your monthly payments are level, so that in the early years each payment is made up mainly of interest with only a small amount of capital paid off. Capital repayment makes up a much larger proportion of the later payments. This process is illustrated in Table 6.4 for a very simplified scenario. If the interest rate were fixed for the whole term of the loan (which is possible but unusual), you would make the same fixed payment each month. Otherwise, when the interest rate changes, the level of payment needed to pay off the whole loan by the end of the term is recalculated and your monthly repayments change.

■ **Interest-only mortgage**. With this type of mortgage, you do not pay off the loan until the end of the term, so the balance outstanding is the same as at the outset and does not fall. Your monthly payments are just interest on the loan. This means the mortgage payments for an interest-only loan will generally be lower than for a repayment loan (as shown in Table 6.3), but you also need to think how you will pay off the loan when the mortgage term is up. Usually you will do this by paying monthly into some kind of savings scheme. A common choice in the past has been to save through an endowment insurance policy (see Chapter 10), forming an endowment mortgage. However, you could save using, for example, stocks-and-shares individual savings (ISA) accounts (see Chapter 9) in which case you have an ISA mortgage, or even a personal pension (see Chapter 7) called a pension mortgage. You might not need any savings vehicle if the property is not your only or main home and you intend to sell it at the end of the term – for example, it is a buy-to-let property or a temporary home for your children while they are at university.

## Table 6.4 Example of a reducing balance loan

*Repayment mortgages work on the reducing balance method. The example here is very simplified, showing a loan of £100,000 repaid over ten years with one repayment a year and the interest rate unchanged at 6 per cent a year throughout.*

| Year | Balance at start of year £ | Interest added £ | Repayment £ | Balance at end of year £ | Capital paid off this year £ | Interest paid this year £ |
|---|---|---|---|---|---|---|
| | A | B | C | D = A + B − C | E = A − D | F = C − E |
| 1 | 100,000 | 6,000 | 13,587 | 92,413 | 7,587 | 6,000 |
| 2 | 92,413 | 5,545 | 13,587 | 84,371 | 8,042 | 5,545 |
| 3 | 84,371 | 5,062 | 13,587 | 75,847 | 8,525 | 5,062 |
| 4 | 75,847 | 4,551 | 13,587 | 66,811 | 9,036 | 4,551 |
| 5 | 66,811 | 4,009 | 13,587 | 57,233 | 9,578 | 4,009 |
| 6 | 57,233 | 3,434 | 13,587 | 47,080 | 10,153 | 3,434 |
| 7 | 47,080 | 2,825 | 13,587 | 36,318 | 10,762 | 2,825 |
| 8 | 36,318 | 2,179 | 13,587 | 24,910 | 11,408 | 2,179 |
| 9 | 24,910 | 1,495 | 13,587 | 12,818 | 12,092 | 1,495 |
| 10 | 12,818 | 769 | 13,587 | 0 | 12,818 | 769 |

The low-risk mortgage choice is a repayment mortgage – provided you keep up the payments, the whole mortgage is paid off by the end of the term. If you take out an interest-only mortgage, you are in effect gambling that you can borrow the money at one rate of interest and get a better return by investing it. You will not be able to beat the borrowing rate with a bank or building society savings account (after all their profit comes from charging borrowers more than they pay savers), so to stand any chance of the gamble paying off you will have to put your savings into stock-market linked investments. Back in the 1970s and early 1980s there were some special reasons why the gamble made sense and this accounts for the popularity at that time of endowment mortgages. But those special reasons no longer apply. This is an example of how products may change over time so that the seemingly familiar in fact transforms into a very different product altogether (see the box overleaf) and underlines the importance of researching products thoroughly if you are acting as your own financial adviser.

### The transformation of endowment mortgages

In the early 1980s, the most popular type of mortgage was an interest-only mortgage combined with monthly savings paid into a low-cost endowment policy. This is a type of life insurance used for investment. The premiums you pay (after the deduction of charges) are invested in the stock market and the aim was that the policy should grow by enough by the end of the mortgage term to pay off the outstanding mortgage. So, in essence, borrowers were gambling that the return on the endowment policy would beat the cost of the mortgage loan. At the time there was a good chance this would happen. The table shows why and also why that is no longer the case, so that endowment mortgages are no longer a good choice for most people.

**Table 6.5 Endowment mortgages then and now**

| Feature | Then (1970s and early 1980s) | Now |
|---|---|---|
| Cost of borrowing | You got tax relief on what you paid in mortgage interest. This reduced the monthly cost of your mortgage | No tax relief. You pay the full cost of mortgage interest |
| Amount you save | Your savings were boosted by the government through the addition of life assurance premium relief | No premium relief. You have to provide the total amount going into your endowment policy |
| How your savings grow | Period of high inflation which was reflected in high stock-market growth | Period of low inflation reflected in lower stock-market returns |

The changes have transformed endowment mortgages so they are no longer the same product they were back in the early 1980s. Despite this, endowment mortgages continued to be sold in high volumes right through the 1990s. In many cases, they were mis-sold (see Chapter 2) without it being made clear to borrowers that the endowment mortgage was linked to the stock market with a risk of the policy failing to produce enough to pay off the loan.

## Interest rate choices

Quite apart from the repayment method, you also face a choice of different interest rate deals which have implications for the amount you pay each month, the risks you are exposed to and the flexibility of the arrangement. They are summarised in Table 6.6.

**Table 6.6 Mortgage interest deals**

| Deal | Description | Advantages | Disadvantages |
|------|-------------|------------|---------------|
| Standard-variable-rate (SVR) | Rate moves up and down in line with rates in the economy as a whole | You should benefit from a fall in the general level of interest rates | Lenders may be slow to pass on rate cuts. Your payments increase if interest rates rise. |
| Tracker-rate | Rate moves up and down automatically in line with a specified rate, such as the Bank of England base rate. This may be for an initial period or the whole term of the loan | You benefit from any fall in the interest rate being tracked | Your payments increase if the rate being tracked rises. There is normally an arrangement fee. Penalty charge incurred if you want to get out of the deal early |
| Discounted-rate | For an initial period – say, the first one to three years – the interest rate is a set percentage lower than the lender's SVR. At the end of the discount period, you revert to the SVR | Your payments are a bit lower in the first few years when money may be especially tight. You should benefit from a fall in the general level of interest rates | Lenders may be slow to pass on rate cuts. Your payments increase if interest rates rise. You need to plan how to manage the increased payments once the discount period ends. There is usually an arrangement fee. Sometimes a penalty charge if you want to get out of the deal early |

▶

**Table 6.6 Mortgage interest deals** *continued*

| Deal | Description | Advantages | Disadvantages |
|---|---|---|---|
| Capped-rate | Rate moves up and down in line with rates in the economy as a whole but is guaranteed not to rise above a set level. This may be for an initial period or the whole term of the loan | You can benefit from a fall in the general level of interest rates, but there may also be a 'collar' built into the deal which is a set minimum rate | Lenders may be slow to pass on rate cuts. Your payments increase if interest rates rise but only as far as the cap. Your payments will not fall if general interest rates go below any collar. There is usually an arrangement fee. Penalty charge incurred if you want to get out of the deal early |
| Fixed-rate (short-term) | Rate is fixed for an initial period, typically two to five years. At the end of the fixed-rate period, you revert to the SVR | You can budget with certainty during the fixed-rate period because your payments do not change even if interest rates rise | You do not benefit from any fall in the general level of interest rates. You need to plan how to manage if your payments increase once the fixed-rate period ends. There is usually an arrangement fee. Penalty charge incurred if you want to get out of the deal early |
| Fixed-rate (long-term) | Rate is fixed for a lengthy period which could be 25 years (i.e. the full length of the most common mortgage term) | You can budget with certainty. Over the years, inflation reduces the real value of your fixed payments (see Chapter 1) | You do not benefit from any fall in interest rates generally. There is usually a hefty charge if you want to get out of the deal |

In many respects, the lowest risk strategy would be to take out a fixed-rate mortgage for the longest available term (see *Stress testing* on p. 168) and there are a few mortgages available for a full 25 years. This is low risk in the sense that you can match your mortgage to your budget with the certainty that, provided your income does not fall, you will continue to be able to meet your mortgage payments. In fact, this approach is not popular in the UK. The main drawback of a very long-term fixed rate is that you are locked into one rate even if the rates available on new mortgages fall to less. A long-term fixed rate might have a few opportunities built in for switching to another mortgage, but apart from that switching would incur penalties. So very long-term fixed-rate mortgages are inflexible.

A more common choice in the UK is a short-term fixed rate for, say, two to five years. This enables you to budget with certainty for a few years, which for a young household might be especially important. At the end of the fixed term, you would normally revert to the lender's standard-variable rate (SVR), if you take no action. But, typically, as the end of the fixed term approaches, you will shop around for the best deal at that time. To ensure you have the freedom to do this, make sure any penalties for switching do not extend beyond the fixed-rate term (called an extended tie-in). The key risk with a short-term fixed-rate mortgage is that, by the end of the term, interest rates may have risen significantly so that your monthly mortgage payments rise by more than you can afford. You may want to consider building up some savings to help you cope with such an increase.

The alternative to a fixed-rate loan is a variable rate mortgage. The disadvantage here is that your monthly payments may rise in an unpredictable way, which can put stress on your household budget. The advantage is that, if interest rates in the economy fall, you benefit. This was particularly evident in 2008–09 when the Bank of England base rate fell to a historical low of 0.5 per cent a year (from 4.5 per cent in mid-2008)[7] and most mortgage customers with SVR loans saw their monthly repayments fall, in some cases by hundreds of pounds a month.

There are variations on the variable-rate theme. With a discounted variable rate, the repayments are artificially low for an initial period – say, the first year or two – which can be a particular help for first-time buyers who may need a period to adjust to the higher monthly outlay of having a mortgage or can anticipate their income increasing as their careers become established.

---

[7] Bank of England, http://www.bankofengland.co.uk/statistics/index.htm. Accessed 27 August 2009.

It is essential to have a plan for affording the repayments once they jump to the SVR at the end of the discount period (see *Stress testing* on p. 168). You also need to check out the competitiveness of the lender's SVR and how long you have to stay with that lender to avoid penalties on switching.

Another important variable-rate variant is the tracker mortgage, where the interest rate you pay is linked to the Bank of England base rate or some other benchmark rate, for example, 1 per cent above the base rate. However, you need to check whether this is subjected to any minimum rate (called a 'collar') at which level you cease to benefit from base-rate cuts.

Capped-rate mortgages are a less commonly used variant where you pay the lender's SVR or a rate linked to it but the rate is guaranteed not to rise above a maximum level (the cap). Normally, also it will not fall below a minimum level (the collar). This is a half-way house that gives you some certainty about budgeting but also enables you to benefit to some extent from cuts in interest rates in the economy as a whole.

With all these possibilities, you might wonder why anyone pays a lender's SVR. There are two particular SVR deals worth a mention: cashback loans and flexible mortgages.

With a cashback mortgage, you pay the SVR but you receive a cash lump sum at the start of the mortgage. This is usually set as a percentage of the sum you have borrowed and might range from hundreds to a few thousand pounds. The cashback could be very useful to help with the immediate costs of moving and setting up home. You could also think of it as an alternative to a discounted variable rate because you could put the lump sum in a savings account and draw down the balance of the account gradually to help you meet your monthly payments. If you pay back the mortgage within the first few years (say, five) you will have to return part or all of the lump sum.

A more important variant to consider is a flexible mortgage. This is designed so that you can overpay and underpay your mortgage and even take payment holidays. Usually you will have to build up a bank of overpayments before you can reduce or miss payments without penalty. Increasingly, ordinary SVR mortgages do let you overpay but do not offer other flexibility features. A full-blown flexible mortgage could be a useful option if your income tends to vary – say, you run your own business – or if you expect to have periods of reduced income, such as taking maternity leave while starting a family. A more sophisticated version of flexibility is the all-in-one mortgage.

## All-in-one mortgage

Variously called current account mortgages, offset mortgages or all-in-one mortgages, with these, you take out a mortgage and also have a current account and/or savings account with the same provider. Instead of interest being charged each month on your outstanding loan, it is charged on your loan after deducting the value of your current account and/or savings account. Your savings do not earn any interest in the conventional sense, but by offsetting the balance of your savings against the mortgage loan, the savings in effect earn the interest rate – moreover they earn this rate tax-free, as the case study shows. You can withdraw or add to your savings at any time, in which case your mortgage payments go up and down in line. The main drawback is that the mortgage rate tends to be a bit higher than the lender's SVR.

## Case study

Rasheed takes out a 25-year repayment mortgage of £100,000 at an interest rate of 6 per cent a year. You can work out from Table 6.3 on p. 155 that his monthly repayments are £644. He also has £10,000 in savings which he has in a savings account, where they earn 2 per cent a year after tax, giving him £200 a year which is just under £17 a month. His mortgage payments less savings interest come to £627.

Rasheed's friend, Rachel, has an all-in-one mortgage. The interest rate is 6.5 per cent a year. She's borrowing £100,000 but has also deposited £10,000 in savings with the lender. This means interest each month is worked out on £100,000 – £10,000 = £90,000. Her monthly repayments are £607.50. Although she is paying a higher mortgage rate than Rasheed, her savings in effect earn 6.5 per cent tax-free, so she is around £20 a month better off than Rasheed.

### Helping your children

In a variation on the all-in-one mortgage, instead of pooling a mortgage and just your own savings, you can also include the savings of other family members or friends that you have elected to be treated as a group. This provides one method by which parents can help their children on to the housing ladder. As a parent, rather than giving a lump sum to your child, you could put your savings into your child's all-in-one mortgage account (and keep the right to have these savings back at any time). You give up the interest on these savings and the interest is in effect used to reduce your child's mortgage payments.

A major problem for first-time buyers often is not managing the repayments but raising enough money for the deposit or convincing the lender to advance a big enough loan. Many parents opt to give their children a lump sum. You could either do this outright or you could buy a home jointly with your children. Another possibility is to agree to act as a guarantor. This means that you become liable to pay the mortgage payments if your child can't. Individual lenders can tell you if this is an arrangement they will consider.

## Shopping around for a mortgage

Once you have chosen the repayment method, the interest deal and any flexibility or offset options, you have the task of choosing a specific lender and mortgage.

Comparison websites provide a useful starting point if you want to shop around for yourself. The Financial Services Authority (FSA) Moneymadeclear Compare Products tables (www.fsa.gov.uk/tables) are an impartial source. If you use commercial internet comparison websites (see Appendix B) bear in mind that they will not necessarily cover the whole market and are unlikely to give sufficient detail for a fully informed choice (see Chapter 1). Therefore, use two or three sites to help you narrow your choice, then gather additional information direct from the lenders. If you do not have access to the internet at home, consider using the internet services at your local library or a cyber-café. If you prefer paper-based resources, personal finance magazines available in newsagents and the personal finance pages of newspapers publish tables of 'best buy' mortgages.

You might decide that, for this stage of your financial plan, you would like the help of an adviser. See Chapter 2 for guidance on using a mortgage adviser. An adviser can be especially useful if your needs are unusual – for example, you do not have a regular pattern of earnings or the property you want to buy has a non-typical construction.

Whether you go to lenders direct or use an adviser, when you express interest in a particular mortgage, as well as any marketing literature, you should be given a Key Facts Illustration. This is a document required under FSA rules which sets out the most important features of the mortgage in a standardised way that makes it easy to compare one mortgage with another. The KFI is personalised to your enquiry and includes sections on:

- **What you have told the lender**: i.e. the information on which the illustration is based, including the amount you want to borrow, the type of mortgage you want, the term and the purchase price of the property.
- **Description of the mortgage**: the lender, the interest-rate deal, the length of any initial fixed-rate, discounted or tracker deal and any special restrictions.
- **The overall cost of the mortgage**: the amount you will repay in total. You will also be given the cost expressed in ways that help you compare this mortgage with others: as the amount you pay back in pounds for each £1 borrowed and as an annual percentage rate (see Chapter 1 for an explanation of this).

■ **What you will need to pay each month**: your monthly repayments. If you have an initial period at a fixed or discounted rate or other special deal, this section will also show what your repayments will be on reversion to the lender's SVR, assuming the SVR is the same as at the time of the illustration.

■ **A section on the risks involved with the mortgage**: see *Stress testing* overleaf.

■ **The fees you must pay**: this will include any administration fee, valuation fee, and so on.

■ **Insurance**: policies you must take out as a condition of the mortgage and whether you must take them out through the lender, and possibly details of optional insurances that you've said you are interested in having.

■ **What happens if you no longer want the mortgage**: details of early repayment charges and what happens to the mortgage if you move house.

■ **Making overpayments**: the impact these have on your outstanding balance and monthly payments.

The KFI is one of the most useful documents you will get as you shop around and is worth looking at in detail. You can easily pick it out from the other literature you get, because it will carry the Key Facts logo (see Figure 6.4).

**Figure 6.4**   The Key Facts logo

*Source*: Financial Services Authority, 2009.

## Case study

Sally is looking at taking out a 25-year repayment mortgage for £160,000 to buy a property valued at £210,000. The balance of the price will come from the sale of her existing home. The interest rate is 6 per cent a year for the first three years, reverting after that to the SVR which is currently 7.4 per cent a year. If she keeps the mortgage for the full 25-year term, based on current interest rates and including charges, she will pay back a total of £345,436. The KFI tells her that this means she will pay back £2.16 for every £1 she borrows. Put another way, the cost of the loan is 7.3 per cent APR. Sally can use these two figures to compare the cost of this mortgage with similar deals from other lenders.

## Shariah-complaint alternative to mortgages

Mainstream mortgages are not acceptable under Shariah law, which prohibits the use of interest. Islamic home finance schemes offer acceptable alternatives, for example:

■ *Ijara* (leasing) combined with diminishing *Musharaka* (equity). For example, you might buy, say, 20 per cent of a property with an Islamic bank buying the remaining 80 per cent. During the term of the agreement, you pay the bank rent and regular capital payments that buy succesive slices of the home until you own the whole property.

■ *Murabaha* (purchase and resale). The Islamic bank buys the property you have selected and immediately resells it to you at a higher price. Instead of paying the whole purchase price as a single lump sum, you agree with the bank to pay in instalments over a number of years.

Because these schemes are offered by Islamic banks, you can be confident that they are not using the money in ways that do not comply with Shariah law, such as investing in industries concerned with alcohol, pork or gambling.

These schemes typically involve a double purchase of the property – once by the bank and then by you, but UK tax law has been amended to prevent stamp duty being charged twice.

## Stress testing

Before you finalise your choice, you need to consider how robust your plan will be if circumstances change. The main risk factors with a mortgage are: your income falls, your mortgage payments rise, or the value of your home falls to less than the outstanding loan (negative equity). This section looks at the steps you might take now, at the point of selecting your mortgage, which could at least partially protect you against these changes, so strengthening your plan.

### A fall in income

The most likely reasons for a fall in income would be unemployment or being off work for a prolonged period due to ill health. Chapter 3 gives guidance on how to plan generally for a loss of income, including whether to take out mortgage payment protection insurance. However, your plan for protecting your income needs to take into account some special help that may be available in the case of mortgage problems. As a result of the financial crisis that started in 2007 and ensuing recession, the government introduced a number of schemes to help homeowners facing difficulty paying their mortgage. These are as follows:

■ **A protocol with lenders.** Lenders have agreed to use repossession only as a last resort and should explore a full range of alternative options with you. If your lender does not follow the protocol, you can complain to the Financial Ombudsman Service (see Chapter 2). The possible alternatives include, for example:

  – *Extending the term of a repayment mortgage.* Looking at Table 6.3 on p. 155, you can see that repaying a loan over a longer term reduces the monthly payments (but will increase the overall total you pay back). This reduces the stress on your monthly budget.

  – *Giving you time to sell your home yourself.* When a lender repossesses a home, it usually tries to sell the property quickly which may mean accepting a knock-down price. This reduces the likelihood of you getting anything back from the sale and increases the risk of negative equity (see p. 173). With extra time to find buyers and perhaps to prepare the house for sale (by, say, decorating a bit, doing repairs, and tidying up the garden), you may be able to get a better sale price.

■ **Homeowners Mortgage Support Scheme.** If the drop in your income is likely to be temporary and your lender has agreed to be part of the scheme, you may be able to defer your interest payments for up to two years. However, the interest will be added to your outstanding balance (and interest will then be charged on the rolled-up interest) so the overall cost of your mortgage will increase. However, this arrangement could give you a useful breathing space while you find another job.

■ **Support for Mortgage Interest**. If you are not working, your income is low and you have savings of less than £6,000 (in 2010–11), you may be able to claim means-tested state benefits, such as income-based jobseeker's allowance or income-based employment and support allowance. If so, after 13 weeks of your claim, you may also qualify for help with your mortgage interest (but not capital) payments. Think about how you could cover the first 13 weeks, for example, through savings or mortgage payment protection insurance.

■ **Mortgage Rescue Scheme**. If your home is being repossessed and, as a result, you will be homeless, your local authority may have a duty to provide you with accommodation. As an alternative, it may put you into this scheme. There are two versions:

  – *Shared equity.* Your council or a housing association pays off part of your mortgage which will reduce your monthly payments for the remaining loan. In return, the council or housing association takes a share of the equity in your home. This means, when you eventually sell, the proceeds will pay off the remaining mortgage, pay the council or housing association and any remainder will be yours.

– *Mortgage-to-rent.* If it looks unlikely that your income will recover soon, the council or housing association may pay off the whole of your mortgage and take over complete ownership of your home. You stay living there and pay rent. Because council and housing association rents are subsidised, your monthly housing costs should fall to a more manageable level. If you can't afford the rent, you may be able to claim housing benefit to cover it (see p. 98).

For details of these schemes, contact your lender, local authority or any of the free, independent debt advice organisations mentioned in Chapter 1. See Appendix B for contact details.

---

### Sale-and-rent-back schemes

Be wary of private firms that claim a 'sale-and-rent-back scheme' is the answer to your mortgage problems. Under such schemes, you agree to sell your property to the firm but carry on living there as a tenant. Superficially, this sounds like the home reversion schemes described later in Chapter 8, but sale-and-rent-back is very different. These schemes have a number of very serious drawbacks:

■ the price you are offered for your home is usually far below its true market price;

■ even though you've probably sold the home at a hefty discount, you have to pay a full commercial rent to stay on;

■ the tenancy agreement is usually for just six- or 12-months. At renewal, the landlord may raise the rent so much that you cannot afford to pay it or not renew the lease at all;

■ because you have voluntarily sold your home, it is not clear whether you would be eligible to claim housing benefit to help with the rent;

■ the landlord may have bought the property with a mortgage and if they don't keep up the mortgage payments, the home may be repossessed and, as a tenant rather than an owner, you have no rights to help from the schemes outlined on p. 169 or to stay in the property.

Problems with these schemes have been so severe, that legislation was hurriedly rushed through so that, from mid-2009, these schemes have been brought within the regulatory regime operated by the FSA. But initially, the FSA is relying on its high-level principles and requirement for firms to treat customers fairly (see Chapter 2). Full regulation will be introduced during 2010. In general, it is best to avoid sale-and-rent-back schemes, but if you do enter into this type of arrangement and are unhappy with it, complain using the procedures outlined in Chapter 2.

## A rise in mortgage payments

A section of the Key Facts Illustration (see p. 166) sets out information about the risks inherent in a mortgage, including an indication of the impact on your monthly payments if the interest rate increases. Figure 6.5 shows an example for a repayment mortgage of £100,000. In this example, a 1 per cent increase in the mortgage rate would increase the monthly repayments by £53 (or £636 a year). You can use Table 6.3 on p. 155 to work out the impact of different rate changes on other variable-rate mortgages.

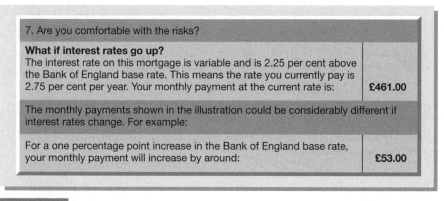

| 7. Are you comfortable with the risks? | |
|---|---|
| **What if interest rates go up?** The interest rate on this mortgage is variable and is 2.25 per cent above the Bank of England base rate. This means the rate you currently pay is 2.75 per cent per year. Your monthly payment at the current rate is: | **£461.00** |
| The monthly payments shown in the illustration could be considerably different if interest rates change. For example: | |
| For a one percentage point increase in the Bank of England base rate, your monthly payment will increase by around: | **£53.00** |

**Figure 6.5**    **Example of risk information from a Key Facts Illustration**

*Source*: Constructed by the author drawing on regulations in the Financial Services Authority Handbook.

Figure 6.6 shows the Bank of England base rate over the past 25 years or so. Although variable mortgage rates are normally a few percentage points higher, they tend to follow the Bank of England rate, so Figure 6.6 gives you an idea of the way that mortgage rates could change. You can see that the Bank of England rate has ranged from nearly 15 per cent a year down to 0.5 per cent, so over the full term of a mortgage you could see considerable variation in your repayments.

Changes that happen many years ahead are less important than changes within the earlier years of your mortgage. Your mortgage debt is a fixed or reducing sum, whereas your earnings will tend to rise at least in line with inflation as the years go by. Thus, your monthly payments will tend to take a smaller proportion of your income in the years ahead, giving you an expanding capacity to cope with any rise in the mortgage rate. But, in the early years of a mortgage, an increase in the mortgage rate can have a big impact on your budget and, as Figure 6.6 shows, it is quite possible for interest rates to change by, say 4 per cent or more over the space of just a few years.

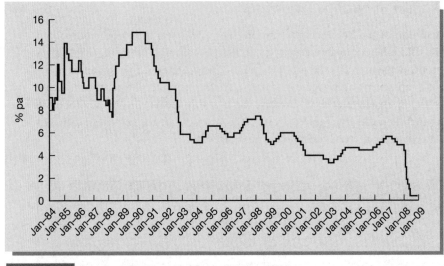

**Figure 6.6**    Bank of England base rate 1984 – 2009

*Source*: Data taken from Bank of England, www.bankofengland.co.uk/mfsd/iadb/Repo.
asp?Travel=NIxIRx. Accessed 27 August 2009.

There are three possible ways to protect yourself against the risk of rising
interest rates:

■ Make sure that your mortgage is not so large that it stretches your
budget to the limit. Leave yourself some spare income or scope for cutting back spending so that you can cope with a rise in repayments.

■ Make sure you have some savings that you can dip into to help you
make the extra payments if rates rise.

■ Opt for a fixed-rate loan, at least for the first few years, so that your
payments do not change if interest rates rise.

As discussed earlier, it is unusual in the UK to take out a very long-term
fixed rate. If you take out a fixed rate for a few years only, you need to
think about whether you will have enough income or savings to help you
cope if interest rates have risen at the time your fixed-rate period comes to
an end and you need to take out a new fix at a higher rate or revert to a
relatively high SVR.

# Case study

> Eleven months ago, Jan took out a fixed-rate repayment mortgage at 4 per cent for a two-year term. The repayments on the £200,000 she borrowed were fixed at £1,054 a month. When the term ends shortly, Jan is due to revert to the lender's standard-variable rate which now stands at 7 per cent and her repayments will jump to £1,389 a month. Jan is looking around for a new fixed-rate deal. The best she can find is another two-year fix, this time at 6 per cent. Her outstanding mortgage balance is currently £190,297 and, at that rate, her repayments will be £1,255 a month. This is still a sizeable jump of £200 a month on the amount she is currently paying.

## *Negative equity*

With any asset you own – be it a home, shares, antiques, and so on – a fall in the market price creates a loss on paper. The paper loss only becomes a real loss if you have to sell when prices are depressed. Therefore a fall in house prices is not necessarily a risk that you need to think about when you are buying a home. But if you know you intend to move again within a few years or that you may have to move at short notice – say, for your work – then it will be important for you to take a view on how house prices might change in future. Figure 6.1 on p. 147 shows house price inflation over a period of nearly 80 years. You can see that there are relatively few periods when prices have fallen and, when they have, the fall has usually been relatively short-lived – just a year or two.

When you are buying a home with a mortgage, there are broadly two ways in which you can try to protect yourself from negative equity:

- put down a larger rather than smaller deposit when you buy;
- if you have to move home, consider renting out your old home and using that income to rent somewhere yourself, in order to defer the sale. (But see Chapter 10 for some issues to think about if you are renting out a property.)

# Review

If any of the changes discussed under *Stress testing* – a fall in your income, a rise in your monthly payments or a fall in house prices that pushes you into negative equity – materialise, they should always trigger a review of your plan. If you have built in some of the protective measures discussed above, this will be the time to claim state benefits or claim on insurance, dip into savings or cut back your spending. If you find you cannot manage your mortgage payments, check whether the special schemes discussed on

p. 169 could apply to you and see the section in Chapter 1 on coping with debt problems.

You will need to review your financial plan whenever you move home. This will include checking you have the resources to meet the costs of sale and repurchase and enough income to meet your new mortgage payments. Generally mortgages are not transferable, so you will pay off your old mortgage from the proceeds of sale and need to shop around for a new deal. In other words, you will go round the financial planning cycle afresh. A major change in your personal circumstances, such as relationship breakdown, will also trigger this type of overall review.

Even if you are not moving, it makes sense to review your mortgage every few years and consider switching if you could get a better deal (called remortgaging). This will give you the chance to check out any newly developed products as well as just changes in the rates for existing ones. You will need to balance any penalties and fees for giving up your existing mortgage against the gains from switching – you can use the calculator in Figure 6.7 to help you do this. If you would gain from moving your mortgage elsewhere, it is always worth discussing your intentions with your existing lender, since they may offer you an improved deal to persuade you to stay. This will probably involve some costs, such as an arrangement fee for the new deal but could work out cheaper and more convenient than switching to another lender.

Another trigger for review is if you come into a large lump sum – for example, as a result of an inheritance or redundancy. One possible use for a lump sum would be to pay off part, or all, of your mortgage. Similarly, if your income increases, you could use your new surplus to pay off your mortgage more quickly. Usually, the cost of borrowing exceeds the return that you can get from savings which means you get a better return from paying off your mortgage (in effect the mortgage rate tax-free) than putting your money into a savings account. However, other points to consider include:

■ **Emergency fund and general financial flexibility**. Having some money in short-term savings gives you the security of knowing that you can draw on funds easily in a crisis or to take advantage of new opportunities. Once you have used the sum to pay off debts, you might find it hard to borrow an equivalent amount if the need arose.

■ **Pension savings**. As you will see in Chapter 7, putting money into a pension scheme is a tax-efficient way to invest. Taking into account the tax advantages, the overall benefit to you might exceed the financial gain from paying off your mortgage.

■ **Mortgage redemption fees.** Before paying off part, or all, of your mortgage early, check what charges you may incur. General charges – such as a deeds fee to cover the legal work – are fairly low. But, if you are part way through a special deal, such as a fixed-rate-interest period, you could face hefty charges if you pay off any of the loan before the end of the period.

| COSTS OF SWITCHING | | £ |
|---|---|---|
| **Your existing mortgage** | | |
| Fees for ending the mortgage early | | |
| Sealing fee/deeds fee for ending the mortgage at any time | | |
| **The new mortgage** | | |
| Valuation fee | | |
| Administration fee/booking fee | | |
| Legal fee | | |
| TOTAL COSTS | A | |

| GAINS FROM SWITCHING | | £ |
|---|---|---|
| Monthly payments for your existing mortgage | B | |
| Monthly payments for your new mortgage | C | |
| MONTHLY SAVING = B – C | D | |

| PAYBACK PERIOD | Months |
|---|---|
| Number of months before you are in profit from the switch = A/D | |

**Figure 6.7**   Weighing up whether to remortgage

# 7

# Building a pension

## Introduction

The need for income in retirement is universal, so saving for retirement should be fundamental to most people's financial planning. However, it is also one of the most difficult areas of financial planning, in part, because you need to plan over a long period. This goes against a common and natural tendency to focus on the short term and hope the future will take care of itself. Such long-term planning also exposes you to high levels of uncertainty, both in terms of how much your pension savings might deliver and how your own personal circumstances will turn out. Therefore, stress testing and regular reviews are especially important stages in building up a pension. This is also a difficult area of financial planning because of the way retirement income you build up through saving interacts with state means-tested benefits, so that for some people retirement saving may not offer value for money.

Although you may view saving for retirement as a household goal, pension schemes are personal to each member of the household. This means, if you are a couple, you should consider what might happen if your relationship were to break down. If you are married or in a civil partnership, your pension rights will be considered as an asset and may be split between you and your ex-partner – though not necessarily in a proportion which you consider to be fair. If you are unmarried, you have no claim on your ex-partner's pension savings and they have has no claim on yours. In either situation, you may find that, following relationship breakdown, you are left on track for a much lower pension than you had expected. You will be especially vulnerable if, for example, in return for taking on the family's caring duties, you had expected to rely on your partner for retirement income. A much more robust plan is to make sure that at least some of the household pension target is built up through savings in your own name that would remain with you even if you and your partner split up.

Figure 7.1 summarises a financial plan for retirement saving that will be developed in this chapter. Having built up your pensions and other savings, Chapter 8 looks at turning them into retirement income.

## Pension saving as a goal

The year 1908 was a watershed in the UK: for the first time, citizens became entitled to an old age pension, payable from age 70, with eligibility dependent on both your means and your morals.[1] Life expectancy then was around age 50, so many people would not live to claim their five shillings (25p) a week. Nevertheless, it was a big improvement on the previous situation where most people had to work until they dropped, rely on the paternalism of employers or fall back on parish poor relief.

The next milestone was in 1948 with the introduction of the Beveridge system of contributory state basic pensions which is still with us today. By contributing towards the state system by paying National Insurance while you work you earn the right to draw a pension when you retire. In February 2009, pensioners received on average £96.62 a week[2] (£5,024 a year) in state retirement pension, which is just 22 per cent of average UK earnings. This is far less than most people would consider adequate for a comfortable standard of living in retirement. Hence the need for additional savings – for example, through an occupational pension scheme available through your work or your own personal savings.

How much income you will need for a comfortable retirement is a very personal choice because only you can decide what lifestyle you will want. Financial advisers often suggest you aim for two-thirds of your pre-retirement earnings, but this is just a rule of thumb and may over-estimate your needs. In theory, there is no harm in having a target that is on the high side; in practice, pensions are expensive and an overly ambitious target

---

[1] Pension Law Review Committee, *Pension Law Reform*, 1993 (the 'Goode Committee').

[2] Department for Work and Pensions, *Tabulation tool: state pension – average weekly amount of benefit*, http://statistics.dwp.gov.uk/asd/tabtool.asp. Accessed 30 August 2009.

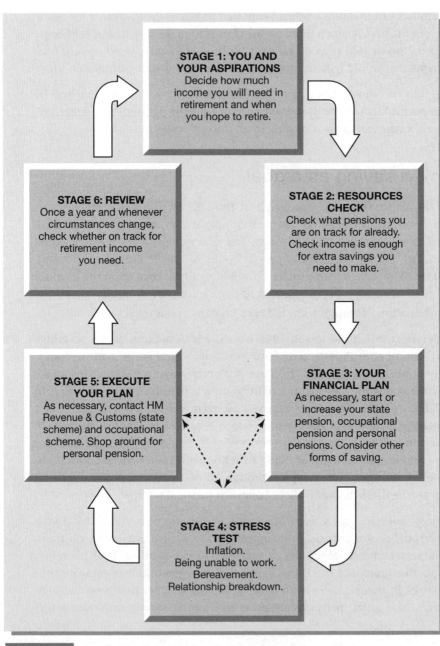

**Figure 7.1**    A possible financial plan for saving for retirement

can make the goal look so daunting that you give up. You can get a more realistic idea of how much you might need if you start by thinking about your likely spending in retirement.

## Spending in retirement

The spending section of the budget template from Chapter 1, which is reproduced in Figure 7.2, is the first step in calculating how much you need to save. Start by filling in the first column with what you spend now. In the second column estimate – still in today's money – what you might spend in retirement, taking into account how your spending pattern might change. As a guide, Table 7.1 compares how people who are currently retired spend their income compared with households of working age, based on a government survey. Of course, the spending shown in the table could involuntarily be constrained if the incomes of the households in the survey are lower than they would like, but the figures do exclude the poorest pensioner households, and give a reasonable guide.

## Before-tax retirement income

If you have completed the template in Figure 7.2, amount B is the net income your household will need in retirement. If you live alone, it is also the net income you personally will need. If you are a couple, in the next step of the calculator you need to decide which of you will provide how much of this income. Splitting the income between you is necessary to work out the gross (before tax) income that you will need. The next stage of the calculator in Figure 7.3 assumes that the tax system when you retire will be the same as it is today. The total, labelled G (to avoid confusion with any of the amounts in the full budget calculator in Chapter 1), is the gross income you are estimated to need in retirement. It is your personal target retirement income. If you are a couple, your partner should repeat the exercise to find their target retirement income.

## Your pension savings target

The next stage of the calculation is to consider what pensions you are already on track to receive, for example, from the State, from occupational pension schemes through work, from any personal pensions and from any other savings that you have earmarked for retirement. All of these types of pension are discussed in detail from p. 187 onwards. Chapter 9 looks at non-pension savings and investments. You may want to read these sections before

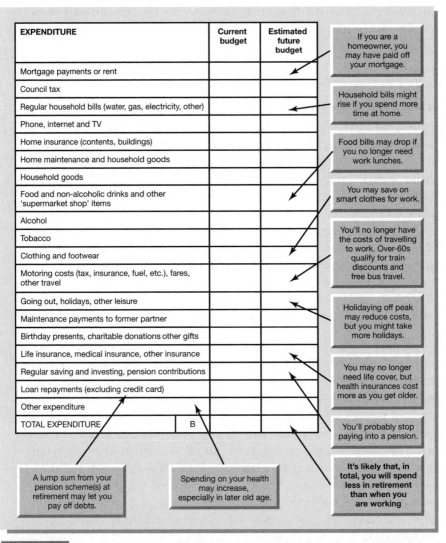

| EXPENDITURE | Current budget | Estimated future budget |
|---|---|---|
| Mortgage payments or rent | | |
| Council tax | | |
| Regular household bills (water, gas, electricity, other) | | |
| Phone, internet and TV | | |
| Home insurance (contents, buildings) | | |
| Home maintenance and household goods | | |
| Household goods | | |
| Food and non-alcoholic drinks and other 'supermarket shop' items | | |
| Alcohol | | |
| Tobacco | | |
| Clothing and footwear | | |
| Motoring costs (tax, insurance, fuel, etc.), fares, other travel | | |
| Going out, holidays, other leisure | | |
| Maintenance payments to former partner | | |
| Birthday presents, charitable donations other gifts | | |
| Life insurance, medical insurance, other insurance | | |
| Regular saving and investing, pension contributions | | |
| Loan repayments (excluding credit card) | | |
| Other expenditure | | |
| TOTAL EXPENDITURE | B | |

If you are a homeowner, you may have paid off your mortgage.

Household bills might rise if you spend more time at home.

Food bills may drop if you no longer need work lunches.

You may save on smart clothes for work.

You'll no longer have the costs of travelling to work. Over-60s qualify for train discounts and free bus travel.

Holidaying off peak may reduce costs, but you might take more holidays.

You may no longer need life cover, but health insurances cost more as you get older.

You'll probably stop paying into a pension.

A lump sum from your pension scheme(s) at retirement may let you pay off debts.

Spending on your health may increase, especially in later old age.

**It's likely that, in total, you will spend less in retirement than when you are working**

**Figure 7.2** Pension calculator Part I: your spending now and in retirement

completing this next stage of the calculator which is set out in Figure 7.4, or alternatively come back to this section when you have read more.

Subtract your savings so far from your target gross income. If the answer is zero or less, you are currently on track for the retirement income you want, You do not need to save extra at present, but because of the uncertainties involved in long-term saving, you should review the position again in a year's time. If the answer is positive, this is the amount by

**Table 7.1  How households spent their money in 2007**

| Expenditure category | Single person[1] | | Couple[1] | |
| --- | --- | --- | --- | --- |
| | Not retired £/ week | Retired[2] £/ week | Not retired £/ week | Retired[2] £/ week |
| Food and non-alcoholic drinks | 24.10 | 25.90 | 49.70 | 49.70 |
| Alcoholic drinks, tobacco and narcotics | 7.00 | 4.60 | 14.30 | 9.30 |
| Clothing and footwear | 10.00 | 6.40 | 23.50 | 12.10 |
| Housing (excluding mortgage interest), fuel and power | 46.80 | 34.10 | 55.00 | 38.60 |
| Household goods and services | 20.60 | 15.80 | 39.50 | 25.40 |
| Health | 2.90 | 4.90 | 7.70 | 8.60 |
| Transport | 40.60 | 13.90 | 79.40 | 45.40 |
| Communication | 8.40 | 5.50 | 12.60 | 8.10 |
| Recreation and culture | 32.00 | 22.70 | 70.50 | 61.30 |
| Education | 3.60 | 1.20 | 3.10 | 0.60 |
| Restaurants and hotels | 23.50 | 9.70 | 48.10 | 25.30 |
| Miscellaneous goods and services | 21.70 | 15.50 | 40.30 | 30.90 |
| Other spending (including mortgage interest) | 66.10 | 24.40 | 99.10 | 44.70 |
| TOTAL | 307.40 | 184.70 | 542.70 | 360.10 |

[1] With no children.
[2] Excluding households mainly dependent on state pensions.

Source: Adapted from Office for National Statistics, Family Spending, November 2008.

which the retirement income you are currently on track for falls short of the amount you need for the retirement you have said you would like – this is your pension savings target.

| FROM NET TO GROSS INCOME | | £ |
| --- | --- | --- |
| Total expenditure in retirement (from Figure 7.2) *Or the share you will provide if you are a couple* | B | |
| Select the appropriate tax factor:<br>If B is up to £11,500, tax factor = 1.0<br>If B is over £11,500 and up to £21,000, tax factor = 1.1<br>If B is over £21,000 and up to £40,000, tax factor = 1.2<br>If B is over £40,000 and up to £53,000, tax factor = 1.3<br>If B is over £53,000 or more, tax factor = 1.4 | F | |
| GROSS INCOME | G | |

**Figure 7.3**   Pension calculator Part 2: gross income you may need in retirement

| FIND THE GAP | | £ |
| --- | --- | --- |
| Gross income needed *From Figure 7.3* | G | |
| State pension *From your state pension forecast – see p. 192* | | |
| Occupational pensions from current and past employers *From last benefit statement – see p. 200* | | |
| Personal pensions *From latest annual statements* | | |
| Income from other savings[1] *From latest statements* | | |
| Total retirement income so far | H | |
| Pension target = G – H | I | |

[1] If your savings will produce a lump sum, you can roughly estimate how much income they might provide in today's money from age 65 by multiplying the lump sum by the appropriate factor from the table below. It assumes your savings grow at a real (after-inflation) rate of 2.4 per cent a year and then buy an index-linked annuity (see Chapter 8 for information about annuities). If you plan to retire later than age 65, see p. 225.

| Years until age 65 | Factor – man | Factor – woman |
|:---:|:---:|:---:|
| 5 | 0.05 | 0.04 |
| 10 | 0.05 | 0.05 |
| 15 | 0.06 | 0.05 |
| 20 | 0.07 | 0.06 |
| 25 | 0.08 | 0.07 |
| 30 | 0.09 | 0.08 |
| 35 | 0.10 | 0.09 |

**Figure 7.4**   **Pension calculator Part 3: your pension target**

# Check your resources

If you are not yet on track for the retirement income you need, you can use Tables 7.2 and 7.3 below to see how much extra you may need to start saving each month to plug the gap. The table is based on assumptions about, for example, how your savings might grow in the run up to retirement and the amount of pension you can then buy. It assumes:

■ You save through a pension scheme either at work (see p. 194) or a personal pension (see p. 206) that you arrange for yourself which means your savings qualify for advantageous tax treatment (see the box on p. 185).

■ The amounts shown in the table are the sums you might need to save after deducting tax relief at the basic rate (20 per cent in 2010–11).

■ You save monthly and once a year increase your savings in line with increases in your earnings which are assumed to grow by 4 per cent a year.

■ Your savings grow at a largely tax-free rate of 7 per cent a year, the deduction of charges reduces your accumulated savings by 1 per cent a year and inflation between now and retirement averages 2.5 per cent a year. Together, these assumptions mean your savings are projected to grow at a real rate of return after charges of 3.4 per cent a year.

■ At retirement, your savings are used to buy an annuity where the income increases each year in line with price inflation in order to maintain its buying power (see Chapter 8 for information about annuities).

If you cannot afford to save the amount Tables 7.2 or 7.3 suggest, you need to rethink your pension target (for example, aim for a lower pension or a later retirement age) or think about ways to boost your budget (see Chapter 1).

### Table 7.2 Single pension: how much you might need to save to meet your target

*The table shows, in today's money, the amount you would need to start saving each month between now and retirement to provide yourself with each £100 a year of pension, based on the assumptions on p. 183.*

| | | | | | Retirement age | | | | | |
|---|---|---|---|---|---|---|---|---|---|---|
| | | | *Men* | | | | | *Women* | | |
| *Age now* | *55* | *60* | *65* | *70* | *75* | *55* | *60* | *65* | *70* | *75* |
| 20 | £3.59 | £2.30 | £1.49 | £0.94 | £0.63 | £3.75 | £2.47 | £1.63 | £1.04 | £0.68 |
| 25 | £4.74 | £2.97 | £1.90 | £1.19 | £0.78 | £4.95 | £3.19 | £2.08 | £1.31 | £0.85 |
| 30 | £6.44 | £3.93 | £2.46 | £1.51 | £0.99 | £6.72 | £4.22 | £2.69 | £1.67 | £1.07 |
| 35 | £9.09 | £5.33 | £3.25 | £1.96 | £1.26 | £9.49 | £5.72 | £3.56 | £2.16 | £1.36 |
| 40 | £13.69 | £7.52 | £4.41 | £2.59 | £1.63 | £14.28 | £8.08 | £4.83 | £2.85 | £1.76 |
| 45 | £23.17 | £11.33 | £6.23 | £3.51 | £2.15 | £24.17 | £12.17 | £6.82 | £3.86 | £2.32 |
| 50 | £52.25 | £19.17 | £9.39 | £4.96 | £2.91 | £54.52 | £20.59 | £10.27 | £5.45 | £3.15 |
| 55 | | £43.24 | £15.89 | £7.47 | £4.12 | | £46.44 | £17.38 | £8.21 | £4.45 |
| 60 | | | £35.83 | £12.64 | £6.20 | | | £39.18 | £13.90 | £6.70 |
| 65 | | | | £28.50 | £10.49 | | | | £31.35 | £11.35 |
| 70 | | | | | £23.66 | | | | | £25.59 |

### Annuities

An annuity is a special type of investment where you exchange a lump sum for an income payable for a defined period. With a pension annuity, the income is usually payable for the rest of your life. See Chapter 8 for more information.

## Table 7.3 Couples: how much you might need to save to meet your pension target

*The table shows, in today's money, the amount you would need to start saving each month between now and retirement to provide yourself with each £100 a year of pension plus a pension for your partner continuing at two-thirds of your pension if you die before them, based on the assumptions on p. 183.*

| | Retirement age (man/woman) | | | | | | | | | |
|---|---|---|---|---|---|---|---|---|---|---|
| | Man buys the annuity | | | | | Woman buys the annuity | | | | |
| Age now | 55/50 | 60/55 | 65/60 | 70/65 | 75/70 | 60/55 | 65/60 | 70/65 | 75/70 | 80/75 |
| 20 | £4.31 | £2.90 | £1.94 | £1.26 | £0.83 | £4.11 | £2.67 | £1.74 | £1.12 | £0.90 |
| 25 | £5.69 | £3.75 | £2.47 | £1.58 | £1.04 | £5.42 | £3.45 | £2.22 | £1.41 | £1.12 |
| 30 | £7.72 | £4.95 | £3.19 | £2.02 | £1.31 | £7.36 | £4.55 | £2.87 | £1.80 | £1.41 |
| 35 | £10.91 | £6.72 | £4.22 | £2.61 | £1.67 | £10.39 | £6.18 | £3.79 | £2.33 | £1.80 |
| 40 | £16.43 | £9.49 | £5.72 | £3.45 | £2.16 | £15.64 | £8.73 | £5.15 | £3.08 | £2.33 |
| 45 | £27.80 | £14.28 | £8.08 | £4.68 | £2.85 | £26.48 | £13.14 | £7.27 | £4.18 | £3.08 |
| 50 | £62.69 | £24.17 | £12.17 | £6.61 | £3.86 | £59.71 | £22.24 | £10.95 | £5.90 | £4.18 |
| 55 | | £54.52 | £20.59 | £9.95 | £5.45 | | £50.16 | £18.53 | £8.88 | £5.90 |
| 60 | | | £46.44 | £16.85 | £8.21 | | | £41.80 | £15.03 | £8.88 |
| 65 | | | | £38.00 | £13.90 | | | | £33.89 | £15.03 |
| 70 | | | | | £31.35 | | | | | £33.89 |

## Tax treatment of pension schemes

A pension scheme, such as an occupational pension scheme at work or a personal pension, is in effect a 'tax wrapper' that ensures the investments inside are treated in the following way:

■ **Tax relief on your contributions:**

- *Most people.* You usually get tax relief on your contributions up to your highest rate of tax. This means, at 2010–11 tax rates, each £100 going into your pensions scheme costs you just £80 if you are a basic-rate taxpayer or £60 if you are a higher-rate taxpayer. (See Appendix A for information about the tax system.) There is maximum limit on the contributions that qualify for relief of 100 per cent of your UK earnings or £3,600 whichever is higher.

▶

– *Non-taxpayers and starting-rate taxpayers*. When you invest through a personal pension (but not an occupational scheme), you get tax relief at the basic rate even if you are a non-taxpayer or pay tax only at the 10 per cent rate.

– *Higher-rate and additional-rate taxpayers*. From 2011–12, additional-rate, and in some cases higher-rate, relief will be gradually reduced if you have taxable income of £150,000 or more. For this purpose 'income' is defined in a special way that means your normal income before tax plus the value of any pension contributions made by your employer on your behalf. However, if your actual income (disregarding any employer contributions) is less than £130,000 you are not affected by these rules. If your income is £130,000 or more and you do fall within the rules, you will still get relief on your pension contributions at the basic rate, but relief at the additional or higher rate will be restricted and, if your income is high enough, withdrawn altogether. Until the rules come into effect on 6 April 2011, a new allowance and tax charge apply to prevent you gaining a tax advantage by bringing forward your pension contributions ahead of the 2011–12 change. These so-called 'anti-forestalling' rules are complex but broadly you will not be caught by them provided you do not change your regular pension contributions or, if you do, the overall amount you save is less than £20,000 a year. 'Regular' contributions are amounts you pay quarterly or more frequently. Less frequent contributions up to £30,000 a year may also be accepted.

■ **Employer contributions**. Any contributions paid by your employer are a tax-free fringe benefit of your job.

■ **Tax relief on some income and all gains from the invested contributions**. Your (and, if relevant, your employer's) contributions are invested. Any income from shares or share-based investments is taxed at 10 per cent (see Chapter 9). But other income and capital gains build up tax free.

■ **Tax-free lump sum at retirement**. Usually you can draw out a quarter of your pension savings as a tax-free lump sum. The rest of your savings must be taken as pension which is taxable. However, older people have higher tax-free allowances than people of working age so tax on your pension may be at a lower rate than the tax relief you had on your contributions.

## Case study

Jessica, aged 25, is a teacher. She estimates that she will need a gross retirement income of £20,000 a year. Through the state scheme and her pension scheme at work, she is currently on track for a pension of £17,000 a year. She has a pension target of £20,000 – £17,000 = £3,000 which she would like to draw from age 65. Table 7.2 (the section on the right headed 'women', row for age 25, column headed 65) shows that she needs to start saving £2.08 a month for each £100 of pension she needs, a total of £3,000/£100 × £2.08 = £62.40 a month.

Russell, currently a self-employed builder aged 55, will receive pensions from several schemes and plans when he retires. Together with his state pension, he is on track for a retirement income of £12,000 a year against the £14,000 he would like. His pension target is £14,000 – £12,000 = £2,000 a year including a two-thirds survivor pension for his wife, who is five years younger than him. Table 7.3 (left-hand section headed 'Man buys the annuity', row 55, column 65/60) shows that if he intends to retire at age 65, to meet his target, he needs to start saving £20.59 a month for each £100 of pension, a total of (£2,000/£100) × £20.59 = £411.80 a month. If he puts off retiring until age 70, the amount he needs to start saving falls to (£2,000/£100) × £9.95 = £199 a month.

# Where your retirement income will come from

Nearly everyone will be entitled to at least some pension from the State (see below), so you can view this as the foundation of your retirement income. As with all financial planning, the next stage is to consider what help you might get from an employer (see p. 194) and lastly what provision you need to make for yourself (see p. 206).

## State retirement pensions

The state pension is made up of two main parts: the basic pension and the additional pension. There were significant changes to the state pension system for people reaching state pension age from 6 April 2010. This section describes these new rules. For details of the previous rules, contact The Pension Service.

All state pensions are index-linked. At present this means that they are increased once a year in line with price inflation as measured by the Retail Prices Index (see Chapter 1). Parliament has passed legislation to allow part of the state pension (the basic pension – see below) to be increased in line with earnings inflation from a future date. Earnings tend to keep pace with the growth of the economy and historically have increased around 1.5 to 2 per cent a year faster than prices, so pensioners would benefit from this change. The original intention was to make the change from 2012 but this will only happen when the Government can afford it.

### Basic pension

Everyone who qualifies for the full basic pension gets the same flat-rate amount, £97.65 a week for a single person in 2010–11. You qualify by paying or being credited with National Insurance contributions during your working life. If you do not have enough contributions for the full pension, you get a reduced amount.

Your working life runs from the tax year in which you reach age 16 to the last full tax year before you reach state pension age. Your state pension age depends on when you were born and may be between 65 and 68 if you are a man or 60 and 68 if you are a woman – see Table 7.4. A tax year runs from 6 April one year to 5 April the next. You can check your precise state pension age and date using an online calculator on the Direct Gov website (see Appendix B).

**Table 7.4 Your state pension age**

| Your date of birth | Your pension age |
|---|---|
| Before 6 April 1950 | 60 (women); 65 (men) |
| 6 April 1950 to 5 April 1955 | Between 60 and 65 (women); 65 (men) |
| 6 April 1955 to 5 April 1959 | 65 |
| 6 April 1959 to 5 April 1960 | Between 65 and 66 |
| 6 April 1960 to 5 April 1968 | 66 |
| 6 April 1968 to 5 April 1969 | Between 66 and 67 |
| 6 April 1969 to 5 April 1977 | 67 |
| 6 April 1977 to 5 April 1978 | Between 67 and 68 |
| 6 April 1978 onwards | 68 |

Each tax year during your working life in which you have been paid or credited with a full year's worth of National Insurance is called a 'qualifying year'. You get the full basic pension if you have 30 qualifying years. If you have less, your basic pension is reduced pro rata. So, in 2010–11, when the basic pension is £97.65, each qualifying year entitles you to £97.65/30 = £3.26 a week of state basic pension, index-linked throughout retirement.

## National Insurance contributions and credits

You pay National Insurance while you are working. Not all contributions count – Table 7.5 shows those which do and don't. You may be credited as if you have paid contributions in some situations, including for example if you are:

■ caring for a child under 12;

■ caring for an adult who is disabled or elderly;

■ unemployed and getting jobseeker's allowance (JSA);

■ an unemployed man, not signed on for JSA, under age 65 but above the women's state pension age (which was 60 but is increasing from 6 April 2010 onwards – see p. 188);

■ off work sick and getting sick pay or employment-and-support allowance;

■ on maternity leave and getting maternity benefit;

■ working on low earnings and getting working tax credit;

■ aged 16,17, 18 and still at school.

You do not get credits while, for example, you are at university, taking a gap year or sabbatical, or running the home without the caring responsibilities outlined above.

### Special rules for couples

If you are married or in a civil partnership, you may be able to claim a state basic pension based on your partner's National Insurance record instead of your own. The maximum you can claim in this way in 2010–11 is £58.50 a week. It will be worth doing this if the best pension based on your own record would be less. From 6 April 2010, the rules are extended to allow husbands to claim on their wife's record and civil partners to claim on their partner's record. Unmarried couples cannot benefit from these rules.

### State additional pension scheme

The state additional pension is paid on top of any basic pension. There has been an additional scheme since the 1960s:

■ 1961–78: graduated pension scheme;

■ 1978–2002: state earnings-related pension scheme (SERPS);

■ 2002–present: state second pension (S2P).

You may have built up some or all of these and they will be combined and paid to you when you start to draw your state pension. The graduated pension scheme provides only a very small top up. SERPS and S2P, which work together, potentially could provide a generous extra sum (over £150 a week in 2010–11). But, in practice, the average SERPS/S2P pension is much lower – the government no longer publish precise figures but in 2008, the average additional pension was around £61 a week for men and £22 a week for women.[3] To understand why actual SERPS/S2P pensions are lower than the maximum, it is helpful to look at how these schemes evolved.

---

[3] Office for National Statistics, 2009, *Pension Trends,* Chapter 5 [online] http://www.statistics.gov.uk/downloads/theme_compendia/pensiontrends/Pension_Trends_ch05.pdf. Accessed 14 December 2009.

**Table 7.5 Which National Insurance contributions count towards your state pension?**

| *If you are:* | *You may pay:* | *These count towards your:* | |
| | | *Basic pension* | *Additional pension* |
| --- | --- | --- | --- |
| An employee | No Class 1 contributions if your earnings are below the lower earnings limit (LEL)[1] | NO[2] | NO |
| | No Class 1 contributions if your earnings are at or above the LEL[1] but less than the primary threshold | YES | NO |
| | Full Class 1 contributions on earnings between the primary threshold[1] and upper accruals point (UAP)[1] | YES | YES |
| | Contracted-out (see opposite page) Class 1 contributions on earnings between the primary threshold and UAP[1] | YES | NO[3] |
| | Married women's reduced rate[4] | NO | NO |
| | Class 1 contributions on earnings above the UAP[1] | NO | NO |
| Self-employed | Class 2 contributions | YES | NO |
| | Class 4 contributions | NO | NO |
| Filling gaps in your past National Insurance record (see p. 192) | Class 3 (voluntary) contributions | YES | NO |

[1] For National Insurance and state pension purposes, your earnings are divided into bands according to the following thresholds (2010–11 rates): lower earnings limit £97 a week; primary threshold £110 a week; upper accruals point £770 a week.

[2] But you might get National Insurance credits if you can claim Working Tax Credit because your earnings are low.

[3] But you will be building up an alternative pension through an occupational scheme or personal pension.

[4] Until May 1977, married women could elect to pay Class 1 contributions at less than the full Class 1 rate and instead rely on their husband's National Insurance record for their pension (see p. 189). Although women can no longer make this election, they can continue with a previous election.

SERPS was set up in 1978 with the support of all the political parties. It aimed to establish:

> *a general structure which will endure and which will enable the State and the occupational pensions movement to get on with the job of developing, in partnership, the provision of proper pensions in retirement, widowhood and chronic ill-health... It will provide pensions at an altogether new level, sufficient to ensure that people in their declining years will be able to spend them in dignity and security.*[4]

Under the original SERPS:

■ Employees were covered by the scheme (but not the self-employed or most people not working or working but on a low income).

■ The maximum SERPS pension would be 25 per cent of the average of your best 20 years' earnings (between limits). For this purpose, earnings were increased between the year you earned them and reaching state pension age in line with national average earnings.

■ Employees could be 'contracted out'. This meant for the contracting-out years they would give up building up SERPS pension but instead build up an equivalent pension from an employer's occupational scheme. Contracted-out employees (and their employers) paid lower National Insurance contributions to reflect the reduced state pension. This is the way the State and occupational schemes worked in partnership to deliver adequate pensions. Thus a low state additional pension would be balanced by a higher occupational pension.

Despite the all-party support for the scheme, within a decade SERPS was deemed too expensive and the benefits were cut back: pensions were to be based on average of all earnings not just the best 20 years and the maximum was reduced to 20 per cent instead of 25 per cent. Moreover, a different type of contracting out was introduced, enabling you to contract out for example into a personal pension, which provided a less certain and secure replacement for SERPS. Instead of the State and occupational schemes working in partnership, you could now, in effect, take a gamble on whether your own personal pension linked to the stock market would do better or worse than the SERPS you gave up.

Further changes were brought in from 2002 when SERPS was adapted and renamed S2P. The S2P changes were not all bad. The scheme was extended

---

[4] Barbara Castle, *House of Commons Debate, 18 March 1975*, Hansard vol. 888, cc1486–583.

to cover more people and the structure altered to deliver more generous pensions to people on low and medium earnings. In particular carers and low earners now have their additional pension worked out as if they have earnings equal to a set level called the low earnings threshold (LET), which in 2009–10 stood at £13,900. Further changes are being made to S2P as follows:

■ From 6 April 2009, the maximum earnings on which your additional pension can be based has been frozen at £770 a week and S2P will gradually move towards being a flat rate pension based, for everyone, on earnings equal to the LET.

■ From 2012, the less certain and secure form of contracting out mentioned above will be abolished (see p. 191).

## How much state pension?

You can probably make a good stab at working out your basic pension, but it is virtually impossible to work out for yourself how much additional pension you will get – not only are the rules and the way changes have been introduced complex, but you would also need a complete record of your earnings and National Insurance position for every tax year since 1978. Therefore, most people have little choice but to rely on the State to have kept accurate records and make the calculations. You can request a state pension forecast at any time by contacting The Pension Service with details. The forecast will tell you, in today's money, how much state pension you are likely to receive when you reach state pension age.

Some occupational pension schemes and personal pensions issue 'combined benefit statements' – these set out how much pension you might get from the scheme and also your state pension forecast as supplied by the government and based on your personal National Insurance record. If you receive a combined benefit statement, you will not need to ask for a state pension forecast.

## Increasing your state pension: extra contributions

If you have fewer than the 30 qualifying years needed for the full basic pension, you may be able to pay extra contributions (called Class 3 voluntary contributions) to fill gaps in your record. Usually, there is a time limit, so that you can go back only six years. However, for people reaching state pension age before 6 April 2015, you can also make a further six years' contributions going back as far as 1975, provided you have at least

20 qualifying years on your record. Class 3 contributions cost £12.05 a week in 2010–11, so £626.60 for a whole year's worth. It does not matter if you have already passed state pension age and started to draw your pension – you can still make voluntary contributions and your pension will then increase.

You cannot fill gaps created because you chose to pay contributions at the married women's reduced rate (see below). Extra contributions do not increase your additional pension.

### Increasing your pension: switching from the married women's reduced rate

The state pension system we have today still reflects it origins in 1948. At that time it was the norm for wives after marriage to rely on their husbands for financial support. Therefore, married women could opt to give up their right to a state pension in their own name and in return pay National Insurance at a reduced rate. This option was abolished in May 1977 but women who had already made the choice by then could continue paying at the reduced rate. The election continues to be effective even if you are widowed, but ends if you divorce or if you stop work for more than two years.

With a variety of changes to the state pension system over the years, continuing to pay at the reduced rate no longer represents a good deal for some women:

■ In particular, married women on low earnings who switch to the full rate, not only build up basic pension but are treated as if they have earnings at the low earnings threshold (£13,900 in 2009–10) for building up additional pension too.

■ From 6 April 2010, every qualifying year counts towards basic pension. So even one year earns you £3.26 a week pension. Before then, you usually had to have around 11 years' worth of contributions to get any basic pension at all.

Set against these advantages of paying National Insurance at the full rate, you need to consider what pension you would get if you stuck with the reduced rate contributions. In that case, you could claim a pension based on your husband's National Insurance record equal to roughly 60 per cent of the amount of basic pension he gets. So if he gets the full pension of £97.65 a week in 2010–11, you can get £58.50 a week. You would need at least 18 years' National Insurance contributions to be entitled to more

basic pension in your own right. If your husband has too few contributions for the full pension, the amount you would get based on his record
would be less and so you would need fewer years on your own record
to beat it. For more information, contact HM Revenue & Customs (see
Appendix B).

### Increasing your pension: defer your pension

You cannot draw your state pension before state pension age, but you can
draw it later. If you put off starting your state pension, when it does start
you can choose to have either a higher pension or a cash lump sum. See
Chapter 8 for details.

## Occupational pensions

Occupational schemes usually provide a package of benefits: a pension for you at retirement, an ill-health pension if you have to stop work
early, lump sum death benefit if you die before retirement, and pensions
for your partner and any dependant children (called survivors' pensions)
if you die before them either while working or after you have retired.
Usually, you can take up to a quarter of your pension savings in the form
of a tax-free lump sum at retirement (see Chapter 8).

The big advantage of occupational pension schemes is that your employer
contributes towards the cost. This means choosing not to join an occupational scheme is like turning down a pay rise. With most schemes, you have
to contribute too, so you will want to weigh up what you get for your money.

There are two main ways that occupational schemes work: on a defined
benefit basis (see p. 195) or a defined contribution basis (see p. 197). Each
of these is considered in detail below, but the key difference is that in
a defined benefit scheme you are promised a level of pension and your
employer is ultimately responsible for ensuring there is enough money
available to meet the pension promise. As such, you are largely shielded
from the risks that could otherwise cause your pension to be less than you
had expected. By contrast, in a defined contribution scheme, you bear all
the risks.

Defined benefit schemes are a particularly valuable perk of a job. The cost
of meeting the promised pensions is usually split between you and your
employer. Typically you pay around 5 or 6 per cent of your salary in pension contributions. Your employer then pays the balance, which, in 2007,
averaged 14 per cent of salary. A defined contribution scheme is usually

a less valuable perk, not only because of risk, but also because employers pay in only 8 per cent of salary on average.[5] So the chance of getting an adequate pension is reduced.

From 2012, the government is proposing to phase in a new national pension scheme to be called the National Employment Savings Trust (NEST). You will have your own personal account, which will work on a defined contribution basis (see p. 197). Employers will be required to pay in just 3 per cent a year. The upshot is that there is a hierarchy of occupational pension schemes, as shown in Figure 7.5.

## Defined benefit schemes

The most common type of defined benefit scheme is a final salary scheme, but there are other types too. What all these schemes have in common is that they promise you a set level of pension:

- In a final salary scheme, you get a fixed proportion of your pay at or near retirement for each year you have been in the scheme. For example, if the proportion is 1/80th, you have been in the scheme 20 years and your pay on leaving is £40,000, your pension would be 1/80 × £40,000 × 20 = £10,000 a year.

- A career average scheme is similar to a final salary scheme, except that your pension is based on your pay averaged over all the time you've been in the scheme rather than your pay at retirement. Usually pay from earlier years will be revalued in line with inflation before the average is worked out. In the state sector, SERPS and S2P are examples of career average schemes.

- Fixed benefit scheme, you are promised a fixed amount of pension for each year of membership. The amount of pension may be increased after payment starts, for example, in line with inflation. Public sector schemes offer a similar arrangement if you want to pay in extra contributions (called additional voluntary contributions or AVCs) – see p. 201.

Because the pension is worked out according to a formula, you know in advance how much pension to expect and, where the pension is linked to your pay or earnings generally while it is building up, you know that your pension will keep pace with inflation. Your pension will be a predictable proportion of your income while working, which helps you to plan ahead.

---

[5] Department for Work and Pensions, *Employers' Pension Provision Survey 2007*, 2008.

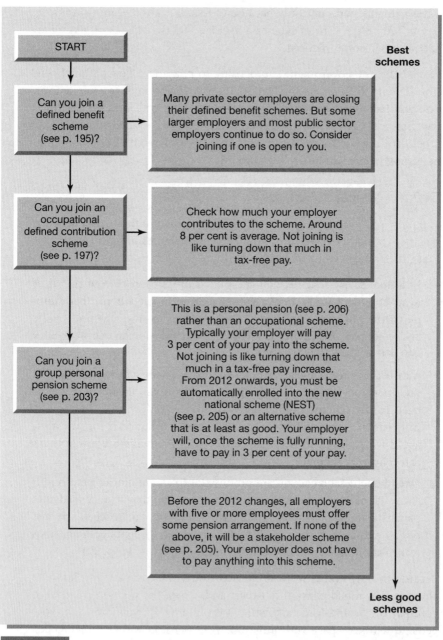

**Figure 7.5**    Joining a pension scheme at work

In a defined benefit scheme, you are unaffected by, say, a fall in the stock market or people living longer (so their pensions have to be paid out for longer) which push up the cost of providing a set level of pension. On the whole, your employer bears these risks and costs, not you. However, if the cost rises, your employer might ask you for higher contributions too. More drastically, in the private sector, many employers have become unwilling to carry on bearing the risks and costs of defined benefit schemes, resulting in scheme closures (see p. 214).

## Case study

Harry works for his local council and belongs to its final salary pension scheme which pays 1/60th of final pay for each year of membership. He has been in the scheme for ten years and based on his current pay of £18,000, he has so far built up a pension of 10 × 1/60 × £18,000 = £3,000 a year, payable from age 65. If he can remain a member until he retires in 20 years' time, he will be on track for a pension of 30 × 1/60 × £18,000 = £9,000 in today's money. Currently he pays just under 6 per cent of his pay towards the pension and the council picks up the rest of the cost.

Seb earns £18,000 a year working for a website design company which runs a defined contribution scheme. He pays in 6 per cent of his pay each month and his employer adds a further 8 per cent. After ten years in the scheme, he has built up a pension fund of £26,600 which, at current annuity rates might buy him a pension of around £1,150 a year from age 65. If he carries on paying in for a further 20 years, his pension fund might grow to £96,600 in today's money (though there is no guarantee of this), which could secure him a pension of nearly £4,200 a year. In addition to the risk, Seb's possible pension is considerably less than Harry expects to get paying the same contributions.

### Defined contribution schemes

The main alternative to a defined benefit scheme is a defined contributions scheme (also called 'money purchase'). With these you build up your own pot of savings (a pension fund) that you use at retirement to buy a pension. You cannot predict with certainty what your pension will be. It will depend on the amount you and your employer pay in, how well the invested contributions grow, how much is lost in charges and the annuity rate at which you can exchange your resulting pension fund for income at the time you want the pension to start. You are directly exposed to the risks of fluctuating stock markets, people living longer (which leads to poorer annuity rates) and your expected pension failing to keep pace with earnings or inflation.

Although the rate of return on the invested contributions will be the major determinant of the pension you get, this is the most difficult of all the factors to forecast (see Chapter 10). Often, it is up to you to choose how your share of the pension fund is invested, typically choosing from a range of investment funds offered by the pension provider – see Chapter 10 for information about investment funds and choosing between them.

Do not underestimate the effect of charges. Even if the main charges quoted are a seemingly small percentage each year, bear in mind that this is an annual percentage of your total pension fund, not the growth in value of the fund. Moreover, the charge is levied year-in-year-out, even in years when your fund has fallen in value. Table 7.6 shows the impact that different levels of yearly charges can have on the amount of pension fund you have available at retirement to turn into a pension. As you can see, building up your fund through regular contributions, charges at 1 per cent a year reduce the value of your eventual pension fund by 3 per cent if you are saving over a period of five years, 5 per cent if you invest over ten years, over a tenth after 20 years and more than a fifth over a period of 35 years. Higher levels of charges take an even larger chunk out of your fund.

**Table 7.6  Example of how charges reduce your pension fund**

*The table shows how charges reduce the pension fund built up through paying a regular monthly sum into a pension scheme.*

| | Level of charges % pa | | | | |
|---|---|---|---|---|---|
| *Years until retirement* | *0.5* | *1.0* | *1.5* | *2.0* | *2.5* |
| 5 | –1% | –3% | –4% | –5% | –6% |
| 10 | –3% | –5% | –8% | –10% | –12% |
| 15 | –4% | –8% | –12% | –15% | –19% |
| 20 | –6% | –11% | –16% | –21% | –25% |
| 25 | –7% | –14% | –21% | –26% | –31% |
| 30 | –9% | –17% | –25% | –31% | –37% |
| 35 | –11% | –21% | –29% | –36% | –43% |

## Hybrid pension schemes

Some occupational schemes combine elements of the defined benefit and defined contribution bases. For example, you might get a modest defined benefit pension with a defined contribution top up.

In a cash balance scheme, you are promised a set level of pension fund at retirement for each year you are in the scheme, which protects you from the risks of stock market fluctuations while your pension rights are building up. It's then up to you to shop around for the best pension at retirement as you would with a defined contribution scheme.

Hybrid schemes are usually designed to share the risks and costs of providing pension between you and your employer. This gives you a more secure pension than you would get from a pure defined contribution scheme but less certainty than a defined benefit scheme.

## When you can draw your pension

Unless you have to retire early due to ill health, the earliest you can draw your pension (from 6 April 2010 onwards) is age 55 and the latest is age 75. Ill health pensions can start from any age. The normal pension age in many schemes is 65. If you start your pension earlier than this, it may be considerably reduced.

Since April 2006, if your employer and pension scheme agree, you can start to draw an occupational pension while continuing to work for the employer who offers the scheme. This could enable you, for example, to gradually cut down on work, balancing the fall in your pay with progressively larger amounts of pension (sometimes called 'phased retirement'). Normally there is nothing to stop you starting your pension and taking a job with another employer or becoming self-employed. It will usually be a condition of an ill-health pension that it stops if you become well enough to resume either your normal work or any work (you need to check the precise conditions that apply in your case). With public sector schemes, your pension might be reduced if, after retiring, you take on work covered by the same pension scheme – for example, you retire from teaching full-time but do some supply work – check the position with your scheme.

## How much occupational pension?

Your current employer's scheme and any previous employer's scheme that will provide you a pension at retirement should provide you with an annual benefit statement. This sets out, in today's money, the amount of pension you are on track to receive from a specified pension age. It might look something like the example in Figure 7.6.

**Yearly statement**
Prepared on 31 December 2009

**ABC Limited**

**Plan number**
000000000

**Date of birth**
17 May 1960

**National Insurance Number**
000000000

**Date plan started**
1 July 2000

**Your selected pension age**
65

**Summary of your plan** from 1 January 2009 to 31 December 2009
...

**What you might get back**
How much pension you get at age 65 depends how much is paid in between now and retirement, how your invested payments grow and the cost of converting your plan into a pension for life at age 65.
Inflation will reduce the buying power of your money in future, so this statement gives you an idea of how much pension you might get in *todays' money*.

**If you continue to make the same contributions to your plan until age 65:**

| | | |
|---|---|---|
| Your forecast starting pension in today's money | £642.44 | a month |
| Alternatively, you might be able to take a lump sum in today's money of | £44,614.00 | |
| And your forecast starting pension in today's money would then be | £481.83 | a month |

**Figure 7.6** Example of a benefit statement from a current employer's scheme

If it is a 'combined benefit statement', it will also include a personalised forecast of the state pension you are due to get from your state pension age. Where it is not a combined benefit statement, it may nevertheless still also draw your attention to the full rate of state basic pension as an indication of the minimum state pension that most people get.

You may have belonged to a previous employer's pension scheme. If you had been in the scheme for less than two years (five years if you left before 25 July 1986), on leaving, you were probably offered a refund of your contributions and your pension rights would have been cancelled. However, if you had been in the scheme longer than this, you had the right to a 'preserved pension'. In most cases, you could choose to transfer that pension to another scheme (see p. 213) but, assuming you did not transfer it, the old scheme remains liable to pay you your preserved pension once you reach the normal pension age for the scheme. This applies even if the scheme has since changed its name, been taken over or merged with another scheme. You should be getting regular benefit statements telling you how much that pension is likely to be. If you have lost touch with the scheme, you can ask the Pensions Tracing Service (see Appendix B) to help you find the relevant contact details so you can re-establish contact and ask the scheme to start sending you statements.

## Increasing your occupational pension: additional voluntary contributions

You may be able to boost your occupational pension by making extra contributions to it – called additional voluntary contributions (AVCs).

In the past, firms had to offer an in-house AVC scheme and, although this is no longer compulsory, many still do so. In the private sector, the AVC scheme is normally a defined contribution scheme. Your AVCs build up a pension fund that you use at retirement to buy extra pension, take as a lump sum or possibly enhance other benefits such as survivors' pensions. Your employer will have chosen the AVC provider and may have negotiated extra features, such as lower-than-normal charges. You choose how the AVCs are invested from the range of investment funds offered by the provider – see Chapter 10 for information about investment funds.

In the public sector, you often have a choice of AVC schemes. You can either pay into a defined contribution scheme as described above or you can often buy additional pension direct – see the case study below. Typically, you buy extra pension in units of £250 which will be paid annually from your retirement age and, in the public sector, increased each year in line with inflation. There may be a maximum amount you can buy, say, £5,000 and you can usually choose whether to pay by monthly instalments or as an immediate lump sum. The cost of the extra pension depends on your age at the time you buy the pension and your sex (because women tend to live longer than men their pensions are on average paid for longer and this costs more). For details of your own scheme, contact the scheme administrators (see Appendix B) or check the scheme's website which will often have an online calculator so you can check how much you would have to pay for extra pension given your particular circumstances.

Alternatively, you might prefer to make your own arrangement for boosting your pension by paying into a personal pension (see p. 206), for example, if the AVC scheme your employer offers has a more restricted choice of investment funds than you would like. However be wary of turning your back on your employer's AVC scheme if your employer offers to match your additional contributions.

## Case study

Cheri, aged 59, works in a hospital and belongs to the NHS Pension Scheme. She is on track for a pension of around £6,000 a year from the scheme but would like to buy an extra £1,000 a year of pension payable from age 65. She uses the NHS Pension Scheme online calculator to check how much the extra pension would cost. One option would be to pay an extra £308.80 a month in contributions for the next five years (a total outlay of £18,528). If she were to pay an immediate lump sum, the cost would be £15,600. The monthly outlay is quite high because Cheri has only a few years left until retirement. For example, Cheri's colleague, Jan, started buying an extra £1,000 a year pension when she was aged 39 and is paying £58.80 a month over a period of 20 years (total cost £14,112).

### Increasing your occupational pension: salary sacrifice

As outlined on pp. 185–6, you normally get tax relief on your pension contributions up to your highest rate of tax. In an occupational scheme, tax relief is given by deducting your pension contributions from your pay before the income tax bill is worked out. But you do not get any relief from National Insurance contributions.

Contributions which your employer pays on your behalf are not only a valuable part of your total pay package but also tax-free, because there is no income tax or National Insurance on the benefit you get from these contributions. Employers, as well as employees, have to pay National Insurance contributions on salary, but there is no employer National Insurance on employer contributions to a pension scheme. A salary sacrifice scheme takes advantage of these rules. You swap part of your pay that is subject to tax and National Insurance for a tax-free benefit, such as your employer paying extra into the pension scheme. The case study below shows how this can make both employee and employer better off.

Provided the salary sacrifice involves a genuine change to your contract of employment so that your pay is permanently reduced, HM Revenue & Customs have indicated that schemes like this are valid tax planning arrangements. However, before, going into a salary sacrifice arrangement, consider carefully the impact the reduction in pay may have on other aspects of your finances. For example, lower pay may mean lower sick pay if you are off work ill, lower maternity pay, lower future pay rises in cash terms if they are given as a percentage of your existing salary, less state additional pension for as long as the right to this remains earnings related (see p. 192), but possibly a higher entitlement to tax credits (see Appendix A).

## Case study

Ajani works for a logistics company. It operates a defined contribution pension scheme, with the employer paying in 6 per cent of pay and employees 5 per cent. The firm has just brought in a salary sacrifice scheme under which employees can agree to a change in their contract which reduces their pay, and in return the employer takes over the employee pension contribution. Because of the saving in National Insurance contributions for both the employer and employees, both gain from the arrangement. For Ajani, the deal works out as shown in Figure 7.7 overleaf.

### Increasing your occupational pension: deferring retirement

If you work on beyond normal pension age, you will usually be able to get a bigger pension, but this will not necessarily be the case:

■ **In a defined benefit scheme**, there may be an overall maximum pension. Contact the HR department to find out the options available in your scheme.

■ **In a defined contribution scheme**, although your fund remains invested and so has longer to grow (and other factors work in your favour – see Chapter 8), other events – such as a slump in the stock market – could reduce the value of your pension fund. Chapter 8 looks at this issue in detail.

### Other pension schemes available through the workplace

If they have five or more employees, employers must offer access to some type of pension arrangement through work. However, this does not have to be an occupational pension scheme, but instead:

■ **A group personal pension scheme (GPPS).** Each employee gets their own personal pension (see p. 206). Your employer may have negotiated a special deal, for example, lower charges or flexible contributions. Your employer must contribute to your GPPS on your behalf, but only 3 per cent of your pay. It's up to you what contributions you make yourself. This pension is attached to you not the job, so stays with you even when you leave. However, your employer contributions will stop when you change jobs.

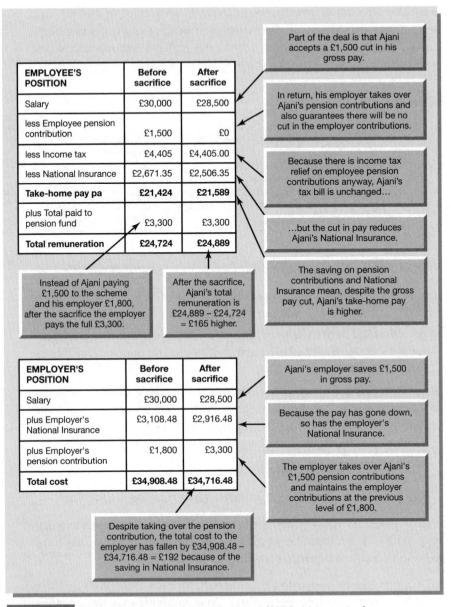

| EMPLOYEE'S POSITION | Before sacrifice | After sacrifice |
|---|---|---|
| Salary | £30,000 | £28,500 |
| less Employee pension contribution | £1,500 | £0 |
| less Income tax | £4,405 | £4,405.00 |
| less National Insurance | £2,671.35 | £2,506.35 |
| **Take-home pay pa** | **£21,424** | **£21,589** |
| plus Total paid to pension fund | £3,300 | £3,300 |
| **Total remuneration** | **£24,724** | **£24,889** |

Part of the deal is that Ajani accepts a £1,500 cut in his gross pay.

In return, his employer takes over Ajani's pension contributions and also guarantees there will be no cut in the employer contributions.

Because there is income tax relief on employee pension contributions anyway, Ajani's tax bill is unchanged...

...but the cut in pay reduces Ajani's National Insurance.

The saving on pension contributions and National Insurance mean, despite the gross pay cut, Ajani's take-home pay is higher.

Instead of Ajani paying £1,500 to the scheme and his employer £1,800, after the sacrifice the employer pays the full £3,300.

After the sacrifice, Ajani's total remuneration is £24,889 – £24,724 = £165 higher.

| EMPLOYER'S POSITION | Before sacrifice | After sacrifice |
|---|---|---|
| Salary | £30,000 | £28,500 |
| plus Employer's National Insurance | £3,108.48 | £2,916.48 |
| plus Employer's pension contribution | £1,800 | £3,300 |
| **Total cost** | **£34,908.48** | **£34,716.48** |

Ajani's employer saves £1,500 in gross pay.

Because the pay has gone down, so has the employer's National Insurance.

The employer takes over Ajani's £1,500 pension contributions and maintains the employer contributions at the previous level of £1,800.

Despite taking over the pension contribution, the total cost to the employer has fallen by £34,908.48 – £34,716.48 = £192 because of the saving in National Insurance.

**Figure 7.7** Example of a salary sacrifice deal (2010–11 tax rates)

■ **A stakeholder pension scheme**. Again, this is a personal pension (see p. 208) attached to you rather than the job. Your employer does not have to pay anything into this scheme on your behalf.

If you join either of these arrangements, normally you can arrange to have any contributions you pay in yourself deducted direct from your pay packet. Your employer then passes the contributions to the provider.

## New pension scheme from 2012

Concerned that many people – especially on low and moderate incomes – are not saving enough for retirement, the government is arranging for a new national scheme to start from 2012. Originally called 'personal accounts', the scheme is now renamed the National Employment Savings Trust (NEST).

Employers will have a new duty to automatically enrol all eligible employees either in the new scheme or in the employer's alternative pension arrangement provided it offers benefits which are at least as good. The duty will be phased in over several years and will apply first to the largest employers. Eligible employees are aged 22 and over but under the pension age for the scheme and with earnings above a specified amount (set at £5,035 in the legislation[6] but likely to be increased at the time the scheme starts). You will have the right to opt out if you don't want to be in the national scheme or your employer's alternative scheme.

The national scheme will work on a defined contribution basis. Your employer will have to contribute at least 3 per cent of your pay between set limits to the national scheme or the alternative arrangement. (The limits are set in the legislation as pay between £5,035 and £33,540, but are likely to be increased at the time the scheme starts.) You will have to contribute at least 4 per cent of your earnings (capped at a maximum of £3,600 a year) and tax relief will add a further 1 per cent or so. Overall, then, around 8 per cent of your pay will go into the scheme once it is fully operational. However, the changes will be phased in with lower contribution rates for both employers and employees in the early years. Even when fully running, the 8 per cent contribution level is considerably less than most employers currently pay into occupational schemes (see p. 194). It is also less than you are likely to need to save to provide yourself with a comfortable retirement – see the case study overleaf.

---

[6] Pensions Act 2008.

At the time of writing, the new national scheme is still being negotiated and designed. It is intended that charges for the scheme will be a lot lower than those for personal pensions and stakeholder schemes (see below). There is expected to be a limited range of investment choices. The scheme is designed primarily for employees who have an employer to help finance the cost of pension saving, but if you are self-employed or not working, you will be able to opt into the scheme if you want to.

If your income is low and expected to remain low after retirement, a concern is whether saving for retirement is worthwhile at all given that the retirement income you build up may mean you lose means-tested benefits once you are retired. Research by the government suggests that 95 per cent of employees will be better off as a result of saving through personal accounts or an equivalent pension scheme, with the addition of the employer's contribution, tax relief and assumed investment growth more than offsetting any loss of benefits.

## Case study

In 2012, Brian is aged 30 and earning £24,000 a year. If he joins the new national scheme, NEST, and total contributions of 8 per cent a year go into his personal account, based on the assumptions below, he can expect a pension of around £6,400, equal to about 16 per cent of his earnings at the time he retires.

This projection is based on the following assumptions: the invested contributions grow at 7 per cent a year, charges average 0.5 per cent a year, the resulting pension fund is used to buy an annuity where the income increases each year in line with price inflation, price inflation averages 2.5 per cent a year and earnings inflation averages 4 per cent a year.

## Personal pensions

You may have a personal pension that you have arranged yourself, for example, because you are self-employed or decided to use this route to boost your occupational scheme. You might also have a personal pension as a result of contracting out of the state additional pension scheme (see p. 191) or through your workplace because your employer had organised a group personal pension or stakeholder scheme. Whatever the route, this type of pension arrangement is personal to you and not linked to any specific job.

All personal pensions work on a defined contribution basis – in other words in the same way as the defined contribution occupational schemes described on p. 197. This means the pension you eventually get depends on how much you (and your employer if relevant) pay in, how well the invested contributions grow, the amount taken away in charges and the rate at which you can convert the resulting pension fund to pension at retirement. So these are schemes where you bear all the risks. Moreover, if you do not have an employer paying into your scheme, you have to bear the full cost yourself of providing your pension this way.

You can choose to make regular payments to a personal pension. Alternatively, you might prefer to make *ad hoc* lump sum payments (called single premiums) – this is often a more convenient option if you run your own business and your profits tend to vary from year to year. See the box below for how you get tax relief on your contributions.

## Tax relief and contributions

What you pay into a personal pension is treated as a contribution from which tax relief at the basic rate has already been deducted (a net contribution). The pension provider then claims the relief from HM Revenue & Customs (HMRC) and adds it to your plan. For example, in 2010–11, if you pay £100 into a personal pension, the provider will claim £25 from HMRC and add this to your plan (since £25 is 20 per cent of the gross contribution of £125). If you are a higher-rate taxpayer, see Appendix A for details of how you get higher-rate relief on your contributions.

Anyone can pay into a personal pension for anyone else – for example, you could pay into a plan for your child or for your partner. Your contribution is, as usual, treated as a net amount and the plan provider claims back and adds the basic-rate relief to the plan in the usual way. But you cannot claim any higher-rate tax relief on a contribution you pay into someone else's plan.

The maximum contributions to the total of your personal pensions and occupational pensions on which you can get tax relief are capped at 100 per cent of your UK earnings or £3,600 if this is higher than your earnings. The limit covers contributions paid by you and anyone else on your behalf, but not contributions from your employer. So, for example, if you are not working because you are bringing up a young family and your partner agrees to pay into your personal pension for you, the maximum they could contribute in 2010–11 is £2,880 a year in net contributions which, with tax relief at 20 per cent come to £3,600.

Unlike occupational defined contribution schemes, there are no automatic extras with personal pensions, such as life cover and survivors' pensions. If you die before starting your pension, the fund you have built up can be paid as a lump sum to anyone you nominate after deduction of tax (at 35 per cent in 2009–10). When you are ready to draw your pension, you can take up to a quarter of your fund as a tax-free lump sum, but what other benefits you have in retirement depends on the choices you make – see Chapter 8 for information.

It's up to you to decide how to invest your pension savings. With an ordinary personal pension offered by an insurance company, you choose from a range of investment funds (see Chapter 10). These may be limited to the company's own funds or sometimes a wider range. For a much wider choice, you could opt for a self-invested personal pension (SIPP) – see p. 210.

Personal pension charges may take a variety of forms. For example, there may be an administration fee each time you invest, charges if you switch from one investment fund to another, charges if you transfer to another provider's plan. But the main charges apply to the underlying investment funds and are usually an up-front or initial charge designed to cover the costs of marketing and paying commission to advisers (see Chapter 2) and an annual management charge, typically between 1 and 2 per cent, but often less once you have built up a large fund. Charges are capped if you choose a stakeholder pension scheme (see below).

Before you invest in a personal pension, you will be given a Key Facts document. This is a document required by rules of the Financial Services Authority, the UK's main financial regulator. It sets out the main features of the plan in a standardised way so that you can easily compare one personal pension with another. It also includes a personal illustration with a projection, in today's money, of how your pension savings might grow and an indication of how all the different charges combined reduce the return you get – see Figure 7.8. The difference between the investment return before and after charges is called the 'reduction in yield' (RIY). The greater the reduction in yield, the higher the charges and the greater the investment growth you will need to pay the charges and leave you with a reasonable return.

The FSA publishes comparative tables (see Appendix B) that are a good starting point when shopping around and comparing different provider's plans.

## Stakeholder pension schemes

You may be offered a stakeholder scheme through your workplace or you can choose to take one out yourself. This is just a personal pension but one that conforms to some minimum standards that are designed to ensure you get reasonable value for money:

■ **Charges**. These are capped at a maximum 1.5 per cent a year for the first 10 years and 1 per cent a year thereafter of the value of your pension fund. Charges can only be levied in this form – for example, no flat fees are allowed.

**ABXY Personal Pension Scheme**

| Illustration for:<br>Mr Joe Bloggs | Date illustration prepared:<br>5 January 2010 | Age:<br>46 next birthday | Selected pension age:<br>65 |

**Contribution details**

| | |
|---|---|
| Regular monthly contribution | £100.00 |
| Less basic rate tax relief at 20% | £20.00 |
| Regular monthly amount to pay | £80.00 |

> The illustration starts by setting out what you plan to pay in and any tax relief to be added to your plan. In this example, the investor pays £80 a month and £20 tax relief is added.

**Effect of changes**

The last two columns of this table assume that your investment will grow at 7.0% a year.

| At the end of year | Total paid in to date £ | Effect of deductions to date £ | What you might get back £ |
|---|---|---|---|
| 1 | 1,200 | 8 | 1,237 |
| 2 | 2,400 | 32 | 2,545 |
| 3 | 3,600 | 75 | 3,928 |
| 4 | 4,800 | 138 | 5,390 |
| 5 | 6,000 | 223 | 6,936 |
| 10 | 12,000 | 1,098 | 16,104 |
| 15 | 18,000 | 3,064 | 28,222 |
| 20 | 24,000 | 6,803 | 44,237 |

> The illustration shows, for selected years, what you will have paid in, the impact of charges, based on the provider's current structure and level of charges, and how your savings might grow, based on an assumption about investment growth and the effects of charges.

**What this table tells you:**

- Deductions cover commission to the adviser or salesperson who sold you this plan, expenses, charges, and other adjustments.
- What you might get back is the transfer value of your scheme at the end of the year shown, assuming your investment grows at 7% a year and after the effect of the deductions shown in the previous column.
- By age 65, expenses, charges and other deductions have th effect of reducing your anticipated return from 7% to 5.8%.

> It shows the overall impact of charges over the full term of your plan. In this example, charges reduce the growth rate from 7 per cent a year to 5,8 per cent, so the reduction in yield is 7% – 5.8% = 1.2% a year.

**Figure 7.8** Extract from an example Key Facts document

*Source:* Constructed by the author drawing on regulations in the Financial Services Authority Handbook

- ■ **Minimum contribution**. This must be set at £20 or less and this applies whether you contribute regularly or as a lump sum.
- ■ **Transfers**. You can transfer your pension fund to another scheme at any time without any early surrender or transfer charge.
- ■ **Investment**. If you do not want to choose how to invest your savings, they automatically go into a default fund which will be a 'lifestyling fund' (see Chapter 10).

## Self-invested personal pensions

Pension schemes may be described as 'tax wrappers' rather than investments in their own right. This is most clearly seen with self-invested personal pensions (SIPPs). The personal pension structure ensures your pension savings get the tax treatment described on p. 185, but you have wide freedom to put whatever investments you like inside the SIPP wrapper – for example, investment funds, UK and foreign shares, bonds, gilts and commercial property. The tax laws do put some restrictions on your choice – in particular, you cannot invest in most forms of residential property through a SIPP, or tangible assets, such as wine, antiques and classic cars. The investments you might want to put into a SIPP are described in Chapters 9 and 10.

SIPPs are offered by insurance companies and other providers, such as stockbrokers and investment managers. Different providers set different terms and conditions for their SIPPs, so not all will allow you to invest in the full range of possible investments. There are often extra charges for having a SIPP compared with an ordinary personal pension – for example, there may be a fee for setting up the SIPP, an annual management charge (on top of any charges for investment funds held within the SIPP), fees for buying and selling investments held within the SIPP, charges if you transfer investments in from another pension scheme or transfer out, and extra charges if you hold more unusual investments, such as commercial property.

However, SIPPs are not all the same. Some are aimed at people with complex investment needs – for example, if you run your own business, you can arrange to hold the property from which your business operates tax-efficiently within a SIPP and the SIPP can also borrow within limits to buy such assets. Some target people who want to have a very wide investment and esoteric choice. Others are designed for people who are happy with investment funds, shares and bonds but want the freedom to choose from across the whole market. If you fall into the latter category, you will be able to find SIPPs with modest charges catering for the DIY investor. Don't pay extra for a SIPP with lots of options and extras that you will not use.

### When you can draw your pension

You can start to draw an income from a personal pension (from 6 April 2010 onwards) at any age from 55 to 75. Ill health pensions can start from any age. The earlier you start to draw the pension, the lower it is likely to be – see Chapter 8.

### How much personal pension?

The provider of each personal pension you have should provide you with an annual statement, showing, in today's money, the amount of pension you are on track to receive from your chosen pension age. If it is a 'combined benefit statement', it will also include a personalised forecast of the state pension you are due to get from your state pension age.

If you have lost touch with a personal pension provider that is still due to pay you a pension at retirement, you can get help finding the scheme through the Pensions Tracing Service (see Appendix B).

## Stress testing

Saving for retirement typically involves investing throughout your working life. When investing over such a long period, it is inevitable that there will be unexpected events and shocks along the way and you cannot prepare in advance for all of them. Instead, regular reviews are a particularly important part of your plan (see below). Stress tests you should undertake at the outset of your plan are:

■ **Value-for-money**. Check whether pension saving makes sense for you at all – see overleaf.

■ **Long-term illness or disability**. Consider how you would cope if your earnings were severely damaged for a prolonged period, for example, because of long-term illness or disability. The most robust solution is to take out income protection insurance (see Chapter 3) for an amount that is enough to cover your ongoing pension contributions. Another option could be to add waiver-of-premium benefit to any regular-premium personal pension you take out – this pays your contributions for you if you cannot work because of illness or disability.

■ **Relationship breakdown**. It is a sad fact that many couples do split up. Try to ensure that you build up pension savings in your own name that would stay with you rather than relying on a partner for your financial security in retirement. Anyone can pay contributions into a personal pension for anyone else, so perhaps your partner would agree to pay into a pension for you in return for you taking on caring duties within the family.

## Will your pension savings give you value for money?

If you are over a qualifying age (60 in 2009–10 but increasing from April 2010 onwards in line with the rise in women's state pension age – see p. 188) and your income and savings are low, you may qualify for a means-tested benefit, called pension credit, to bring your income up to the minimum that the government deems you need to live on. In addition, you can get other means-tested help, for example council tax benefit to cover all, or part, of your council tax bill, housing benefit to cover your rent and, if you still have mortgage payments, help meeting the interest part of them.

In 2010–11, pension credit will top up your income to a guaranteed level of £132.60 a week if you are single and £202.40 a week if you are a couple. In the same year, the full state basic pension is £97.65 a week for a single person and £156.15 for a couple. Therefore, a single person needs to have built up extra retirement income of more than £34.95 a week (£1,817 a year) to start to benefit from any saving, otherwise the extra savings simply displace means-tested benefits. And the situation is similar for a couple. You are most likely to be in this situation if you expect to live in rented accommodation when you are retired and/or you are in middle age or older with relatively little time left to build up your savings.

In fact, the pension credit system does build in some reward for small levels of saving. However, taking into account the other means-tested benefits such as council tax benefit and housing benefit, in general it is fair to say that, if you can only make very modest savings for retirement, you are unlikely to see much if any benefit from them under the current system. Of course, the problem in planning many years or even decades ahead, is whether to assume that the current system will still apply when you reach retirement. There is no way of knowing, though given the structure of society and the economy in the UK, it seems likely that a means-tested minimum income might persist even if the precise form changes.

# Review

In general, rather than stress testing at the outset for a vast array of potential events, you should aim to review your plan regularly – say, once a year – so that you can check progress against your retirement income target and adjust your plan year-by-year to stay on track.

In addition, you will need to review your plan whenever your circumstances change, for example, your income changes, a relationship breaks down, and so on. Two particular situations that should trigger a review are whenever you change job and if your pension scheme closes down.

## Changing job

Whenever you apply for a new job, you should always look at the pension arrangements as part of the pay packet on offer. The chance to join a good pension scheme – particularly a defined benefit scheme – is a valuable perk.

If you leave a job and you have been a member of your old employer's pension scheme for two years or more, you have the right to a preserved pension. This means the scheme will still pay you a pension when you eventually reach the normal pension age for the scheme. If the scheme you are leaving is a defined benefit scheme, your pension will be worked out based on your pay at or up to the time you leave the scheme and then increased in line with price inflation between the time you leave and the pension starting. However, with most schemes, the inflation increases are now capped at a maximum of 2.5 per cent a year. So, if prices rise on average more than that, your preserved pension will be losing buying power as the years go by. You will need to take that into account in your financial planning, otherwise you will overestimate the real value of your expected retirement income.

If you leave a defined contribution scheme, your pension fund remains invested and (hopefully) carries on growing by enough to cover the charges and provide a real increase in the fund, but no new contributions are paid in.

Instead of leaving your preserved pension in the old scheme, you have the right to transfer it to a new scheme – this could be a personal pension or a new employer's occupational scheme if it is willing to accept the transfer. With a defined benefit scheme, the old scheme will work out a 'cash equivalent transfer value' (CETV) which is the lump sum the scheme estimates it would have to invest today to provide the promised benefits. This lump sum can either be invested in a defined contribution scheme or used to buy benefits, if applicable, in your new employer's defined benefits scheme. When you leave a defined contribution scheme, the value of your fund, less any transfer charges, is the amount available to transfer to a new scheme.

Deciding whether or not to transfer a preserved pension is not an easy decision. Here are some of the factors you will need to weigh up:

■ **Risk**. A defined benefit scheme promises you a predictable pension. If you transfer to a defined contribution scheme, you will be giving up that promise and taking on the risk of ending up with a lower pension, but also the chance that it could be higher.

■ **Charges**. In general, charges tend to be lower in occupational schemes than in personal pensions, so be wary of transferring to a personal pension.

■ **Risk of scheme closure**. If you are worried that your old employer might go out of business and its defined benefit pension scheme might not be able to meet all the pension promises (see below), it might be better to transfer out.

This is an area where you might prefer to seek professional advice (see Chapter 2) rather than be your own adviser.

## Occupational scheme closure

If you are in an occupational defined contribution scheme, you bear the risks of the stock market going down or people living longer or runaway inflation – you simply end up with less pension for your money. Your employer does not have to pay in extra or protect you from these risks, so defined contribution schemes are neither under strain nor expected to close down.

The situation is very different with defined benefit schemes. The scheme promises to pay set pensions. Your employer sponsors the scheme and, as such, must pay in whatever is required to meet the cost of the pension promises. If the stock market falls so that the pension-fund investments are worth less than needed, the employer must pay in extra. If people look like they are living longer so the cost of paying pensions rises, the employer must pay in extra. Many employers in the private sector have decided that the costs and uncertainties of running defined benefit schemes are too great and, as a result, have been closing the schemes to new members. Some are also now closing these schemes to existing members too. In that case, the usual practice is to wind up the scheme and buy special contracts that guarantee the pension you had built up to the date of closure will be paid when you reach retirement.

The pension you have built up to the date of closure is usually the same as the preserved pension you would have had if you had left the scheme. This could be substantially less than the amount you had been planning to build up had the pension scheme remained open. Your employer may well offer membership of a replacement pension arrangement, but this is likely to be a defined contribution or hybrid scheme offering lower or less certain benefits. You may need to take steps to boost your pension (see p. 201).

When a pension fund's investments are insufficient to meet the cost of all the promised benefits, the scheme is said to be in deficit. The deficit is often large and employers may be allowed up to 10 years to channel in additional funds to plug the gap. If the employer goes out of business in the meantime, the pension fund could be left with a hole in its finances and no way left to fill it. In this situation, the fund would be able to claim compensation from the Pension Protection Fund (PPF).

The PPF is a centralised fund, financed by levies on all occupational defined benefit schemes. It will pay out enough so that a pension fund can pay 100 per cent of all the pensions in payment up to a maximum limit and the promised pensions for members who have yet to reach retirement up to 90 per cent of the maximum limit. In 2009–10, the limit is £31,936.32 if you are aged 65 at the time the compensation is provided but with lower limits applying for younger members and higher limits for older members. This means for most people, the PPF would cover at least nine-tenths of their whole pension, but if you were in line to get a large sum, you could find your pension planning blown badly off track. Once it starts to be paid, the pension is increased in line with inflation up to a maximum 2.5 per cent a year, which could be less than you had been planning for. For more information, contact the Pension Protection Fund (see Appendix B).

# 8

# Retirement choices

## Introduction

Chapter 7 focused on the accumulation of wealth to finance your eventual retirement. This chapter focuses on the decumulation – in other words, the mechanics of turning that wealth back into income – which starts when you reach retirement. Figure 8.1 summarises a possible structure for a financial plan to provide yourself with sufficient income at this stage of life. Apart from pension rights and pension funds that you have built up during your working life, the other major asset you may now have is a home. The second part of the chapter looks at whether this asset too could be a viable source of income or cash during retirement, particularly through the use of equity release schemes. You will find information about investing non-pension and housing wealth to provide income in Chapters 9 and 10.

First, it is useful to clarify what the term 'retirement' means, both generally and as used in this book.

## The changing nature of retirement

In years gone by, 'retirement' meant the complete cessation of work. Maybe marked by a leaving party and gold watch, it was a cliff-edge, where one day you were in work, the next a person of leisure. Drawing a pension made this possible, so retirement and starting your pension were usually synonymous. Retirement is still like that for some people, but, for others, there is a spread of years in which you ease away from your full-time normal job and experience paid work in a different form. This might

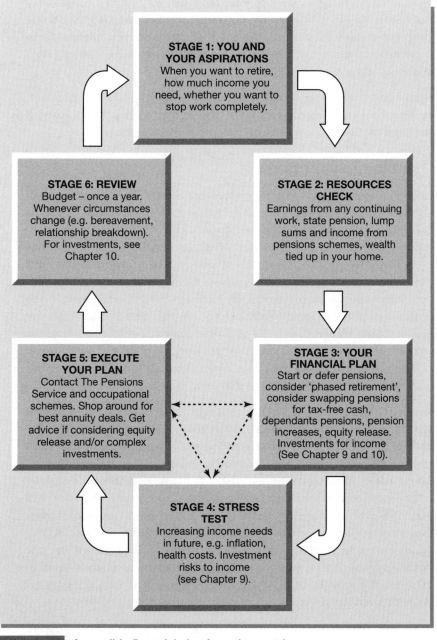

**STAGE 1: YOU AND YOUR ASPIRATIONS**
When you want to retire, how much income you need, whether you want to stop work completely.

**STAGE 2: RESOURCES CHECK**
Earnings from any continuing work, state pension, lump sums and income from pensions schemes, wealth tied up in your home.

**STAGE 3: YOUR FINANCIAL PLAN**
Start or defer pensions, consider 'phased retirement', consider swapping pensions for tax-free cash, dependants pensions, pension increases, equity release. Investments for income (See Chapter 9 and 10).

**STAGE 4: STRESS TEST**
Increasing income needs in future, e.g. inflation, health costs. Investment risks to income (see Chapter 9).

**STAGE 5: EXECUTE YOUR PLAN**
Contact The Pensions Service and occupational schemes. Shop around for best annuity deals. Get advice if considering equity release and/or complex investments.

**STAGE 6: REVIEW**
Budget – once a year. Whenever circumstances change (e.g. bereavement, relationship breakdown). For investments, see Chapter 10.

**Figure 8.1** A possible financial plan for retirement income

be working fewer days a week in your usual job, shifting to a consultancy basis, switching to a different type of work probably part-time, or starting your own small-scale business. During this transition, you might start to draw some of the pension you have built up, postponing – often called deferring – the rest.

Unless stated otherwise, for convenience, this chapter refers to 'retirement' as the point in time when you start to draw at least some pension, without implying that you have necessarily stopped work completely.

## Your right to carry on working

Hopefully, if you expect to carry on working in later life, this will be from choice. However, if your retirement income from other sources is low, it could be a financial necessity. Earnings can top up a low pension; they might also enable you to defer your pension so that it will be bigger once it does start (see p. 220 onwards). But work can be about more than just pay. Work can be a source of identity, self-esteem, companionship, purpose, challenge and achievement so, for many people, retirement in the sense of stopping work altogether is not an ambition at all. Often, the goal is greater choice: the choice to do the work you enjoy; the choice to work more suitable, flexible and shorter hours; the choice to have longer holidays at more convenient times. Unless you opt for self-employment, exercising that choice requires the jobs to be available.

Since 1 October 2006, it has been illegal for employers to discriminate against people in the workplace on the grounds of age. This means that age should not play a part in advertisements for jobs, interview and selection processes, training and promotion opportunities, or redundancy, unless it can be objectively justified. For example, a theatre company might justifiably require a young person to play a young character in a play. However, although the law may be on your side as an older worker, it can be very hard to challenge age discrimination: for example, it may be impossible to prove that you were not called for an interview because of your age. Moreover, when it comes to retirement, as matters stood in 2009, the law provides only weak protection because it includes a national default retirement age of 65.

In general, you cannot be forced to retire before age 65. In theory, an employer can set a default retirement age for staff that is lower but must be able objectively to justify this. While, health, strength, eyesight and so on may all affect your ability to do a job and have a tendency to deteriorate with age, they are not an inevitable result of reaching some particular age. Therefore, it is hard to see how, in practice, employers could justify setting a lower default retirement age than 65. Employer's can set a default retirement age that is higher than 65 or have no default age at all.

Note that retirement age in this context is not the same as pension age. Pension schemes can legally set a normal age at which your full pension becomes payable and this may be different from your employer's default retirement age.

A potential new employer can justifiably refuse to interview or employ you if you are over, or within six months of, that employer's default retirement age. If you are already employed and want to work on beyond the employer's default retirement age, you have the legal right to ask to do this (see box) and your employer must consider your request. But your request can be turned down and your employer does not have to say why.

Originally, the national default age of 65 was due to be reviewed in 2011. But, following a legal challenge by, Heyday (part of Age Concern–Help the Aged, a voluntary sector organisation that campaigns for older people), the government has said it will bring forward the review to 2010 and this might result in the raising or removal of the default age. Until then, you cannot be sure that you will be considered for work beyond age 65.

### Asking to stay on

Between 12 and six months of your reaching the retirement age for your workplace (which will normally be 65 or older), your employer should write to you notifying you of your retirement date and reminding you that you have the right to request to stay. At least three months' before the retirement date, you should make your request in writing. Your employer must consider your request and should normally meet with you to discuss it. If your employer has not made a decision by the time the retirement date arrives, you continue to be employed until your employer tells you the outcome. If your employer does not agree with your request, you can appeal and your employer must consider your appeal – this can take place after you have retired. If your employer does not follow the correct procedure, you may be able to claim compensation for unfair dismissal by taking a case to an Employment Tribunal. For more information, contact the Advisory, Conciliation and Arbitration Service (ACAS). (See Appendix B for contact details.)

# Choices at the point of retirement

The months in the run up to retirement will be a busy time. You may face some or all of the following choices:

■ whether to start your state pension or defer it to earn extra pension or a cash lump sum (see below);

■ when to start your occupational or personal pension (see p. 225);

■ whether to take a tax-free lump sum from any occupational and personal pension schemes (see p. 226);

■ possibly choices about survivors' benefits from a final salary scheme or other defined benefit occupational scheme (see p. 230);

■ if you have any defined contribution schemes – whether occupational or personal pensions – how to draw the best income and other benefits from them (see p. 231).

---

**Pensions and tax**

Your state, occupational and personal pensions are all taxable income. The state pension is paid without any tax deducted. The provider of your main occupational or personal pension normally deducts tax using the Pay-As-You-Earn (PAYE) system. As well as tax on the occupation or personal pension itself, PAYE may be used to collect tax due on other income you have, such as your state pension. For more information about tax, see Appendix A.

---

## Deferring your state pension

You cannot draw your state pension before state pension age (see Chapter 7), but you can draw it later. If you put off starting your state pension, when it does start you can choose to have either a higher pension or a cash lump sum. Even if you have already started your state pension, you can change your mind and cancel it to earn extra pension or lump sum. But you can only cancel it once, not repeatedly. Deferring your pension could be particularly worth considering if you will carry on working beyond state pension age and so might not need your pension straight away.

You have to defer your whole state pension, including any additional pension you get as well as basic. If your husband, wife or civil partner gets a pension based on your contribution record (rather than their own), they will have to defer their pension too and will also benefit from the deferral.

There is no limit to the extra pension or lump sum you can have and you can defer your pension for as long as you like. You must defer for at least five weeks to earn extra pension and at least a year to earn a lump sum. You choose whether to take the extra pension or the lump sum at the time the deferral comes to an end and you are ready to start your pension.

## The extra-pension option

If you opt for extra pension, your state pension is increased by 1 per cent for each five weeks you defer, giving an increase of 10.4 per cent for each complete year of deferral. For example, in 2010–11, the full state basic pension is £97.65 a week. If you deferred starting it for one complete year, you would get a pension of £97.65 + (10.4% × £97.65) = £107.81 a week once it did start. The extra pension is index-linked and taxed in the normal way (see Appendix A). Table 8.1 shows by how much each £100 of deferred state pension would increase, depending on how long you defer for.

**Table 8.1 Extra pension or lump sum from deferring your state pension**

*This table shows, for each £100 of the pension you defer, how much extra pension you will get when the pension starts. It also shows how much lump sum you might get instead of extra pension. All amounts are in today's money.*

| How long you defer your pension | How much pension you would give up in total | If you choose extra pension: your pension once it does start | If you choose a lump sum: how much you might get[1] |
|---|---|---|---|
| 6 months | £2,600 | £105.20 | n/a[2] |
| 1 year | £5,200 | £110.40 | £5,266 |
| 18 months | £7,800 | £115.60 | £7,948 |
| 2 years | £10,400 | £120.80 | £10,664 |
| 3 years | £15,600 | £131.20 | £16,196 |
| 4 years | £20,800 | £141.60 | £21,867 |
| 5 years | £26,000 | £152.00 | £27,680 |
| 10 years | £52,000 | £204.00 | £58,997 |

[1] Assuming your deferred pension earns interest at a rate of 2.5 per cent a year throughout the deferral period and inflation was 0 per cent – this broadly reflects economic conditions in 2009.

[2] You must defer your pension for at least a year to be eligible for the lump sum option.

Whether you win or lose from the extra-pension option depends on how much pension you give up during the deferral and how long you survive after your higher pension starts to be paid. You earn extra pension at the same rate (10.4 per cent a year) whatever your age when you defer your pension and however long you defer it for. This means everyone faces the same deal and the same break-even point: you need to survive nine years and seven months before the amount of extra pension you get equals the amount of pension you have given up – see the case study below. Table 8.2 below shows the average life expectancy for men and women of different ages. As you can see, your chance of living long enough to break even are excellent in the early stages of retirement but diminish as you get older. But, looking back to Chapter 1, you'll recall that in this type of situation the lump-sum option is likely to look more attractive if you tend to be risk averse, because you avoid taking any gamble on how long you might survive.

**Table 8.2 Average life expectancy**

| When you have reached this age: | On average, you can expect to live this many more years: | |
|---|---|---|
| | Men | Women |
| 60 | 25.4 | 28.1 |
| 65 | 21.0 | 23.4 |
| 70 | 16.8 | 18.9 |
| 75 | 12.7 | 14.3 |
| 80 | 9.0 | 10.1 |
| 85 | 6.3 | 7.0 |
| 90 | 4.3 | 4.6 |
| 91 | 3.9 | 4.2 |
| 95 | 2.9 | 3.1 |

*Source*: Data taken from http://www.statistics.gov.uk/downloads/theme_population/ interim_life/period_cohort_tables_index08.pdf

# Case study

> Sadie reached state pension age of 60 in May 2009 and was entitled to receive £130 a week. But she is still working as a research chemist with a drugs company and does not need her pension yet. Therefore she has deferred the pension and plans to start drawing it at age 65 when she retires. Giving up £130 a week (index-linked) for five years (260 weeks) means giving up total pension of 260 × £130 = £33,800 in today's money. When her pension does start in five years time, she will get an extra amount each week of 5 × 10.4% × £130 = £67.60 in today's money. Dividing £33,800 by £67.60 comes to 500. This means she needs to survive for 500 weeks in order to receive as much in extra pension as she has given up during deferral. 500 weeks is the same as nine years and seven months. Looking at Table 8.2, Sadie can see that average life expectancy for a woman aged 65 is 21 years, so she fully expects to profit from deferring and choosing extra pension.

## *The lump-sum option*

Opting for the lump sum rather than extra pension is in some ways a more certain bet because once your pension starts, you get the cash straight away (see case study overleaf). But, planning ahead, the amount you get is less certain because it depends on interest rates during the deferral period.

The lump sum is worked out as if you had put the deferred pension in a savings account where it earns a return of 2 per cent above the Bank of England base rate. At the time of writing (autumn 2009), the Bank of England base rate was at a historically low 0.5 per cent a year, so at that time your deferred pension would have earned interest at a rate of 2.5 per cent a year. Table 8.1 shows the lump sum you would get if your deferred pension earned this rate. Of course, money paid in future years may have a lower buying power than money today because of rising prices (see Chapter 1), so it is necessary to think about what real value this future lump sum might have. In 2009, the low Bank of England base rate was accompanied by low – at times negative – inflation, so the figures in Table 8.1 assume that the future lump sum you get might has the same buying power as an identical sum today: in other words, the amount shown is simultaneously both the cash sum and the value in today's money. If the Bank of England base rate rose to, say 4 per cent, the return on your deferred pension would rise to 4% + 2% = 6% a year, but inflation would probably also be higher and so the real value of the lump sum might not be much greater than shown in Table 8.1.

The amounts shown in the table are before tax. The lump sum is taxable but only at the top rate you would have paid without the lump sum. So if your top rate was 10 per cent, the whole lump sum would be taxed at

10 per cent; if 20 per cent, the whole lump sum would be taxed at 20 per cent; from 2010–11 onwards, if your top rate is 40 per cent, the whole lump sum would be taxed at 40 per cent and not 50 per cent. In other words the lump sum can't push you into a higher tax bracket. In addition, you can start your state pension but opt to receive the lump sum in the next tax year when your top tax rate might be lower, for example, because you have stopped work.

## Case study

> Frank reached state pension age of 65 in August 2009 and was entitled to receive £141 a week. As he is still working, he has decided to defer his pension. He is not sure how long for – maybe three years or so. When he does decide to start his pension, if he opts to take a lump sum, his pension will be paid at the same rate of £141 a week plus the normal state pension inflation-linked increases since 2009 that all pensioners get, in other words, it will have the same buying power as £141 today.

### *Extra pension or lump sum?*

Which is the better choice: extra pension or lump sum? As you can see from the discussion above, both options have an element of uncertainty. The extra pension is a predictable weekly amount in today's money, but you don't know how long you will survive to claim it. At the time you start to defer your pension the lump sum is an uncertain amount, but you can claim it in full as soon as the deferral period ends.

However, you should bear in mind that you do not need to make the choice at the time you start to defer your pension. Assuming you defer for at least a year, you make the choice only when you decide the time has come to start your pension. At that time, you will know exactly how much lump sum you are being offered and it may be worth more or less than the examples shown in Table 8.1. So, at that stage, you will have better information for weighing up the lump sum against the extra pension, as shown in the case study on p. 225.

Unless you defer the pension for many years or your health or family history suggest your life expectancy is shorter than average, the extra pension will often look the superior deal financially. But you need to consider the choice in your own context. For example, if not having the lump sum means you could not fulfil another goal – perhaps your once-in-a-lifetime round-the-world cruise – or you would borrow to do so, then the lump sum could be the better choice for you.

## Case study

Assume that George in the previous case study decides to start his state pension after deferring it for three years. He then has the option to take an enhanced pension of £141 + (3 × 10.4% × £141) = £185 a week in today's money. Assuming his deferred pension earned a better return than the examples in Table 8.1, he is offered the alternative of a lump sum worth £22,332 in today's money.* He knows that, on average, he is likely to live long enough for the extra pension to be a good deal – average life expectancy for a man aged 68 is 18.5 years. But is the cash lump sum a better deal? The extra pension is £44 a week. Dividing £22,332 by £44 comes to 508. So provided he survives 507.55 weeks (nine years and nine months), he will get a better deal from the extra pension than from the lump sum.

* This example assumes the pension earns 6 per cent a year during deferral and the inflation rate is 2.5 per cent a year.

## When to start your occupational or personal pension

Most occupational pension schemes have a normal pension age at which the full pension becomes payable. You can usually start your pension earlier – though not before age 55 unless you are retiring on ill health grounds – but your pension will nearly always be lower if you do.

In a defined benefit scheme (see Chapter 7 for a reminder of how these work), retiring early will mean you have been in the scheme for fewer years which will feed through to the amount of pension you get. In addition, your pension might be subject to an 'actuarial reduction' which is a cut to reflect the extra costs to the scheme of paying out your pension for longer. For example, consider a final salary scheme that pays a pension of 1/60th of your pre-retirement pay for each year you have been in the scheme. If you joined the scheme at age 50 and worked to age 65 by which time your salary was, say, £60,000 a year, your pension would be 1/60 × £60,000 × 15 = £15,000 a year. If you decided to stop early at age 60, even if your pay was the same, you pension according to the normal formula would be 1/60 × £60,000 × 10 = £10,000 a year. But, in addition, the scheme might impose an actuarial reduction of say 5 per cent for each year you retire early. Since you are retiring five years early, the reduction would be 5 × 5% = 25%, so you would get only 75% × £10,000 = £7,500 a year pension. Retiring five years early has halved your pension from £15,000 to just £7,500 a year.

In some situations, employers offer to enhance an early retirement pension, for example, if you have already completed a minimum number of years of service or if your employer wants to encourage voluntary redundancy. Ill-health pensions are often more generous, for example, they may be based on the number of years you would have worked if you could have stayed on until normal pension age and usually there will be no actuarial reduction. The precise rules differ for each scheme. If you are thinking about early retirement, you need to check the rules for your own scheme and request a benefit statement showing the pension you can expect from the early retirement age you are thinking about.

In a defined contribution scheme, you build up your own pot of savings – your pension fund – which you use to buy your pension at retirement, usually by buying an annuity. (An annuity is an investment where you give up a lump sum and in exchange get an income typically for life.) If you retire early, your pension is likely to be lower because:

■ less money goes into the fund when your and your employer's contributions stop early;

■ the fund has less time to grow, so you lose a substantial chunk of potential investment growth;

■ the amount of yearly pension you can buy with your fund will be less because the pension has to be paid out for longer. This will be reflected in a lower annuity rate (see p. 232).

Conversely, if you retire later than the normal pension age, your defined contribution pension is likely to be higher because you and your employer may continue paying in contributions, the fund has longer to grow and you may get a better annuity rate because the pension is likely to be paid out for fewer years.

The impact of later retirement on a defined benefit pension is less clear cut and depends on the rules of your particular scheme. For example, in a final salary scheme, the maximum pension from normal pension age is often 40/60th (two-thirds) of your pre-retirement pay. If you put off starting the pension to a later age, you might be able to earn extra but perhaps only to an absolute cap of, say, 45/60th of final pay. Once the cap has been reached, you might as well start the pension even if you will still carry on working.

Tax legislation requires you to start drawing a pension from any occupational scheme or personal pension no later than age 75.

## Tax-free cash from occupational and personal schemes

With occupational schemes and personal pensions, when you come to draw your pension before age 75, you can opt to swap part of it for a tax-free cash sum. The maximum lump sum is a quarter of your pension savings or benefits, though you can take less if you want. The larger the tax-free cash sum, the smaller your pension will be.

Taking a tax-free sum is popular and there are many ways you might use it, for example:

- **Pay off debts**. You might clear any remaining mortgage or pay off a car loan or credit card debts. This will reduce your outgoings, improving your budget and freeing up income for other purposes.

- **Spend it**. For example, you might want to replace perks you had through your job, such as a company car. Alternatively, you might just want to have some fun – take a big holiday or buy something you've always dreamed of (a boat, flying lessons, and so on). More pragmatically, you might want to update appliances such as kitchen equipment or add an extension to your home.

- **Give it away**. Your priority might be to help family members, for example, providing children or grandchildren with a deposit on a home or funding for school fees or university. See Chapter 11 for guidance on making lifetime gifts tax-efficiently.

- **Save and invest**. For example, you might want to set some aside as an emergency fund or invest to provide extra income. Chapters 9 and 10 consider saving and investing for income as a goal, but see also the box overleaf.

### Defined contribution schemes

In a defined contribution scheme, it will nearly always be worth taking the tax-free cash, since – as the box overleaf explains – even if you need income, you can probably invest it to provide more after tax than the pension you give up. But this may not be the case if your scheme offers you a pension that is guaranteed to be a minimum amount and that guarantee is higher than the income you could get through investing the lump sum.

### Using tax savings to boost your income

In any defined contribution scheme, which includes many occupational schemes and all personal pensions, even if you need the maximum possible pension, taking the tax-free lump sum could still make sense. This is because the pension you give up is taxable. You may be able to invest the lump sum to provide a tax-free income. Even if the income is taxable, you still have the benefit of the capital being tax-free – this is most easily seen if you look at the example of buying a purchased life annuity.

An annuity is an investment where you use a lump sum to buy an income, typically payable for the rest of your life. As you will explore on p. 232, annuities are a common way of providing pensions. But, when you use a pension fund to buy a pension annuity, the whole of the income you get is taxable. By contrast, when you use money from other sources to buy a purchased life annuity, only part of the income is taxable – the rest is treated as the gradual return of your capital and is tax-free. This means that the after-tax income you get from investing your tax-free lump sum can end up being higher than the after-tax income from the pension you gave up. See Chapter 9 for more ideas on investing tax-efficiently.

## *Defined benefit schemes*

In a defined benefit scheme, taking the tax-free lump sum is often not a good deal. The amount of lump sum you can have is worked out using a 'commutation factor' – this tells you the amount of lump sum you get for each £1 a year of before-tax pension you give up. For example, if the commutation factor is 16 then you would get £16 of lump sum for each £1 of pension.

A way to see if you are being offered a good deal is to compare the commutation factor with the amount of pension you could get if you used the lump sum to buy an annuity. In making this comparison, you need to compare like with like. For example, under current rules, the pension you are giving up would have been increased each year – usually by at least inflation up to 2.5 per cent a year. In a public sector scheme, the increases are normally in line with inflation without an upper limit. Therefore, you need to compare against an annuity that would provide an income that increases in a similar way.

Table 8.3 shows annuity rates in autumn 2009 and the commutation factors to which they are equivalent. You can think of these as break-even commutation factors – if your scheme offers you that factor or better, the deal is good. If your scheme offers you less – which is commonly the case – financially the deal is not great, so you should think carefully about whether you really want the lump sum (see the case study). For more information about annuities, see p. 232.

## Table 8.3 Break-even commutation factors

| If your scheme offers you this type of pension | The annuity rate for an equivalent income is[1] | | | | The break-even commutation factor is[2] | | | |
|---|---|---|---|---|---|---|---|---|
| | Man aged | | Woman aged | | Man aged | | Woman aged | |
| | 60 | 65 | 60 | 65 | 60 | 65 | 60 | 65 |
| Pension just for you increasing by up to 3 per cent a year | £408 | £480 | £372 | £444 | 25 | 21 | 27 | 23 |
| Pension for you and half-rate survivor's pension for your partner, increasing by 3 per cent a year | £348 | £408 | £360 | £420 | 29 | 25 | 28 | 24 |
| Pension just for you increasing in line with inflation | £348 | £420 | £312 | £384 | 29 | 24 | 32 | 26 |
| Pension for you and half-rate survivor's pension for your partner, increasing in line with inflation | £288 | £348 | £300 | £360 | 35 | 29 | 33 | 28 |

[1] The rate shows the amount of yearly income in the first year for each £10,000 of lump sum invested – see p. 232 for more information. Rates for non-smoker, for survivor pension male assumed to be five years older than woman.

[2] This is the cost of the annuity (£10,000) divided by the rate. For example, if £10,000 buys an annual income starting at £408, then £1 of income given up is worth a lump sum of £10,000/£408.

*Source*: Author's own work, annuity rates from Financial Services Authority, www.fsa.gov.uk/tables. Accessed 5 September 2009.

## Case study

> Adam, 64, is a senior planning officer with a local council. He has been in the final salary pension scheme 18 years and earns £35,000 a year. When he retires shortly, he will get a pension of 18 × 1/60 × £35,000 = £10,500 a year. He has the option to swap part of this for a tax-free lump sum and the commutation factor is 12. This means, for example, he could give up £1,000 a year of pension and get a lump sum of £12,000. The pension would be fully index-linked and includes a survivor's pension for his wife. Adam checks annuity rates and sees that, if he were to buy this type of pension for himself, he would have to pay around £29 for each £1 of income. The commutation factor of 12 that his scheme uses is a lot less than the factor of 29 that represents the true value of the pension. Adam decides to take the maximum pension without any lump sum.

## Other defined benefit scheme choices

Defined benefit schemes are designed to provide a package of benefits to all members. In general, the pension on offer is better than you would get from other types of scheme and so you can simply take up the pension at retirement with a minimum of fuss and few big decisions to make.

The section above looked at the key decision of whether or not to take a tax-free lump sum. The other major choice you might be offered concerns survivors' pensions. Typically, part of the package will be a pension for your husband, wife or other partner that would carry on being paid from the scheme if you were to die first. The pension would normally be half or two-thirds of the amount you had been getting before you died.

Some schemes give you the option to give up the pension for a surviving partner and instead receive a higher pension for yourself. So your pension will be lower if you include a pension for a surviving partner and higher if you don't. If you are a single person, opting out of the survivor's pension is likely to be a good idea. But, if you are married, in a civil partnership or live with somebody, think very carefully before opting out of the survivor's pension. Would your partner be able to cope financially if you died first? See Chapter 4 for more about this aspect of your financial planning.

If you have been in a pension scheme for many years, the benefits may have improved from time to time and this often applies with survivors' pensions. However, improvements will not necessarily have been backdated. For example, traditionally public sector schemes did not pay a survivor's pension at all to an unmarried partner. In general, this was changed from the start of 2007, but only your pension scheme membership from 2007 onwards counts towards the survivor's pension which could mean the pension for a surviving unmarried partner would be very low. You may be offered the choice at retirement of increasing the survivor's pension in exchange for a reduction in your own retirement pension. In making this choice, once again you need to think through what resources your partner would have if you die first and Chapter 4 will help you with this area of planning.

## Defined contribution scheme choices

In all types of defined contribution scheme, you will get a statement several months before your pension is due to start setting out the amount of pension the scheme will offer given the size of your pension fund. However, you do not have to accept this offer. Along with the statement, you'll get a letter explaining that you have the right to shop around and buy your pension elsewhere. This right is called your open market option (OMO). In most cases, you should definitely take this opportunity to shop around – it could easily increase your income for life by a fifth or even more.

After drawing out any tax-free lump sum (see p. 226), there are two main ways in which you might turn your remaining pension fund into pension:

▪ **Buy an annuity**. You can fairly easily shop around yourself for the annuities offering the best rates – a good, impartial source is the Compare Product tables on the Financial Services Authority's Moneymadeclear website (www.fsa.gov.uk/tables). Some internet comparison sites (such as www.moneyfacts.co.uk) also publish comparative tables. However, if you are not confident doing this or your circumstances are complicated (for example your health is very poor), this is an area where you might want the help of an independent financial adviser (see Chapter 2). Information to help you either choose your own annuity or get the best from using an adviser starts on p. 232.

▪ **Use income drawdown**. You keep your pension fund invested and draw an income direct from it. This option, which is explained on p. 241, is suitable only if you have a large pension fund or other sources of retirement income. This is not really an area where you should go it alone – get help from an IFA.

To find IFAs, including those who specialise in annuities and income drawdown, see the contact details in Appendix B.

The type of annuity or other choices you make now determine the whole package of benefits you have in retirement – for example, whether your pension increases over the years and whether it includes any pension for a partner if you die first.

## Choosing an annuity

There are two broad types of annuity:

- **With a lifetime annuity**, you give up a lump sum – in this case, your pension fund – and in exchange get an income for the rest of your life.
- **With a short-term annuity** (also called a 'temporary annuity'), you give up a smaller lump sum – a slice of your pension fund – and get an income payable for a fixed period.

With both, once you have bought the annuity, you can't change your mind and there is no way to cash in the annuity early to get a lump sum back. On the other hand, you lock into the annuity at the terms on offer at the time you buy and you are unaffected by any subsequent deterioration. So buying an annuity is an important decision that sets the financial circumstances for your whole retirement.

Most people use their pension fund to buy a lifetime annuity. If you do, then you are not just making an investment; you are also buying insurance against living a long time. To see how this works, imagine reaching retirement with savings of £100,000. You could invest this and live off the income but, at the end of your life, there would still be a capital sum of £100,000 that in a way has been wasted because it could have been providing you with extra income. To avoid this problem, you could instead estimate that you would live, say 20 years, and each year you could draw off the investment income and just enough of the capital so that after 20 years your savings have been run down to zero. That maximises your income, but what do you do if you survive longer than 20 years? You would have no income left. Essentially an annuity maximises your pension by using the investment income and capital but also guarantees to carry on paying that income even if you live beyond the point at which your money would have run out.

Annuities are offered by insurance companies. They group similar customers together in a pool and base the annuity rate on the average life expectancy of the people in the pool. The people who do not live as long as average subsidise the pensions for the people who live longer than average. This is exactly the same as the way, say, life insurance works, where the people in the insurance pool who do not die subsidise the cost of paying out to the survivors of the people who do die.

## Level annuities and annuity rates

The most basic type of annuity pays out the same income year after year and is therefore called a level annuity. It tends to be the most popular choice because it is straightforward and, compared with other annuities, gives you the highest starting income. The main drawback is that, as retirement progresses, rising prices eat into the buying power of the income.

# Case study

Ewa, aged 65, has a pension fund of £50,000. She shops around to find the best level annuity rate which is £624 a year for each £10,000 of pension fund. This gives her a pension of (£50,000/£10,000) × £624 = £3,120 a year. If inflation averages 2.5 per cent a year, by the time Ewa is 75, the pension will have only the same buying power as £2,437 today. This means the pension would then buy a fifth less than it does today.

The amount of income you get from an annuity is usually expressed as a rate stating the number of pounds of income you will get for each £10,000 you invest. This is the amount of income you get before tax. In the case of an annuity bought with a pension fund (sometimes called a 'compulsory purchase annuity'), the whole of the income is taxable. Annuity income can be paid monthly, quarterly or less frequently: you choose the period which is most convenient for you.

The annuity rate you can get is influenced by a variety of personal factors:

■ **Your age at the time you invest**. The older you are, the higher the income. This is because average life expectancy reduces with age, so the pension is likely to be paid out for a shorter period than for a younger person. The way rates are linked to age is one of the reasons why you will usually get a lower pension if you retire early and a higher pension if you retire later.

■ **Your sex**. Women tend to live longer than men, so they get a lower pension than a man for any given sum invested.

■ **Your health**. Some providers offer enhanced annuities (sometimes called 'impaired life annuities') that pay extra income if you have a health condition that is likely to reduce your life expectancy, for example, heart problems or diabetes. These annuities are assessed on a case-by-case basis and if your health problem is severe, the income you get could be much higher than for a healthy person.

■ **Lifestyle factors**. Some providers offer extra income to people who smoke because this reduces their life expectancy.

■ **Your occupation**. At least one provider offers higher annuities to people who have worked in the construction industry because life expectancy tends to be lower for people who have had tough manual jobs.

■ **Your postcode**. As a proxy for health and lifestyle, some providers now vary the rate according to your postcode, with higher levels of income being offered to people living in inner city areas than those living in leafy suburbs.

Table 8.4 shows some examples of the impact of some of these personal factors on the annuity rate you could get in autumn 2009. In addition, annuity rates are affected by broader social, economic and commercial factors:

■ **Increasing longevity**. People in general are tending to live longer due to better diet, advances in medicine and other factors. This means that a pension for someone of a specified age will have to be paid out for longer these days than it would have been in the past. This tends to push annuity rates down.

■ **Long-term interest rates**. Providers ensure they have the money to pay you the promised income by investing it into relatively safe, long-term, income-generating investments, such as UK government bonds and high quality corporate bonds – basically loans to the UK government and to companies (see Chapter 9). The return on these is sensitive to inflation. In a period of low inflation, such as the UK has experienced since the early 1990s, returns tend to be low and this depresses annuity rates.

■ **Insurance company reserves**. Just like a prudent household, insurance companies must keep some money in reserve in case of bad times. This money is put into safe, easily accessible investments but there is a cost to doing this because the invested reserves earn only a very low return. In 2009, new European laws were under discussion which, if adopted in the UK, would increase the level of reserves that annuity providers would have to hold. As a result, the providers were predicting that annuity rates might have to fall by as much as a fifth.[1]

Because of these broader factors, especially fluctuating interest rates, annuity rates are changing all the time, so when you are ready to buy, you need to check rates at that time. But there are also long-term trends in annuity

---

[1] Financial Times, *Insurers fear need for £50bn cash call*, 2 September 2009.

rates. Increasing longevity and a low-inflation environment in particular have contributed to a more than halving of annuity rates over the last 20 years: in 1990, a man, non-smoker, aged 65 could get a level income of around £1,500 a year for each £10,000 invested;[2] by 2009, this had fallen to just £672 a year.[3]

The final factor affecting the annuity rate you get is shopping around. Table 8.4 shows the best rates available at the time the data was gathered. But, for example, the worst rate for a man aged 65 was £571 a year for £10,000 invested.[4] This is 17 per cent lower than the best rate of £689 for a non-smoker and 28 per cent worse than the best rate for a smoker. People buying at the worst rate would have permanently denied themselves of one-fifth (non-smoker) or nearly a third (smoker) of the income they could have had. It really does pay to shop around.

**Table 8.4 Examples of how personal factors affect level annuity rates[1]**

| Age | Man | | Woman | |
| --- | --- | --- | --- | --- |
| | Non-smoker | Smoker | Non-smoker | Smoker |
| 55 | £563 | £598 | £541 | £587 |
| 60 | £616 | £682 | £584 | £651 |
| 65 | £689 | £792 | £644 | £754 |
| 70 | £793 | £945 | £728 | £897 |
| 75 | £966 | £1,183 | £853 | £1,127 |

[1] Annual income for each £10,000 invested.

Source: Data taken from Moneyfacts, *Investment, Life & Pensions Moneyfacts*, August 2009.

## Increasing annuities

You can at least partially avoid the problem of inflation eroding the buying power of your annuity income if you choose an increasing rather than level annuity. The main choice is between:

[2]  FT Business Information Ltd, *Money Management*, July 1990.

[3]  Financial Services Authority, www.fsa.gov.uk/tables. Accessed 5 September 2009.

[4]  Moneyfacts, *Investments, Life & Pensions Moneyfacts*, August 2009.

■ **An escalating annuity**. This increases by a fixed percentage every year – for example 3 or 5 per cent. This protects you from modest price rises, but leaves you still exposed if inflation climbs to high rates.

■ **An RPI-linked annuity**. This provides full inflation-proofing. The income you get rises each year in line with changes in the Retail Prices Index (see Chapter 1). During the rare periods when prices fall (as in 2009), technically your income should also fall, unless the terms and conditions for the annuity specifically rule this out. However, during 2009, several annuity providers waived their right to cut the income from RPI-linked annuities and maintained the income at an unchanged level.

The drawback with increasing annuities is that the starting income is a lot lower than you would get from a level annuity – see Table 8.5. (Annuity rates for increasing annuities tell you the amount of income you will get in the first year for each £10,000 invested.) It will usually be many years before the income catches up and even longer before you have received the same total income from the increasing annuity as you would have had from a level annuity, as shown in Table 8.5. For example, the table shows that a man aged 65 could get a level annuity paying an income of £672 a year for each £10,000 he invests. If instead he chose an RPI-linked annuity, the income would start at a much lower level of £420 a year but would increase in line with inflation. If inflation averaged 5 per cent a year, after 11 years the income would have increased to £684, just about the level of income being paid out by the level annuity. At that stage, the level annuity would have paid out 11 × £672 = £7,329 in total while the RPI-linked annuity would have paid out £5,967. It will be another eight years before the total paid out under the two annuities is roughly the same. With an average life expectancy of 21 years, this man would be marginally better off choosing the RPI-linked annuity. If prices increased at a faster rate than 5 per cent a year, he would be even better off. But if inflation were lower than 5 per cent a year, the level annuity would start to look the better deal.

Whether or not choosing an increasing annuity turns out well depends on the level of increases and how long you live. If you are risk averse, your inclination may be to take the level annuity, but in that case you do need to consider how you will cope with the effects of inflation as the years go by.

**Table 8.5  Level and increasing annuity rates[1] compared**

|  | Level annuity | Annuity with income increasing at 3% a year | RPI-linked annuity if inflation averages 5% pa |
|---|---|---|---|
| *Man aged 65* | | | |
| Starting income | £672 | £480 | £420 |
| Income catches up with level annuity | | Income in Year 13: £684 | Income in Year 11: £684 |
| Total paid out catches up with level annuity | | Year 23 | Year 19 |
| Life expectancy | | 21.0 | 21.0 |
| *Woman aged 60* | | | |
| Starting income | £564 | £372 | £312 |
| Income catches up with level annuity | | Income in Year 15: £563 | Income in Year 13: £560 |
| Total paid out catches up with level annuity | | Year 28 | Year 23 |
|  | | 28.1 | 28.1 |

[1] Annual income for each £10,000 invested.

*Source*: Author's own work, annuity rates from Financial Services Authority, www.fsa.gov.uk/ tables. Accessed 5 September 2009.

## Investment-linked annuities

Another way to try to beat inflation could be to choose an investment-linked annuity. With these, your income rises and falls in line with the value of investments in an underlying fund. When the annuity starts, you select a rate at which you expect the fund to grow each year and this determines your starting income. If you choose a high growth rate, your starting income is relatively high. If you choose a low growth rate, the starting income is lower. Each year, the actual growth rate of the investments is compared with the rate you selected. If the actual growth rate is higher, your income increases; if it is lower, your income falls. The higher the growth rate you selected at the outset, the bigger the chance that the income will fall.

There are two ways in which the underlying investments may be organised: on a with-profits or a unit-linked basis. These are described in detail in Chapter 10. The essential difference is this:

■ **With a with-profits fund**, some of the return from good years is held back to boost the return in poor years – a process called smoothing. The provider decides how much of the return should be passed to investors each year in the form of bonuses. The lowest possible bonus is nothing at all. So, if you choose a zero assumed growth rate at the outset (called the 'assumed bonus rate'), your income cannot fall and will rise if any bonus at all is declared.

■ **With a unit-linked fund**, the value of the underlying fund can fall as well as rise, so even if you choose a zero assumed growth rate, your income could still fall. But, in years when the fund does well, you will get the full benefit of the increase.

Not many people would be comfortable with a retirement income that varies unpredictably from one year to the next, especially if the income can fall. Therefore, investment-linked annuities are only suitable if you have a large pension fund to invest (well into six figures) or you have other more stable sources of income as well. If investment-linked annuities do appeal, then you might instead be interested in income drawdown (see p. 241).

### Capital protection

In general, the income from an annuity dies with you. This may put you off the idea of buying one for fear that you will die soon after taking it out and so not have had value for money. There are two types of annuity that let you guard against this:

■ **Capital protected annuity**. With this type, the annuity is guaranteed to pay out at least as much as you originally invested. For example, if you invest £10,000 for a level annuity of £672 a year, the annuity is guaranteed to pay out at least £10,000. After about 15 years you will have received that much in income. If you died after, say, ten years, you would have had £6,720 in income and the balance of your investment, £10,000 – £6,720 = £3,280 would be paid out as a lump sum to your heirs less income tax at a rate of 35 per cent (see Chapter 4 for information about tax on payments from pension arrangements to survivors).

■ **Annuity with guarantee.** This guarantees to pay out an income for a minimum number of years, usually five, but up to ten is allowed, even if you die within that period. The income would continue to be paid to whoever you nominate to receive it.

The price of these guarantees is usually a lower annuity rate, but the price is not necessarily high. If the period over which the guarantee will operate falls easily within the average life expectancy for someone of your age, the guarantee may cost little or even nothing to add. For example, in autumn 2009, a 65-year-old man (with an average life expectancy of 21 years) could get £672 a year for each £10,000 invested from a level annuity without any guarantee, the same income with a five-year guarantee, and a slight reduction to £660 a year with a ten-year guarantee.

## Short-term annuities

Another worry you might have is investing all of your pension fund at a time which, with hindsight, turns out to be a period when annuity rates were unusually low. To keep your options open, you could use just part of your pension fund to buy a short-term annuity. This runs for a maximum of five years which must end before you reach age 75. When the annuity comes to an end, you can use a further slice of your fund to buy another short-term annuity provided that too finishes before you reach age 75, a lifetime annuity, or move into income drawdown (see p. 241).

While short-term annuities protect you from locking your whole pension fund into a poor deal, equally they expose you to the risk of deteriorating annuity rates as the years go by. However, when you buy each successive annuity, you are a little bit older and benefit from the increase in annuity rates that comes with age.

## Providing for a partner

So far, this chapter has looked at annuities in terms of providing an income for your own lifetime (single-life annuities), but you can also buy joint-life-last-survivor annuities (often abbreviated to 'joint life annuities'). These pay out an income until the second of a couple dies. On the first death, the income may continue at the same rate or reduce by, say, one-third or a half. Joint-life annuities can pay out a level or an increasing income.

As with all annuities, the rate you get is heavily linked to life expectancy. For example if a man takes out a joint-life annuity to cover himself and his female partner who is the same age, the annuity rate will be reduced because the likelihood is that his partner will outlive him and so the annuity will have to pay out for longer than an equivalent annuity for his life alone. On the other hand, the reduction in income will be smaller for a woman buying an annuity that will pay out for her own life and that of a male partner of the same age, because on average he is likely to die before her. If your partner is much younger than you are, you may not be able to get a joint-life annuity at all. See Table 8.6 for some comparisons of single and joint-life annuity rates.

If your partner is financially dependent on you, or co-dependent (for example, you share household bills), a joint-life annuity is a good way of ensuring that they would be financially secure if you died. Don't be tempted to rely on an annuity with guarantee (see p. 239) which would pay a continuing income for a maximum of ten years – if your partner survived for longer, they would be left without enough income. See Chapter 4 for more information about planning to protect your family.

**Table 8.6  Single life and joint-life annuity rates[1] compared**

|  | Single life annuity rate | Joint-life-last survivor annuity rate[2] | Difference in annual income between single-life and joint-life rates |
|---|---|---|---|
| Level annuity bought by a man aged 65 with female partner aged 65 | £660 | £588 | £72 |
| Level annuity bought by woman aged 65 with male partner aged 65 | £612 | £576 | £36 |
| RPI-linked annuity bought by man aged 65 and female partner aged 60 | £420 | £324 | £96 |

[1] Annual income for each £10,000 invested.

[2] Income reducing by one-third on first death.

*Source*: Author's own work, annuity rates from Financial Services Authority, www.fsa.gov.uk/ tables. Accessed 5 September 2009.

## Income drawdown

Instead of buying an annuity, when you want to start your pension you could leave your pension fund invested and draw an income direct from your fund. As a concept, this is called 'income drawdown' or 'income withdrawal'. Because of tax legislation, you will also see this called taking an 'unsecured pension' if you use income drawdown before age 75 and having an 'alternatively secured pension' if you are aged 75 or over. At any time, you can move out of income drawdown and use the remaining pension fund to buy an annuity.

To prevent your pension fund running out before the end of retirement, the tax laws set limits on the income you can have:

■ **Before age 75 (unsecured pension).** The minimum pension you can draw is nothing. This means, at this stage of life, you could go into income drawdown purely to draw out the tax-free lump sum (see p. 226) but defer any pension until later. The maximum pension you can have is 120 per cent of the amount that a level annuity for someone of your age could have. Your income will be automatically reviewed every five years or sooner if you ask.

■ **Age 75 and over (alternatively secured pension).** The minimum pension you can have is 55 per cent of the amount of level annuity which a person aged 75 would have been able to get. The maximum is 90 per cent of that amount. Your income will be automatically reviewed every year but the limits will continue to be based on the annuity for a person aged 75, rather than your actual age.

Income drawdown may appeal if you enjoy being in control of your own investments (for example, while building up your pension savings, you may have opted for a self-invested personal pension), you think annuity rates offer a poor deal which you do not want to be locked into and/or you are hoping your family can inherit your remaining pension fund when you die. However, income drawdown is suitable only if you have a large pension fund (into six figures) or other sources of stable retirement income and you are not risk-averse. Moreover, a tightening of the tax rules in recent years means that the scope to leave your pension fund to your heirs is now severely limited if you die after age 75. To appreciate these limitations, you need to know something of how income drawdown works.

Earlier (p. 232), this chapter explained how annuities are a combination of an investment and insurance against living too long. Income drawdown is purely about investment and there is no insurance element. This means you get no cross-subsidy from people who die younger than you and you are reliant only on your own pension fund for your income. This means your investments have to work harder than they would have done within the framework of an annuity if they are to provide a comparable income. This extra return you need because you have not bought an annuity is called 'mortality drag'. The insurance company invests annuity investors' money in long-term gilts and high-quality corporate bonds (see p. 234). To get the extra return you need, you will have to invest in more risky investments, typically shares and share-based funds, which are explained in Chapters 9 and 10.

Bear in mind that the value of shares can go up and down. As part of the income drawdown process, your income is regularly reviewed. Between reviews, you may have drawn income from the fund and the value of the remaining investments may have gone up or down. At review, the income drawdown provider checks the value of the fund to see how much it could now buy if it were used to purchase a level annuity and this benchmark sets the lower and upper limits for your income for the next period. If the value of your pension fund has fallen, the maximum income you can draw will also fall. So income drawdown is suitable only if you can cope with an income that may fluctuate greatly from one review to the next.

Compared with buying an annuity, there are extra costs, in particular, charges for managing the investments in your fund and fees for the regular reviews. Therefore some of the return from investing your pension fund will be swallowed up in charges.

All in all, investment drawdown is more risky and more expensive than buying an annuity.

When it comes to inheritance, if you die before age 75, among other options (see Chapter 4 regarding pensions for survivors), the balance of your fund can be paid to your heirs after the deduction of income tax at a special pension scheme rate of 35 per cent. This is designed to claw back the tax reliefs that apply to pension savings – see Chapter 7 – since they were not intended to subsidise inheritance. Less benign rules apply if you die on or after age 75. In that case, unless your remaining pension fund is used to provide a pension for your partner or donated to charity, it is subject to both income tax and inheritance tax. The resulting tax charge may be as high as 82 per cent in 2009–10. Such high tax rates rule out using income drawdown as an effective route for inheritance planning.

---

**Third-way products** |

In recent years, providers in the USA and the UK have been experimenting with 'third-way products' that aim to combine some of the security of annuities with the opportunity that income drawdown offers for a higher investment-linked pension. Typically they combine lifetime annuities or short-term annuities with an element of income drawdown and offer either a guaranteed minimum income each year or a guaranteed minimum sum at age 75 which you can then use to buy a lifetime annuity. To date, these products have not been particularly successful because the extra charges for providing the guarantees and managing the investment elements eat too heavily into the extra income that might be generated. Also ensuring that the guarantees can be met limits the extent to which you can use share-based investments to provide the potential for extra income.

For now, third-way products do not look attractive. You can, in any case, create your own third way by splitting your pension fund, using some to buy an annuity to provide yourself with a secure minimum income and using the rest to buy investment-linked annuities or for income drawdown.

---

## Stress testing and review

Retirement security is about balancing your income and spending needs. Therefore stress testing involves looking at possible threats to your income and areas where your spending might rise as retirement progresses.

Probably the largest spending threat is the possibility of deteriorating health which may require increased spending on personal care. Chapter 5 looks in detail at financial planning for health and care needs. In the more general context of retirement planning, a key way to plan for health needs is either to set aside savings in earlier retirement for use later on or to organise your retirement income so that it increases in stages as retirement progresses – a process called 'phasing'. The same approach can also be used to deal with another more general and major risk, which is inflation eroding the buying power of your income. There are several ways you could phase your income, for example:

■ **Staggered buying of annuities**. You do not have to use your whole pension fund in one go to buy an annuity. You could use part to buy a lifetime annuity when you start retirement. The rest of your pension fund could be left to carry on growing and you could even still be paying in contributions up to age 75. In one or more later stages, you can annuitise the remaining fund.

■ **Increasing annuity** (see p. 235). If you opt for an annuity that increases by a fixed percentage each year or an annuity that increases with inflation, to some extent you have built-in phasing so that your income increases over time.

■ **Investment-linked annuity with low assumed growth rate** (see p. 237). By selecting a zero growth rate at the outset and an annuity where the underlying investment fund is invested on a with-profits basis, you set a minimum income which will not fall and which is likely to rise as retirement progresses.

■ **Income drawdown** (see p. 241). This gives you the flexibility to vary the income you draw from your pension fund, so you could start by taking just a small income, increasing the amount you draw off as the years go by.

If you have opted for investment-linked annuities or income drawdown, you are exposed to investment risk. You will find a lot more information about this and strategies for dealing with it in Chapters 9 and 10. More generally, you can partially protect yourself from investment risk by ensuring that your retirement income comes from a spread of sources, some of which – for example, a defined benefit pension from a work-based scheme or a level or increasing annuity – provide a stable, non-investment-linked income.

Where your retirement income planning is thrown off track – for example, because of investment returns being worse than you had allowed for – a possible fall-back position if you are a homeowner could be to release some of the equity tied up in your home.

## Using the equity tied up in your home

By the time Britons reach age 65, 77 per cent own their home, 70 per cent with no mortgage.[5] Their home is often the most valuable asset they have. Yet people over state pension age are more likely than the rest of the population to have an income below the poverty line. This situation is often called being asset-rich but income-poor. It is possible to use the equity tied up in your home to boost your income or provide a large lump sum in later life. In addition, housing equity is sometimes seen as a potential solution for society as a whole to the problems of pensioner poverty and paying for care in old age (see the box). But releasing equity will not be a suitable option for everyone and the products available – equity release schemes – need to be approached with caution.

[5] Department for Work and Pensions, *Family Resources Survey 2007–08*, 2009.

## Housing equity and social policy

### Pensions

In 2002, the government appointed a Pensions Commission to look into the problem of providing adequate pensions for all. In its final report, the Commission made the following points:

> Housing wealth...has major implications for appropriate pension system design. But it is not in itself a sufficient solution to problems of pension adequacy... A 55–59 year old with an income of between £17,500–£24,999 owned housing assets (net of mortgage debt) with a median value of around £150,000 in mid 2002. And while today only a very small proportion of these are used to fund retirement via equity release or trading down, with home ownership now reaching over 60% among those aged over 80, there will be an increasing flow of inheritance of housing assets, often by people who already own one house. For many people therefore, housing assets (either accumulated or inherited) could play a significant part in the provision of resources for consumption in retirement. But the ownership of these housing assets is not negatively correlated with pension rights: i.e. there is no significant tendency for those with inadequate pension rights to own larger houses. Home ownership therefore, while clearly relevant to pension provision for many people, cannot be seen as providing a total substitute for earnings-related pension provision.

> Source: Pensions Commission, A New Pension Settlement for the Twenty-First Century. The Second Report of the Pensions Commission, 2005 ('Second Turner Report').

### Long-term care

In 2009, the government launched the 'Big Care Debate' to explore how a new system could be created to provide care and support for elderly and frail people. One of the suggestions it had already floated in discussion groups was the idea that the system could be funded at least in part through the equity people have tied up in their homes:

> Internationally, several countries have introduced systems that focus on funding care and support for older people through contributions by older groups in the population... This recognises the fact that in many countries in the developed world there has been a shift in wealth from younger people to older people. This shift has also occurred in England. The generation currently in their 50s and 60s, or older, has benefited in particular from massive increases in property prices... In 2004, people over 60 held £932 billion in equity in their homes. This is likely to have dropped slightly with the fall in property prices, and we know that there is very wide inequality among older people. But the group of people over 60 remain the wealthiest generation that this country has ever seen... At our engagement events there was heated discussion... Many people ... did not believe that older people, who had worked all their lives, should have to pay for their care and support. There was a strong sense that it was not fair that people should have to use their housing assets to pay for any part of their care and support. But others, particularly younger people... argued that the increase in older people's housing wealth was not something that they had earned, so it was not fair that they should have an automatic right to keep it, at the expense of younger generations. The arguments on this point were probably the most heated at any of the events. There were very strong views on both sides.

> Source: Department of Health, Shaping the Future of Care Together, July 2009.

## Check your resources and circumstances

The only resource you need to be eligible for equity release is a suitable property. From the provider's point of view, your home must hold its value and be easy to sell when the time comes. Homes that might not be acceptable include: those with an unusual construction, leasehold properties with a lease of less than, say 80 years, sheltered housing since it typically has restrictions on who can buy which could make it hard to sell, and shared-ownership homes (where you own part and your council or housing association owns the rest). Your home must be in a reasonable state of repair. You must own your home outright or have only a small mortgage left which you will have to pay off with part of the money raised through the equity release. Usually you need to be aged at least 60 to be eligible for equity release but you get a better deal if you are older. Equity release schemes can be for couples as well as single people.

Depending on your needs and circumstances, there may be other options open to you that you should consider before deciding on equity release:

■ **Downsizing**. The easiest way to release the equity in your home is to sell and move somewhere cheaper.

■ **Grants and loans**. If the reason you are looking at equity release is to raise cash to pay for home repairs, adaptations or improvements, first check whether you are eligible for a grant or loan from, say, your local council. You are most likely to qualify if your income is low and/or you have a disability. Contact your local Home Improvement Agency (see Appendix B) for advice.

■ **Interest-only mortgage**. If you want to raise just a small sum (a few thousand pounds), an interest-only mortgage may be more suitable than an equity release scheme. These loans are available from building societies and banks. You pay interest on the loan – so you need to check that you can afford these payments out of your monthly income – and the capital is repaid only when the home is eventually sold. If you are eligible for pension credit (see p. 212), this may be increased to cover the interest payments, if the money raised is used for 'essential' work on your home, such as repairing your heating system or a badly leaking roof, or replacing dangerous wiring.

■ **A lodger**. If you have space, you could boost your income by letting a room in your home. Under the 'rent-a-room scheme', you can have up to £4,250 a year in rent tax-free. For information, contact HM Revenue & Customs (see Appendix B).

# Equity release schemes

Equity release schemes are financial products that enable you to raise an income and/or lump sum from the value of your home while retaining the right to live there for as long as you need to – usually until you die or move into long-term residential care (see Chapter 5 for care options). If you take out a scheme as a couple, it continues until the second of you no longer needs the home.

There are two main types of scheme: lifetime mortgages and reversion schemes.

## Lifetime mortgages

You borrow against the value of your home. Typically, you use a 'roll-up mortgage' which means that instead of paying the interest each month, the interest is added to the outstanding loan. Because of compounding – in other words, the fact that interest is charged on the rolled-up interest not just the amount originally borrowed – the loan can increase alarmingly over the years, as demonstrated by the example in Table 8.7. When you eventually no longer need your home, it is sold. The equity-release firm collects the amount it is owed. The remainder passes to your heirs. Whether or not there is any remainder depends on:

■ **How house prices have changed.** If they have risen, even though the rolled-up loan has increased, there may still be some of the proceeds from selling your home left to pass on.

■ **No-negative-equity guarantee.** In the late 1980s, some consumers were badly burned by poorly designed lifetime mortgages which left the borrowers owing more than their homes were worth when house prices fell in the early 1990s (see Figure 6.1 on p. 147). As a result, most lifetime mortgages since then have, as a built-in feature, a no-negative-equity guarantee. This is a promise that the loan outstanding will be capped at the value of the home. However, in 2009, following another fall in house prices – which this time hurt the providers rather than the consumers – some providers were talking about reverting to schemes without this type of guarantee.

A popular variant on the standard lifetime mortgage is a drawdown scheme. With this, instead of borrowing a single large amount, you arrange a facility to borrow but draw off the loan in a succession of small sums. You can either do this in an *ad hoc* way or make regular withdrawals to in effect provide yourself with an income. A big advantage of the drawdown scheme is that interest is charged only on the amount you have actually borrowed so the outstanding loan builds up more slowly than with a standard scheme.

**Table 8.7 How a roll-up mortgage could grow**

| Years since loan taken out | How each £10,000 borrowed would grow with interest charged at: | | | | | |
|---|---|---|---|---|---|---|
| | *5% pa* | *6% pa* | *7% pa* | *8% pa* | *9% pa* | *10% pa* |
| 1 | £10,500 | £10,600 | £10,700 | £10,800 | £10,900 | £11,000 |
| 5 | £12,763 | £13,382 | £14,026 | £14,693 | £15,386 | £16,105 |
| 10 | £16,289 | £17,908 | £19,672 | £21,589 | £23,674 | £25,937 |
| 15 | £20,789 | £23,966 | £27,590 | £31,722 | £36,425 | £41,772 |
| 20 | £26,533 | £32,071 | £38,697 | £46,610 | £56,044 | £67,275 |
| 25 | £33,864 | £42,919 | £54,274 | £68,485 | £86,231 | £108,347 |

### Why negative equity may be important

Assume you might take out a lifetime mortgage to provide yourself with extra income and live in your home until you die. Suppose the house is then sold and the proceeds fall short of the amount owed on your mortgage. The shortfall becomes a debt of your estate, so other assets may have to be sold to pay it off. If your estate is not big enough to clear the whole debt, the balance has to be written off. So, without a no-negative-equity guarantee, your heirs do not inherit your home and may inherit less from your other assets. In the extreme, they might not inherit anything at all. Whether or not this matters, is a personal decision for you and your heirs. It is a problem for your heirs if they have been relying on an inheritance, but a problem for you only if helping your heirs features as a high priority in your financial plan.

However, negative equity *is* a problem for you if you may need to move after having taken out the lifetime mortgage. For example, you might decide to move closer to your children or to switch to somewhere with a smaller garden. Then negative equity becomes your problem because you would have to find assets over and above the sale proceeds of your home to clear the debt before you could move. Therefore, you should be very wary of taking out a lifetime mortgage that does not have a no-negative-equity guarantee. Even with a guarantee, you may find that after paying off a lifetime mortgage, you have too little equity left for a deposit on a new home.

## *Home reversion schemes*

The other type of equity release scheme is the home reversion scheme. With this, you sell part, or all, of your home in return for a lump sum. If you need income, you can invest the sum to provide this (see Chapters 9 and 10). You become a tenant with the right to remain in your home for as long as you need, either rent-free or paying just a trivial sum.

You do not get full value for the part of the home you sell – for example, you might sell half your home worth, say, £100,000 and get a lump sum of £50,000. The precise amount you get depends on your age and sex. You can think of this shortfall as representing the commercial rent a tenant would normally pay. The reversion company instead of receiving regular rent gets a larger share of the sale proceeds when your home is sold. Because the company has to wait – maybe many years – to get this money, there is also the sense of interest rolling up with the rent. The longer you are expected to live, the longer the company expects to have to wait to see a return on its investment (the purchase of your home). For this reason, the longer your life expectancy – in particular, the younger you are – the lower the sum you will get relative to the amount of your home that you sell.

# Stress test and review

Once you have taken out a home reversion scheme, you cannot buy your property back. Although you can in theory pay off a lifetime mortgage early, the potentially large sum involved may make this impossible. This makes the opportunity for and need for review very limited. Therefore, it is essential that you check before you buy that a scheme would be suitable for you, thinking about both your circumstances now and how they might change in future.

Home reversion schemes are not the best choice when house prices are low, since you will be selling part of all of your home for less than you would get when prices are more buoyant and it will be the provider not you who benefits from any subsequent recovery in prices. Lifetime mortgages do not suffer from this drawback. Although a low valuation may restrict the amount you can borrow, any subsequent rise in house prices goes to you rather than the equity release provider.

There are a number of important issues to take into account with any equity release scheme, including any impact on your tax and benefits position (see the box overleaf), what charges you will have to pay and ensuring that your property is independently valued (especially in the case of a home reversion scheme). You may also want to discuss your intentions with your family if they might be expecting to inherit the home from you – this could save disputes later on.

It is essential to check your on-going obligations. With both types of equity release, you will be expected to keep your home in a state of reasonable repair. With a reversion scheme, you become a tenant, so you should check the tenancy agreement carefully to understand your rights and obligations, and you are strongly advised to get help from a solicitor with this. With both lifetime mortgages and reversion schemes, check whether there are any restrictions on how you use the property (for example, running a small business, keeping a pet, leaving the property empty for an extended period if say you over-winter in Spain), restrictions on who can live there (such as a lodger, someone who becomes your carer or your partner if you form a relationship after you have taken out the scheme). Also check what happens if you want to move: can you transfer the scheme to another suitable property?

If you are using equity release to provide yourself with extra income, be aware that the buying power will tend to fall over the years because of inflation – see p. 243 for general guidance on planning your retirement income to deal with inflation.

### Tax and benefits

In general, income you raise through equity release schemes counts as taxable income. The effective tax rate on this income could be high if it causes you to lose any tax-free allowance. When you reach age 65, you become eligible for a higher tax allowance (see Appendix A) but the extra allowance is progressively withdrawn if your income exceeds a set limit (£22,900 in 2010–11). From 2010–11 onwards, even the standard personal allowance that everyone gets will be withdrawn if your income exceeds £100,000 a year. Lump sums you raise through equity release do not count as income. You could avoid tax problems by, for example, using a drawdown lifetime mortgage.

Any income or capital you raise through equity release will normally count when working out your eligibility for means-tested benefits, such as pension credit or council tax benefit. The Pension Service or your local Citizens Advice Bureau (see Appendix B) can check the impact of equity release on your benefits for you.

If you take advice about equity release from either a provider or a financial adviser, the firm must consider the impact of the scheme on your tax position and benefits or refer you to someone else who can advise you on this aspect.

## Choosing equity release

Equity release schemes and their impact on your finances are complex, so you may want to get help from an independent financial adviser (IFA). Even if you don't use an IFA, you should use a solicitor to check the legal side of the mortgage or sale of your home.

If you want to shop around yourself, you can find comparative tables of schemes in the print publications *Moneyfacts* and *Investments, Life & Pensions Moneyfacts* published by Moneyfacts, and occasional surveys in personal finance magazines, such as *Money Management*. Many equity release providers belong to Safe Home Income Plans (SHIP), a trade body which requires its members to abide by a code of conduct and can provide a list of its members. The charity, Age Concern–Help the Aged, produces a detailed free information booklet called *Equity release and income-related benefit*. (See Appendix B for contact details.)

When you express interest in a particular lifetime mortgage or home reversion plan, the provider or adviser must give you a personalised Key Facts Illustration, setting out the main features of the scheme in a standardised format that helps you compare one scheme with another.

See Appendix B for all contact details.

# 9

# Saving and investing

## Introduction

The core of much financial planning is building up (accumulating) or using (decumulating) wealth. Thus, virtually all goals can be reduced to creating or increasing a lump sum – growth – or investing to provide a stream of income. This is the case whether you are, for example, building up a pension, saving to pay for your child's education, establishing an emergency fund, saving for a wedding, boosting your income as a student, paying for care or drawing an income in retirement.

This chapter and Chapter 10 look at the products and strategies you can use to meet saving and investing goals. In addition to the focus of the goal – growth or income – other key factors, which will drive your choice of product or strategy are:

- **Timeframe.** Over what period do you need to save or draw income – is this a short-, medium- or long-term goal?
- **Risk.** What is your attitude towards risk?
- **Tax.** What is your tax position?

The first half of this chapter looks at the impact of these factors on basic investment strategies. The second half of the chapter describes the key building blocks of saving and investment: cash products, bonds and shares. Chapter 10 considers how these and other investments, including property, investment funds and derivatives, can be built into strategies for managing your wealth.

**Investment funds**

These are ready-made portfolios that let you pool your money with other people's in order to invest in a wide range of underlying investments.

# Timeframe and risk

Chapter 1 briefly considered risk, by which most people mean 'capital risk', in other words, the risk of losing some or all of your original investment (your capital). This chapter develops the idea of risk and considers the trade-off all investors face between different types of risk.

Central to saving and investing is the concept that risk and return go hand in hand. This means if you are risk averse (see p. 8), you must be prepared to accept a lower return; if you want the chance of a higher return, you must take on extra risk. There are three core risks involved in this concept:

- **Capital risk.** This can be defined more widely as the risk of losing your original capital or the return that you have already built up. This risk is associated particularly with investments, such as shares, that are traded on a stock market where their price can fall rather than rise.

- **Liquidity risk.** This is the risk that you cannot get your money back at the time you need it. This may be because you have invested for a set term – maybe a building society savings bond where you have tied up your money for two years. Alternatively, you might be able to get at your money but only by paying a penalty charge that in effect wipes out any extra return you would have had.

- **Income risk.** This is a risk where you have invested for an income whose value can fall. This may arise because you have invested in savings products that offer a variable rather than fixed rate of interest and the rate is cut. It could also occur because you have chosen, say, share-based investments where the income (dividends) may be cut or missed altogether rather than the reasonably secure fixed returns offered by government bonds.

If you are investing for the long term, you might consider taking on any of these risks in order to boost your chance of a superior return. If you are investing for the short term, whatever you attitude towards risk, it is usually inappropriate to take on capital risk and any liquidity risk should be avoided or minimised by matching the term of your savings and investments to the time horizon you have for needing your money back. Short-term investors may, however, be comfortable taking on income risk.

The core risks above are balanced against the 'nominal' return from your investment, in other words the return in cash terms. But you'll recall from Chapter 1 that inflation is an important factor in all medium- and long-term financial planning. The need to maintain the buying power of your money, whether you are a growth or an income investor, is another major driver pushing you to take on these core risks in order to generate returns that are positive in 'real' (inflation-adjusted) terms, not simply nominal.

While you can estimate what inflation will be in the future and make your investment decisions accordingly, you cannot know whether your forecast will turn out to be right. This uncertainty makes rising prices not just a factor to be dealt with but another area of risk – inflation risk – that you need to take into account.

The impact of inflation is not usually an issue for short-term investors, unless inflation reaches very high levels (as for example it did in the UK in the later 1970s).

### Bond confusion

The word 'bond' is used throughout the financial world as a name for many different types of saving and investment. In its purest sense a bond is a loan issued by a government or company and traded on the stock market (see p. 285). But the term has also been taken up to describe savings products (such as premium bonds – see p. 282 – and bank and building society fixed-term accounts – see p. 281). In addition, it is commonly used by insurance companies to describe some of their investments, where typically you invest a lump sum for income or growth (such as with-profits bonds and unit-linked bonds – see p. 320). This book generally uses 'bonds' to mean government and corporate loans traded on the stock market and makes clear if the word is being used in another sense.

## Risk and return

The three core risks outlined above – capital risk, liquidity risk and income risk – are collective terms that hide the underlying sources of risk. For example, capital risk may be implicit in an investment because: it is traded on a market where its price can fall (what most people mean by capital risk); it is offered by a company that might go out of business and renege on its debts (default risk, also called credit risk); it is denominated in a foreign currency and the exchange rate moves (exchange rate risk); and so on.

Given the many potential sources of risk and the fact that investment products can often be used in different ways that may increase the inherent risk, there is no neat, definitive way to rank products in order of their risk–return balance. You will always have to look at each product individually to assess precisely where the balance lies. Nevertheless, Figure 9.1 gives an indication of rank as a rough starting point. The letters after each investment indicate the predominant risks in each case.

# Balancing risks

It is impossible to eradicate all risk from your saving and investment strategies. For example, a saver who wants to avoid all capital risk will usually avoid bonds and shares whose price can fall but, in doing so, must accept a lower return which increases inflation risk – and also the risk of failing to meet any pre-set target (in this book, called shortfall risk). An investor who wants to reduce inflation risk must either accept the liquidity risk of locking into index-linked returns or the capital risk of investments traded on the stock market. Therefore, the first step in building a strategy is to decide how you want to balance the core risks against inflation risk and shortfall risk.

## Inflation risk v liquidity or capital risk

The most widely used strategy for an investor who wants to reduce inflation risk is to accept the capital risk inherent in shares. Shares reflect the profits of the company that issues them. Profits are the gap between revenue and expenses, both of which can be expected to rise broadly in line with inflation. Therefore, over time shares can be expected to give returns that tend to at least keep pace with inflation and this has generally been the case over the last hundred years, as demonstrated in Table 9.1. The table reports the results of research carried out by Barclays Capital. It shows the before-tax real return – that is, the return over and above gains due simply to inflation – from equities (shares), gilts (government bonds), index-linked gilts and cash (building society savings account) since 1908. There are just three decades – 1908–18, 1968–78 and 1998–2008 – when shares failed to beat inflation. The first of these decades encompasses the First World War; the second includes the early 1970s when mushrooming inflation, rising unemployment and industrial action pushed Britain into political and economic turmoil; and the third period is dominated by the dotcom crash of 2000–03 and the global financial crisis that hit the world in 2007. In 1908–18, cash was hit even harder than equities, so it is only during 1968–78 and 1998–2008 that cash turned out to be the better investment than shares. In all the remaining decades, shares outperformed cash, often by a very large margin.

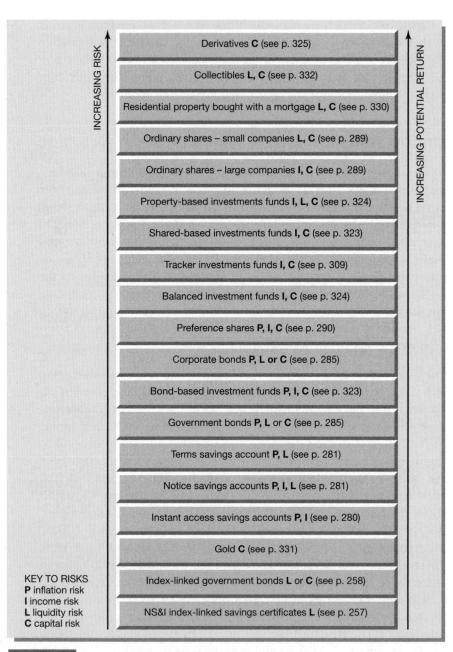

**Figure 9.1** Investments ranked by risk and return

**Table 9.1  Real return from investments each decade since 1908**

| Decade | Equities % pa | Gilts % pa | Index-linked gilts % pa | Cash % pa |
|---|---|---|---|---|
| 1908–18 | –3.5 | –7.4 | | –4.8 |
| 1918–28 | 10.3 | 7.0 | | 6.9 |
| 1928–38 | 3.6 | 6.7 | | 2.4 |
| 1938–48 | 3.9 | 0.8 | | –2.6 |
| 1948–58 | 7.1 | –4.5 | | –1.8 |
| 1958–68 | 11.0 | –1.4 | | 1.9 |
| 1968–78 | –3.5 | –3.3 | | –2.7 |
| 1978–88 | 12.4 | 5.8 | | 3.8 |
| 1988–98 | 11.1 | 8.7 | 6.0 | 4.7 |
| 1998–2008 | –1.5 | 2.4 | 1.9 | 2.4 |

*Source*: Barclays 2009 Equity Gilt Study, Barclays Capital.

However, there is another strategy for protecting yourself against expected future price rises: inflation-proofed investments. In the UK, there are just two main investments of this type, both issued by the UK government. They are National Savings and Investments (NS&I) index-linked certificates and index-linked gilts. NS&I is an agency that issues savings products on behalf of the government. Its index-linked certificates allow savers to invest for a fixed term (three or five years for certificates taken out in 2009) during which they earn interest. The interest is set at a fixed rate (1 per cent in 2009) plus any increase in the Retail Prices Index (RPI). For example, if inflation as measured by the RPI were 2 per cent a year, your return would be 1% + 2% = 3% a year. If inflation were 10 per cent a year, you would get 1% + 10% = 11%. The value of the certificates does not fall, so if inflation were negative (deflation), you would just earn the flat 1 per cent a year.

Unlike shares which increase the likelihood that you will beat inflation but make no guarantees, NS&I index-linked certificates remove the uncertainty completely. Your return will always beat inflation by the 1 per cent margin whatever the rate of inflation turns out to be and whatever disasters befall the economy. (Being a government agency, NS&I is backed by the UK government and the risk of default is considered negligible.)

Although the certificates enable you to remove inflation risk, there is a price for this in terms of a potentially low return (1 per cent nominal) compared with other savings products. There is also an increase in liquidity risk, because you must tie up your money for the full term in order to get the full promise of inflation-proofing.

Index-linked gilts are a type of government bond (see p. 285). All bonds have broadly the same structure: you lend money to the government or company that issues the bond and usually receive regular fixed amounts of interest. The bond typically has a fixed lifetime (the term) at the end of which the loan is repaid (redeemed). But you do not have to hold bonds for their full term because they can be bought and sold on the stock market. It is important to appreciate that, if you buy a bond (either when it is first issued or on the stock market) and hold it until redemption, the return you get is fixed at the time you buy because the interest is fixed and so is the redemption value. But, if you sell bonds on the stock market, your return is not fixed because bond prices rise and fall and you cannot predict in advance what price you will be able to get.

Index-linked bonds follow the normal bond format except both the interest payments and the redemption value change in line with changes in the RPI. (Unlike the NS&I certificates, the payments from index-linked government bonds would fall if the change in the RPI were negative, in other words, there was deflation.) This means if you buy an index-linked bond and hold it to redemption, the return you get is fixed but in real, rather than nominal, terms – see the case study. As with other bonds, if you sell an index-linked bond before redemption, your return ceases to be fixed because you cannot know the price at which you can sell and so you lose the guarantee of inflation-proofing.

As with the NS&I certificates, the interest offered by index-linked gilts before the inflation-proofing is added looks low relative to the return from competing non-inflation-proofed investments. So, once again, the price of removing inflation risk is a potential reduction in return and an increase in liquidity risk, because the only way to guarantee the inflation-proofing is to hold to redemption. You can sell the gilts before redemption but then you trade liquidity risk (being unable to access your money immediately) for capital risk (being able to get some money back now but only by accepting the market price, which could mean making a loss or a profit).

## Case study

In 2008, Ed invested £40,000 in an index-linked government bond, 1¼ per cent Index-Linked Treasury Gilt 2055, which pays out interest every six months. In May 2008, he received interest of £184.46. Between May and November, inflation increased by 2.8 per cent and his next interest payment in November 2008 increased in line to £189.62. Between November 2008 and May 2009, inflation fell by 3.1 per cent, and his interest payment also fell to £183.78.

## Inflation risk v liquidity, income and capital risks

One of the most challenging investment goals is to produce income over a long period of time. The ideal would be to make a single investment at the outset that would produce a stable, adequate income for as long as you need it. A traditional way to do this, much favoured in the nineteenth century, was to invest in government stocks. But both the fixed income these provide and the fixed capital you tie up in them until redemption are eroded by inflation. A stable income has to be one that is capable of maintaining its buying power as time goes by.

A choice not open to nineteenth century investors was the index-linked government bonds discussed above, which were introduced in the UK in 1981. Income seekers can now invest for a long-term, inflation-proofed income either by buying these bonds direct or indirectly by opting for an RPI-linked annuity (see Chapter 8). Annuities (an investment where you swap a lump sum for an income paid either for the rest of your life or a set period) are offered by insurance companies. To ensure they can deliver the promised income, the companies invest your lump sum payment in suitably matched investments. If the company has promised to pay you an RPI-linked income, it will invest the bulk of your money in index-linked government bonds. This is the lowest risk strategy for providing yourself with a stable income. However, it is also the most expensive. The return from index-linked gilts is modest and the starting income from RPI-linked annuities is low. So the price of eradicating inflation risk is a reduction in return – that may simply make this goal far too expensive – and liquidity risk. The latter is taken to an extreme in the case of buying an annuity because, once bought, you cannot reverse the deal or sell your annuity in an open market to get your original capital back – you are locked in permanently.

The alternative is to look at investments that offer the chance, though not the guarantee, of both income growth to protect your buying power and capital growth to protect your underlying capital from erosion by inflation. Once again, shares are a main candidate, alongside investing in property to generate rental income. In both cases, you must however accept that both your income and your capital may fall as well as rise – in other words, you are exposed to both income and capital risk.

## Shortfall risk v capital risk

As Table 9.1 on p. 257 shows, over the long-term, shares tend to outperform those investments, such as bonds and savings accounts, which are characterised by lower capital risk. This is the other main reason, apart from protection against inflation, why investors opt to take on additional risk. Some goals – such as paying off an endowment mortgage (see Chapter 5) or saving for retirement (see Chapter 7) involve building up a target lump sum. Although in theory this could be achieved using low-risk products, such as savings accounts, in practice the probable lower return would mean your having to save impossibly large amounts. Table 9.2 shows the amount you would need to save each month to build up £10,000 over different time periods and given different rates of return. As you can see, if you were saving for a pension over a period of 30 years and the return averaged 2 per cent (the average from cash over the last 50 years, according to the Barclays Capital research), you would need to save twice as much each month as you would if the return were 6 per cent (close to the average return from equities over the past 50 years). If you were saving over 25 years to pay off a £100,000 endowment mortgage, you would need to save £260 a month (on top of your mortgage interest payments) if the rate of return were 2 per cent a year compared with £150 a month if the return were 6 per cent a year. If your return would be reduced by tax (see below), you would need to save even more.

Opting for lower risk investments either involves a commitment to saving large amounts or taking a gamble that the return from savings accounts will buck the historical trend and produce a high enough return for you to reach your target. If returns from savings accounts over the long-term are likely to be similar to those for the past 50 years, there is a high risk that you will fail to reach your target – in other words, an increase in shortfall risk. To reduce shortfall risk, you would need to embrace the additional capital risk inherent in investments such as shares.

# How savings and investments are taxed

So far, this chapter has looked at the return from investments without any explicit discussion of tax. But if you have to pay tax on your

### Table 9.2  How much you need to save

*The table shows the amount you would need to save each month to generate a lump sum of £10,000 (as a nominal value) after various numbers of years at different rates of return.*

| | Term (years) | | | | |
|---|---|---|---|---|---|
| Rate of return %pa | 10 | 15 | 20 | 25 | 30 |
| 1 | £79 | £51 | £38 | £29 | £24 |
| 2 | £75 | £48 | £34 | £26 | £20 |
| 3 | £72 | £44 | £31 | £22 | £17 |
| 4 | £68 | £41 | £27 | £20 | £15 |
| 5 | £65 | £38 | £25 | £17 | £12 |
| 6 | £61 | £35 | £22 | £15 | £10 |
| 7 | £58 | £32 | £20 | £13 | £9 |
| 8 | £55 | £29 | £17 | £11 | £7 |
| 9 | £52 | £27 | £16 | £9 | £6 |
| 10 | £50 | £25 | £14 | £8 | £5 |

income or profits, an investment will have to work even harder to give you the returns you need. Therefore, the varied tax treatment of different investments is a major factor to take into account in your planning. Tax treatment does not depend simply on the tax features of the investment concerned but the way this interacts with your personal tax position. Appendix A sets out the basics of the UK tax system as a whole and enables you to work out what type of taxpayer you are – this is summarised in Table 9.3, together with an indication of the types of investment that are most likely to suit you or not based on tax grounds.

The rest of this section describes how broad types of investment are taxed and how this relates to your own tax status. The taxation of an investment becomes more favourable if it can be put inside a tax wrapper (see p. 270). The most common wrappers are pension schemes and individual savings accounts (ISAs).

**Table 9.3  Types of taxpayer**

| Type of taxpayer[1] | What this means | Good investment features | Poor investment features |
|---|---|---|---|
| Non-taxpayer | Your income is too low for you to pay income tax. | Government bonus added (e.g. personal pensions, Saving Gateway). Income paid gross (e.g. some NS&I products, offshore savings accounts, government and corporate bonds). Tax already deducted is reclaimable (e.g. savings accounts). | Tax already deducted cannot be reclaimed (e.g. shares, share-based investment funds, investment-type life insurance). |
| Starting-rate taxpayer | Your income is low and your top rate of income tax is 10 per cent in 2010–11 (on savings income). | Tax-free investments (e.g. cash ISAs, personal pensions). Income paid gross (e.g. some NS&I products, offshore savings accounts, government and corporate bonds). Tax already deducted is reclaimable (e.g. savings accounts). | Tax already deducted at more than 10% cannot be reclaimed (e.g. investment-type life insurance). |
| Basic-rate taxpayer | Your top rate of tax is 20 per cent in 2010–11. | Tax-free investments (e.g. some NS&I products, cash ISAs, pension schemes). Tax is already deducted (convenient) (e.g. most savings accounts, shares, most investment funds). Income is paid gross (delay before tax has to be paid) (e.g. offshore accounts). Return is capital gain rather than income.[2] | Capital gains tax already deducted cannot be reclaimed (e.g. investment-type life insurance). |

#### Table 9.3 Types of taxpayer *continued*

| Type of taxpayer[1] | What this means | Good investment features | Poor investment features |
|---|---|---|---|
| Higher-rate and additional-rate taxpayers | For higher-rate taxpayers: your top rate of tax is 40 per cent in 2010–11.<br><br>For additional-rate taxpayers: your top rate is tax is 50 per cent from 2010–11. | Tax-free investments (e.g. some NS&I products, cash and stocks-and-shares ISAs, pension schemes).<br><br>Income is paid gross (delay before tax has to be paid) (e.g. offshore accounts).<br><br>Return is capital gain rather than income (e.g. growth investment funds (other than life-insurance based).[2] | Return taxed as income while return from competing investments taxed as capital gain (e.g. most types of investment-type life insurance).<br><br>Capital gains tax already deducted cannot be reclaimed (e.g. investment-type life insurance). |

[1] Income tax position.

[2] You have a substantial capital gains tax allowance (£10,100 in 2009–10) and, at the time of writing in 2009–10, the capital gains tax rate was 18 per cent. However, the capital gains tax rate for 2010–11 was yet to be announced and it was strongly expected that the government would increase the rate.

## Capital gains and tax

Some investments – for example, shares, most investment funds and buy-to-let property – produce a profit because you can sell them at a higher price than you bought them at. This difference is called a capital gain and there may be capital gains tax (CGT) to pay on any such profit. However, there are some reliefs you can claim (see Appendix B) and everyone has a fairly large yearly CGT allowance (£10,100 for 2009–10) which is usually increased each year in line with inflation. Most people do not make full use of their allowance and do not pay CGT. Therefore, you often have scope to save tax if you choose investments that produce a capital gain rather than income.

Even where you do pay CGT – for example, on the sale of a rental property – tax was charged at a flat rate of 18 per cent in 2009–10 which was usually lower than the rate you would pay on income. This made investments producing gains look more attractive on tax grounds than those which produce income. However it was expected, at the time of writing, that the rate might be increased in 2010–11.

## Income tax and savings

Savings accounts and some other investments (such as government and corporate bonds) pay interest and this is classified for tax purposes as 'savings income'. Savings income may be taxed in one of three ways: tax-free; taxable but paid gross (before any tax is deducted); or taxable and paid net (with some tax already paid).

### Tax-free savings income

The interest from some NS&I products – cash ISAs, NS&I certificates, premium bonds and children's bonus bonds – is always tax-free. The interest from bank and building society savings accounts is normally taxable, but becomes tax-free if you invest through a tax wrapper, such as an individual savings account (see p. 272).

### Savings income paid net

Usually, savings income is paid with basic-rate tax already deducted and this applies, for example, to most bank and building society accounts.

If you are a non-taxpayer, you can claim back this tax or arrange to have the interest paid gross (see the box). If you are a basic-rate taxpayer, the tax deducted exactly matches your tax bill, so there is no further tax to pay and none to reclaim. If you are a higher-rate taxpayer or, from 2010–11, an additional-rate taxpayer, you must pay extra tax (usually via the self-assessment system – see Appendix A) to bring the tax paid up to either 40 or 50 per cent of the gross interest.

You can convert the net interest you receive into the gross amount either by adding back the tax deducted or by 'grossing up' – see box. For example, if you receive net interest of £80 from which £20 tax has been deducted, the gross dividend is £100. Using the grossing-up method, the gross dividend is £80/(1 – 20%) = £80/0.8 = £100.

> ### Non-taxpayer and starting-rate taxpayers
>
> If you receive interest with tax at the basic rate already deducted, you can claim back all of this tax if you are a non-taxpayer or half of the tax if you are a starting-rate taxpayer. To do this, use form R40 'Claim for repayment of tax deducted from savings and investments'. Either download the form from the HM Revenue & Customs website or ask your tax office to send you a copy (see Appendix B).
>
> If you are a non-taxpayer, instead of claiming tax back each year, you can register to receive the interest gross without any tax deducted. To do this, complete form R85 'Getting your interest without tax taken off', which you can get from your savings account provider or the Revenue website. Return the completed form to the savings provider.

**Grossing up**

You receive some types of income net of tax, for example interest from savings and dividends from shares. To convert the net amount you receive to the gross, divide the amount you receive by (1 – tax rate). Table 9.4 gives some examples.

**Table 9.4 Grossing up net income**

| Tax rate (%) | Grossing-up factor | Examples |
|---|---|---|
| 10 | 1/(1 – 10%) = 1/0.9 | Net dividend of £450 is equivalent to gross dividend of £450/0.9 = £500. |
| 20 | 1/(1 – 20%) = 1/0.8 | Net interest of £400 is equivalent to gross interest of £400/0.8 = £500. |
| 41 | 1/(1 – 41%) = 1/0.59 | A slice of earnings net of tax at 40% and National Insurance at 1% equal to £295 is equivalent to gross earnings of £295/0.59 = £500. |

## Case study

Arif and Sarah have a joint savings account with a bank which pays net £346 interest in the 2010–11 tax year. Arif is a basic-rate taxpayer but Sarah is a non-taxpayer, so they ask the bank if it will pay half the interest with tax deducted and the other half without. They know that some banks will do this, but theirs say it can't. Therefore, after the end of the tax year, Sarah completes form R40 to claim back the tax deducted from her £173 share of the net interest. Including tax at 20 per cent, this is equivalent to gross interest of £216.25, so she gets a tax refund of £216.25 – £173 = £43.25.

### Savings income paid gross

More unusually, savings income may be paid gross to all savers. This applies, for example, to most accounts you have with offshore banks. Although the interest is paid gross, as a UK resident, you are nevertheless liable for tax and should declare this income to the Revenue. Savings accounts and income bonds from NS&I pay gross interest.

If you are a non-taxpayer, it is convenient to receive interest gross because it saves you claiming tax back. However, it is easy to register to receive gross interest from accounts that would normally pay net interest, so you do not need especially to seek out products that always pay interest gross.

If you are a taxpayer, you get a small advantage from receiving gross interest because there is a delay until you have to pay the tax due and, in the meantime, you can earn interest on the tax not yet handed over.

## Income tax and dividends

Dividend income is income from shares and investment funds where the underlying investments are mainly or wholly shares. Dividend income is the return paid out by a company to its shareholders. It is paid out of the company's profits which have already been subjected to corporation tax while in the hands of the company. In recognition of the tax already paid, dividend income comes with a tax credit equal to 10 per cent of the gross dividend. The gross dividend is the amount you actually receive (the net dividend) plus the tax credit. For example, if you receive £90, the tax credit is £10 which is 10 per cent of £90 + £10 = £100. Using the grossing-up method (see the box on p. 265), the gross dividend is £90/(1 – 10%) = £100.

Unlike the tax paid on savings income, you cannot reclaim the tax credit if you are a non-taxpayer. If you are a starting-rate or basic-rate taxpayer, the tax credit exactly matches the tax due on the dividend income. If you are a higher-rate taxpayer, you must pay extra tax to bring the total up to 32.5 per cent or 42.5 per cent of the gross dividend.

Even if you invest in shares through a tax wrapper, such as an ISA or pension scheme (see p. 270), the tax credit cannot be reclaimed.

## Income tax and life insurance

Life insurance companies are major providers of investment products in the UK. They provide a route for putting your money into investment funds. Some, such as pensions, are taxed in a special way (see *Tax wrappers and incentives* on p. 270), but most are taxed according to the special rules for life insurance described in this section. A variety of changes to the UK tax system since the mid-1980s mean that life insurance is now seldom a tax-efficient form of investment. Most people would do better to choose other forms of investment fund, such as unit trusts and open-ended investment companies (see p. 313), investment trusts (see p. 314) and exchange-traded funds (see p. 319).

With investment-type life insurance, you take out an insurance policy. The amount you pay is called the premium and this can be either regular premiums or a single cash sum at the start of a policy, called a single premium. Some of the premium will pay for life cover, though often only a very small amount; some is deducted in charges; the remainder is invested in one or more investment funds. A fundamental aspect of investment-type life insurance is that the life insurance company pays tax on the income and any capital gains from the investments in the fund. You, in effect, get a credit for this tax but cannot reclaim any of the tax already deducted. (So, in some ways, the tax treatment of life insurance income is similar to that of dividend income.) You are treated as if the income has already been taxed at the basic rate (20 per cent in 2010–11). How the income is then taxed in your hands depends on two factors: the type of policy concerned and the type of taxpayer you are.

## Regular-premium policies

Most investment-type life insurance policies where you pay regular monthly or yearly premiums meet the conditions to be 'qualifying policies'. These conditions are:

■ this is a regular-premium policy with payments due yearly or more frequently;

■ you keep the policy going for at least ten years or three-quarters of the original term, whichever is less.

If the conditions are met at the start, but are broken later (for example, you stop paying into the policy before the first ten years or three-quarters of the term are up), the policy reverts to being 'non-qualifying' and is taxed as described below for single premium policies.

With a qualifying policy, whatever type of taxpayer you are, there is no tax to pay in your hands. This does not mean the investment is tax-free because it has already suffered tax in the life insurance company's hands at 20 per cent. Bear in mind that tax has been levied not just on income from the investments in the underlying fund but also on any capital gains. This means, if you have unused capital gains tax allowance (see Appendix B), as most people do, your investment will have been more heavily taxed than it would if you invested in, say, a unit trust (see Figure 9.2).

## Single-premium policies

Single-premium policies are all 'non-qualifying' meaning that they do not qualify for the freedom from extra tax that applies to regular-premium policies. However, there is extra tax to pay only if you are a higher-rate taxpayer, from 2010–11 an additional-rate taxpayer, or your income (including that from the investment) is in the region where you are losing personal allowance (see Appendix A and the case study below).

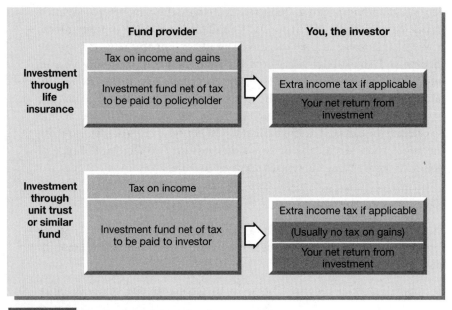

**Figure 9.2**    Tax on investment funds compared

The extra tax, if applicable is charged on the proceeds you receive from the policy less the premium you paid – confusingly this is called a 'charge-able gain', even though it is taxed as income. For example, if you receive £10,000 and you paid a premium of £6,000, your chargeable gain is £4,000. Although the life company has paid tax on the underlying invest-ments, you do not gross up this gain. You are treated as if basic rate tax has already been paid and so just pay the difference between your top rate of tax and the basic rate. For example, if you are a higher-rate taxpayer, at 2010–11 tax rates, you pay tax of 40% – 20% = 20% on the chargeable gain. From 2010–11, an additional-rate taxpayer will pay at a rate of 50% – 20% = 30%.

If adding the gain to your other income for the tax year takes you over a tax-rate threshold, you are automatically given 'top-slicing relief' which may reduce your tax bill. This relief works by calculating the tax on the gain in an alternative way. The total gain is divided by the number of years the policy has run to find the average yearly gain or 'slice'. This slice is added to your other income for the year to work out the tax due, if any, on the slice. Tax on the whole gain is then tax on the slice multiplied by the number of years the policy has run. See the case study opposite.

There is a special feature of non-qualifying policies that is heavily used to market these investments. That is an ability to draw a regular income while deferring tax until the year in which the policy ends. This is relevant only to higher-rate taxpayers, additional-rate taxpayers and those who would lose personal allowance (since otherwise there is no tax to defer). The maximum income you can draw each year for a maximum of 20 years is 1/20th (5 per cent) of the premium paid. If you do not draw the full 5 per cent in any year, you can carry it over to be drawn out in a later year. When the policy comes to an end, the chargeable gain is worked out as the final proceeds plus the income drawn in earlier years less the premium paid.

Whenever you make a chargeable gain on a policy, the life company will give you a 'chargeable event certificate' stating the amount of the gain, so you will know what to declare to the Revenue.

Note that, unless top-slicing relief applies, the rates of income tax charged on life insurance gains were higher than the 18 per cent tax rate in 2009–10 on capital gains. This meant that even for higher-rate taxpayers, an investment that produced capital gains was more tax-efficient than investment-type life insurance. This may change if the CGT rate is increased in 2010–11.

## Case study

Ruth, aged 66, has an income of £22,900 in 20010–11. This is the maximum she can have without losing any personal allowance so she qualifies for the full amount for someone aged 65 to 74 of £9,490 and her tax bill for the year is set to be £2,682. However, she decides to cash in a single-premium life-insurance policy, making a gain of £2,000. This increases her income to £24,900. Although she is still a basic rate taxpayer and there is no tax for her to pay on the gain itself, her tax bill increases to £2,882. This is because her personal allowance is reduced by £1 for every £2 of income above £22,900. Therefore the £2,000 gain reduces her personal allowance by £1,000. This puts an extra £1,000 of her income into the basic rate tax band adding £200 to her tax bill.

In 2010–11 Jim, aged 48, has earnings of £43,000 and also makes a life insurance gain of £5,000 on a policy that has run for five years. At first sight, £875 of the gain falls within Jim's basic-rate band, leaving £4,125 to be taxed at 40% – 20% = 20%, a tax bill of £825. However, because the gain takes Jim over a tax-rate threshold, top-slicing relief applies. The gain of £5,000 is divided by the number of years the policy has run, which is five. This gives an average gain or 'slice' of £1,000. So £875 of the slice falls within Jim's basic-rate band, leaving £125 to be taxed at 40% – 20% = 20%. Therefore, tax on the slice is £25 and tax on the whole gain is reduced to 5 × £25 = £125.

## Tax wrappers and incentives

You can boost the return from many savings and investment products by investing through a 'tax wrapper'. This is not itself an investment but is like a layer that you wrap around investments which means they then benefit from advantageous tax treatment. The main tax wrappers are pension schemes (see Chapter 7), ISAs (see p. 272) and child trust funds (see p. 274). The government's aim in offering tax wrappers is to encourage certain types of saving and investment behaviour, such as providing for your own retirement and introducing children to the concept of saving. In addition, there are some other incentive schemes aimed at, for example, encouraging low-income households to get into the savings habit and wealthier investors to put money into small and growing businesses. The main wrappers and incentive schemes are summarised in Table 9.5.

**Table 9.5 Tax wrappers and other incentive schemes**

| *Scheme* | *Aims* | *Tax incentives* |
|---|---|---|
| Pension scheme | Encourage everyone to build up retirement income. | Tax relief on amounts paid in or, with personal pensions, bonus added for non-taxpayers and starting-rate taxpayers. Gains and some income from the investments in the scheme are tax-free. Part of proceeds can be taken as a tax-free lump sum. See Chapter 7. |
| Individual savings account (ISA) | Encourage saving and investing. | Gains and some types of income from investments in the ISA are tax-free (see below). |
| Child trust fund (CTF) | Help young people start adult life with some resources and teach children about saving. | Government gives child money at birth and age seven to put in CTF account. Parents and others can add more. Gains and some types of income from the investments in the CTF are tax-free. See p. 274. |
| Friendly society tax-exempt plan | Encourage saving and investing. | Gains and some types of income from investments in the plan are tax-free. Maximum investment is £270 a year. See p. 276. |

**Table 9.5 Tax wrappers and other incentive schemes** *continued*

| *Scheme* | *Aims* | *Tax incentives* |
| --- | --- | --- |
| Saving Gateway | Encourage low-income households to build up savings. | Saver opens an account which earns interest. Government adds bonus of 50p for each £1 saved up to a maximum bonus of £300. Interest and bonus are tax-free. See p. 277. |
| Enterprise investment scheme | Encourage investment in new and young, growing companies. | Tax relief on amount invested. Gains when shares sold may be tax-free. See p. 277. |
| Venture capital trust | Encourage investment in new and young, growing companies. | Tax relief on amount invested. Dividends, if any, are tax-free. Gains when shares sold may be tax-free. See p. 277. |

The government contains the cost of the tax advantages from using tax wrappers and other incentive schemes by setting limits on the amount you can invest in each type. The government also often tries to ensure that your savings and investments meet the aims of the scheme or wrapper by imposing restrictions on when or how the proceeds can be used. Whenever you consider savings or investments, it makes sense to look first at using a tax wrapper before considering direct investment. But the restrictions mean that a tax wrapper might not always be a suitable choice. Charges from providers may also reduce the attractiveness of the wrappers. In general, provided you are happy with the restrictions, the most tax advantaged way of investing is through a pension scheme, for example a self-invested personal pension (SIPP) – see Chapter 7. Unless you prefer to invest all your money through a pension scheme, you should normally try to use at least some of your annual ISA allowance each year.

### 'Tax-free' investments

The government usually describes ISAs and CTFs as giving tax-free returns. This is not really accurate, because income from shares and share-based investments comes with tax at 10 per cent already deducted and this cannot be reclaimed. This is an important point because the 10 per cent tax affects your choice between using these tax wrappers or not. Interestingly, life companies, whose investments are in a similar position given that the return reaches you with tax at 20 per cent already deducted are (correctly) not allowed to describe their investments as tax-free.

## Individual Savings Accounts

Individual savings accounts (ISAs) were introduced in April 1999 to replace two earlier tax-incentivised schemes/wrappers (tax-efficient special savings accounts and personal equity plans) both of which have now been absorbed into the ISA regime. There are two types of ISA:

- ■ **Cash ISAs.** These are savings accounts which typically come ready wrapped in the ISA. Interest from the account is tax-free. You can have a cash ISA from age 16 onwards.

- ■ **Stocks-and-shares ISAs.** Inside this type, you can put stock-market investments, such as shares and bonds, and investment funds. Some investment funds come ready wrapped in an ISA. More often you select an ISA provider, which may be a fund provider, an independent financial adviser, stockbroker or wealth manager and can then choose what investments to put inside the wrapper. Your choice may be constrained by the range offered by that provider. Gains and savings income from investments within this type of ISA are tax-free, but dividend income is taxed at a flat-rate 10 per cent (with no higher- or additional-rate tax to pay). You must be 18 or over to have a stocks-and-shares ISA.

Each tax year you have an annual ISA allowance – see Table 9.6. If you do not use part or all of your allowance, it is lost for good as it cannot be carried forward into a future year. The government has said that ISAs will continue indefinitely, so once you have put investments into an ISA they can be tax-free for life or until you withdraw them from the wrapper (or the government of the day changes its mind about continuing the scheme).

**Table 9.6 Your annual ISA allowance**

| Type of ISA | 2009–10[1] | 2010–11 onwards |
|---|---|---|
| Cash ISA | £3,600 | £5,100 |
| Stocks-and-shares ISA | £7,200 less any amount you have put into a cash ISA | £10,200 less any amount you have put into a cash ISA |

[1] The higher amounts for 2010–11 apply from 1 October 2009 for anyone aged 50 or over between that date and 5 April 2010.

Each year, you can either take out a cash ISA or a stocks-and-shares ISA or one of each and you must choose one provider only for each ISA. The allowance applies to the amount you pay in during the tax year, not the net sum invested. For example, if you put £3,000 into a cash ISA and draw out £500 in the same year, you have £600 of allowance remaining for the year (not £1,100). If you want to switch an ISA to a new provider in the year you take it out, you must transfer the whole sum. But, for ISAs you started in earlier tax years, you can ask the providers to transfer just part of your savings if you want a new provider and have as many different providers as you like.

The tax rules do not put any restrictions on withdrawing money from your ISAs, but the individual providers might. For example, a cash ISA could be a term account where you agree to leave your money invested for a set number of years.

There are no charges for cash ISAs – the provider's costs are reflected in the interest rate you are offered. There may be charges for a stocks-and-shares ISA wrapper (in addition to whatever charges apply to the underlying investments), though often the ISA wrapper around investment funds is free.

---

### Warning! ISA transfers

You must instruct the providers of the old and new ISAs to make the transfer for you. Do not withdraw the money with the intention of reinvesting it yourself because on withdrawal your savings will permanently lose their ISA status and the tax advantages that offers.

---

Many people use their cash ISA allowance, fewer take out stocks-and-shares ISAs, and you should bear these points in mind:

■ **Non-taxpayers**. The incentive offered by ISAs is tax saving. If you don't pay tax anyway, you get nothing from this incentive. However, the tax savings are due to exist indefinitely, so if you may be a taxpayer at some time in the future, it could still be worth using your ISA allowance – for example, young people from age 16 should consider starting cash ISAs if they have savings even though it may be a while before they start to pay tax. The market for cash ISAs tends to be competitive, so from time to time the rates on cash ISAs may be better than on non-ISA accounts, in which case they would be a good choice even if you do not pay tax.

■ **Starting-rate and basic-rate taxpayers.** There is a clear advantage in taking out a cash ISA because you save tax on the interest earned. But you will not necessarily get any advantage from using a stocks-and-shares ISA. Gains will be tax-free but, if you are not using your full capital gains tax allowance (see Appendix A), you will not currently be paying tax on gains anyway. However, if you are expecting your ISA investments to perform very well, you might perhaps have large gains in future. Any savings income – for example from government or corporate bonds held within the ISA – will also be tax-free, but dividend income from shares and investment funds will be taxed at 10 per cent, which is the same rate you would pay if you held the shares or funds without the ISA wrapper.

■ **Higher-rate and additional-rate taxpayers.** Tax on dividend income is capped at 10 per cent which is less than you would pay if you held shares and investment funds direct. Coupled with the tax-free savings income, this means you do get an income-tax advantage from holding investments through a stocks-and-shares ISA as well as cash ISAs. You may also save CGT, if you regularly use your whole allowance.

■ **Admin savings for all taxpayers.** ISA income and gains do not have to be declared to the Revenue. Therefore you do not have to fill in forms and keep paperwork for tax purposes.

■ **Alternatives for taxpayers.** If your main aim is saving for retirement, the tax advantages of pension schemes are better than those for ISAs (see Table 9.7). However, ISAs are more flexible because you can withdraw your money at any time and in the form of tax-free cash sums, whereas with pension schemes you cannot usually get your money back until age 55 at the earliest and most must be drawn in the form of taxable pension.

The Financial Services Authority's Moneymadeclear website (see Appendix B) includes comparative tables for savings accounts, including cash ISAs, and stocks-and-shares ISAs for investment funds. Most comparison websites include cash ISAs.

## Child trust funds

Child trust funds (CTFs) have been introduced for every child born from 1 September 2002 onwards as part of a drive to improve the financial capability of the nation. The scheme has the twin aims of ensuring young people enter adult life with some resources and stimulating school-age children to start taking an interest in saving and so hopefully develop a

**Table 9.7 Pension schemes v ISAs**

| Feature | Pension scheme | ISA |
|---|---|---|
| *Tax features* | | |
| Tax relief or bonus on money paid in | ✓[1] | ✗ |
| Investments grow largely tax-free | ✓ | ✓ |
| Can withdraw money as tax-free lump sum(s) | ✓ (¼ of fund only) | ✓ |
| Don't have to withdraw money as taxable income | ✗ (¾ of fund[1]) | ✓ |
| *Flexibility features* | | |
| Can make withdrawals at any time | ✗ | ✓ |

[1] Tax relief on money paid in May at a higher rate than tax on the income drawn out.

lifelong savings habit. To support the latter aim, schools periodically run teaching and activities based around the CTF scheme.

Shortly after the birth of a new child, you receive a voucher from the government for £250, or £500 if your household income is low, which you can use to open your child's CTF account. If, after a year, you have not opened the account, HM Revenue & Customs (who administer the scheme) will open an account instead. When your child reaches age seven, the government pays in a further £250 or £500. Children with a disability receive a higher government endowment. You, relatives, friends and anyone else can also add up to £1,200 a year in total to the account.

Your child can take control of the account from age 16, but cannot withdraw the money before reaching 18. At that age, the account closes and the young person can do anything they like with the proceeds, including spending the lot or rolling the money over into an ISA (which would be in addition to their normal annual ISA allowance).

During the 18-year term of the account, the money invested has the same tax advantages as an ISA: gains and savings income are tax-free; and dividend income is taxed at 10 per cent. There is a choice of ways to invest:

■ **Savings CTF.** The money goes into a savings account with a bank, building society or credit union.

■ **Stocks-and-shares CTF.** The money is invested in stock-market investments, such as shares, bonds and investment funds. This type of CTF tends to be offered by friendly societies and stockbrokers.

■ **Stakeholder CTF.** The money is invested in stock-market investments for the first 13 years and gradually shifted to lower risk investments during the last five years (a process called lifestyling), though your child (or you on their behalf) can opt out of this shift if they want to. Charges are capped at 1.5 per cent a year of the value of the fund. Nearly all CTF providers offer the stakeholder option.

The 18-year term makes this a long-term investment, so the stocks-and-shares or stakeholder option is likely to be the more suitable choice. If the Revenue opens the account for your child, it will always select a stakeholder CTF, though you can change this if you want. Either you or your child can switch between the different types of CTF and between providers at any time.

Some points to bear in mind when considering a CTF are:

■ **Government contribution.** There are no catches – this is genuinely free money from the government.

■ **Extra money from family and friends.** Although money invested in a CTF grows largely tax-free, most children are non-taxpayers anyway so do not gain any advantage from the CTF wrapper. The position is different for parents because gifts to your own children can create a tax bill for you (see Chapter 11), but gifts you pay into a CTF do not.

■ **Stakeholder charges.** Although charges for stakeholder CTFs are capped at 1.5 per cent a year of the value of the investments, this is not a low charge. For example, even if the CTF grew by an average 7 per cent a year, after 18 years charges at 1.5 per cent would have swallowed up over a fifth of the resulting fund – see Table 10.4 on p. 309.

For information about CTFs and a full list of providers, visit the Government's CTF website or call the CTF Helpline (see Appendix B).

### Friendly society plans

Friendly societies are mutual organisations owned by their members. The origins of the movement go back to the seventeenth century, to an era without a welfare state. Friendly societies grew up as mutual self-help organisations to help members in times of trouble, such as illness and bereavement. These days, UK friendly societies offer similar products to insurance companies, but some of their history lingers both in their names and a few of their products. One such product is the tax-exempt plan which promotes small-scale saving.

You pay regular savings into the plan, usually monthly or yearly. The plan is designed to run for a set term, commonly 10 or 25 years, at the end of which it pays out a lump sum. Your savings are invested in one or more investment funds where they grow largely tax-free. 'Tax exempt' is the common name for these plans, but is not entirely accurate. Like ISAs and CTFs, dividend income from the investments in the plan is taxed at 10 per cent, but otherwise income and gains are tax-free.

The maximum you can pay in is low at just £25 a month (or £270 a year). You need to watch out for charges – with such a low level of saving any fixed fees tend to take a big chunk out of your money in percentage terms. Some providers offer 'feeder' accounts so that you can invest a lump sum rather than saving regularly. The feeder account pays out a monthly or yearly income direct to the friendly society plan. The return on the feeder account is not tax-free.

## Saving Gateway

This is new incentive scheme due to start in April 2010 to encourage low-income households into the savings habit. The account is open to people claiming means-tested state benefits, disability benefits or carer's allowance.

You save up to £25 a month with a bank, building society or credit union for a period of two years. Your savings earn interest and, at the end of the two years, you also get a 'maturity payment' from the government. Both the interest and the maturity payment are tax-free. At the end of two years, you can roll over the proceeds into an ISA.

The maturity payment equals 50p for each £1 of your highest balance (excluding interest) during the two-year term. You can withdraw your money at any time, but you get the maximum maturity payment only if you pay in the maximum £25 a month and make no withdrawals, in which case it would be (24 × £25) × 50p = £300.

## Investing in new companies

The enterprise investment scheme (EIS) and venture capital trusts (VCTs) both offer tax savings if you invest in the newly issued shares of trading companies that are not yet traded on the stock exchange. These types of shares are high risk. You are gambling on the company growing into a successful concern that may in time pay dividends to its shareholders and eventually become traded on a stock market. In the meantime, you are unlikely to get any income at all and it may be difficult to sell the shares in which case you could lose your original investment or a large part of it (liquidity risk and capital risk). Such losses may come to more than the tax relief that you have had.

With the EIS scheme, you get income-tax relief (at a rate of 20 per cent in 2009–10) on up to £500,000 a year of your investment, provided you hang on to the shares for at least three years. In addition, there is no CGT on any gain you make when you sell the shares. You can also use the EIS scheme to put off paying CGT that you have made on other assets by claiming CGT deferral relief. You can get this relief if, having sold something at a profit, you reinvest the proceeds in EIS shares. There is a window for making the reinvestment which runs from one year before you sell the original asset to two years after.

With the VCT scheme, instead of investing direct in the underlying companies, you invest in a fund – the VCT – which invests in a range of companies and is quoted on the stock market. The idea behind this scheme is to make it easier for you to sell when you want to. However, in practice, VCT shares are not very actively traded so liquidity risk is still a problem. You get income-tax relief at a rate of 30 per cent (in 2009–10) on the amount you invest in VCTs up to a maximum investment of £200,000 (in 2009–10), provided you hold the VCT for at least five years. There is no CGT on any gains you make when you sell. If in the meantime you get any dividends, these are tax-free.

For more information about these schemes, see the HM Revenue & Customs website and contact the British Business Angels Association (see Appendix B).

# The building blocks of saving and investing

This section describes the basic ingredients of saving and investing. You can invest in these direct, but often you will invest indirectly, for example, using the investment funds or more sophisticated investments described in the next chapter. If you are already familiar with these building blocks, you may prefer to turn straight to Chapter 10 for ideas on turning them into investment strategies.

# Savings products

Savings products are offered mainly by banks, building societies, credit unions and National Savings & Investments (NS&I). These low-risk products are the foundation of saving investing. They provide the obvious home for an emergency fund, money in transition between one use and another, and short-term saving over periods of less than five years. They are also useful as a counter-balance to more risky investments when you are building a portfolio of investments (see Chapter 10).

## Savings accounts and bonds

The return is in the form of interest, which may be variable or fixed. Watch out for returns that are boosted with a bonus for the first few months or year. After the bonus period is over, the rate might not look attractive. Typically, interest rates are tiered so that higher balances earn a higher-rate of interest. The highest rates are usually offered on accounts you operate by internet, phone or post. Some accounts target particular groups – for example, the over-50s – but the returns offered are not necessarily better than those available elsewhere.

Interest is taxed as savings income (see p. 264), though you can avoid tax by using a tax wrapper. For example, you can choose ISAs (see p. 272). Similarly, you might hold part of a self-invested personal pension (SIPPs) – see Chapter 7 – in the form of savings products though not all savings providers will accept money from SIPPs. This is because savings products are often designed to be held direct by individuals, whereas SIPP money is usually in the name of the SIPP provider who is acting on your behalf.

These are all deposit-based products, meaning that your capital is not at risk, unless the provider goes bust. Even then, you will usually be fully or partially protected by a compensation scheme (see Chapter 2) but to be ultra safe you could: restrict your investments to UK institutions and ensure that, with any one provider you have no more than £50,000 (the UK compensation cap in 2009); and/or stick to NS&I products which are ultimately backed by the UK government without limit. The return on NS&I products tends to be lower than the rates available elsewhere, reflecting their very safe status.

Deposits are vulnerable to inflation which reduces the buying power of your savings, especially if you are drawing off the interest rather than reinvesting it. An exception is NS&I index-linked certificates which promise a return that increases with inflation (see p. 257). Guaranteed equity bonds

– see the section *Structured products* on p. 283 – aim to offer you some of the superior return of shares without capital risk, but are not completely risk-free, though the NS&I offering comes close.

The most liquid products are instant-access savings accounts, so this should be the baseline against which to compare other savings products. Where products restrict your liquidity by requiring you to give notice of withdrawals (notice accounts) or to leave your money invested for a set number of years (term accounts or bonds), you should expect to be compensated with a higher rate of interest. Table 9.8 gives a broad outline of the main products available.

To compare savings products, use online comparative tables, including those from the Financial Services Authority's Moneymadeclear website and the specialist provider Moneyfacts (see Appendix B). 'Best buy' tables are also published regularly in the personal finance pages of newspapers and in personal finance magazines available from newsagents.

**Table 9.8 Savings products**

| Type | Minimum investment | Return | Tax | Term | Access |
|------|--------------------|--------|-----|------|--------|
| Instant access account | Varies, from £1 | Variable | As savings income paid net (see p. 264)<br><br>Tax-free if cash ISA | None | Immediate |
| NS&I easy access account | £20 | Variable | As savings income paid gross (see p. 265) | None | Immediate (up to £300 daily through post offices) |
| NS&I investment account | £100 | Variable | As savings income paid gross (see p. 265) | None | Immediate |
| NS&I premium bonds | £100 | Chance to win prizes | Tax-free | None | 8 working days |

## Table 9.8  Savings products *continued*

| Type | Minimum investment | Return | Tax | Term | Access |
|------|-------------------|--------|-----|------|--------|
| Notice account | Varies, from £1 | Variable | As savings income paid net (see p. 264)<br><br>Tax-free if cash ISA | None | Give specified notice – e.g. 30, 60, 90 or 120 days – or lose some interest |
| Regular savings account | Often between £10 and £500 a month | Variable or fixed | As savings income paid net (see p. 264)<br><br>Tax-free if cash ISA | May be instant access or fixed term, (e.g. 1 year) | Only limited withdrawals if any, otherwise loss of interest or account closed |
| Monthly income account | Varies, often £1,000 to £5,000 | Variable, paid out as income | As savings income paid net (see p. 264) | None | Either immediate or give specified notice |
| NS&I income bonds | £500 | Variable, paid out as income | As savings income, paid gross (see p. 265) | None | Immediate |
| NS&I guaranteed income bonds* | £500 | Fixed, paid out as income | As savings income paid net (see p. 264) | 1, 2, 3 and 5 years | Loss of interest on early access |
| Term account (bond) | Varies, from £1 but often £500 or £1,000 | Fixed | As savings income paid net (see p. 264)<br><br>Tax-free if cash ISA | Usually 1 to 5 years | Either no earlier access or lose some interest |

▶

Table 9.8 **Savings products** *continued*

| Type | Minimum investment | Return | Tax | Term | Access |
|------|------|------|------|------|------|
| NS&I savings certificates | £100 | Fixed or fixed percentage plus inflation | Tax-free | 2 or 5 years (fixed return)<br><br>3 or 5 years (index-linked) | Loss of interest on early access |
| NS&I children's bonus bonds | £25 | Fixed | Tax-free | 5 years | Loss of interest on early access |
| NS&I guaranteed growth bonds | £500 | Fixed | As savings income paid net (see p. 264) | 1, 2, 3 or 5 years | Loss of interest on early access |
| Guaranteed equity bond | Varies, from say £500 to maximum ISA limit | Linked to change in a stock market index or value of a basket of shares | As savings income paid net (see p. 264)<br><br>Tax-free if cash ISA | Usually 3 to 6 years | Often no early access. If allowed, risk of capital loss |

*These products were withdrawn in December 2009 because the NS&I funding targets had been met, but new issues are likely in future.

## Premium bonds

Premium bonds are an unusual savings product offered by NS&I. Instead of receiving interest, you have the chance each month to win prizes. The interest that would have been paid out creates a prize fund – the size of this fund and the number of prizes go up and down with the underlying variable interest rate. Each £1 you invest buys one bond. Prizes range from £25 up to a single jackpot each month of £1 million.

In October 2009, the interest rate underlying the prize fund was 1.5 per cent a year and the chance of a bond winning any prize was 1 in 24,000 each month. Just under nine-tenths of the prizes were for £25. There was a 1 in 40.6 billion chance each month of any one bond winning the jackpot.

When premium bonds first went on sale in 1956, some postal workers refused to handle them because they were perceived to be gambling rather than saving. Technically, premium bonds are an 'interest lottery'. You are not gambling with your capital which you can get back in full at any time. But you are gambling with the interest that you would otherwise have earned. You could create your own interest lottery by putting money in a bank or building society savings account and drawing off the interest each month to buy National Lottery tickets. Interestingly, this can give you a better chance of winning a life-changing amount – see the case study.

## Case study

Claire is thinking about investing £1,000 in premium bonds, purely because she likes the idea of winning £1 million. If she does, she will have a 1 in 40 million chance each month of winning the jackpot. Alternatively, she could invest the £1,000 in a cash ISA at 1.5 per cent a year interest. This would give her £15 interest a year, more than enough to buy one National Lottery ticket a month. One ticket would give her a 1 in 14 million chance of winning the jackpot – significantly better odds than the premium bonds.

### Structured products

If you are a cautious investor who does not want to lose any capital but you want a better return than savings accounts are offering, you may be tempted by guaranteed equity bonds, which are a type of 'structured product'.

These bonds have a fixed term of three to six years. Provided you hold them for the full term, you get your capital back in full plus interest which is based on the rise in a stock-market index or basket of shares. Stock-market return without the risk? You'll recall that risk and return always go hand in hand, and you need to look closely at any structured product to see what is really happening 'under the bonnet'.

Although the offer sounds simple, guaranteed equity bonds are complicated products that typically combine some kind of corporate bond (see p. 285) and a derivative (see p. 325). Most of your investment buys a bond that will grow to repay your capital at the end of the term. The remainder is used to buy a derivative that will deliver the stock-market growth. The bond and derivative are usually bought from an outside firm, often an investment bank, who is called the 'counterparty'. When you buy a guaranteed equity bond, you should bear these points in mind:

■ The guarantee to return your capital is only as good as the counterparty's promise. Usually the counterparty is a sound financial institution that is highly unlikely to fail, but Lehman Brothers did (see Chapter 1) and, during the global banking crisis, other banks came close to collapse, so this risk cannot be entirely ignored. (NS&I guaranteed equity bonds are, in effect, underwritten by the UK government which should be sound.)

■ Your stock-market returns are in reality only partial returns. For example, many bonds promise to pay a maximum of, say 60 per cent of the change in a stock-market index. Even where a bond will pay you 100 per cent of the change, this is still not the full return that you would get from investing in shares direct because you are getting only the rise in share price and none of the dividend income. The Barclays Capital research mentioned earlier in this chapter found that the value of £100 invested in shares in 1945 ignoring the income would have grown to £5,721 (including growth due to inflation) but, including the reinvested dividend income, the investment would be worth £92,460. So guaranteed equity bonds don't really promise you such a great return.

Provided you are a long-term investor, you would do better to construct your own portfolio with some of your money invested in savings and some direct in the stock market to give you a balance of returns, rather than using structured products. See Chapter 10.

## Shariah-compliant and ethical savings products

A fundamental principle of Shariah law is a prohibition on earning or paying interest (*Riba*). Therefore, Shariah-complaint savings products work on a profit-sharing basis. Typically, a saver's money goes into a pool along with money from other savers. The pool is then used by the bank to finance business ventures. When the ventures make a profit, this is split between the bank and the pool. Savers then share the profit between them, for example, with longer-term savers getting a larger share than short-term savers. If the business ventures make a loss, the pool may have to pay its share of the loss. There are a number of banks offering Shariah-complaint products in the UK, for example, the Islamic Bank of Britain and HSBC Amanah Finance (see Appendix B).

Shariah-compliant products are not restricted to Moslem savers and might be suitable if you are looking for ethical savings products. This is because Shariah law also prohibits the use of funds for certain purposes including businesses connected with alcohol, gambling and pornography.

There are also mainstream savings products that comply with ethical principles. For example Co-operative Bank (which includes the online provider, Smile) does not invest in businesses involved in tobacco, the arms trade, uncontrolled genetic modification or which are unecological or fail to uphold human rights. Triodos Bank lends only to organisations that have social aims and support communities. And Ecology Building Society is committed to using its funds to improve the environment through sustainable houses and communities. See Appendix B for contact details.

---

### Saving without banks

When you put money in a savings account, you are lending to a bank or building society which then lends your money on to people who want to borrow. You can cut out the bank or building society as middleman and lend direct to borrowers through a website called Zopa (see Appendix B for contact details). Borrowers are graded according to their credit status and for how long they want to borrow. As a saver, you decide which grade of lender you want to lend to and the rate you want to receive. Then you wait for borrowers to take up your offer. Your money is spread across a range of borrowers to reduce the risk of losing money if someone defaults – for example, if you lend £500, it will be spread across at least 50 borrowers. To date default rates are low, for example between 1 and 4 per cent of loans made.

---

## Bonds

Bonds are loans you make to the government (called government bonds or gilts) or companies (called corporate bonds). Most bonds have a set date on which the loan will be repaid (the redemption date). In the meantime, you receive interest, typically every six months. You do not have to hold the bond until redemption, but can sell it early on the stock market. Similarly, although you can buy bonds direct from the borrower when the bonds are first issued, you don't have to do that. Instead you can buy on the stock market bonds that have already been issued.

For convenience, bonds are usually described in terms of units called £100 nominal, but you can buy and sell in larger and smaller amounts and in fractions of a unit. The return you get from a bond is made up of two parts:

■ **Interest**. The name of a bond will usually include the interest rate it pays. For example, if the name includes the words '3 per cent' this means that, for each £100 nominal you hold, the bond will pay out 3 per cent a year interest. This would normally be paid in two equal amounts of 1.5 per cent at six-monthly intervals. When interest is expressed like this as a rate for each £100 nominal, it is often called the 'coupon' (because in days gone by you had to clip and present a coupon in order to claim your interest). Now, here is the tricky part: when you buy a bond, you may pay more or less for each unit than £100. This means the interest you get may be more or less than the coupon rate suggests, depending on the amount you paid – see the example in Table 9.9. Interest is taxed as savings income and normally paid gross but is tax-free if you hold the bonds through a stocks-and-shares ISA.

■ **A gain or loss at redemption or sale**. If you hold a bond until it is redeemed, you normally get back £100 for each £100 nominal that you hold. If you originally paid less than £100 for each unit, you will make a capital gain at redemption. If you paid more than £100 per unit, you will make a loss on redemption. If you sell a bond before redemption, what you get back depends on the market price at the time which may be higher or lower than the nominal value of £100 and higher or lower than the amount you originally paid. Any capital gain on bonds is usually free of CGT whether or not held through an ISA.

**Table 9.9  Example of a government bond**

| Feature or situation | The bond | Notes |
|---|---|---|
| Bond name | 5% Treasury gilt 2018 | The name tells you the coupon is 5% and the redemption date is in 2018. |
| Coupon | 5% | Coupon is the interest as a percentage of the nominal value of £100. |
| Interest payment each six months for each £100 nominal | £2.50 | Each six-monthly payment is half the coupon. |
| Interest yield if the market price is £100 for each £100 nominal | $= 5/100 \times 100$ $= 5\%$ pa | If the market price equals the nominal value, the interest yield is the same as the coupon. |
| Interest yield if the market price is £88 for each £100 nominal | $= 5/88 \times 100$ $= 5.68\%$ pa | If the market price falls, the interest yield (and the redemption yield) goes up. |
| Interest yield if the market price is £112 for each £100 nominal | $= 5/112 \times 100$ $= 4.46\%$ pa | The market price rises, the interest yield (and the redemption yield) falls. |
| Redemption yield if the market price is £112 for each £100 nominal | 3.37% pa | The redemption yield in this case is lower than the interest yield because there will be a capital loss at redemption. |

There are two measures of the return you get from a bond. The interest yield (also called the running yield or income yield) is the interest expressed as a percentage of the current stock-market price. This is a useful measure of the income you would get if you invested at that price. If you are investing for income, you could compare this yield with, for example, the interest you would get from a savings account. The redemption yield is a measure of the total return you would get from a bond if you held it until redemption, taking into account not just the interest but also the capital gain or loss you would make, if you bought at the market price today.

You can find government bond yields on the Debt Management Office website. Yields for both government and corporate bonds are published in specialist newspapers, such as the *Financial Times* and are available from stockbrokers.

Bonds are often thought of as investments primarily for generating income. That certainly is one way to use them. But some bonds pay a very low rate of interest and so may be more useful if you are looking for growth. In fact bonds are very flexible – some can even be 'stripped'. A bond normally produces a flow of payments: interest every six months and redemption payment at the end. When a bond is stripped, each interest payment and the redemption payment are peeled off and sold as separate bonds. So each stripped bond comprises a single payment to be made on a future date. By combining strips with a variety of payment dates, you can generate your own tailor-made income stream – for example, a monthly rather than six-monthly income, or payments to coincide with the dates on which school fees are due.

If you intend to hold a bond until it is redeemed, at the time you invest you know exactly what payments you will get so your return is fixed and guaranteed. The price of the guarantee is being locked into the bond until redemption, so this is an illiquid investment. You always have the option of selling early on the stock market but then you cannot know what price you will get, so you face capital risk. The ability of bonds to deliver a fixed return if held to redemption means that generally bonds are considered relatively low risk investments. They can be useful as part of a portfolio to counterbalance more risky investments, such as shares.

Bonds are not devoid of all capital risk because the government or company that issued them might fail to make the promised payments. This is an aspect of capital risk mentioned earlier in this chapter and is called default risk (or credit risk). The UK government is considered very unlikely to default (because it could raise extra money through taxes or by printing money), so government bonds are considered low risk investments.

Corporate bonds are riskier because companies do from time to time default on their payments. To compensate for the extra risk, they normally offer a higher rate of return.

While investors do sometimes hold government bonds direct, they more often invest in bonds through investment funds (see Chapter 10) – this applies especially when it comes to corporate bonds which are typically traded in amounts that exceed most private investors' budgets. For information on buying and selling government bonds direct, visit the Debt Management Office (DMO) website or contact a stockbroker (see Appendix B).

### Buying and selling stock-market investments

When you buy and sell investments quoted on a stock exchange, you normally pay two types of charges:

■ **Spread**. This is the difference between the price at which you can buy a share or bond and the lower price at which you can sell it. This difference goes to the intermediaries who guarantee to ensure that there is a ready market. The more liquid the market for a particular share or bond, the smaller the spread.

■ **Dealing charges**. You usually buy through a stockbroker or other dealing service which will either take a flat fee for each transaction (say, £10 to £15 per deal) or charge commission as a percentage of the amount you are trading (say, 0.7 per cent). See Table 9.10 for an example.

**Table 9.10 Cost of buying and selling government bonds through the DMO service**

| Deal type | Commission rate | Minimum charge |
|---|---|---|
| Costs up to £5,000 | 0.7% | £12.50 |
| Costs over £5,000 | £35 plus 0.375% of the amount in excess of £5,000 | £35 |
| Proceeds up to £5,000 | 0.7% | None |
| Proceeds over £5,000 | £35 plus 0.375% of the amount in excess of £5,000 | £35 |

Source: Debt Management Office, 2009, Purchase and Sale Service. Terms and Conditions, http://www-uk.computershare.com, Accessed 30 September 2009.

You may also have to pay other charges. For example, there is a 0.5 per cent stamp duty charge on share purchases and a £1 'PTM levy' on transactions of £10,000 or more to fund a regulatory body called the Panel on Takeovers and Mergers. Stockbrokers may charge regular fees for holding shares on your behalf and will usually charge a transfer fee if you want to move your holdings to another broker – these fees vary from one broker to another, so check and compare before you commit to one broker or another. You may be required to have a deposit account with a stockbroker in order to pay for purchases and the rate paid on money in the account may be low or zero, which is in effect another charge.

## Shares

When you buy shares, you become part-owner of a company along with all the other shareholders. Your return may be made up of:

■ **Dividends**. Regular income paid out to shareholders which represents a slice of the profits the company has made. See p. 266 for details of how dividends are taxed.

■ **Capital gain or loss on sale**. Unlike bonds, shares do not normally have a redemption date. Therefore, normally the only way to cash in your investment is to sell the shares on the stock market. You can't be sure in advance what price you will get. If you get less than you originally paid, you will make a loss. If you get more, you will make a capital gain. You may have to pay capital gains tax (CGT) on any gains – see Appendix A for how CGT works. Sometimes, a company will buy back its own shares and make you an offer that is typically higher than the market price. And, in some situations, a rival company mounting a takeover bid will offer to buy your shares.

Shares are at the riskier end of the investment spectrum. Large well-established companies usually pay dividends every six months, but there is no guarantee that dividends will be maintained at previous levels or paid at all, so there is income risk. Companies that are growing and building up their business may not pay any dividends at all, so you may be pinning all your hopes on selling the shares for a profit. The uncertainty over the price at which you can buy and sell shares creates capital risk. The market for some – especially those in smaller companies – is often not very active, so you might have to wait to find a buyer and/or accept a much lower price than you had expected (liquidity risk). Shares in private companies are not quoted on a stock exchange at all and it might be impossible to find anyone willing to buy them.

In addition to differences in the companies that issue shares, there are also different types of share. Most commonly, you will buy ordinary shares. But there are also preference shares which carry additional rights

– see Table 9.11. Preference shares straddle the border between bonds and shares, offering some of the security of bonds with some of the growth potential of shares.

**Table 9.11 Preference and ordinary shares compared**

|  | *Preference shares* | *Ordinary shares* |
|---|---|---|
| Income (dividends) | Most preference shares pay dividends up to a fixed rate, similar to the fixed interest you would get from a bond. | Dividends are paid out only once all obligations to preference shareholders have been met in full. The amount paid out may vary from year to year. |
|  | The dividends to the preference shareholders up to that fixed rate must be paid before the ordinary shareholders can have any dividends. |  |
|  | Unlike a bond, there is no promise to pay the dividend which could be cut or missed. If these are cumulative preference shares, any dividends which are missed must be made good in future years before any dividends to ordinary shareholders can restart. | There is no guarantee of any dividend. If dividends are missed, they are not made good in later years. |
|  | 'Participating' preference shares, in addition to the fixed-rate dividend, may also receive an extra share of the company's profits if specified conditions are met. |  |
| Capital | You can sell your shares on the stock market. Some preference shares are redeemable which means they have a fixed life at the end of which you get back, say, £100 for each £100 nominal of shares you hold – again, very similar to bonds. | Normally, the only way to get your capital back is to sell your shares on the stock market. |
| If the company is wound up | All the debts of the company must be paid off. If any money is left over, preference shareholders are first in line to get any money back. | Ordinary shareholders are last in line and will get anything back only after all the preference shareholders have been paid in full. |

Both the ordinary shares of large, well-established companies (often called 'blue-chip' after the most valuable token in poker) and preference shares can be useful for investors seeking income. Ordinary shares generally, and especially those of smaller, growing companies, are useful for investors seeking growth.

Companies are the main drivers of economic growth, so share performance tends to rise and fall with the state of the economy. But different industries respond in different ways. Some shares are called 'defensive' because they tend to fall less than the stock market in bad times. They include shares in sectors such as food, fuel and water, because these are all things that people still need to buy even in a recession. Small luxury goods may also be resilient because when consumers cannot afford big-ticket items they may console themselves instead with small, affordable treats. In the past these used to be items like lipstick; these days it may be a coffee in Starbucks. By contrast, 'aggressive stocks' are shares that tend to outperform the market on its way up and fall harder when the market goes down. They tend to be smaller then the blue chip companies with, investors hope, the potential to grow to that size.

# 10

# Managing your wealth

## Introduction

The key to many financial goals is successfully investing your money. Chapter 9 describes the risks involved, tax considerations and the main building blocks of investment. This chapter focuses on selecting and building these blocks and other more sophisticated instruments into successful investment strategies. As you know from Chapter 9, there is no way simultaneously to avoid all risks. Inevitably your strategies will involve trading off one risk against another or accepting a lower potential return as the price of reducing risk. The strategies described in this chapter show you ways of achieving a balance, drawing on some of the techniques used by professional advisers and fund managers. Figure 10.1 summarises at a high level a financial planning approach to investment.

Your attitude towards risk will be an important factor in the strategies you choose. But, however naturally cautious you are, there are some situations in which you will have to take some risks if you are to stand a reasonable chance of achieving your goals. Failing to embrace risk at the expense of your goals could be called 'reckless caution' – for example, relying on savings accounts to deliver an income over the long term may seem low risk but embeds the near certainty that your living standards will have to fall over time because of the effects of inflation.

Conversely, even if you enoy taking risks, higher risk strategies will not be suitable for all goals. By all means speculate using derivatives (see p. 325) – just don't do it with the children's education money or your pension fund. You need also to be alert to the true nature of the risks involved in

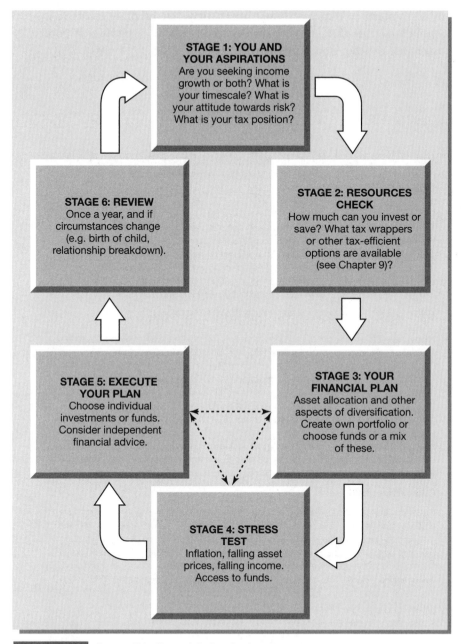

**Figure 10.1**  A possible financial plan for investment

any investment, so that you do not unwittingly take on more risk than is appropriate either through your own decision making or because of poor advice – see the case studies below.

The first, most fundamental, risk-balancing strategy is diversification.

## Case study

Mr and Mrs H had a number of complaints about the endowment policy sold to them in April 1992, the main problem being that they considered the sale unsuitable because they did not wish to take any risk.

**Complaint upheld**

The firm had been unable to produce any documentation from the time of the sale. We therefore used the endowment mortgage questionnaire and established that the policy was too high-risk for Mr and Mrs H. They described themselves as 'cautious' people, who had no previous experience of mortgage endowments. They had no other investments and there was nothing to support the firm's view that the couple had been prepared to accept the risk associated with endowments.

*Source*: Financial Ombudsman Service, *Ombudsman News*, August 2001.

Mr M was 72 and living on a modest pension when he was advised to invest £5,000 in a high-income bond. The firm's product literature for the bond warned that investors could lose a small amount of capital. The 'fact find' completed by the firm recorded that Mr M was 'seeking capital growth' and was prepared to take a medium/high level of risk with his investment. However, Mr M had not signed the 'fact find' and there was no record that the adviser had discussed any alternative type of investment with him. Several years later, alerted by press reports about some of the disadvantages of high-income bonds, Mr M contacted the firm. He discovered that the value of his investment had dropped considerably. Although the level of growth he had been promised was guaranteed, he now realised that the return of his original investment was not. So he complained to the firm.

**Complaint upheld**

We noted that Mr M had little experience of stock market investment and had never had any medium/high risk investments before. At the time he was advised to put his money into the bond, his capital was all in a deposit account, apart from £1,000 in premium bonds and £3,200 in a low-risk personal equity plan (PEP) that included some shares. Although, after investing in the bond, Mr M still had some funds put by for emergencies, nearly 75% of his capital was in equity-based investments. We upheld this complaint on the grounds that the firm's advice had been inappropriate and had exposed Mr M to too great a degree of financial risk, in view of his circumstances.

*Source*: Financial Ombudsman Service, *Ombudsman News*, March 2003.

# Diversification

At its simplest, diversification means: don't put all your eggs in one basket. However, underlying this statement is a tricky question: if not one basket, what others should you should use? Diversification can mean choosing a range of investments (see below), a range of asset classes (see p. 299) and also a range of timing (see p. 304).

## Investment diversification

Chapter 9 suggests that, for superior returns over the long term, you need to look at investing in shares (equities). Which shares should you choose and how many companies should you invest in?

Suppose you invest £10,000 in the shares of Taylor Wimpey (a house builder) and the price falls by 10 per cent, you will make a loss of £1,000. If you invest £5,000 in Taylor Wimpey shares and £5,000 in Tesco (a food retailer) and its shares rise 5 per cent, then a £500 loss on Taylor Wimpey shares would be offset by a gain of £250 on the Tesco shares. Holding two stocks in your portfolio instead of one has reduced the impact of a loss on one of them. On the other hand, you could think of the Taylor Wimpey holding as having reduced (in this case, more than offset) the £500 gain you would have made if you had invested your whole £10,000 in Tesco. So diversification has a smoothing effect which reduces the risk of loss but also reduces the chance (risk) of gains. If you are a cautious investor, you are likely to welcome the risk reduction. If you are an aggressive investor, you might prefer to concentrate your money rather than diversify.

In the example above, the chance of Taylor Wimpey and Tesco shares behaving differently is reasonably high. Taylor Wimpey is a 'cyclical stock', meaning that the company's fortunes tend to move up and down with the state of the economy generally. If the economy is growing, the housing market tends to boom and the volume and profitability of the housebuilding business tends to rise. If the economy moves into recession, fewer people can afford new homes and home construction companies' activity and profits tend to fall. Tesco, by contrast, as a food retailer, is in a traditionally 'defensive' sector – people eat whether the economy is in boom or bust, so food retailers' shares can be expected to hold up well in a downturn but will not necessarily be the brightest stars in a boom. When shares respond differently to events, they are said to be 'uncorrelated' and it can be shown statistically that the risk of a portfolio containing such shares is lower than the risk of each of the component shares (see the case study). In practice, different shares are never completely uncorrelated, but a weak correlation will still produce a reduction in risk. So diversification is not just about spreading risk – it can actually reduce the amount of risk you bear for any given level of return.

If you had split your money between Taylor Wimpey and Persimmon (another house builder), chances are that Persimmon shares might also fall at the same time as Taylor Wimpey. In this case, the shares are strongly correlated and diversification does not significantly reduce risk. Therefore, for diversification to work best, you need to select companies which are likely to respond in different ways to changing business and economic conditions and events. This could mean spreading your money across a range of business sectors. Taking diversification a stage further, why stick to the shares of companies linked to just one economy? Spreading your money across the shares of companies based in the UK, the rest of Europe, the USA and Asia increases diversification even further.

If you are interested in selecting your own shares, two particularly good free sources of share data are the websites ADVFN and Yahoo Finance. For profiles setting out the basics of companies listed on the UK main market, visit the London Stock Exchange website. (See Appendix B for contact details.)

## Case study

Rebekah likes to manage her own investments and is interested in the mathematics behind performance and risk measurement. Risk can be measured using a statistic called 'standard deviation' which is calculated from price data for the past few years (usually three or five). If standard deviation is small, then the future return from an investment is likely to be within a narrow range, so risk is low. If the standard deviation is high, future returns could be in a much wider range and so the risk is high. Rebekah thinks she has found two investments that are completely uncorrelated. One has a risk level (standard deviation) of 10 and the other of 8. She can work out that if she combines them in a portfolio, putting half her money in each of the investments, the risk level will be 6.4. In other words, combining the two investments produces a portfolio that has lower risk than either of the investments independently.

### How much diversification do you need?

Diversification as a method of reducing risk has its limits. On a day-to-day basis, different companies' shares may seem to respond to different events or to the same events in different ways. But step back and they all tend to follow the big market trends in a similar way. This is because companies these days are complex organisations often operating across a range of markets and using similar financial management tools, so the big-picture business and economic factors that affect one company usually affect other companies too. Even different markets around the world tend to move in tandem, especially as businesses and economies become more globalised. Figure 10.2 shows the main stock market index for four different stock markets in different parts of the world over the years 2005 to 2009. What is striking about the indices is that they display a broadly similar pattern of movement. Spreading your money across these different markets would not necessarily have resulted in losses in one market being offset by gains in another, though individual stocks in any of the markets could have bucked the overall trend. Therefore, financial experts distinguish two types of risk:[1]

■ **Specific risk** (also called idiosyncratic risk). This is the extent to which a share's price or return moves independently of the stock market as a whole. A share's 'alpha' is a measure of this type of risk.

■ **Market risk** (also called systematic risk). This is the extent to which changes in a share's price or return simply reflect changes in the market as a whole. It is measured by a share's 'beta'.

Diversification can help you get rid of specific risk, but it cannot remove market risk. To see this, imagine if you held every share in the market: you would in effect be holding the market itself, so all the specific risks would have combined to produce only the market risk. In practice, you do not need to hold every share in the market to eliminate specific risk. An influential academic study found that by the time you have around ten or so shares in your portfolio – even if these are randomly selected rather than carefully looking for uncorrelated shares – you will have eliminated most of the specific risk.[2]

---

[1] See, for example, Sharpe, W., 1981, *Investments*, Englewood Cliffs: Prentice Hall Inc.

[2] Evans J. L. and Archer S. H., 1968, 'Diversification and the reduction of dispersion: an empirical analysis' in *Journal of Finance*, December.

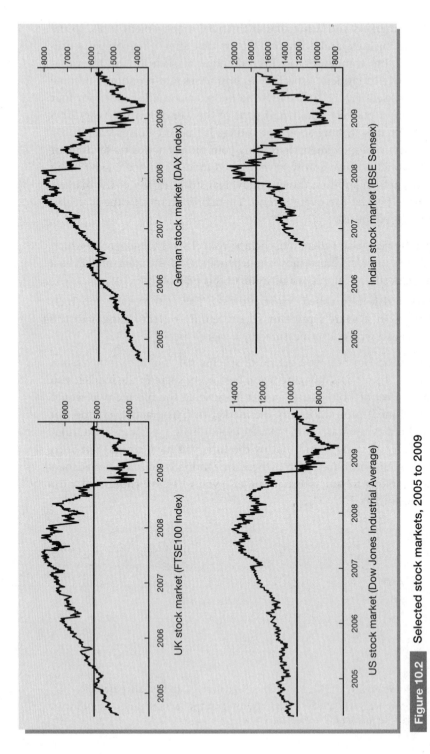

**Figure 10.2**    Selected stock markets, 2005 to 2009

*Source:* ADVFN, www.advfn.com/index/StockMarketIndices.asp. Accessed 3 October 2009.

## Interpreting beta

'Beta' is an indicator of relative risk. It measures the sensitivity of the return on a share (or other investment) to changes in the market as a whole. It is worked out statistically using data from, typically, the past three or five years. The beta for the market is by definition 1.

Although the theory which underpins the measure beta is based on the returns from investments, the published betas for shares are based on price movements only (and not dividends as well). Movements in the share price are measured relative to a stock-market index: for example, in the UK, the FTSE All Share Index would be a typical choice.

If a share has a beta greater than 1, its price will tend to rise by more than the stock market as a whole when the market is rising and fall by more when the market is falling. A beta greater than 1 is typical of growth stocks and cyclical stocks. Taking the example earlier in this chapter, in October 2009, the published beta for Taylor Wimpey was 2.98.[3] This means that, based on past data, when the stock market moves by 1 per cent, on average the Taylor Wimpey share price will move by 2.98 × 1% = 2.98%.

If a share has a beta of less than 1. its price will tend to rise and fall by less than the market. This is typical of defensive stocks. Using the earlier example, the beta of Tesco in October 2009 was 0.83.[4] Therefore a 1 per cent change in the stock market would on average cause a 0.83 × 1% = 0.83% change in the Tesco share price.

The higher the beta, the higher the relative risk of the stock and the greater the returns you should expect. The lower the beta, the lower the risk and the lower the expected return. An aggressive investment strategy would focus on shares with betas greater than 1 when you expect the stock market to rise. A cautious investor might prefer shares with betas of less than 1 since based on past performance they are less volatile than other shares.

You can compare betas for shares only in the same market. Betas calculated relative to different stock-market indices are not comparable.

## Asset allocation

Although investment diversification has been described above in the context of shares, it applies equally to any other type of investment that is traded on a market, such as bonds and even residential property (see the discussion of buy-to-let on p. 330). Diversification also applies across the boundaries of different investments. Just as combining uncorrelated or weakly correlated shares reduces risk for any given level of return, combining different types of investments – called asset classes – also improves the risk-return balance, provided the classes are uncorrelated or only

---

[3] www.advfn.com. Accessed 3 October 2009.

[4] www.advfn.com. Accessed 3 October 2009.

weakly correlated. Traditionally, there are four main asset classes which, in ascending order of capital risk, are:

■ **Cash**, meaning deposit-type investments where you earn interest and the risk to your capital is usually negligible. For private investors, accounts with banks, building societies and National Savings & Investments would count as cash.

■ **Bonds**. These are the government bonds (also called gilts when issued by the UK government) and corporate bonds considered in Chapter 9, including index-linked bonds.

■ **Property**. Normally this refers to commercial property, for example, holding of office blocks, shopping centres and industrial parks or shares in companies that specialise in owning and managing these. Private investors often hold residential property as an investment.

■ **Equities**. These are shares in companies.

In general, these four classes tend to be sufficiently uncorrelated – responding to economic events in different ways – to improve the risk-return balance when they are combined in a portfolio. For example, equities and property tend to do well in times of inflation, unlike cash and bonds. But cash and bonds may produce solid returns in an economic downturn, while property and equities tend to suffer.

The extent to which different investments or assets are correlated can be measured and represented by a statistic called a 'correlation coefficient'. A coefficient of 1 would mean that two asset classes moved in exactly the same way (so there would not be any point combining the assets). A coefficient of zero would mean the asset classes were completely uncorrelated. Most coefficients lie between these two extremes. A negative coefficient means that positive performance for one asset class is associated with negative performance from the other. (A coefficient of –1 would mean the assets were perfectly negatively correlated with the risk of losses on one asset being completely offset by the chance of gains on the other, so eliminating risk altogether for a portfolio made up of these two assets.) Table 10.1 on p. 301 shows the correlation coefficient for different pairs of asset class using data for the period from 1997 to 2009. The ideal for investors is to combine asset classes that have low or negative correlations, say, less than 0.5.

The global financial crisis that hit the world in 2007 demonstrated that, in some situations, the relative independence of the asset classes can break down, with all delivering poor performance simultaneously. Even before this, investment professionals have been on the hunt for new asset classes and it is variously claimed that gold (see p. 331), art (see p. 332), hedge funds (see p. 328) and a variety of other investments all fit the bill. In practice, it is not always clear that they do provide the benefits of diversification that are claimed. For example, the global crisis cast doubts on the ability of hedge funds to deliver uncorrelated returns.

**Table 10.1 How asset classes are correlated**

*Asset classes with a relatively low correlation (less than 0.5) are shown in bold.*

|  | *Cash* | *UK government bonds* | *Property* | *UK equities* | *International equities* |
|---|---|---|---|---|---|
| Cash |  |  |  |  |  |
| UK government bonds | **0.25** |  |  |  |  |
| Property | **0.29** | **0.02** |  |  |  |
| UK equities | **−0.03** | **0.28** | 0.53 |  |  |
| International equities | **0.06** | **0.28** | **0.44** | 0.96 |  |

*Source*: Author's own work based on yearly return data from *Money Management* (January 1998–December 2009).

There are two ways to approach asset allocation. If you follow the teachings of academic theory, you can construct a relatively low-risk portfolio by combining assets that have a low correlation. This works even if the constituent assets are fairly high risk as long as the correlation between them is low enough. This to a large extent explains the traditional popularity of commercial property as part of a portfolio – although usually a higher-risk-higher-return asset than bonds, its correlation with cash and gilts is low (0.29 and 0.02, repectively in Table 10.1) and even the correlation with equities falls well short of 1.0 (0.53 for UK equities and 0.44 for international equities in Table 10.1), making it a good partner with shares in a portfolio. But practice is harder than theory. Measurements of correlation are based on data from the past which, to use the common regulatory warning, is no guide to the future. If the assets that seemed to be uncorrelated in the past become more closely correlated because of a change in economic conditions, the risk inherent in your portfolio will be higher than you had expected or wanted.

Many investors, both private and professional, take a less theoretical approach to asset allocation. Convential wisdom suggests that you should hold several asset classes, but vary the mix according to the level of risk appropriate to your situation and investment timescale. When you are young with plenty of time to ride out dips in the stock market and many years of earnings ahead, you can afford to put a high proportion of your wealth into equities. When you are older, you will still need some exposure to equities (to provide protection against inflation) but should hold a higher proportion of cash and bonds. There are some rough rules of thumb. For example, one rule suggests that taking your age away from 100 per cent gives you the proportion you should invest in equities. Thus, if you are 20, you should have 100 – 20 = 80 per cent of your wealth in equities; if you are 60, 40 per cent, and so on.

The asset mix will also depend on your personal attitude towards risk and the nature of your goals. In general, equities are good for capital growth, whereas bonds and property come into their own particularly for income investors. Table 10.2 below shows examples of three portfolios for different types of investor. These are average portfolios compiled by the Association of Private Client Investment Managers and Stockbrokers in summer 2009 from a survey of the recommendations its members make to their clients. The first portfolio is for income investors, the second for growth investors and the third (called a 'balanced portfolio') is for investors seeking both income and growth. In the aftermath of the global financial crisis and ensuing recession, commercial property was still not performing well, which probably explains the low percentage of the portfolio in property even for income investors. The main differences between the portfolios are the proportions invested in bonds (more for income seekers), the split of equities between UK and international (a higher proportion in international for growth seekers) and the use of hedge funds for growth.

Asset allocation is highly personalised. The mix that works for one investor cannot simply be transported across to another. You can find a useful free online tool to help you select an asset allocation that may be suitable for you at the website of the Iowa Public Employees Retirement System, www.ipers.org/calcs/AssetAllocator.html. Although this is a US site and the tool is denominated in dollars, you can interpret it as if it were in pounds. The US tax rates are different, so you will have to approximate these for UK rates. But overall the suggested allocations are as relevant to investors in the UK as in the USA.

**Table 10.2 Examples of portfolios for different types of investor**

|  | Income portfolio % | Growth portfolio % | Balanced portfolio % |
|---|---|---|---|
| UK shares | 45.0 | 47.5 | 42.5 |
| International shares | 10.0 | 30.0 | 22.5 |
| Bonds | 37.5 | 7.5 | 20.0 |
| Cash | 5.0 | 5.0 | 5.0 |
| Commercial property | 2.5 | 2.5 | 2.5 |
| Hedge funds | – | 7.5 | 7.5 |
| **Total** | **100** | **100** | **100** |

*Source*: Association of Private Client Investment Managers and Stockbrokers, 2009. http://www.apcims.co.uk/investors/private_investor_indices.php. Accessed 3 October 2009.

### Commercial property as a source of income

Commercial property includes shopping centres, office blocks, business parks, industrial units and the like. An important part of the return is generated by rents paid by the tenants of these shops, offices, factories and workshops. Commercial leases tend to be written so that, when reviewed, rents can only be revised upwards not down. So, unlike the fixed interest offered by bonds, income from property has a built-in tendency to rise. Therefore, commercial property is often looked on as a good investment for private investors seeking income.

A further part of the return comes from any rise or fall in the value of the properties themselves. This will be influenced by the demand for shop premises, office space, and so on. Therefore it is sensitive to the state of the economy. In boom times, existing businesses expand and new businesses spring up creating extra demand for premises, pushing prices higher, which attracts growth investors to the sector. In recessions, businesses fail; shops and office blocks stand empty, so commercial property prices tend to fall.

Private investors normally invest in commercial property through investment funds (see p. 307).

## Rebalancing

As some investments do better than others, your portfolio will drift from the asset allocation you have chosen. Rebalancing is the process of selling some assets and buying others in order to restore the intended allocation.

However, rebalancing is a controversial topic. Advocates claim that it encourages sound investment behaviour. If one asset class – say, shares – does well relative to the others, it will become over-represented in your allocation. Therefore, you should sell shares and buy more of the assets that have done less well. This means you are forced to sell high and buy low, which is the basis of all buy-and-hold investment strategies. (See the case study below).

Opponents of rebalancing question why you would sell investments that are doing well and buy into poor performers. One wit likened this to picking the flowers and leaving the weeds. There is also the question of how often rebalancing should take place. If you rebalance often – say, every six months – dealing costs will eat more heavily into your returns than if you rebalance infrequently.

A middle course might be to consider rebalancing as an option when you review your investments, say, once a year, but defer rebalancing if it looks premature given investment conditions at that time.

## Case study

> Faz, in his mid-50s and investing for growth, allocated his £100,000 portfolio as follows: shares 45 per cent, property 20 per cent, bonds 30 per cent and cash 5 per cent. At the end of a year, the shares have grown by 15 per cent, property by 8 per cent, the bonds have fallen by 10 per cent and the cash has remained fairly static. Overall his portfolio is now worth £105,350 and the allocation has drifted as shown in Figure 10.3 opposite. He has to decide whether to sell some equities and property and buy bonds to restore his original allocation.

## Time diversification

As a buy-and-hold growth investor (also called investing 'long'), your aim is to buy investments when their price is low and sell when they are high. Sounds simple enough, but in practice it is either difficult or impossible – depending on which school of thought you believe (see p. 309) – to get the timing right. And private investors are notorious for waiting so long after a change in market direction that they tend to invest when the market is near its peak and sell shortly before it hits rock bottom.

Time diversification removes the risk of getting the timing completely wrong – but also removes the chance of getting the timing absolutely right. You can use timing diversification on the way into the market, the way out or both. It can be used with any investment that is 'fungible'

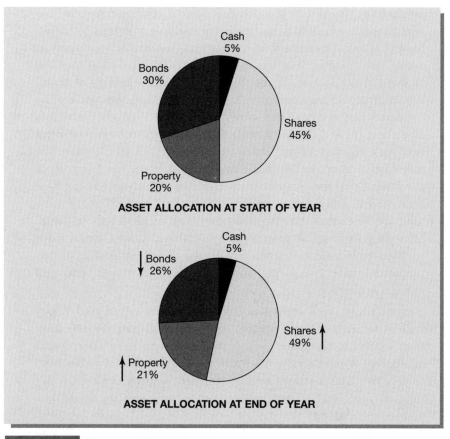

**Figure 10.3**  How portfolio allocation can drift

(divisible into units where one unit is the same as another), such as shares and bonds, units in an investment fund, and so on.

On the way into the market, instead of investing a single lump sum, you invest in regular smaller amounts – for example, monthly. A claimed advantage for this approach is 'pound cost averaging', which simply means that the weighted average price you pay for the investment is lower than the unweighted price over the period. This arises because when the price is low, the same sum of money buys more units than when the buying price is high – see the case study opposite.

When you come to withdraw money from the market, the principle is the same – take your money out in several small stages rather than as a single lump sum. There are two popular ways of doing this:

■ **Lifestyling**. This can be used where you need your money to be in a liquid form at a certain future time. For example, you may be investing to produce a pension fund that you will use to buy an annuity at age 65 (see Chapter 8) or managing your child's trust fund that will be spent at age 18 (see Chapter 9). Lifestyling is the process of gradually shifting your asset allocation from equities into bonds and cash as the date when you need the money approaches. Typically the shift is made over the last five years or so of the investment term. The effect is to lock in gains already made from the equities and insulate the investments from any fall in the stock market in the last few years of the term. Of course, if stock markets are in a downturn at the time lifestyling is due to start, you might want to suspend the process (and maybe extend the investment term) rather than lock in losses. Lifestyling within a pension fund, by shifting you into bonds, helps to align your fund investments with the investments that underpin annuity rates (see p. 234) and so insulate you from the effects of changes in annuity rates.

■ **Target dating**. Target-date investment funds aim to return your money on a set future date. They employ lifestyling, by shifting the allocation from equities to bonds and cash, in the last few years as the target date approaches. You select the fund with the target date that corresponds to your desired investment term. If you want your money back earlier or later, you switch to another target-date fund with the target date you are now seeking.

The main drawback of time diversification is that it may increase dealing costs because you are trading frequently in smaller amounts.

## Case study

In 2007, Carol wanted to invest in the shares of several companies but was unsure when would be the best time to buy. She could not predict how share prices would move in future, but now with hindsight she can see how her strategies would have worked out.

Take just one of the companies, International Power. Table 10.3 shows International Power's share price at six-monthly intervals during the period 2007 to 2009. Carol had £10,000 to invest in this company. If she had invested the full £10,000 in one go, she would have done best if she had waited and invested in January 2009. She would then have picked up the shares cheaply, paying 271.75p per share and six months later her holding would have been worth £15,189. The worst month to buy would have been July 2007 when the price hit a peak of 413.75p per share. By July 2009, Carol's shares would have been standing at a loss and valued at £9,976.

If instead, Carol had ignored timing and invested £2,000 every six months, by July 2009, she would have 2,760 shares valued at £11,393. While this is not as good as the gain she would have made investing the whole sum in January 2009, it is a good deal better than the loss she would have made investing in July 2007.

The pound-cost-averaging enthusiasts claim the alchemy of the regular investments is paying an average price for the shares of £10,000/2,760 = 362.32p which is less than the average share price over the period of (360.25 + 413.75 + 399.00 + 412.75 + 271.75)/5 = 371.50.

**Table 10.3 Example of pound cost averaging**

| | | | Invest full £10,000 in month shown | | Invest £2,000 a month | |
|---|---|---|---|---|---|---|
| Year | Month | International Power share price (pence) | Number of shares | Value of holding in July 2009 | Number of shares purchased | Value of holding in July 2009 |
| 2007 | Jan | 360.25 | 2776 | £11,457 | 555 | |
| | July | 413.75 | 2417 | £9,976 | 483 | |
| 2008 | Jan | 399.00 | 2506 | £10,345 | 501 | |
| | July | 412.75 | 2423 | £10,000 | 485 | |
| 2009 | Jan | 271.75 | 3680 | £15,189 | 736 | |
| | July | 412.75 | | **Total** | **2760** | **£11,393** |
| Average share price | | 371.50 | | Average share price paid | | 362.32 |

# Investment funds – the basics

You do not have to go to the trouble of constructing your own portfolio from scratch. You can instead buy into ready-made portfolios: investment funds. You may still want to combine different funds to achieve the spread of investments and asset allocation that is right for you.

## Pros and cons of using investment funds

An investment fund pools your money with that of lots of other investors. One advantage of investing in this way is that you can access a well-spread portfolio of shares and/or other investments with only a small outlay. Many investment funds accept minimum investments as low as £500 as a lump sum or £25 a month in regular savings. If you were to build your own diversified portfolio of shares, you would need holdings in at least ten companies (see p. 297) and dealing charges make purchases under around £1,000 each uneconomic, so you would need to have at least £10,000 to invest.

Because the investment fund is buying in bulk, it will usually be able to negotiate lower dealing charges than you would have to pay as a private share investor.

Using an investment fund may save you a lot of time and trouble. If you believe it is possible to pick stock-market winners and time buying and selling accurately, being a DIY investor will involve you in a lot of detailed research into companies and their shares. That's fine if you have the time and enjoy stock-picking (perhaps as part of an investment club – see p. 314), but if not you can leave this task to professional fund managers.

Investment funds can give you access to strategies that are difficult or impossible for private investors. For example, if you want to invest in the whole stock market, this would be impossible if you were buying each share yourself, but a fund can do this. If you want to invest abroad, it can be difficult trading on foreign stock exchanges and storing foreign shares safely. Investment funds have the contacts and know-who to invest over-seas efficiently and safely.

The main drawback of using an investment fund is charges. Some of the return from your investments will be drawn off to pay for the professionals who run the fund. Charges can come in a variety of forms – see the discussion of each type of fund on pp. 311–22 – but all funds will levy some type of annual management charge (AMC). This typically varies from less than 0.5 per cent for exchange-traded funds up to 1.5 per cent or even more for other funds. In addition, there will be other yearly charges associated with running the fund. The AMC and most of these other charges can be collectively measured by looking at the total expense ration (TER) – see the box.

It is important to appreciate that annual charges are levied as a percentage of your investment fund, not as a percentage of your return. You pay the charges whether your investment has grown or not and, in effect, the same pool of assets is being charged over and over again. This means a small-sounding AMC or TER can in fact take a big slice out of your investment over the long term – see Table 10.4. For example, if you invest £10,000 for 15 years and the annual charge is 1 per cent a year, you would (based on the assumptions in Table 10.4) get back just under £19,400 compared with the £23,616 your fund would have grown to without charges. The 1 per cent a year charge has cumulatively taken 18 per cent of your potential fund.

**Table 10.4 The impact of annual charges on a lump sum investment**

*The table shows the value of a £10,000 investment at the end of the term shown in the first column, after charges have been deducted. The investment is assumed to grow at 7 per cent a year and all amounts are shown in today's money assuming that inflation averages 2.5 per cent a year.*

| Investment term | No charges | Annual management charge % pa | | | | |
|---|---|---|---|---|---|---|
| | | 0.50% | 1% | 1.50% | 2% | 2.50% |
| 1 | £10,439 | £10,387 | £10,336 | £10,285 | £10,235 | £10,185 |
| 2 | £10,897 | £10,790 | £10,684 | £10,579 | £10,476 | £10,374 |
| 3 | £11,376 | £11,208 | £11,043 | £10,881 | £10,722 | £10,566 |
| 4 | £11,875 | £11,642 | £11,414 | £11,192 | £10,974 | £10,762 |
| 5 | £12,397 | £12,093 | £11,798 | £11,511 | £11,232 | £10,962 |
| 10 | £15,367 | £14,624 | £13,919 | £13,250 | £12,617 | £12,016 |
| 15 | £19,050 | £17,684 | £16,421 | £15,252 | £14,171 | £13,171 |
| 20 | £23,616 | £21,385 | £19,372 | £17,557 | £15,918 | £14,437 |

**Total expense ratio**

The total expense ratio (TER) is a measure of the annual cost of operating an investment fund. The main component is the annual management charge, but also included are trustee fees, custodian charges for holding the underlying investments, cost of the annual audit, and so on. Dealing charges for buying and selling the underlying assets are not included.

The expenses are expressed as a percentage of the value of the investment fund to give a ratio. The TER, which typically lies in the range 0.5 to 2 per cent, will tend to be higher for smaller rather than larger funds and for those holding overseas investments.

## Active versus passive funds

An academic debate that has important consequences for practical investing through funds is the question of whether stock markets are efficient. An efficient market will ensure that the prices of all shares accurately reflect the balance of risk and return. For example, investors will have to pay a relatively high price for a stable blue-chip share, like Marks & Spencer, so the scope for large price movements and high gains will be reduced to reflect the low-risk nature of the shares. Conversely, investors will pay a relatively low price for the shares of a high-risk growth company. If a share price looks too cheap (so that the return that can be expected looks too high), investors will almost instantly snap up this bargain. This demand from investors will drive the price up to its 'correct' price. If a share price looks too high (expected returns look too low), no-one will want to buy and lack of demand will drag the price down until it reaches the 'correct' level.

For the market to work in this efficient manner, investors must have all the information they need to price shares correctly. What academics call the 'efficient market hypothesis' assumes this is the case and that a company's share price encapsulates all that is known about the company, its shares, the markets it operates in and all relevant economic and other factors. In its strongest form, the argument claims that the share price also already encapsulates investors' expectations about how these factors will change in future and that the only thing that can move the share price is new, totally unpredictable information.[5] If markets really are efficient, then there is no opportunity for investors, be they private individuals or fund managers, consistently to pick stocks in order to make superior returns or to predict the timing of changes in market prices. In other words, there is no way consistently to exploit the specific risk of individual shares to make 'alpha' gains.

In that case, there is little point exposing yourself to specific risk. It would be better to get rid of it through diversification. Although specific risk can be substantially reduced by holding relatively few shares, it can be completely eradicated by holding all the shares on the market – in other words, holding an investment fund that simply aims to track the market as a whole. If you want to adjust the risk–return balance, then you can split your money between the market and a risk-free or nearly risk-free asset such as cash. So to reduce risk you hold the market and cash; to increase risk you borrow extra cash to buy more of the market. This strategy is called 'passive' investing.

The main tools of passive investing are tracker funds. A tracker fund is constructed to reproduce the performance of a selected stock market index. Some funds do actually hold every single stock in the market. But an alternative technique – there are others – is 'representative sampling'. A reduced number of shares held are those that account for the majority

---

[5] Fama, E., 1970, 'Efficient capital markets: a review of theory and empirical works' in *Journal of Finance*, May.

of a stock market's movements. The published 'tracking error' for the fund gives a measure of how closely it succeeds in reproducing the underlying market movements.

Not surprisingly, many fund managers reject the efficient market hypothesis and related theories. 'Active' fund managers believe they can, through their research and skills, pick winners and deliver better performance than the market as a whole. The occasional Warren Buffetts of the world do suggest there may be something in this view. However, most academic studies into fund performance have found little evidence that fund managers do consistently add value, especially once the managers' charges are deducted from the investment returns.

A plus point for tracker funds is that their charges tend to be lower than for active funds, because most of the expert input is at the outset in constructing the portfolio, whereas an active portfolio requires the ongoing research and attention of its managers. The turnover of underlying investments is also likely to be lower in a tracker fund, resulting in lower dealing charges.

## The different forms of investment fund

Investment funds come in a variety of forms Table 10.5 gives sources of information about each form and Table 10.6 summarises the differences. The form of fund you choose affects the tax treatment and the level of charges you face. But once tax and charges are stripped away, the types of fund (see p. 323) you can choose are broadly similar. A good strategy is to work from the type of fund upwards, in other words decide on the type of portfolio that will help you meet your goals, then look for the form of fund or tax wrapper that will give you the best tax and charges treatment.

### Table 10.5 Information about investment funds

*The easiest way to access information about investment funds is to use the internet.*

| Website | Type of site | Type of fund |
|---|---|---|
| www.fsa.gov.uk/tables | Regulator | UTO (ISAs only), LF |
| www.fundsdirect.co.uk | Fund supermarket | UTO |
| www.morningstar.co.uk | Information | NUTO, IT, LF, PF, ETF |
| www.trustnet.co.uk | Information | UTO, IT, PF, LF, OF, ETF, VCT |
| www.fundsnetwork.co.uk | Fund supermarket | UTO |

▶

**Table 10.5 Information about investment funds** *continued*

| Website | Type of site | Type of fund |
|---------|--------------|--------------|
| www.citywire.co.uk | Information | UTO, IT, LF, PF, ETF |
| www.investmentuk.org | Trade body | UTO |
| www.theaic.co.uk | Trade body | IT, VCT |
| www.abi.org.uk | Trade body | LF, PF |

Type of fund: UTO = unit trusts and oeics; IT = investment trusts; PF = pension funds; LF = life funds; OF = offshore funds; ETF = exchange traded funds; VCT = venture capital trusts.

**Table 10.6 Forms of investment fund**

| Fund | Tax treatment | Charges tend to be: | Other |
|------|---------------|---------------------|-------|
| Unit trusts and open-ended investment companies | Can be held direct or through a tax wrapper (pension scheme, individual savings account, child trust fund – see Chapters 7 and 9). | Medium; lower for tracker funds (see p. 311) | |
| Investment trusts | Can be held direct or through a tax wrapper (pension scheme, individual savings account, child trust fund – see Chapters 7 and 9). | Usually lower than for unit trusts | Fund can borrow, so leverage increases risk and potential returns. |
| Exchange-traded funds | Can often be held direct or through a tax wrapper (pension scheme, individual savings account, child trust fund – see Chapters 7 and 9). | Very low | Some funds borrow, so leverage increases risk and potential returns. |
| Insurance funds (non-pension) | Ready wrapped. Tax treatment often unfavourable (see Chapter 9). | High | With-profits option available (see p. 321). |
| Insurance funds (pension) | Ready wrapped. Along with other pension wrappers, usually most tax-advantageous way to invest (see Chapter 7). | High | With-profits option available (see p. 321). |
| Friendly society tax-efficient plans | Ready wrapped. Advantageous tax treatment (see Chapter 9). | High | With-profits option available (see p. 321). |

## Unit trusts and open-ended investment companies

With a unit trust, your money is pooled and used to buy investments which are held in a fund run by the unit trust management company. You are allocated units which represent a share of the underlying fund. Unit trusts are 'open-ended'. This means that, if more people want to invest than cash in their units, the manager will create new units and the fund will buy additional investments with the net new money coming in. If more people want to cash in than buy units, the manager will cancel units and the fund will sell investments to meet the outflow of funds. This means that the number of units in issue rises and falls directly in line with the underlying investment fund and the price of each unit is directly linked to the value of the underlying investments.

The fund is set up as a trust, so the investments are legally owned by the trustee but held on behalf of the investors. Some unit trusts are set up as 'umbrella funds' with a range of different types of fund within a single trust. But usually each type of fund is a separate trust so, to move from one fund to another, you would need to sell your units in the old fund and buy new units in the new one. If you are a capital gains taxpayer this could trigger a tax charge; however most investors do not pay this tax (see Chapter 9).

An open-ended investment company (OEIC) is similar to a unit trust but is a structure more familiar to non-UK investors. Therefore, management companies that wish to market themselves across Europe tend to favour the OEIC structure. The investments are held and managed by a company. The company can issue different shares corresponding to different types of fund and it is relatively easy to switch between the different shares in order to transfer money from one fund to another. Like unit trusts, OEICs are open-ended funds, so the value of the shares you hold directly reflects the value of the underlying investments in the fund. Mutual funds in the USA are the equivalent of UK unit trusts and OEICs.

When you buy a unit trust, there will usually be an up-front charge which mainly comprises a bid–offer spread. This is the difference (usually around 5 per cent) between the price at which you buy the units or shares and the lower price at which you could immediately sell them back. This charge typically covers the cost of marketing the fund and any commission paid to an adviser. If you buy unit trust through a discount broker or fund supermarket, the bid–offer spread is usually reduced or cut altogether. OEICs are single-priced with no bid–offer spread, so buyers and sellers pay the same amount, which is usually set mid-way between where the bid and offer prices would have been.

The other main charge is an annual management charge that pays the fund management company. Often this charge is between 1 and 1.5 per cent, though in 2009 some much lower charging funds began to emerge. There are other charges which are deducted from the fund itself and you can get a measure of the collective effect of most of the charges by looking at the TER.

When you choose a unit trust or OEIC, you will be given a Key Facts document, which sets out information about the investment in a standardised way, and this will include details of any up-front charge and annual management charge, and will show the effect on your investment of the TER.

### Cash and carry

You can buy unit trusts and OEICs direct from the fund management company or through a financial adviser. However, you can usually buy more cheaply if you go to a discount broker (who you might deal with by phone, post or the internet) or fund supermarket (an online store). In either case, you buy without advice and so make your own decisions about which funds to choose. Most discount brokers and fund supermarkets offer an individual savings account (ISA) tax wrapper within which you can mix and match the funds from any provider. Some offer other tax wrappers too, such as self-invested personal pensions. For information, Appendix B gives contact details for a selection of discount brokers and fund supermarkets, but this should not be taken as a recommendation to use these firms over any others.

### Investment clubs

If you enjoy selecting your own investments but are attracted to the advantages of pooling your money with other investors, you might consider starting or joining an investment club. Usually, you organise a club as a private unit trust, so each member has units in the club's fund in proportion to the amount they have invested. For information and comprehensive guidance on setting up and running an investment club, contact Ifs Proshare (see Appendix B).

## Investment trusts

An investment trust is a company quoted on the stock exchange whose business is running an investment fund. You invest by buying shares in the investment trust company. Like any other company, and in contrast to a unit trust, there will be a set number of shares in issue at any time. This makes the fund 'close-ended' and means there is only an indirect relationship between the share price you pay and the value of the under-lying investments in the fund. For example, if buyers exceed sellers, this will tend to push the share price up until it rises above the 'net asset value per share' (NAV). The NAV is the value of the underlying fund divided by the number of shares in the investment trust company. If the share price is higher than the NAV, the shares are said to be trading at a premium. Conversely, if sellers outnumber buyers, this will tend to push the share price down. If the price goes below the NAV, the shares are said to be trad-ing at a discount – in other words, you will be paying less for the shares than you would get back if the trust company were wound up. Investment trusts standing at a discount may seem like bargain buys, but there is no guarantee that the discount will disappear in future. Some investment trusts trade at a discount for many years.

Another important difference between unit trusts and investment trusts is that, being a company, an investment trust can borrow money. This means that investment trusts can make leveraged investments (see Chapter 1). Leverage magnifies the size of any gains but also any losses. Therefore, it is important to check the degree of leverage involved before you invest. A highly leveraged investment strategy will make the invest-ment trust a more risky investment. A measure called 'gearing' is used to indicate the extent of an investment trust's leverage. Gearing is a term used throughout the corporate world and is measured in a variety of ways. The convention with investment trusts is to use an index number that indicates the amount by which shareholders funds will change in response to a change in the value of the total assets. A value of 100 indicates there is no leverage and thus shareholders benefit directly in line with any rise or fall in assets. A value above 100 indicates there is leverage and the higher the value, the greater the borrowings – see the box for an example. Therefore, an investment trust with a gearing figure of, say, 130 would be a more risky investment than a trust with a gearing figure of 110.

Since investment trusts are quoted companies, you normally buy and sell their shares through a stockbroker, so you need to allow for dealing costs (see Chapter 9). However, many investment trust management compa-nies operate savings schemes through which you can either invest lump sums (from around £250 upwards) or regular savings (from £50) and get the benefit of lower-than-normal dealing charges. An investment trust company's charges are deducted from the investment fund and include an annual management charge, typically around 1 per cent and the other costs of operating the fund. Total expense ratios (see p. 309) are published for investment trusts.

> ### An example of the effects of leverage
>
> Suppose an investment trust issues £50 million of shares and also borrows £30 million. Its total funds are £80 million and its gearing is calculated as total funds divided by shareholder funds and expressed as an index number = 80m/50m × 100 = 160.
>
> If over the next year, the fund grows by 10 per cent, the value of the assets rise to 110% × £80m = £88m. For simplicity ignoring interest on the borrowing, after the debt of £30 million has been repaid, shareholders are left with £58 million. So, because of leverage, the 10 per cent rise in asset values has produced a 16 per cent rise in shareholder funds.
>
> If, on the other hand, the fund had fallen in value by 10 per cent, by the end of the year it would have been worth only £72 million. The £30 million would still have to be repaid, leaving shareholders with £42 million. In this case the 10 per cent fall in the fund would have created a 16 per cent loss for the shareholders.
>
> The gearing figure not only tells you the proportion of total funds (debt plus shareholders' funds) to total funds, it can also be used to work out by how much the shareholders' funds will increase or decrease given a rise or fall in total assets. In this case 160/100 × 10% = 16%.

## Split-capital investment trusts

Investment trusts are companies so, in their most basic form, they issue ordinary shares. But they can also issue different types of shares, for example preference shares and shares that carry different rights. There can be a great deal of variation from one trust to another, but in its simplest form a split capital trust is a company with a fixed lifetime, issuing two types of shares:

■ **Income shares**. These carry the right to receive the income from the underlying investments. This is paid out in the form of dividends. When the trust is wound up at the end of its fixed life, shareholders might be promised a fixed amount from the proceeds from selling the underlying assets or nothing at all. These shares are useful for investors seeking income.

■ **Capital shares**. These do not pay any income, but when the trust is wound up, they receive most or all of the proceeds from the sale of the assets. These shares are useful for investors seeking growth.

A variation that was popular some years ago and has started to make a small comeback is the zero-dividend preference share. 'Zeros' as they are known are a type of capital share and pay no income. Because they are preference shares, when the trust is wound up, they are first in line to receive a set pay-out before any ordinary shareholders see p. 290. And, because they pay out a capital gain and no income, the return for many investors is tax-free. Zeros used to be marketed especially as a low-risk way of meeting school fees or providing retirement income. Parents or pensioners would invest in a portfolio of zeros maturing on staggered dates to coincide with the dates when fees would fall due or income was required.

The popularity of zeros was tarnished in the early years of the millennium when many investors lost money despite the supposedly low-risk nature of these shares. It turned out that many split-capital trusts were involved in a 'magic circle' where they were investing in each other's shares (called 'cross-holding'). When the stock market took at nosedive in the year 2000 as a result of the dotcom crash, the value of the investments in the trusts' funds fell with the market. But the fall was then exacerbated by the fall in value of the investment trust shares held within the portfolios of other investment trusts (see the example overleaf). The regulatory position of investment trusts is complicated, because they are treated largely in the same way as Taylor Wimpey, Tesco or any other quoted company and not subject to the same type of rules as, say, unit trusts. This meant investors were not necessarily entitled to redress, unless they had received misleading advice (see case study overleaf), though after negotiation with the Financial Services Authority, a number of trusts agreed without admitting any liability to pay some £195 million in compensation to investors.

An outcome of the split-capital trusts debacle was that zeros were shunned as a risky investment. That true picture is more complex. Zeros in themselves are not necessarily high risk. The risk depends entirely on the investment strategies being adopted in the underlying investment fund. High leverage and cross-holdings increase risk, as the example overleaf demonstrates, but not all investment trusts adopt these strategies. If you are interested in zeros, you need to check carefully the level of risk inherent in any investment trust you choose, including the level of gearing and of cross-holdings. A key published statistic is the 'hurdle rate'. This is the yearly rate of growth in assets that the investment trust must achieve in order to be able to pay the promised capital sum when the zeros are due to be repaid and taking into account costs and charges that are deducted from the capital in the fund (rather than from the income it generates). However, the hurdle rate on its own can be misleading because you also need to know how much of that growth would be syphoned off to make the promised income payments on any income shares. And the hurdle rate tells you nothing about the level of risk in the fund. If the investment trust is highly geared and/or invested in other trusts that are geared, there may be a high risk that even a modest hurdle rate will not be achieved. So you need to do your homework before investing in zeros.

### Example of the effect on return of cross-holdings

Table 10.7 shows the holdings of two seemingly similar investment trusts. Both have an investment fund of £100 million with half financed from borrowing and half from shareholder funds (gearing of 200). But Trust B's assets are all invested in the stock market generally, whereas £30 million of Trust A's assets are invested in Trust B.

Suppose the stock market falls by 20 per cent. Trust B's investments fall in value to £80 million. The £50 million of borrowing still has to be repaid, so the shareholders now have just £30 million of their original £50 million invested, so they have made a loss of 40 per cent. Now look at what has happened to Trust A. The £70 million of the fund invested in the stock market has fall in value by 20 per cent to £56 million but the £30 million invested in Trust B has fallen by 40 per cent to just £18 million. The £50 million of borrowing has to be repaid, leaving investors with £24 million out of their original £50 million invested – a fall of 53 per cent.

The effect of the cross-holding in Trust B has been to magnify the losses, because the investors in Trust A are exposed to the gearing of Trust B as well as Trust A.

**Table 10.7  Impact of a 20 per cent fall in the stock market**

|  | TRUST A | | TRUST B | |
| --- | --- | --- | --- | --- |
| Source of the trust's funds | Before £m | After £m | Before £m | After £m |
| Borrowing | £50 | £50 | £50 | £50 |
| Shareholders' funds, of which: | | | | |
|    Invested in stock market generally | £20 | £6 | £50 | £30 |
|    Invested in investment trust B | £30 | £18 | £0 | – |
| **Value of the trust's assets** | £100 | £74 | £100 | £80 |
| Change in value of shareholders' funds | | –52% | | –40% |

# Case study

Mr R had invested in a split capital investment trust without first taking investment advice. He later discovered that the trust held shares in other split capital investment trusts, forming a so-called 'magic circle' of cross-holdings. Mr R disapproved of this practice and complained to us that it had not been made clear to him that his investment would be managed on this basis.

We explained to Mr R that we have no authority to investigate these cross-holdings. Investment trusts are quoted companies (PLCs). Their business is the management of investments and their share price fluctuates in line with supply and demand, rather than according to the value of the underlying investments. Cross-holdings are, effectively, a commercial decision taken by the investment trust company. Firms' commercial decisions are not within our jurisdiction.

Even if such matters were within our jurisdiction, we would not have been able to look into this particular case. This is because Mr R had not taken investment advice but had relied solely on his own judgement in deciding that the investment was suitable for him.

*Source*: Financial Ombudsman Service, *Ombudsman News*, May 2002.

## Exchange-traded funds – the basics

To date, most exchange-traded funds (ETFs) are tracker funds designed to follow the movement of an underlying index. This could be an index for the market as a whole (for example, the FTSE100 Index which records the movement of the largest 100 shares quoted on the London Stock Exchange), or an index for a sector of the stock market, or an index for some other asset class, even art.

To see how ETFs work, take the example of a fund tracking the FTSE100. The fund manager creates ETF shares and swaps them with large institutions, not for cash, but for a portfolio of the actual shares that make up the FTSE100. ETFs are open-ended funds, so the manager will create and issue new shares if more institutions want to buy than sell. Similarly, the fund manager will buy back and cancel shares if there are more institutions wanting to sell than buy. There is no cash in these transactions – the fund manager and institutions trade only ETF shares for portfolios of the FTSE100 shares, and vice versa.

The institution may want to hold the ETF shares itself, but more often acts as a market-maker (a firm that stands ready to buy shares from and sell shares to investors, making a profit through small differences in the buying and selling price). You, the investor, buy ETF shares on the stock market either from a market-maker or from investors who have previously bought the shares and are now looking to sell.

Although the price you pay on the stock market is determined by the balance of buyers and sellers, unlike an investment trust the price is usually very close to the net asset value (NAV) of the investments in the underlying fund. This is because any difference in price represents a profit opportunity for the market makers and is soon traded away. For example, if the market price of an ETF's shares is higher than its NAV, it will pay the market-maker to buy FTSE100 shares on the stock market, swap them with the fund manager for ETF shares, and then sell the ETF shares on the stock market. This extra supply of ETF shares will dampen the market price until it returns close to the NAV. In a similar way, if the market price of the ETF shares is lower than the NAV, the market-maker can profit by taking ETF shares back to the fund manager, getting FTSE100 shares in return, and then selling the FTSE100 shares on the stock market. The reduction in supply of ETF shares will tend to push the price up until it returns to the NAV.

The fund manager and the institutions trade shares directly between themselves without paying dealing charges to a broker and these are tracker funds with low management costs. The result is that the annual charges for an ETF tend to be very low, often below 0.75 per cent. Referring back to Table 10.4 on p. 309, you can see that this is a big advantage leaving far more investment growth in your hands. However, you buy ETF shares through a stockbroker so incur dealing charges on your own trades (see Chapter 9), which can eat into your profits if you trade often. Unlike other share purchases, there is no stamp duty when you buy ETF shares.

Low charges and the ease of buying and shares on the stock market give ETFs the edge over other forms of investment fund. If you are wondering why a financial adviser has never recommended them to you, it is most likely because they do not pay usually any commission to intermediaries, whereas the adviser does get paid if they recommend unit trusts, OEICs or life insurance funds.

However, ETFs are relatively new and they are evolving fast. While many are still essentially tracker funds, other ETFs are more exotic and follow the higher-risk strategies adoped by hedge funds (see p. 328). So always check out the nature of the fund thoroughly before you buy.

## Life insurance and pension funds

The business of a life insurer is to collect premiums from policyholders, invest them in a fund and use that fund to meet claims as and when they fall due. Therefore, it was a small step for insurers to create policies that not only paid out on death but would instead pay out during the policy-holder's lifetime a share of the underlying investment fund.

There are two main sorts of investment-type life insurance: whole-of-life policies, designed to run until death but with the option to cash in earlier; and endowment policies designed to run for a set period of years. As described in Chapter 9, these may be qualifying or non-qualifying for tax purposes, but in either case are not tax-efficient for most investors. However, life insurers also operate pension schemes. Once the life insurance fund is put inside the tax wrapper of a pension scheme, it does become a tax-efficient way to invest (see Chapter 7). However, bear in mind that you can hold other types of investment fund in a pension wrapper.

You share in the underlying investment fund on one of two bases. With a unit-linked fund, you are allocated units in the same way as if you were investing in a unit trust. The value of your units rises and falls with the value of the investments in the fund. You can choose from a range of different funds and switch between them either freely or at low cost. (With some insurers, instead of investing in the insurer's own funds, you do actually invest in a range of unit trusts.)

The second basis, with-profits, aims to offer a lower risk alternative. Instead of being linked to a specific pool of investments, your return depends on the overall profitability of the insurer's life business once its charges, claims and dividend shareholders (if it is a company rather than a mutual organisation) have been met. The return will depend largely on the performance of the investments in the pool, which are usually a mix of shares, commercial property and bonds. The insurer's actuary (an expert at dealing with data and probabilities in order to forecast future claims and profits) determines each year how much of the profits should be allocated to investors. The actuary uses a process of smoothing, so that part of the profits from good years are held back in reserve and used to boost the allocation in years of poorer business and investment performance. You receive your share of the profits in the form of bonuses. The reversionary (yearly) bonuses, once added to your policy cannot be taken back unless you cash in before the policy has matured. A terminal bonus is added at maturity. Thus, the idea is that your policy will tend to grow smoothly over time, insulating you from the ups and downs of the stock market. While this sounds like a good investment for cautious investors, with-profits policies have a number of drawbacks:

■ **Market value reduction or MVR** (sometimes more euphemistically called a market value adjustment or MVA). Most policies are designed to run for a set number of years or until you reach an agreed age (such as 65). If you surrender (cash in) or transfer the policy early, you may have to pay an MVR, which is an early surrender charge. This aims to claw back part of the reversionary bonuses previously allocated to your policy if stock markets have fallen back since then.

■ **Lack of transparency**. It is hard to estimate what return you might get from a with-profits policy because the company has the discretion to award whatever bonuses it deems appropriate. On request, you should be given a document called the Principles and Practice of Financial Management (PPFM) which gives information about the factors that influence bonus rates, including, for example, the allocation of the underlying fund between different assets classes, charges in recent years, and so on. Although this guide comes in a consumer-friendly, as well as a technical, version, it is still difficult to predict what return you might get.

■ **Terminal bonus**. This bonus often makes up a high proportion of your total return, for example, a quarter or more. The terminal bonus varies greatly from one year to the next reflecting stock market performance. This heavy reliance of the overall return on the rate of terminal bonus means that you are not really as insulated from the ups and downs of the stock market as you might have expected.

The charges for insurance-based funds tend to be much higher than for other forms of fund. There will typically be a policy fee deducted from your premiums. Don't be surprised if more than 100 per cent of your money is allocated to units – the allocation is often expressed as a percentage of your premium after deduction of the policy fee. For unitised funds, there will be a bid-offer spread, typically 5 per cent, which allows for up-front commission paid to an adviser (whether you use one or not) and an annual management charge (AMC), usually around 1 to 1.5 per cent. However, the AMC may be less if you have a large sum invested. Be wary of capital units (common in the past but less so now), which are simply units that have a higher than normal AMC for the first few years of the policy. Often the first one or two switches from one unit-linked fund to another are free, but thereafter there is usually a charge. Finally, there may be a surrender fee if you withdraw your money early or other than on pre-set dates.

# The choice of funds

With the exception of the with-profits basis of investing (which is only available through insurance and pension funds), whichever form of investment fund you choose, you have a very similar range of underlying investment choices. Each fund offers you a particular type of investment or strategy. Examples of the main types of fund available are given in Table 10.8: p. 327 looks at some more complex types of fund.

You can mix and match funds to suit your own goals. Alternatively, some funds offer a ready-made mix of assets or funds.

In general, most investment funds are reasonably liquid investments, so you can withdraw your money within a few days though, of course, you may not get the price you want. The exception among the funds listed in Table 10.8 is property funds. Because the fund may have to sell physical properties in order to realise the cash to repay investors, most funds reserve the right to impose a waiting period of six months (longer if the FSA agrees). Property funds that invest in the shares of property funds rather than physical property are more liquid.

**Table 10.8 Main types of investment fund**

| Type of fund | Description | Particularly useful for |
|---|---|---|
| *Specialised funds (in roughly ascending order of risk)* | | |
| Money market | Short-terms loans to banks, companies and government. Broadly equivalent to a bank savings account. | Liquidity. |
| | | Preserving capital. |
| | | Income. |
| | | Temporary store awaiting reinvestment. |
| | | Asset mix. |
| Fixed income | Government and corporate bonds. | Income. |
| | | Asset mix. |
| Equity income | Shares that have a track record of paying high dividends. | Income with growth. |
| | | Asset mix. |
| Equity – UK | Shares in UK companies. | Growth. |
| | | Asset mix. |

▶

**Table 10.8 Main types of investment fund *continued***

| Type of fund | Description | Particularly useful for |
|---|---|---|
| Property | Shares in companies in the property sector (usually commercial property). Alternatively funds investing direct in commercial property. | Income. Growth. Asset mix. |
| Equity global | Shares in companies across the world. | Growth. Asset mix. |
| Equity – specified countries | Shares in companies in a specified country or geographical region, such as Europe, Japan, BRIC (Brazil, Russia, India and China). | Growth. Asset mix. |
| Equity – sector | Shares in companies in particular sectors, such as pharmaceuticals or mining. | Growth. |
| Equity – smaller companies | Shares in relatively young companies that are expected to grow. | Growth. |
| Equity – emerging markets | Shares in companies in countries that are undergoing rapid development and expected to deliver high growth, such as India and China. | Growth. |
| Commodities | Investments may be in commodities direct or via derivatives (see p. 325). | Growth. Asset mix. |
| *Funds that choose an asset allocation for you* | | |
| Asset allocation | Funds that invest in a spread of cash, bonds, equities and possibly other assets. The name of the fund indicates its aim; for example, defensive and cautious funds are for low-risk investors; balanced, aggressive and flexible funds suit higher-risk investors. | Income. Growth. |
| Lifestyle, lifecycle, target date | Fund starts by investing mainly in equities and shifts towards bonds and cash as a pre-set maturity date approaches (see p. 306). | Growth. |
| Fund-of-funds | Fund investing in a selection of other funds chosen by the manager. Be aware that this means two sets of charges are deducted from your investment. | Income. Growth. |

If you are interested in choosing funds that invest ethically – for example, avoiding the arms trade or supporting fair employment policies – the Ethical Investment Research Service is a good source of information (see Appendix B).

# Derivatives

So far, this and the preceding chapter have focused on investments that you buy individually or in funds and hold, possibly indefinitely, in order to generate income or profit or both. When you use derivatives, you buy some sort of claim to an underlying investment rather than the investment itself. Moreover, you are gaining exposure to a movement in the price of the underlying investment during a specified, often short, period of time. Derivatives can either be used as a sort of insurance (hedging) or to speculate (gamble).

The main derivatives used by professionals are options and futures. It is useful to understand a little of how these work in order to understand some of the products available to private investors, such as structured products and hedge funds. In general, few private investors buy options and futures themselves, though spread betting and covered warrants offer the opportunity for similar investment strategies. These are outside the scope of this book, but Appendix B suggests some sources of information if you would like to explore this area of investment.

## Futures and options

Futures probably go back to the Ancient Greeks but first came into widespread use among the nineteenth century farmers of the US Midwest (which is why one of the pre-eminent derivatives exchanges is based in Chicago). Prices for crops would fluctuate widely, leaving farmers uncertain whether it would be worth sowing seed for the season ahead. To remove the uncertainty, the practice developed of selling the crop in advance at a price fixed now. The farmers knew what income they would get. While they did not get the benefit of a price rise, they were protected from price falls. The buyers could either take delivery of the crops after harvest or sell their right to someone else before then. If the price of the underlying crop had risen above the price fixed in the contract, the buyer would be able to sell the futures contract for a profit.

Options are similar to futures except that you have the right, rather than an obligation, to buy an underlying commodity or investment at a fixed price at a future time. If you do not stand to make a profit from exercising an option, you can simply let it lapse. An option that gives you the right to buy an underlying commodity or investment is called a call option. You can also buy options that give you the right to sell an investment at a set price in future and these are called put options. Taking delivery of the underlying commodity or investments is called exercising the option. But you do not have to hold the option until the exercise date. Instead you can sell it on a derivatives market. The main market is the UK is LIFFE (originally the London International Financial Futures Exchange) which is now part of an international group, NYSE-Euronext. What you are selling is your right to buy or sell, not the underlying assets themselves.

## Using options for hedging

Suppose you own 10,000 shares in a Company X. Currently their price stands at £1 per share. You are worried that their price might fall. You could just sell the shares now and realise the £10,000 while you can. But suppose the shares rise rather than fall? You will then have missed out on the increase. Instead of selling, you could buy a put option giving you the right to sell the shares in future at the current price. If the price does fall as you feared, you will then be able to exercise your option and get the £10,000. If the price rises, you can let the option lapse and sell the shares on the stock market for a better price. Used this way, options are very like taking out an insurance policy. Just like a policy, you have to pay a premium for the option and you claim (exercise) only if you incur a loss.

Here is another hedging strategy. Suppose you do not own shares in Company Y, but think there is a good chance they will rise in value. You could buy the shares, but if you are wrong and the price falls, you stand to make a sizeable loss. An alternative would be to buy a call option giving you the right to buy the shares on a future date at or near the current price. If the shares do rise, you exercise the option and can, if you want, immediately sell Company Y's shares at a profit. If Company Y's share price falls, you let the option lapse and all you have lost is the premium for the option. Of course, if Company Y's shares do rise in value, the option to buy at the current price will become increasingly valuable, so rather than waiting to exercise the option, you could just sell the option to another investor and so make your profit that way.

The two strategies above are described in terms of investment in a single company, but you can also buy options on the whole market. These are called index options and the underlying asset is the shares that make up a particular stock-market index, such as the FTSE100. But, with index options, you never take delivery of the shares themselves. Instead you receive or pay cash according to the change in the stock-market index.

Using the first strategy above, you could protect a whole portfolio of shares against adverse movements in the stock market by buying a put index option. Using the second strategy, you could protect yourself against the timing risk of investing in shares at the wrong time.

### Using options for speculation

It is clear from the second strategy above, that you can make a profit from options without ever owning the underlying assets, but you need to understand the risks involved. For example, with index options, you could buy the right to buy the market in future at a price fixed now. If the market rises above the exercise price plus the premium you paid then you stand to make a profit (called being 'in the money') and can either sell the option or exercise it. If the market does not rise as you had hoped, you lose the premium you paid and nothing more. But bear in mind that the premium was 100 per cent of your capital outlay for the deal.

A big advantage of introducing options into an investment strategy is the opportunity to make money from falling as well as rising prices and markets, whereas conventional strategies rely on markets rising.

# Complex investment funds

While most investment funds tend largely to use conventional buy-and-hold strategies, there is a growing tendency to use derivatives and other techniques, such as short selling, to boost returns. Short selling means selling shares you do not own with the hope of buying them back later at a lower price. Private investors are barred from short selling, but professional investors can borrow shares from other large investors (in return for a fee) in order to sell and buy back later. You need to be aware when these strategies are being employed because they have implications for the risks you are taking on when you invest.

## Guaranteed and protected products

Guaranteed and protected products are examples of structured products. You might invest in them as unit trust funds, say, or as high-income or growth bonds issued by an insurance company.

In a guaranteed fund, your money is invested for a cycle of, say, three months. Part of the fund is invested in, say, zero-coupon bonds from an investment bank. These make no regular interest payments but promise to pay a fixed sum on redemption in three months' time which will be enough to replace the original capital. The residue of the fund buys call index options which will provide a return linked to the stock market if it rises and no return if the market falls.

A protected fund is similar but, instead of guaranteeing the full return of your capital, only part is protected. For example, the fund may promise to return 90 per cent of your capital plus a return linked to the stock market. As with the guaranteed fund, the capital is paid back by using a zero-coupon bond. In this case, a larger slice of the fund can be used to buy call options, which boosts your return if the stock market rises. But, if the market falls, all you get back is 90 per cent of your capital at the start of the cycle. If the market falls for several cycles, these losses compound. For example, after three cycles (nine months) of falling stock markets, you would get back only 90% × 90% × 90% = 73% of your original capital.

High-income bonds and guaranteed growth bonds offered by life insurance companies work in similar ways. For example, with a high-income bond – designed to pay you a regular income in excess of the return from a building society – the insurer might invest the bulk of your money in corporate bonds to provide the income. The residue buys, say, a call index option with an exercise price significantly higher than the current level of the market. As long as the stock market increases by a target amount, your capital is returned in full. If it rises by less, only part of your capital is returned and, in effect, the extra income you have received will have been funded out of your capital.

## Hedge funds

Hedge funds use gearing, derivatives, short-selling and a wide range of other techniques to pursue a variety of strategies. Types of hedge fund include:

■ **Absolute return funds.** These funds aim to produce either a target level of return or to beat the return on savings accounts, whether stock markets are rising or falling. A variety of techniques may be employed, for example, the fund may invest in corporate bonds and use put options to protect against a fall in their prices. It may invest in a portfolio of shares and sell short when it expects price falls. Some experts think this form of investment fund will become the bedrock of investment in future years. They argue that the long bull markets of the last century will not be repeated and so it will no longer be possible to make money consistently out of simple buy-and-hold strategies. Absolute return funds will provide a medium-risk core for long-term investors in the same way that with-profits funds aimed to do in the past. Others question the ability of absolute return funds to deliver the promised returns. Most funds do not claim to meet their target month by month, but over an average period of a year or more.

■ **130/30 funds.** These funds are using something similar to leverage in order to magnify the gains from successful buy-and-hold investments. However, rather than borrowing to invest, the fund short sells investments to the value of 30 per cent of the fund. It then uses the proceeds of these sales to buy more of its buy-and-hold investments. The success of the strategy relies on the fund manager being able to stock pick successfully.

■ **Covered call funds.** The aim of these funds is to provide a high level of income. The fund is invested in shares with a record of paying good dividends – in much the same way as a conventional equity income fund. But, in addition, the fund sells call options on the shares it owns. When you buy a call option, you have the right to buy shares in future at a set price and you are likely to exercise the option if the share price rises. If you sell call options, you are on the other side of the deal and obliged to hand over the shares if the option is exercised. This is a relatively safe position for the fund because it already owns the shares that might be bought (called a 'covered' position). Provided the stock market is stable or falling, the options are unlikely to be exercised and the premiums received from selling the options provide the extra income the fund boasts.

Because hedge funds frequently set up strategies involving derivatives that are designed to yield results over a set period of time, you may not be able to get your money out of the fund on demand and may have to wait several months.

Hedge fund charges are much higher than the charges for traditional investment funds. Typically, there is an annual management charge of, say, 2 per cent of the value of the fund. In addition, the fund manager may get a performance-related fee that could take up to a quarter of any profit made by the fund.

## Other investments

A few other investments which interest private investors are covered in this last section. The most important is residential property.

## Residential property

According to a survey in 2009, around 3 million Britons are relying on their home to fund their retirement.[6] Despite, the fall in house prices following the global financial crisis of 2007, it is easy to see why residential property looks so attractive. As Figure 6.1 in Chapter 6 shows, since the 1960s, in most years, house prices have risen, often by substantial amounts. Typically property is bought with a mortgage, so gains are magnified through the effects of leverage (see Chapter 1). Not surprisingly, nearly half of the people in the UK see housing as the most significant part of their future financial security.[7]

If owning your own home has delivered such good returns, it is a small step to consider rental property as a superior investment. But is this view justified?

The return from rental property takes two forms: income from rents and a capital gain or loss when you sell the property. According to a survey of landlords by the Association of Residential Letting Agents (ARLA), just over 6 per cent invested for the rental income, 45 per cent were seeking a combination of rent and capital growth and the remainder had capital growth as their main goal.[8] ARLA tracks the return on buy-to-let investing and, despite the housing market downturn, the average annual return over the five years to summer 2009, including capital appreciation, was 9.13 per cent for landlords who bought outright and 22.18 per cent for those who bought with a mortgage and so benefited from the effects of gearing.[9] While these are persuasive rates of return, some points to bear in mind are:

■ **Capital risk and liquidity**. Investing in a single buy-to-let property is a high-risk strategy. Regardless of what happens to the housing market as a whole, you have not diversified away any of the specific risks relating to that property, for example, flooding, subsidence, declining neighbourhood, planning permission for a major road or industrial estate nearby, and so on. If you are buying with a mortgage, gearing magnifies losses as well as gains.

---

[6] Baring Asset Management, 2009, *UK property pension pots lose £29 billion in past year*, London: Baring Asset Management.

[7] Aviva, 2008, *Understanding consumer attitudes to saving*, London: Aviva.

[8] Association of Residential Letting Agents (ARLA), 2009, *The ARLA History of Buy-to-Let Investment 2001 to 2007*, Warwick: ARLA, Q2.

[9] Association of Residential Letting Agents (ARLA), 2009, *The ARLA Review and Index*, Warwick: ARLA, Q2.

▪ **Income risk**. You will not necessarily be able to generate rental income in a continuous stream. The ARLA survey shows that the average void period (time without paying tenants) is 30 days a year.[10] Void period may be especially problematic is you have borrowed to invest and need the income to meet the mortgage payments.

▪ **Costs**. As the landlord, you are responsible for repairs and maintenance to the property and keeping it insured. You may want to delegate the job of finding and dealing with tenants, hiring builders, etc. to deal with repairs, and so on to a letting agent, in which case you will need to factor into your calculations the agent's fees.

▪ **Tax**. Capital gains when you sell your own home are tax-free, but any profit you make selling a buy-to-let property is subject to capital gains tax – at 18 per cent in 2009–10 and this may rise in future (see Appendix A). Rental income is subject to income tax but you can deduct all the expenses of running your rental business. You will need to fill in a tax return each year, declaring your rental income and any gain on sale.

## Gold

Gold is a traditional safe haven in times of economic and political unrest and viewed by many as a hedge against inflation. This largely stems from gold's historic role as a currency in its own right. Gold (and silver) coins were used for centuries; until the last century paper currencies were backed by gold, and many central banks still keep stores of gold in their vaults. Some investment experts put gold among the safest of assets and recommend that it should form part of every portfolio.

What underpins gold's special role is confidence that, even when paper currencies and economies collapse, gold holds its value and can still be exchanged for goods and services. As long as that confidence persists, the argument will hold true, just as the acceptability of paper currencies rests in the belief that other people will exchange them in return for goods and services. But, at the end of the day, gold is just a commodity. It is used commercially – for example, in jewellery – but that alone is not enough to justify the remarkable prices that gold sometimes achieves. The main driver of the gold price is sentiment.

---

[10] Association of Residential Letting Agents (ARLA), 2009, *The ARLA Review and Index*, Warwick: ARLA, Q2.

If you are attracted to holding gold as an investment, choose your timing carefully. When fearful investors have already driven gold to peak prices, you may buy only to realise a quick loss when the price falls back. Bear in mind that gold does not provide an income. Consider, too, how you will invest. Physical gold is heavy, making it awkward to transport. It needs to be stored, which means either paying for storage or ensuring you have your own secure store and insurance. An alternative way to invest is through investment funds, such as unit trusts and exchange-traded funds. These may hold physical gold or possibly invest in derivatives linked to the gold price.

## Collectables

Unlike stocks and shares, there are few ways to buy into the overall market for collectables. Instead, you must select individual antiques, works of art or fine vintages. Unless you have very large sums to invest, your scope for spreading risk across a wide range of different pieces may be limited. Therefore, it is essential that you either have the expertise to select good quality items or find a reliable source of advice.

Even then, returns are unpredictable. There is an argument that, since the supply of good genuine antiques and old masters is finite, they will always retain their value. But demand – and so prices – can still vary considerably as particular styles and genre go in and out of fashion. If you opt for contemporary art (say, 1940s onwards), you are taking a considerable gamble on whether the particular artists you choose will in time become sought after. In general, you should only buy what you like. If it turns out to be a good investment, well and good. But, unless you are buying at the very top end of the market, profit should not be your main motive.

Standard investment advice applies: do not put all your eggs in one basket. Spread your risks by having a range of different investments, with antiques or art being just part of your overall portfolio.

There are four main ways to buy collectables. First, you could visit dealers' shops or galleries. Choose reputable dealers, preferably ones that belong to a trade association, such as BADA or the Association of Art and Antiques Dealers (LAPADA), and who follow a code of practice (see Appendix B). Make sure you get a proper invoice for your purchases, showing the dealer's name and address, date of purchase, price paid and – importantly – a description of the item including any details that influenced the price you paid, for example if the item had been restored. A way to access lots of dealers all in one go is through fairs, for example, the Affordable Art Fairs bring together hundreds of dealers and galleries. Another possibility is auctions. Finally, the internet is becoming an increasingly important way to buy and sell, through websites such as eBay or more formal auctions run by big name houses, such as Sotheby's and Christie's. Their websites carry full instructions on how to take part. Make sure you understand the arrangements for payment, who is responsible for delivery costs and insurance, and that payments are made over a secure server (look for a closed padlock or similar symbol and 'https' in the address bar).

An advantage of buying from a dealer or at a fair is that there are few hidden costs. You simply pay the price on the tag. However, the dealer has a living to make, so the price at which you buy is inevitably higher than the price at which the dealer would immediately buy back the piece. If you buy at auction, be aware that you pay a buyer's premium (typically 10 to 15 per cent plus VAT but sometimes more) as well as the hammer price. For example, if your bid for £588 is successful, you actually pay £588 if the premium is 15 per cent. When you sell, you pay a commission to the auction house.

If you have bought a large item, you must also allow for the costs of delivery and insurance in transit. And, once you've got your items home, you'll also need insurance. A typical home contents policy has fairly limited cover for 'valuables'. Check your policy carefully and, if you need more cover, contact your insurer or a broker. You may also need to spend extra to protect your investments. If you have invested in furniture or paintings, check that you can keep them in the right conditions in terms of light, humidity and so on. BADA and LAPADA have useful guidelines on their websites. Dealers can also advise you and there are numerous books on the care of antiques.

Most alternative investments count as 'tangible moveable assets' for tax purposes, so any gain may be tax-free (see Appendix A). If not, it may still fall within your yearly capital gains tax allowance (£10,100 in 2009–10). If you buy and sell regularly, there is a risk that HM Revenue & Customs might consider you are carrying on a trade and try to tax your gains as income.

## Stress testing and review

Whatever your goals and whatever products or portfolios you choose to meet them, you should always ensure that you understand the risks involved. The main task of stress testing is to consider what will happen to your investments if relevant risks materialise and whether you need to take steps to adjust your plan to cope with them. For example:

■ Is there a possibility that you would need quick access to your money? Do the investments you have chosen give you that access? If they do, would you get back your money in full or is there a risk of capital loss?

■ If you are investing for a higher return than a savings account would offer, why is the return higher? What risks are involved? In what circumstances might you lose capital and how much might you lose? Are there extra charges which will reduce the promised return?

■ If you are investing for income, can the income vary? Can you cope if the income goes down? What protection do you have from inflation?

It is impossible to predict the future. Events will inevitably have an impact on your savings and investments. This area of planning is rather like keeping a temperamental classic car on the road. You need to be alert to strange noises in the engine, be ready to tweak the settings and diligently carry out an annual service.

# 11

# Passing it on

## Introduction

A goal for many people is being able to help their children and other family members even after they have gone. Leaving an inheritance can do this and may also give you the pleasure in your lifetime of a sense of growing financial achievement. However, even if you built up considerable wealth by the time you stop work, it may not be possible to hold on to it as retirement progresses. To some extent governed by luck, you may find your accumulated wealth is used up paying for long-term care, though – as Chapter 5 points out – planning for care can help to preserve at least some of your wealth. You may also find that you draw down your assets during retirement in order to boost your income, though hopefully Chapters 8 to 10 have given you ideas for simultaneously providing income and protecting capital. Assuming you do reach later life with a sizeable portion of your wealth intact, this chapter looks at how you can effectively and efficiently cascade it to those you leave behind. Figure 11.1 outlines a basic plan for this area of your finances.

## Who inherits?

The first, most fundamental step in inheritance planning is to write a will. If you don't (called dying intestate), the law rather than you will dictate how your wealth is passed on. Figure 11.2 summarises who would inherit under the intestacy laws for England and Wales. The rules are slightly different in Northern Ireland and this is indicated in the footnotes to the chart. The rules are very different in Scotland – see the box on p. 338.

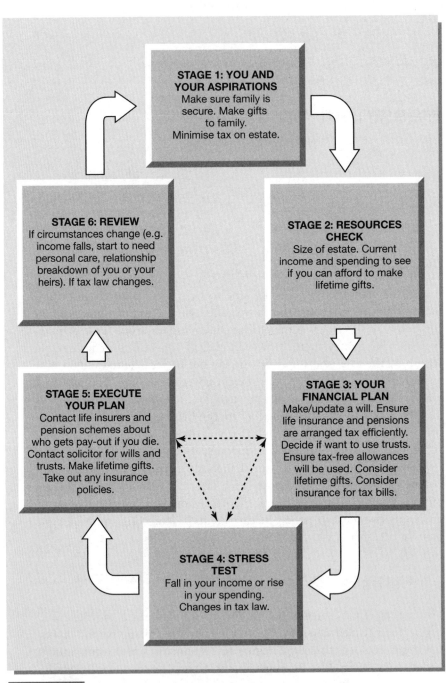

**Figure 11.1**    A basic financial plan for passing on your wealth

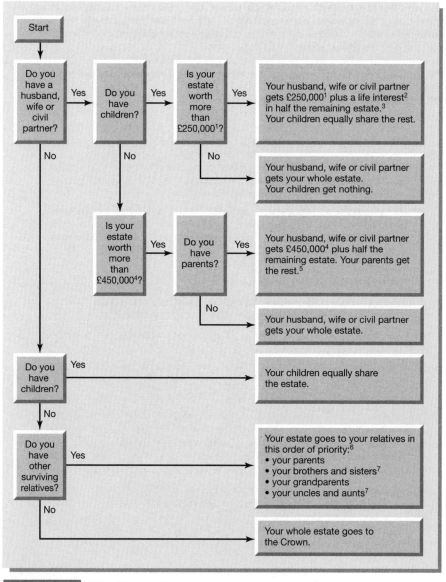

**Figure 11.2**   Who inherits if you do not leave a will[1]

---

[1] £125,000 in Northern Ireland.

[2] Your spouse or civil partner may use the assets or spend the income from investing them. On the death of your spouse or civil partner, the assets pass to your children.

[3] The rules are different in Northern Ireland: your husband, wife or civil partner gets £125,000 plus half the remainder if there is one child (outright not just a life interest) or one-third of the remainder if there are two or more children.

[4] £200,000 in Northern Ireland.

[5] The rules are different in Northern Ireland: if your parents have died before you, the remainder goes instead to your brothers and sisters (and if any of them have died before you, to their children instead). If there are no parents, brothers, sisters, nephews or nieces, your husband, wife or civil partners gets the whole estate.

[6] The rules are different in Northern Ireland: even more distant relatives may inherit.

[7] If any of these relatives has died before you but leaves children, the assets pass to their children instead.

[8] Different rules apply in Scotland – see below.

---

### Dying intestate in Scotland

The intestacy rules in Scotland are very different to those which apply in the rest of the UK. Scottish law gives your husband, wife or civil partner 'prior rights', in other words a first claim on the estate up to these limits:

■ your share of a home you shared with your spouse or civil partner plus furniture and furnishings up to the value of £24,000 – if the home is valued at more than £300,000, your spouse or civil partner has the right to £300,000 rather than the home itself, plus

■ the first £42,000 of the rest of the estate if you have children (or their descendants) or £75,000 if there are none.

In addition, your husband, wife, civil partner and any children have 'legal rights' to your moveable estate (basically your estate other than land and buildings) as follows:

■ if you have a partner and children, your spouse or civil partner gets one-third and the children get one-third;

■ if you have a partner and no children, your spouse or civil partner gets one half;

■ if you have no partner but children, your children get one half.

The remainder of your estate goes to any surviving relatives in this order of priority: children, parents and siblings if both survive; siblings if no parents; parents if no siblings; spouse or civil partner; and aunts, grandparents, great uncles and aunts, and remoter ancestors. If any relative has died but had children, their children inherit in their place. If you have no relatives, the remaining estate goes to the Crown.

If you make a will, the prior rights no longer apply, but your husband, wife, civil partner or children can claim their legal rights and these would then replace any bequest you had made to them in your will.

---

## Problems of intestacy

The intestacy rules are designed mainly to protect your surviving husband, wife or civil partner and any children. This may be exactly what you would have planned anyway, but there are a number of potential problems:

■ **An unmarried partner.** If you live with a partner, but you are not married or in a civil partnership, they have no automatic right to inherit any part of your estate. They may be able to make a claim for support under the Inheritance (Provision for Family and Dependants) Act 1975 if they lived with you for at least the two years before death or can show you provided financial support. The amount they would be awarded would depend on the particular circumstances of the case. Your partner would have to make a claim within six months of probate and any case could be lengthy and costly.

■ **Step children**. Under the intestacy laws, 'children' includes those related to you by blood or legally adopted but does not include step children. Again, to get any financial help from your estate, your step children would have to rely on a claim under the Inheritance (Provision for Family and Dependants) Act 1975.

■ **A separated spouse or civil partner**. If you are separated but not divorced from a former husband, wife or civil partner, they would still inherit under the intestacy laws.

■ **Different needs**. Children inherit in equal shares, regardless of whether they have equal needs or, if adult, equal ability to manage money.

■ **Minor children**. A child is a minor if under 18 and unmarried. Any inheritance under the intestacy laws does not go direct to the child but must be held in trust for them (see p. 340 for more about trusts). The costs of running the trust may be high relative to the amount they inherit.

■ **Your home**. Where your estate comprises mainly a single valuable asset, such as your home, the asset may have to be sold so that the proceeds can be split between different people in accordance with the intestacy laws. This could mean, for example, your husband or wife being unable to stay in the family home.

■ **Distant relatives**. If you have no husband, wife, civil partner or children, your estate may go to relatives you did not know or, worse, did not like. Without a will, your estate cannot be passed to friends or charity.

■ **The Crown**. If you have no living relatives, the State gets the lot! That's equivalent to a 100 per cent tax bill on your wealth.

## Reasons to have a will

Apart from giving you the chance to avoid the problems of intestacy outlined above, a will is also the opportunity to express other wishes, for example, about your remains and guardians for your children. A will is also a tool you can use to set up more complex arrangements, such as trusts: for example, if you wish to give some of your heirs the use, but not outright ownership, of assets during their lifetime or you want to appoint someone to make decisions about when children or grandchildren need financial help. Last but not least, a will can help you plan away or reduce tax on your estate.

There is no reason not to have a will. You could even write one yourself, though this is not recommended. The Guinness Book of Records used to cite the shortest will ever written as simply saying 'All to Mother'. Unfortunately, this led to a protracted family row because it was not clear whether 'Mother' was the man's wife or his parent. It shows how, even a simple will can be expressed badly. Another pitfall to avoid is getting someone you would like to benefit under your will also to act as a witness – the will remains valid in other respects but the witness is not allowed to receive anything under the will. For reasons like these, it is generally a good idea to get a solicitor to draw up your will and if your circumstances are simple this should cost only around £75. You'll pay more if your affairs are complex.

# Using trusts

Popular history has it that trusts originated in the Middle Ages when knights went off to the Crusades and would place their wealth with a trusted relative with instructions to make sure the knight's wife and children were provided for. Whether this is true or not, trusts are still used today and remain arrangements that pass the legal ownership of assets (the trust assets) from one or more people (the settlors) to others (the trustees) with instructions (the trust deed and rules) to use the assets for the benefit of one or more specified people (the beneficiaries). In this way, trusts let you give away assets either in your will or during your lifetime, but maintain some control over how the assets are used.

There are no restrictions on the roles that people have in a trust. For example, the settlor can also be a trustee, the settlor can even be a beneficiary (though this affects the way the trust and the settlor are treated for tax purposes), and beneficiaries can be trustees.

There are two basic types of trust: interest-in-possession (also called life interest trusts) and discretionary trusts.

With an interest-in-possession trust, one or more people have the right (called a 'life interest') to use the trust assets or receive income from the invested trust assets. Typically this right lasts for as long as they live, but the trust rules could specify that it ends on some earlier event, such as remarriage. When the life interest ends, the assets pass to whoever has the 'reversionary interest' – usually this will be a different person to the one who had the life interest but it could be the same person. For example, a very common trust arrangement is to leave your husband or wife a life interest (maybe the right to live in the family home and income from your investments) with the assets passing to your children on your spouse's death. Under the intestacy rules for England and Wales (see Figure 11.2), if you leave a spouse and children, part of your estate over £250,000 goes to your spouse in trust and, on their death, to your children, so this is an example of an interest-in-possession trust.

Any trust which is not an interest-in-possession trust must be a discretionary trust. Here, the trustees have a free hand within the framework of the trust deed and rules to decide who should benefit from the trust assets and when. The trust deed and rules will set out who the potential beneficiaries are. At the time the trust is set up, at least one beneficiary must be alive, but others could be unborn. For example, provided you have at least one grandchild already, you could set up a trust for the benefit of your grandchildren. As more are born, they automatically become potential beneficiaries. A discretionary trust could be useful where a child or family member needs financial help but is not good at managing money. You could set up a discretionary trust for the benefit of someone who has a disability – and this is treated in a favourable way for tax purposes. You could also set up a discretionary trust to make gifts to charities and again this would benefit from favourable tax treatment. You can specify in the trust deed and rules the sort of situations in which the trustees should make payments to beneficiaries, for example to help with their education or on marriage, and even specify how the trust assets are invested. If there are no investment instructions, there are laws that require trustees to act in a prudent way.

Setting up a trust is not really a DIY task. The wording of the trust deed and rules needs to be precise and the taxation of trusts, which is complex, needs to be carefully considered. Get help from a solicitor (see Appendix B).

# Inheritance and tax

There are three taxes you need to be aware of when planning for inheritance: inheritance tax, income tax (including pre-owned assets tax) and capital gains tax. The interaction between these taxes is important for efficient inheritance planning.

## Inheritance tax

This is a tax on gifts, whether made in your lifetime or at death. Whatever you leave in your will or through the intestacy rules after your debts have been paid – called your 'estate' – is treated as a final gift you make.

### Inheritance tax basics

Inheritance tax does not tax each gift in isolation, but puts each one into the context of a running total of taxable gifts made over the last seven years. The first slice of your running total, called the 'nil-rate band' is tax-free. The nil-rate band is £325,000 in 2009–10 and is frozen at this level for 2010–11. The remainder of the running total is subject to tax either at the death rate of 40 per cent or the lifetime rate of 20 per cent. Figure 11.3 illustrates how the process works. You can see that, as the years roll by, earlier gifts drop out of the running total. The nil-rate band may cover all of the taxable gifts within the seven-year period or just part. If the latter, any part of the current gift that falls within the taxable section of the running total is subject to tax.

Inheritance tax is charged on the loss to the giver, so if tax is due on a gift and you pay it, the tax itself forms part of the gift.

You may be surprised to realise that in theory any gift you make – even the smallest birthday gift or Christmas present – is within the scope of inheritance tax and would be taxable if the legislation did not make a number of exemptions. These are set out in the box below. In fact, birthday and Christmas presents escape tax because generally they fall within the normal expenditure out of income or £250 per person exemptions.

If a lifetime gift is not covered by one of the exemptions in the box, then normally it would be a taxable gift to be added to your seven-year running total. But some gifts count as 'potentially exempt transfers' (PETs). A PET is treated initially as if it is exempt and actually becomes exempt provided you survive for seven years after making it. If you die within seven years, it becomes a taxable gift after all and joins your seven-year running total (see below for the implications of this for both your estate and the recipient of the gift). Gifts you make to people are PETs and also those you put into a discretionary trust for a disabled person (provided the trust meets certain rules).

Gifts to most other types of trust or to, say companies, are not PETs and count as taxable gifts. There is no tax to pay if they are covered by your nil-rate band. If not, there will be a tax bill at the time you make the gift and there could be a further tax bill on death (see p. 344) if you die within seven years of making the gift.

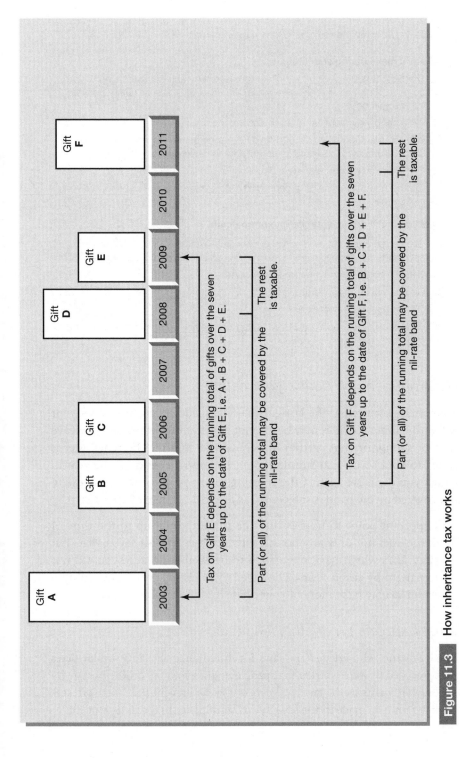

Figure 11.3 How inheritance tax works

## Gifts which are exempt from inheritance tax

**Gifts you make during your lifetime**

■ The first £3,000 a year of any gifts not covered by another exemption. If you do not use part or all of this allowance, the unused bit can be carried forward for one year only.

■ £250 per person per year to any number of people.

■ Gifts on marriage up to £5,000 if you are a parent of the bride and groom, £2,500 if you are a grandparent and £1,000 for anyone else.

■ Gifts that count as normal expenditure out of your income (see p. 352).

■ Gifts for the maintenance of your family, including a former husband, wife or civil partner.

**Gifts you make during your lifetime or on death**

■ Gifts to your husband, wife or civil partner (but limited to £55,000 if their permanent home is outside the UK). Gifts to an unmarried partner are not exempt.

■ Gifts to charities or community sports clubs.

■ Gifts to most political parties.

■ Gifts to housing associations.

■ Gifts of heritage property (such as stately homes and art works deemed to be of national importance).

## What happens on death: your estate

Your estate is treated as the last gift that you made. Some gifts under your will or the intestacy rules may be exempt, for example, whatever you leave to your spouse or civil partner or bequests to charity. The remainder is added to your seven-year running total. The nil-rate band for the year in which you die is set against the running total and any part of the estate not covered by the band is subject to tax at the death rate of 40 per cent.

An important point to note is that the running total up to the time of death includes not only any taxable gifts made in the last seven years but also any PETs which have now failed to be exempt because you did not survive them by seven years. The failed PETs use up part of the nil-rate band and so may push more of your estate into the taxable band.

## What happens on death: lifetime gifts

The legislators who created the laws for inheritance tax (and similar taxes that preceded it) were worried that people might avoid tax on their estate by making hefty gifts in the last few years of life. To prevent this, there are special rules for gifts made in the seven years running up to the date of death.

## Case study

In May 2007, Keith gave a holiday cottage he owned to his daughter. The cottage was worth £206,000. There was no inheritance tax on the gift at the time because £6,000 was exempt (using two £3,000 a year exemptions) and the rest counted as a potentially exempt transfer (PET). Keith died in August 2009, leaving an estate valued at £310,000. On its own the estate came to less than the nil-rate band for 2009–10 of £325,000 but, to work out if tax is due, the estate must be added to any taxable gifts made in the last seven years including failed PETs. Keith's running total comes to £200,000 + £325,000 = £525,000. The PET has used up £200,000 of the nil-rate band leaving only £125,000 to set against the estate. This means £310,000 – £125,000 = £185,000 of the estate is taxable and the tax charge is 40% × £185,000 = £74,000.

You have already seen above how failed PETs can use up the nil-rate band and so cause extra tax to become due on the estate. In addition, there may now be tax to pay on the failed PETs themselves because, with hindsight, it has become clear that they should not have been exempt after all.

Tax on a failed PET is worked out by looking at the running total over the seven years up to the date on which the gift was made but then using the nil-rate band and tax rate that apply at the date of death – see the case study below. The tax due is reduced if the PET was made more than three years before death – see Table 11.1. Initially, the person who received the gift is expected to pay the tax that has now become due on it. If they can't or will not pay, your estate will have to foot the bill instead.

**Table 11.1 Taper relief on PETs and chargeable gifts**

| Number of complete years you survived after making the gift | Percentage reduction in the tax bill |
| --- | --- |
| Less than 3 | 0 |
| 3 | 20 |
| 4 | 40 |
| 5 | 60 |
| 6 | 80 |
| 7 or more | 100 (i.e. no tax) |

There may also be extra tax to pay on any lifetime gift that was taxable at the time you made it, if you have failed to survive at least seven years. If the running total of the taxable gifts up to the time of the gift was more than your nil-rate band at that time, you would have paid tax at the lifetime rate of 20 per cent. On death within seven years, the calculation is redone, still using the running total up to the time of the gift, but now applying the nil-rate band and tax rate for the year of death. The nil-rate band tends to increase each year, so it could be that the gift is now covered by the band, in which case there will be no extra tax to pay after all. But if all or part of the gift falls within the taxable band, tax at 40 per cent is worked out. The tax bill is reduced if the gift was made more than three years before death – see Table 11.1. If the final tax charge is greater than the tax you paid at the time of the gift, extra tax is now due. Initially, the person who received the gift is expected to pay this but, if they can't or will not, your estate will have to pay instead. If the newly worked out tax bill is less than the tax originally paid, there is no more tax to pay but you cannot claim any refund.

Note that, although the death bands and rates are used to work out tax on a failed PET or a taxable gift within the previous seven years, this is a completely separate calculation from tax on the estate. In particular, you cannot claim taper relief to reduce tax on the estate.

## Case study

Reema gave one of her two nieces £250,000 in February 2003 and the other £250,000 in March 2004. There was no tax on the gifts at the time they were made because they counted as PETs. Apart from using her £3,000 a year exemption, Reema made no other lifetime gifts. Reema died in June 2009 which was less than seven years after making the gifts, so they were reclassified as taxable gifts.

Reema's seven-year running total up to and including the February 2003 gift was just £250,000. This falls comfortably within the £325,000 nil-rate band that applies in the year she died.

Her running total up to and including the March 2004 gift was £250,000 + £250,000 = £500,000. This means £500,000 − £325,000 = £175,000 of the gift to her second niece falls within the taxable band and tax is initially worked out as 40% × £175,000 = £70,000. However Reema died more than five complete years after making the gift, so the tax bill is reduced by 60 per cent, reducing the tax bill to £28,000. The niece is asked to pay this but, if she can't, Reema's estate will.

### Gifts with reservation

A gift will not count as genuine for inheritance tax purposes if you can still use or benefit from it. In that case it is called a gift with reservation and still counts as part of your estate for inheritance. This might apply if, for example, you give your home to your children but you carry on living there rent-free or you give away a painting but it carries on hanging on your wall.

Something you continue to use or benefit from is not a gift with reservation if you pay the full market rent for your use or, if you share the item, you pay your full share of the costs. For example, if a relative came to live with you and you gave them a half share of your home, you should not be deemed to benefit from the half-share you had given away provided you paid at least half the household bills.

## Capital gains tax

Capital gains tax (CGT) is a tax on the increase in value of an asset during the time you have owned it. Tax becomes due when you dispose of the asset, which could be when you sell or when you give it away. If you acquire or dispose of an asset as a gift, it is usually valued for tax purposes at its market value at the time of the gift.

There is no CGT on what you leave on death. However, CGT could be due on lifetime gifts that you make. Some lifetime gifts are exempt from CGT, in particular:

■ gifts to your husband, wife or civil partner (but not an unmarried partner);

■ gifts to charity;

■ part or all of your only or main home;

■ cash (in sterling) rather than possessions or assets;

■ investments held in an individual savings account (see Chapter 9) up to the time of the gift;

■ possessions that have a predicted useful life of at most 50 years;

■ cars, motorbikes or other private motor vehicles;

■ more durable possessions worth no more than £6,000 each.

There could be CGT to pay on most other lifetime gifts, but the first slice each year is covered by a tax-free allowance (£10,100 in 2009–10). Anything above that is taxed at 18 per cent in 2009–10. (The CGT rate of 18 per cent is a great deal lower than the top rate of income tax, which is 50 per cent from 2010–11 onwards, providing a strong incentive for tax planning schemes to save tax. As a result, at the time of writing, there was considerable speculation that the CGT rate might be increased from 2010–11 onwards.)

Note that, although a gift with reservation (see above) is not effective for inheritance tax, it is still a genuine gift for CGT purposes – see the case study.

## Case study

In November 2002, Gerald gave his home to his son, Stuart. At the time, it was valued at £160,000. Gerald carried on living in the place and did not pay any rent to Stuart, so this counted as a gift with reservation. When Stuart died in July 2009, the house – by then valued at £210,000 – was treated as still being part of his estate and inheritance tax of £84,000 was due on it.

Following his dad's death, Stuart decided to sell the house. In the depressed housing market, he was lucky to get the full £210,000 asking price. He had assumed because the house was part of Gerald's estate and there is no capital gains tax on what is left on death, that there would be no capital gains tax bill on the sale of the house. However, Stuart had a nasty shock. Under the tax rules, the gift of the home in 2002 was valid for capital gains tax purposes. This meant Stuart, who had never lived in the property so could not claim any main-home exemption, was treated as having made a capital gain of £210,000 – £160,000 = £50,000. After setting his tax-free allowance against this, he was left facing a tax bill of (£50,000 – £10,100) × 18% = £7,182.

## Income tax

In general, income tax does not affect gifts made in your lifetime or on death, but there are two important exceptions: gifts to minor children; and gifts that you still benefit from unless they are caught by the gift with reservation rules. These exceptions both arise because of rules that aim to curb tax avoidance.

### Gifts to minor children

Everyone, however young, is within the scope of income tax and has a tax-free personal allowance. This means children can have up to £6,475 a year of income in 2009–10 and 2010–11 without having to pay any tax. However, if you give money or assets to your own child under the aged of 18 (or under 16 if married), if the gift generates more than £100 a year of income, the whole of the income will be treated as yours for income tax purposes, not income of your child.

This £100-rule does not apply if your gift is invested in a child trust fund or certain other investments that provide a tax-free income (for more information, see Chapter 9). The rule also does not apply to gifts from anyone other than parents – for example, grandparents and family friends.

If you set up a trust (see p. 340) from which your own minor child can benefit, you will be treated as having a 'retained interest' in the trust and will be taxed as if any income and capital gains made by the trust are yours.

## Gifts you still benefit from

If you give something away and can still benefit from it, usually for inheritance tax purposes, it will be caught by the gift with reservation rules (see p. 346). But, over the years, insurance companies and professional advisers have developed a range of clever schemes to get around the gift with reservation rules. HM Revenue & Customs challenged many of these arrangements and, as fast as new effective avoidance schemes arose, the Revenue would change the inheritance tax rules to close them down. But this always left a rump of people who had succeeded in saving tax before the law was changed. As a result, in 2005, a new tax, the pre-owned assets tax (POAT) was introduced which unusually, rather than being yet another amendment to inheritance tax, is an income tax. Another unusual and unwelcome feature of POAT is that it is retroactive, meaning that, instead of just taxing arrangements you set up from 2005 onwards, it also imposes a tax charge on arrangements you may have made many years ago.

Under the POAT rules, if you benefit from something you have given away at any time since 18 March 1986 that is not caught by the gift with reservation rules or that was bought with money you provided within the last seven years, a yearly value is put on the benefit you are deemed to get. For example, if you continue to live in a property, the yearly value is the commercial rent you would otherwise be paying. With other assets, the benefit is deemed to be the market value multiplied by an official rate published by the Revenue (4.75 per cent in autumn 2009).

If the value of all the benefits you are deemed to still enjoy is less than a set limit (£5,000 in 2009–10), the amount is disregarded. If it comes to more, the value less anything you actually pay for the use of the assets, is added to your taxable income for the year and income tax is then charged under the normal income tax rules (see Appendix A).

You can escape paying the POAT charge in three ways: start paying the full market rent for any assets caught by POAT; unwind the arrangement so that you no longer benefit from an asset you gave away, for example, by bringing the asset back into your estate; or elect to be treated as if the gift with reservation rules do apply to the arrangement. Normally an election must be made by 31 January following the year in which you first became liable for POAT but the Revenue is able to accept late elections.

# Reducing inheritance tax on your estate

You do not have to worry about inheritance tax on your estate if the value of everything you own less all your debts comes to less than the nil-rate band (£325,000 in 2009–10 and 2010–11). Married couples and civil partners can have double that (£650,000 in 2009–10 and 2010–11) before they have to worry (see p. 351).

Even if your estate is worth more than the nil-rate band, bear in mind that inheritance tax is a problem for your heirs rather than you and that they will usually be in the fortunate position of having come into an inheritance so maybe can afford to pay any tax due. Keep inheritance tax in perspective and don't take steps to save it that would put your financial security during your lifetime in jeopardy.

In some situations, an inheritance tax bill for your survivors can cause real hardship. This is particularly the case where you share your home with someone other than your spouse or civil partner, such as an unmarried partner, brother, sister or adult child (see pp. 104 and 354).

Always bearing the above thoughts in mind, this section looks at a number of straightforward strategies for saving inheritance tax. There are also far more complicated techniques which may be appropriate if your estate is large and/or your affairs complex. These are outside the scope of this book and you should seek professional advice from, for example, a member of the Society of Trust and Estate Practitioners (see Appendix B).

## Bypass your estate

Death may trigger lump sum payments from pension schemes and life insurance policies (see Chapter 4). In the absence of any other instruction, these payments will be made to your estate and swell its value for inheritance tax purposes. In most cases, you can prevent this happening.

With occupational and personal pension schemes, you will normally be invited to nominate who you would like to receive any lump sum death benefit. Provided the trustees or provider have discretion to decide who gets the payment and your nomination is just an expression of your wishes, rather than a legal instruction, the payment can go direct to whoever you nominated without going through your estate. This is likely to speed up the payment as well as save tax. Although the trustees or provider do not have to follow your wishes, they usually will, unless someone else makes a claim to be dependent on you.

Similarly, you can ask for life insurance policies to be 'written in trust'. The trustees then decide who should receive the pay out but will normally follow your wishes. Once again, the payment then goes direct to the intended beneficiary, bypassing your estate. Most insurers have standard paperwork for writing a policy in trust, so there should be no extra charge.

## Make tax-free bequests

The value of your estate for inheritance tax is reduced by any bequests you make which are tax-free. Commonly, husbands and wives leave the bulk of their estate to each other and this means there is often no tax bill when the first of them dies. Bequests to charity are also tax-free. See p. 344 for other gifts that are tax-free on death.

## Use your nil-rate band

Bequests to people other than your spouse, civil partner or charity – such as your children – are not tax-free, but there will still be no tax to pay if they are covered by your nil-rate band.

In the past, married couples wasted the nil-rate band of the first to die if the whole of the estate was left to a surviving spouse. However, this problem disappeared when the law was changed with effect from 9 October 2007. When the second of a couple dies on or after this date, they can inherit any unused nil-rate band from their late husband, wife or civil partner whenever that person died. For example, suppose a husband died and had used only half of the nil-rate band that applied in the year of his death. If his wife dies in September 2009, instead of the usual nil-rate band of £325,000, her estate will have the benefit of a 1.5 × £325,000 = £487,500 nil-rate band. If the husband had not used any of his nil-rate band, her estate would have a double band of £650,000 in 2009–10. To make use of this rule, the people sorting out your estate will need to have paperwork to prove how much nil-rate band had been left unused on the first death, so make sure you store the relevant documents safely and where whoever will deal with your affairs can find them.

When unmarried couples leave their estate to each other, these bequests are not tax-free and so automatically use up some or all of the nil-rate band.

## Make lifetime gifts

One way to reduce the value of your estate at the time of death is to give some of it away during your lifetime. This is a viable approach only if you can afford to manage without the assets that you give away. Bear in mind that, if you give something away but carry on using it, this would either not be effective for saving inheritance tax because of the gift with reservation rules (see p. 346) or could trigger a pre-owned assets tax charge (see p. 349). For inheritance planning, your gifts do need to be genuine.

Also be aware that tax law contains rules about associated operations to prevent you artificially saving tax. For example, if you give £250 each (making use of the small-gift exemption) to several different people on condition that they pass these gifts onto your child, the Revenue will treat these all as a single gift from you to your child.

With lifetime gifts, there is a hierarchy of tax effectiveness as shown in Figure 11.4. Your first choice should always be a tax-exempt gift if this is possible. Particularly useful are the £3,000 a year and normal expenditure out of income exemptions. There is no cash limit on the latter, so you could use it to make large gifts. To count as normal expenditure out of income, the gifts must:

■ **Form a regular pattern**. This could be, for example, paying regular premiums for life insurance to benefit someone else or regular contributions to a personal pension scheme for your partner, children or grandchildren. Less frequent payments can also form a regular pattern, such as a cash sum to each grandchild on their 18th birthday or a similar gift to the same person every Christmas. It may not be obvious when you make the first gift that it will be part of a regular pattern, so you should keep records that later on will demonstrate the pattern.

■ **Be paid out of your income**. The exemption will not count if your gifts are funded through the sale of assets or from 'income' that technically is not income for tax purposes (such as the capital element of payments from a purchased life annuity or drawdown from a lifetime mortgage, as described in Chapter 8, pp. 228 and 247).

■ **Leave you with enough to maintain your normal lifestyle**. The Revenue will challenge the normality of the payments if they leave you so short of income that you have to cut back on your usual spending.

## Limit the growth of your estate

There are several ways you could do this. For example, if you are giving away assets outright, give those which are more likely to increase in value. Consider making interest-free loans and letting the recipient keep any return from investing the loans.

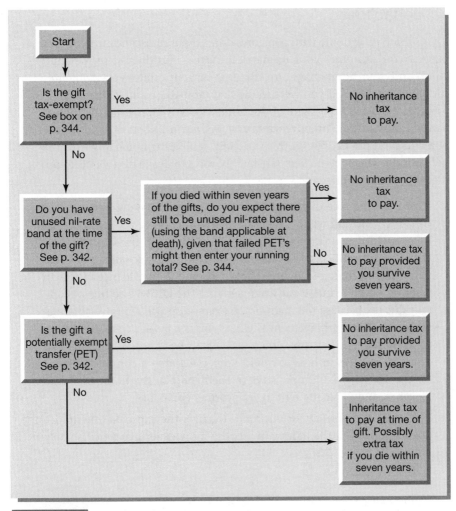

**Figure 11.4**   A hierarchy of tax-efficient giving

More complex inheritance tax schemes often involve paying regular premiums into a life insurance policy. The money is invested to build up a fund with the bulk of the proceeds passing either on death or at the end of a specified term to whoever you have nominated. Often there is a facility for you to draw back your original investment in the form of regular payments that provide you with income. The regular premiums you pay are typically covered by your £3,000-annual exemption or count as normal expenditure out of income.

## Protect cohabitees

If you share your home with someone other than a husband, wife or civil partner (for example, your unmarried partner, brother, sister or adult child) and your home makes up the bulk of your estate, your cohabitee could face problems if you were to die first (and you could if they were to predecease you). If your share of the home is worth more than the nil-rate band, there could be inheritance tax to pay but no assets other than the home to fund the tax bill. In this situation, selling the home might be the only option. There are no very satisfactory ways to deal with this situation. A couple of possibilities are:

■ If you are the sole owner of the home, consider giving part to your cohabitee. The gift will count as a PET for inheritance tax and so is tax-free provided you survive for seven years. You will need to take care that the gift with reservation rules do not apply, so make sure you pay your full share of the household bills and keep evidence of this in case the Revenue query the arrangement. The gift will be free of capital gains tax because the main-home exemption will apply. A potential weakness of this arrangement is what happens if your cohabitee wants to move out. In that case, you would again be at risk of the gift with reservation rules unless you paid your cohabitee a commercial rent for the use you would now have of their share of the home or, say, a lodger moved in paying rent to your former cohabitee.

■ You could perhaps pay for insurance to cover the expected inheritance tax bill. However, the older you are, the more expensive cover is likely to be.

---

### Equity release and inheritance planning

Some advisers suggest that equity release schemes (see Chapter 8) can be a useful way to save inheritance tax. It is certainly true that, if you take out a lifetime mortgage against your home and spend the money raised, the value of your estate will be reduced. Your home is still part of your estate but the mortgage debt is deducted. Similarly, a home reversion scheme cuts the size of your estate because your home passes out and into the ownership of the reversion company. But you should bear in mind that equity release schemes do not give you the full value of the equity you give up. This difference is likely to more than match any amount you save in inheritance tax. The upshot is that you do not have anything extra to leave to your heirs. Equity release can be useful if your primary aim is to raise income or cash, but not primarily as a method of inheritance planning.

# Stress testing and review

A will can be altered relatively easily if the need arises so can be dealt with through reviews rather than stress testing. The major potential problem is giving away assets that you find you need later on. Before making any lifetime gifts, take time to consider your budget now and how it might change in future: the template in Chapter 1 will help you to do this. Make sure you have a wide margin of financial flexibility to cope with, for example, a possible rise in health-related spending or the impact of inflation on the buying power of your income.

Be cautious about complex tax planning schemes. Providers who develop these have to notify them to the Revenue (and you have to declare on your annual tax return if you are using any such schemes). There is always a risk that such schemes could be closed down and the Revenue has shown, with the introduction of the pre-owned assets tax, that it is prepared to use measures that have a retrospective effect on planning that seemed effective at the time.

If you cannot plan away an actual or potential tax bill, an option is to take out insurance to ensure that the bill can be paid. For example, you could take out term insurance to provide a lump sum to cover the tax that may be due on a PET if you die within seven years. Because the tax on the PET reduces with taper relief (see p. 345), you need reducing term insurance where the potential pay-out decreases in line with the tax bill. Ensure the policy is written in trust (see p. 351) with the recipient of the PET nominated to receive the pay-out. That way the pay-out by-passes your estate. Because you are paying premiums for a policy to benefit someone else, this in itself is a gift, but can be covered by the normal expenditure out of income or £3,000 annual exemption.

Similarly, you could take out insurance to cover the expected tax bill on your estate at death with the pay-out going to whoever your heirs will be so that they have enough to pay the tax. In this case you need a whole-of-life policy rather than term insurance.

It's a good idea to review your inheritance planning strategy once a year in the light of changes in your wealth and possible alterations to tax law. In addition, you will need to make a major review whenever the circumstances of you or your heirs changes. This should include reviewing and, if necessary, updating your will. In particular, if you are married or in a civil partnership and your relationship breaks down, be aware that, although bequests to a divorced spouse become invalid, those to a separated spouse remain unless you alter your will.

# Appendix A: The UK tax system and tax credits

## Introduction

Tax is an integral factor in financial planning. Governments offer tax incentives to encourage you to act or plan in particular ways and the way different savings, investments, insurance products and other payments are taxed can have a big impact on the outcome of any plan. But you cannot just look at each product in isolation. The tax relief you personally will get or the tax you will have to pay depends on your overall tax position and varies from person to person. This appendix explains how the UK tax system creates your personal tax position with respect to income (income tax and National Insurance) and capital gains. If you spend some of your time abroad and/or have wealth located in another country, you may need to take that country's tax system into account as well. The UK tax system is complicated and this appendix gives only a simplified outline. For more detailed information, see the *FT Guide to Personal Tax* (available from bookshops).

Tax credits (in their current form) were introduced in the UK in 2003. They follow the spirit of a theoretical concept, called 'negative income tax'. In a negative income tax system, paying less tax as your income falls is extended so that, at a threshold low level of income, you actually start to receive payments from the government instead of handing over tax. UK tax credits are a type of means-tested state benefit, administered by HM Revenue & Customs, where entitlement depends on your income worked out in broadly the same way as for tax purposes. Unlike most means-tested benefits, especially if you have children, you can qualify for tax credits at relatively high levels of income, for example, £50,000 a year or more in 2009–10. In fact, nine out of ten families with children in the UK can claim tax credits. You may also be eligible if you work, but your earnings are low.

Tax credits are included in this section (see p. 381) because the government tends to treat tax and tax credits as integrated for policy purposes. For example, when a 10 per cent tax band on earnings was abolished in

2008–09, in calculating the numbers of people adversely affected, the government excluded those who would be eligible for an increase in tax credits implemented in the same year.

Throughout the chapters of this book, tax and tax-credit implications are discussed wherever relevant.

This book was finalised in early 2010 – i.e. during the 2009–10 tax year. At that time, some tax allowances, rates and other details had been announced for the 2010–11 tax year, but not all. A further complicating factor was that a General Election was due to be held in mid-2010 and, depending on which political party or parties then hold power, further tax charges for 2010–11 could be made by a new government. Therefore, this appendix focuses largely on tax year 2009–10, but includes information for 2010–11 where this has been announced.

# Income tax

Income tax in the UK is a 'progressive' system – this means that higher tax rates apply to higher incomes. Income is divided into bands and the tax rate you pay on your highest band determines whether you are classified as a 'non-taxpayer' (too little income to pay any tax), 'basic-rate tax-payer', 'higher-rate taxpayer' or, from 2010–11 'additional-rate taxpayer'. The suitability of different types of financial products and strategies often depends on which category of taxpayer applies to you.

## Working out your tax bill

As the name makes clear, income tax is a tax on income. However, it is not always obvious what counts as income; and some types are tax-free. Table A.1 lists the main tax-free and taxable income in the UK in the 2009–10 tax year. (A tax year runs from 6 April one year to the following 5 April.)

Broadly, to work out your tax bill, you add together your income, deduct any spending that qualifies for tax relief and a tax-free personal allowance. What is left is the income on which tax is due. In practice, the process is a bit more complicated and is explained in the steps below.

**Table A.1 Main types of tax-free and taxable income**

| Source of income | Tax-free income | Taxable income usually paid with tax deducted | Taxable income usually paid without any tax deducted |
|---|---|---|---|
| Work | Some fringe benefits with a job (e.g. childcare vouchers, your employer's contributions to a pension scheme). Up to £30,000 of redundancy pay. | Earnings from a job. Sick pay. Maternity pay. | Profits from self-employment. |
| Insurance | Income protection insurance pay-outs from a policy you bought for yourself. Pay-out from term insurance, including family income benefit. Long-term care insurance pay-outs paid direct to a carer. | Income protection insurance pay-outs from a scheme at work. Pay-outs from payment protection policies (including those to meet mortgage payments). | |
| Pensions | | Occupational pension. Personal pension. | State pension. |
| Savings and investments | Cash individual savings accounts (ISAs). Government and corporate bonds held in ISAs and child trust funds (CTFs). National Savings & Investments certificates. Saving Gateway accounts. Premium bond prizes. | Interest from savings accounts. Part of the income from purchased life annuities. Dividends from shares and share-based investments (even if held within an ISA or CTF). Pay-outs from investment-type life insurance plans and bonds. | Offshore savings accounts. Interest from government and corporate bonds. Property income dividends (PIDs) paid by some types of investment fund. |

▶

### Table A.1 Main types of tax-free and taxable income *continued*

| Source of income | Tax-free income | Taxable income usually paid with tax deducted | Taxable income usually paid without any tax deducted |
|---|---|---|---|
| State benefits | Child benefit. Tax credits. Pension credit. Housing benefit. Council tax benefit. Maternity allowance. Income-related employment and support allowance. Attendance allowance. Disability living allowance. | Contributory employment and support allowance. | |
| Other sources | Student grants and loans. Maintenance from a former partner. Gambling winnings. Rent from lodgers up to £4,250 a year through the Rent-a-Room Relief scheme. Cashback on a mortgage. | | Profits from renting out property. Benefit you are deemed to get if you still use something you have given away (see Chapter 11). |

## Step 1: Add up your income

The first step in working out your tax bill is to decide what income to include in your tax calculation. Do not include any tax-free income. If you have income from which tax has already been deducted (net income), you should add back the tax and include the before-tax (gross) amount in your calculation.

Next, divide your income into the categories shown in Figure A.1. You may find it easier to start from the right and work through the columns moving to the left:

**Income**

|  | Other income | Savings income | Dividend income | Life insurance income |
| --- | --- | --- | --- | --- |
| Income from each source |  |  |  |  |
| TOTALS | A1 | A2 | A3 | A4 |

**DEDUCTIONS THAT QUALIFY FOR FULL TAX RELIEF**
Set the deductions below against each category of income, following the order indicated by the numbers in each column.

|  | Other income<br>1st | Savings income<br>2nd | Dividend income<br>3rd | Life insurance income<br>4th |
| --- | --- | --- | --- | --- |
| Pension contributions to occupational scheme |  |  |  |  |
| Charitable donations through payroll giving |  |  |  |  |
| Personal allowance |  |  |  |  |
| TOTALS | B1 | B2 | B3 | B4 |
| INCOME TO BE TAXED = A – B | C1 | C2 | C3 | C4 |

**Figure A.1** Tax calculator: income and deductions

■ **Life insurance income** is the income or lump sum payment (confusingly, for tax purposes called a 'gain') that you get from life insurance plans and bonds, unless the plan counts as a 'qualifying policy' (see Chapter 9). These plans and bonds might be, for example, endowment policies, with-profits bonds or single premium bonds. Contrary to normal tax rules, you include only the income you actually receive without adding any of the tax already paid by the life insurance company (see Chapter 9).

■ **Dividend income** is income from shares and from share-based investment funds (rather than funds investing in bonds or property).

■ **Savings income** is the interest you get from savings accounts, most National Savings & Investment products (other than those which are tax-free), government and corporate bonds, and part of the income from purchased life annuities (but not annuities that you buy with a pension fund).

■ **Other income** is whatever has not been put into the three columns described above. It will usually include the bulk of your income, such as earnings, pensions, profits from self-employment, rents if you let out property and property income dividends from investment funds invested in property.

## Step 2: Deductions that qualify for full tax relief

The tax system includes a variety of tax reliefs, often aimed at encouraging certain types of action or spending, such as saving for retirement or giving to charity. You can deduct what you spend on some of these items, called 'outgoing', from your income before tax is worked out. This ensures that the spending gets full tax relief right up to your top rate of tax. The two main items you can deduct are: contributions you make to an occupational pension scheme (but not any personal pensions) and donations you make to charity through a payroll giving scheme run by your employer.

You can get tax relief on some other types of spending but the relief is given in a different way – see *Tax bands and rates* below.

In 2009–10, everyone gets a tax-free allowance, which is an amount of otherwise taxable income that you can have tax-free. In other words, your personal allowance also gives you full tax relief, so you deduct it from your income at this step in the calculation. The amount of personal allowance you get depends on your age and income. As Table A.2 shows, people aged 65 and over get a higher allowance. But the extra they get is reduced if their 'adjusted net income' is more than a set limit (£22,900 in 2009–10 and 2010–11). 'Adjusted net income' is basically income less any pension contributions and donations to charity that you make. The extra allowance is reduced by £1 for each £2 of income over the limit until it has fallen back to the amount of allowance that people under age 65 get.

From 2010–11, not everyone will get a personal allowance. If your adjusted net income is £100,000 a year or more, you lose £1 of the allowance for each £2 of income over that limit, until the allowance is reduced to zero.

### Table A.2  Personal allowances

| Your age[1] | 2009–10 | 2010–11 |
| --- | --- | --- |
| Under 65 | £6,475 | £6,475 |
| 65 to 74 | £9,490[2] | £9,490[2] |
| 75 or over | £9,640[2] | £9,640[2] |

[1] This is the age that you reach during the tax year. For example, even if you reach age 65 on 5 April 2010, you still qualify for £9,490 for the whole 2009–10 tax year.

[2] Reduced by £1 for each £2 of your adjusted net income above £22,900. But it will not be reduced to less than £6,475.

You deduct your outgoings from your income in a very specific order. First you deduct them from 'other income'. If the outgoings come to more than your 'other income', you deduct the unused part from your 'savings income'. If any outgoings remain unused, you next deduct them from dividend income and lastly life insurance income. You do the same with your personal allowance. There is a case study on p. 367 to show you how this works.

### Step 3: Tax rates and bands

Now you know what income is to be taxed, you split the income into different bands – see Figure A.2 and the case study on p. 367.

**INCOME SLICES**
Set each tax band from Table A.3 (adjusted if necessary) against each category of income, following the order indicated by the numbers in each column.

| | Other income 1st | Savings income 2nd | Dividend income 3rd | Life insurance income 4th |
|---|---|---|---|---|
| Starting rate | C1.sr | C2.sr | C3.sr | C4.sr |
| Basic rate | C1.br | C2.br | C3.br | C4.br |
| Higher rate | C1.hr | C2.hr | C3.hr | C4.hr |
| Additional rate | C1.ar | C2.ar | C3.ar | C4.ar |

**TAX DUE ON EACH SLICE**
Multiply each slice of income from the table above by the relevant tax rate from Table A.3 following the order indicated by the numbers in each column.

| | Other income 1st | Savings income 2nd | Dividend income 3rd | Life insurance income 4th |
|---|---|---|---|---|
| Starting rate | C1.sr × 20% | C2.sr × 10% | C3.sr × 10% | C4.sr × 0% |
| Basic rate | C1.br × 20% | C2.br × 20% | C3.br × 10% | C4.br × 0% |
| Higher rate | C1.hr × 40% | C2.hr × 40% | C3.hr × 32.5% | C4.hr × 20% |
| Additional rate | C1.ar × 50% | C2.ar × 50% | C3.ar × 42.5% | C4.ar × 30% |
| TOTALS | D1 | D2 | D3 | D4 |

| | |
|---|---|
| TOTAL TAX DUE | |
| TOTAL TAX BILL D1 + D2 + D3 + D4 | |
| Less tax already paid | |
| TAX NOW DUE | |

**Figure A.2**   Tax calculator: tax due

In 2009–10, there are three bands: the starting rate band, the basic rate band and whatever remains is the higher-rate band. From 2010–11, there is one more band with the introduction of an additional rate of 50 per cent. Normally, the tax bands change each year in line with price infla- tion measured as the change in the RPI to the preceding September. In September 2009, the change in the RPI was negative and the government decided to leave the tax bands unchanged, as shown in Table A.3. Table A.3 sets out the standard tax bands. However, in your own personal case, your basic rate band might be extended. This is because of the way tax relief is given on some types of spending, in particular, contributions to a personal pension and donations to charity using the Gift Aid scheme. In both cases, the amount you pay is treated as being net of tax relief at the basic rate. The pension provider or charity claims the relief from the Revenue and adds it to your pension scheme or donation. If you are a higher-rate taxpayer, you qualify for extra tax relief and this is given by adding the gross value of your payments to the standard basic rate band. This takes exactly the correct amount of your income out of the higher- rate tax band so you get the tax relief due. See the case study below for how this works.

## Case study

Hannah pays a lump sum of £10,000 into her personal pension in 2009–10. This is treated as being net of tax relief at the basic rate and the provider claims £2,500 (20 per cent of the gross contribution of £12,500) to add to her scheme. Since Hannah is a higher-rate taxpayer, she qualifies for 40 per cent tax relief on this contribution: 40% × £12,500 = £5,000. She has already had £2,500 of this by paying the contribution net. To give her the remaining relief, the Revenue extends her basic rate tax band from £37,400 to £37,400 + £12,500 = £49,900. This means an extra £12,500 of Hannah's income is taxed at 20 per cent rather than 40 per cent, saving her (40% – 20%) × £12,500 = £2,500. In total, £12,500 has gone into Hannah's pension scheme at a cost to her of £10,000 – £2,500 = £7,500.

In exactly the same way that you set your outgoings and personal allow- ance against the different categories of income in a set order, each tax band is also set first against your 'other income', next against 'savings income' and so on. As you can see in Table A.3, different tax rates apply depending on both the category of income and the tax band. For example, if the whole of your starting rate band is used up against 'other income' (tax rate 20 per cent), it will be impossible for any of your savings income to fall within that band, so you will not get the benefit of the 10 per cent tax rate on savings income (see the case studies on p. 367).

## A.3 Tax bands and rates

*2009–10*

| Band | Other income | Savings income | Dividend income | Life insurance income |
|---|---|---|---|---|
| Starting rate £0–£2,440 | 20% | 10% | 10% | 0% |
| Basic rate £2,441–£37,400 | 20% | 20% | 10% | 0% |
| Higher rate Over £37,400 | 40% | 40% | 32.5% | 20% |

*2010–11*

| | Other income | Savings income | Dividend income | Life insurance income |
|---|---|---|---|---|
| Starting rate £0–£2,440 | 20% | 10% | 10% | 0% |
| Basic rate £2,441–£37,400 | 20% | 20% | 10% | 0% |
| Higher rate £37,401–£150,000 | 40% | 40% | 32.5% | 20% |
| Additional rate Over £150,000 | 50% | 50% | 42.5% | 30% |

Once you have split your income into the appropriate bands, multiply each slice by the appropriate tax rate to find the tax due on that slice. Add the tax due on every slice to find the total tax bill. From this, you can deduct tax relief due on some less common items, such as amounts you invest in high-risk shares through the enterprise investment scheme (see Chapter 9). You also deduct any tax you have already paid (for example, tax already deducted from savings interest and dividends or from your earnings – see p. 380).

The case study below pulls together how the whole process works.

## Case study

In 2009–10, Jim, aged 66, has an income of £11,000 made up of a state pension of £5,000 and savings income of £6,000. None of his spending qualifies for tax relief, but he gets a personal allowance of £9,490. The personal allowance is set first against his state pension (which counts as 'other income'). The remaining £4,490 of allowance is deducted from his savings income, leaving £1,510. There is no 'other income' left to use up any of the starting rate band, which can be set against the £1,510 of savings income which is, therefore, taxed at 10 per cent. Jim pays total tax of 10% × £1,510 = £151.

Ling, 52, has a part-time job and earns £10,000 a year. She also has £1,000 savings income. Her personal allowance of £6,475 is completely used up against her earnings (which count as 'other income'). So too is her starting-rate band which carries a tax rate of 20 per cent when used against 'other income'. The remaining £1,085 of earnings and her £1,000 savings income both fall within the basic-rate band and are taxed at 20 per cent. Her total tax bill is 20% × (£2,440 + £1,085 + £1,000) = £905.

## Case study

Arif, 46, had the following income in 2009–10: earnings of £46,000 on which he paid tax of £8,330, rental income of £4,000, savings income of £3,000 from which tax of £600 had already been deducted, dividend income of £1,800 paid with tax of £200 already deducted (making gross dividends of £2,000), and a life insurance gain of £1,000. He paid £500 a month into a personal pension – this is net of basic rate tax relief, so equivalent to a gross contribution of £625 a month. Using the steps outlined on pp. 360–7, his tax bill is worked out as shown in Figure A.3. He has a balance of £1,186 tax to pay.

**Income**

|  | Other income | Savings income | Dividend income | Life insurance income |
|---|---|---|---|---|
| Earnings | £46,000 |  |  |  |
| Rents | £4,000 |  |  |  |
| Savings |  | £3,000 |  |  |
| Dividends |  |  | £2,000 |  |
| Life insurance |  |  |  | £1,000 |
| TOTALS | A1 £50,000 | A2 £3,000 | A3 £2,000 | A4 £1,000 |

**DEDUCTIONS THAT QUALIFY FOR FULL TAX RELIEF**

|  | Other income 1st | Savings income 2nd | Dividend income 3rd | Life insurance income 4th |
|---|---|---|---|---|
| Personal allowance | £6,475 |  |  |  |
| TOTALS | B1 | B2 | B3 | B4 |
| INCOME TO BE TAXED = A – B | C1 £43,525 | C2 £3,000 | C3 £2,000 | C4 £1,000 |

**INCOME SLICES**

|  | Other income 1st | Savings income 2nd | Dividend income 3rd | Life insurance income 4th |
|---|---|---|---|---|
| Starting rate £2,440 | C1.sr £2,440 | C2.sr £0 | C3.sr £0 | C4.sr £0 |
| Basic rate £34,560 + £7,500[1] | C1.br £41,085 | C2.br £975 | C3.br £0 | C4.br £0 |
| Higher rate | C1.hr £0 | C2.hr £2,025 | C3.hr £2,000 | C4.hr £1,000 |

[1] Basic rate band is extended by the gross pension contributions.

## TAX DUE ON EACH SLICE

| | Other income 1st | | Savings income 2nd | | Dividend income 3rd | | Life insurance income 4th | |
|---|---|---|---|---|---|---|---|---|
| Starting rate | £2,440 × 20% | £244 | £0 × 10% | £0 | £0 × 10% | £0 | £0 × 0% | £0 |
| Basic rate £34,560 + £6,000 | £41,085 × 20% | £8,217 | £975 × 20% | £195 | £0 × 10% | £0 | £0 × 0% | £0 |
| Higher rate | £0 × 40% | £0 | £2,025 × 40% | £810 | £2,000 × 32.5% | £650 | £1,000 × 20% | £200 |
| TOTALS | D1 | £8,461 | D2 | £1,005 | D3 | £650 | D4 | £200 |

## TOTAL TAX DUE

| | |
|---|---|
| TOTAL TAX BILL £8,461 + £1,005 + £650 + £200 | £10,316 |
| Less tax already paid £8,330 + £600 + £200 | £9,130 |
| TAX NOW DUE | £1,186 |

**Figure A.3** Example of an income tax calculation for 2009–10

# National Insurance

National Insurance (NI) is a tax on employment income. There is no NI to pay on pensions, income from savings and investments or rental income. NI contributions are paid by employees, their employers and the self-employed. You can be liable for NI between the ages of 16 and state pension age. If you work on beyond state pension age, you do not pay NI on your earnings or profits.

There are four different classes of NI contribution. With three of them you build up an entitlement to claim certain state benefits, but the other is just a tax:

■ **Class 1**. Paid by employees and employers as a percentage of earnings. Employees do not pay NI on fringe benefits, such as a company car or medical insurance. Contributions may entitle you to claim jobseeker's allowance, employment and support allowance, state basic and additional pension and give your widow or widower the right to bereavement benefits.

■ **Class 2**. Paid by the self-employed at a flat rate. Contributions may entitle you to claim the same benefits as employees (see above) with the exception of jobseeker's allowance and state additional pension, neither of which you can claim.

■ **Class 3**. These are voluntary contributions which you can choose to pay if you have gaps in your record (see Chapter 7). They may entitle you to state basic pension and your widow or widower to bereavement benefits.

■ **Class 4**. Paid by the self-employed as a percentage of profits. These do not carry any entitlement to state benefits.

Table A.4 shows National Insurance rates for the tax year 2009–10 and 2010–11. Unusually (and due to inflation as measured by the RPI being negative in 2009), nearly all of the National Insurance thresholds are unchanged between 2009–10 and 2010–11. The government has announced that all the rates shown in the table will increase by 1 per cent from 2011–12 onwards.

**Table A.4  National Insurance for 2009–10 and 2010–11**

| Class | Additional information | Rate |
|---|---|---|
| 1 (employees) | Earnings up to £110 a week | 0%[1] |
| | Earnings between £110 and £844 a week | 11%[2] |
| | Earnings above £844 a week | 1% |
| 2 (self-employed) | Flat rate | £2.40 a week[3] |
| 3 (voluntary) | Flat rate | £12.05 a week |
| 4 (self-employed) | Profits up to £5,715 | 0% |
| | Profits between £5,715 and £43,875 | 8% |
| | Profits above £43,875 | 1% |

[1] Earnings between £95 and £110 a week in 2009–10 and between £97 and £110 a week in 2010–11 count towards state benefits even though you pay no NI.
[2] You pay a lower rate if you are contracted out of the state additional pension scheme or at the married women's reduced rate (see Chapter 7).
[3] You can opt out of paying if your profits are no more than £5,075 for the year.

# Capital gains tax

Capital gains tax (CGT) is a tax on a rise in the value of an asset during the time you have owned it. From the 2008–09 tax year onwards, the calculation of CGT was greatly simplified and a new flat rate introduced which had a major impact on investment decisions. Although relatively few people pay CGT (some 350,000 people a year compared with nearly 30 million who pay income tax), it is an important tax for financial planning, particularly investment and inheritance planning, because:

■ gains are taxed more lightly than income – where you have a choice, for example, between different routes for investing in investment funds (see Chapter 9), you can often save tax by selecting an asset which produces capital gain rather than income;

■ the ability to transfer assets between spouses and civil partners free of CGT (and usually inheritance tax too as explained in Chapter 11) enables couples to spread their assets tax efficiently;

■ the tax exemption for your main home opens up some planning possibilities for second-home owners and buy-to-let investors.

## How gains are taxed

A brief outline of CGT is given in Chapter 11 in the context of lifetime gifts. But CGT may arise whenever you dispose of an asset, not just as a gift, but when you sell or even where you receive compensation for an asset that is lost or destroyed. However, some assets and disposals are tax-free. Chapter 11 mentioned the main exemptions, but a more detailed list is given in the box below. The process for working out tax on any gain is described in the steps below and summarised in Figure A.4.

---

### Tax-free capital gains

- Your only or main home.
- Private cars.
- Assets with a predictable useful life of 50 years or less.
- More durable 'tangible moveable assets' (such as personal possessions, jewellery, art and antiques) you sell for less than £6,000.
- British money (including post 1837 sovereigns).
- Foreign currency for your personal spending (but not savings).
- Gambling and lottery winnings.
- Cashback received as an inducement to buy (for example, cashback with a mortgage).
- Gains on life insurance policies (but income tax applies – see p. 266).
- Gains on investments held with ISAs and child trust funds.
- Gains on shares held in enterprise investment schemes for at least three years and venture capital trusts.
- Gains on British government bonds and most corporate bonds (and options to buy or sell them).
- Gifts to charity and some sports clubs.
- Gifts to museums and similar organisations and of heritage property.
- Disposals of land and/or buildings to a housing association.
- Sale of business assets if covered by entrepreneur's relief.
- Assets you leave on death.

---

### Step one: Basic gain

The starting point for working out tax is the price or market value of the item on disposal – called the 'final value'. From this, you deduct the price you paid or the market value of the item when you first acquired it – the 'initial value' – and any allowable expenses. This gives you a basic capital gain or loss.

| BASIC GAIN (EACH DISPOSAL) | | |
|---|---|---|
| Final value | A | |
| Initial value | B | |
| Allowable expenses | C | |
| BASIC GAIN OR LOSS = A – B – C | D× | |

| EXEMPTIONS (EACH DISPOSAL) | | |
|---|---|---|
| Basic gain | D× | |
| Main-home exemption (see p. 377) | | |
| Lettings relief (see p. 378) | | |
| Entrepreneur's relief | | |
| Other exemptions | | |
| TOTAL EXEMPTIONS | E | |
| CHARGEABLE GAIN = D× – E | F× | |

| LOSS RELIEF (ALL DISPOSALS) | | |
|---|---|---|
| Total chargeable gains = sum of all the values F× | F | |
| Total losses this tax year = sum of all the losses D× | D | |
| SUB-TOTAL = F – D | G | |
| Annual allowance[1] | H | |
| SUB-TOTAL = G – H | I | |
| Losses brought forward | J | |
| Brought-forward losses used. The lower of I and J | K | |
| NET CHARGEABLE GAINS = G – K | L | |

[1]  £10,100 in 2009–10. The allowance is usually increased each tax year and the new amount is announced in the annual Budget (see Appendix B).

**Figure A.4**   Capital gains tax calculator

| ANNUAL ALLOWANCE AND TAX | | |
|---|---|---|
| Net chargeable gains | L | |
| Annual allowance[1] | H | |
| TAXABLE GAINS = L – H | M | |
| Tax rate[2] | N | |
| TAX NOW DUE = M × N | O | |

[1] £10,100 in 2009–10. The allowance is usually increased each tax year and the new amount is announced in the annual Budget (see Appendix B).
[2] 18% in 2009–10. The rate is changed infrequently. Any change is announced in the annual Budget (see Appendix B).

**Figure A.4**   Capital gains tax calculator *continued*

Allowable expenses are costs you have incurred buying and selling the asset, for example, stamp duty, broker's or agent's fees, valuations and advertising the sale. Also allowable are the costs of improvements to the asset as long as the improvement is reflected in the sale price you could get, for example, the cost of adding an extension to a property but not just normal maintenance.

There are special rules for 'tangible moveable property' (also called 'chattels'), essentially personal possessions, including artwork and antiques. Any gain is tax-free if the item is predicted to have a useful life of less than 50 years ('wasting assets'). On more durable items, a gain is tax-free if the final value of the item is less than £6,000. If the final value is higher, then any gain is the lower of the actual basic gain or 5/3 of the excess of the final value over £6,000 – see the case study. A loss is restricted to £6,000 less the initial value and allowable expenses, even if the actual final value was less than £6,000. Anti-avoidance legislation prevents you splitting a set into separate components for the purpose of these rules.

There are also special rules for shares – see the box.

## Case study

Jane has been investing in art. She sells a picture that she bought for £4,000 two years ago for £7,500. She has buying and selling costs of £700. Her basic gain is £7,500 – £4,000 – £700 = £2,800. Using the special rules for chattels, the gain would be 5/3 × (£7,500 – £6,000) = £2,500. Since this is lower, her gain for CGT is £2,500.

**Valuing shares for capital gains tax**

Shares of the same type in the same company, and units of the same type in the same unit trust, all look the same. If you have bought some of them at different times from others, and sell only part of a holding, you need a way of identifying which shares or units you are selling. CGT solves this problem by having special rules for matching shares. Your disposals are matched to the shares of units you bought in the following order:

■ shares or units bought or given to you on the same day;

■ shares acquired in the next 30 days: this is an anti-avoidance rule to prevent you selling shares one day and buying them back the next to create a gain or loss purely to save tax;

■ all other shares go into a pool and are treated as if they are a single asset: the initial value and allowable expenses are the averages for the pool.

## Step two: Exemptions

If you have made a gain, you deduct any exemptions and reliefs that apply, for example the main home exemption (see p. 377), lettings relief if you have let out part or all of your home, or entrepreneur's relief if the items have been used in a business. The exemption might cover just part of the gain or the whole amount. You can't use exemptions to create a loss.

## Step three: Loss relief

You add together all your capital gains for a tax year and subtract any losses you have made in the same year. If this reduces the balance to zero and you still have some unused losses, you can carry the losses forward to use in future years.

Next you look at any losses you have carried forward from earlier years and deduct these from any remaining gain. But, in this case, you do not deduct any more than is needed to reduce your remaining gain to the value of the tax-free allowance for the year (£10,100 in 2009–10). Any unused losses continue to be carried forward for use in future years.

## Step four: Tax-free allowance and tax

If, having worked through the steps above, you still have gains left, you next deduct your annual tax-free allowance (£10,100 in 2009–10) and multiply the remainder by 18 per cent to find the tax due. The case study below shows the whole process in action.

## Case study

Felipe inherited a house from his parents ten years ago valued at £100,000. He lived there for one year and let it out for the remaining nine. In 2009–10, he sold the house for £250,000. The costs of selling were £5,000. He made no losses in 2009–10, but he is carrying forward losses from previous years of £20,000. He works out his capital gains tax bill as shown in Figure A.5. For details of the main-home relief and lettings relief he claims, see p. 378. His CGT bill for the year is £3,042.

| BASIC GAIN (EACH DISPOSAL) | | |
|---|---|---|
| Final value | A | £250,000 |
| Initial value | B | £100,000 |
| Allowable expenses | C | £5,000 |
| BASIC GAIN OR LOSS = A – B – C | Dx | £145,000 |

| EXEMPTIONS (EACH DISPOSAL) | | |
|---|---|---|
| Basic gain | Dx | £145,000 |
| Main-home exemption (see p. 377) | | £58,000 |
| Lettings relief (see p. 378) | | £40,000 |
| Entrepreneur's relief | | |
| Other exemptions | | |
| TOTAL EXEMPTIONS | E | £98,000 |
| CHARGEABLE GAIN = Dx – E | Fx | £47,000 |

| LOSS RELIEF (ALL DISPOSALS) | | |
|---|---|---|
| Total chargeable gains = sum of all the values Fx | F | £47,000 |
| Total losses this tax year = sum of all the losses Dx | D | £0 |
| SUB-TOTAL = F – D | G | £47,000 |
| Annual allowance[1] | H | £10,100 |
| SUB-TOTAL = G – H | I | £36,900 |
| Losses brought forward | J | £20,000 |
| Brought-forward losses used. The lower of I and J | K | £20,000 |
| NET CHARGEABLE GAINS = G – K | L | £27,000 |

[1]  £10,100 in 2009–10. The allowance is usually increased each tax year and the new amount is announced in the annual Budget (see Appendix B).

| ANNUAL ALLOWANCE AND TAX | | |
|---|---|---|
| Net chargeable gains | L | £27,000 |
| Annual allowance[1] | H | £10,100 |
| TAXABLE GAINS = L – H | M | £16,900 |
| Tax rate[2] | N | 18% |
| TAX NOW DUE = M × N | O | £3,042 |

[1]  £10,100 in 2009–10. The allowance is usually increased each tax year and the new amount is announced in the annual Budget (see Appendix B).
[2]  18% in 2009–10. The rate is changed infrequently. Any change is announced in the annual Budget (see Appendix B).

**Figure A.5**   **Example of a capital gains tax calculation**

By 2009–10, the difference between the CGT rate of 18 per cent and the top rate of income tax of 40 per cent – due to rise to 50 per cent from 2010–11 onwards – had become very wide. This was providing a strong incentive for taxpayers to arrange their affairs to produce gains rather than income. As a result, at the time of writing, there was considerable speculation that the government would announce an increase in the CGT rate in the 2010 Budget, probably with effect from 2010–11 onwards.

## Special CGT rules for your main home

There is normally no CGT on any gain you make when you sell your only or main home – this is called 'private residence relief'. However, there may be tax to pay if you have used part of your home exclusively for business, let out part or all of it, or you have spent extended periods living away from home. The general rule is that relief is then apportioned on a time basis and, in the case of business use, whatever basis you agree with the Revenue (say, area). For example, if a property counted as your main home for four out of ten years, 6/10th of any gain would be taxable. If you used one out of seven rooms exclusively for business, 1/7th of any gain could be taxable.

Because of the way these rules work, if you buy or inherit a property and decide to let it to generate income, it is worth thinking about making it your own main home for a while. That way, you will be able to reduce or even eliminate any capital gain when you sell – see the case study on p. 379.

## Periods away from home

In general, for periods when you live somewhere else, your home does not qualify for relief. But some periods away are ignored:

■ the first year (sometimes extended to the first two) if your home is not yet ready to move into because of building work or modernisation;

■ the last three years of ownership (whether you are then living there or not);

■ periods of any length if you have to live elsewhere in job-related accommodation, provided you intend to live in your own home eventually;

■ provided you live in the home before the first absence and after the last:

  – periods up to four years in total if your employer requires you to live elsewhere in the UK;

  – periods of any length if your employer requires you to work abroad;

  – any other absences up to a total of three years.

## Lettings relief

Taking in a lodger who has their own room but shares your living space does not jeopardise CGT relief on your home. However, taking in more than one lodger might, because the Revenue could argue that you are running a business. (In either case, you could claim Rent-a-Room relief for the income you make in rents, see p. 15.)

If you let out part of your home as a self-contained unit, while you live in the rest, you get private residence relief only on the part you still live in. And, if you let out your whole home for a time, the whole of any gain for that period is potentially taxable. However, provided the property has been your main home for at least some of the time during which you have owned it, you can claim lettings relief. This is a deduction in your CGT bill equal to the lower of:

■ the amount of the gain;

■ the amount of private residence relief you do get; or

■ £40,000.

# Case study

Felipe inherited a house from his parents ten years ago valued at £100,000. He lived there for one year and let it out for the remaining nine. In 2009–10, he sold the house for £250,000, making a basic gain of £145,000, after deducting the costs of selling the home. He works out the proportion of the gain which is eligible for private residence relief:

■ the one year he lived in the home;

■ the last three years he owned the home, even though he had moved out years earlier.

Therefore, 4/10th × £145,000 = £58,000 of the gain qualifies for relief. The remaining £87,000 is attributable to the letting. Because the property was his main home for a while, Felipe can claim lettings relief. This is the lower of the actual gain £87,000, an amount equal to the private residence relief of £58,000, and £40,000. In this case, the lettings relief is £40,000.

Therefore, the chargeable gain on the house is £145,000 – £58,000 – £40,000 = £47,000.

## *More than one home*

At any one time, only one property can be your main residence. If you have more than one home, unless you elect otherwise, your main home will be the one which, on the facts, seems to be the one where you mainly live. This would be decided on, for example, where you are registered to vote, where your post and phone calls go, where you usually sleep at night, and so on.

However, within two years of acquiring a new home, you can elect which is to be treated as your main home. In this case, the facts are disregarded and you can elect whichever home you like – even if the one you elect as your main home is not the one where you spend most of your time. But whichever you elect must be a place where you genuinely reside at least some of the time – it can't be, for example, a buy-to-let property that you own but never live in.

Once you have made the election, you can then change it whenever you like and as often as you like.

If you missed the two-year window for making an election, you can create a new opportunity by acquiring a new home. The rules do not depend on you owning the home – it could be somewhere you rent for a while.

A husband and wife or civil partners who live together can only have one main home between them for CGT purposes. An unmarried couple can each elect to have a different main home.

## Case study

Carol and Ted live in Somerset but also have a small flat in London which Ted has been using on business trips. When they moved to the country, they elected for their Somerset home to be their main home. Now they are planning to sell the London flat. They alter their election so that the London flat is their main home; a week later they alter the election again making the Somerset house their main home. The effect of these changes is that:

■ Since the London flat has been their main home (albeit for a week), the last three years of ownership now qualify for private residence relief. This reduces the CGT due as a result of the sale.

■ When they eventually dispose of the Somerset home, one week's worth of any gain will be subject to CGT. This is likely to be a trivial sum easily covered by their annual tax-free allowances.

# How tax is collected

If you work for an employer or receive a pension from an occupational scheme or personal pension, the employer or pension provider will operate Pay-As-You-Earn (PAYE). This is a system of deducting what you owe in tax and, if applicable, National Insurance direct from your pay or pension before the remainder is paid out to you. PAYE is used to collect not just tax on the pay or pension itself, but also tax due on other income you have, such as higher rate tax due on savings income and tax on your state pension.

If it is not possible to collect part or all of the tax you are due to pay through PAYE, instead it is collected through the self-assessment system. This will apply, for example, if you are self-employed or you have income from renting property or taxable capital gains. Each year you must fill in a tax return. Tax is usually collected in two instalments (called payments on account) on 31 January and 31 July, with a final balancing charge or refund on the following 31 January. For example, in the 2009–10 tax year, payments on account are due on 31 January 2010 and 31 July 2010 with the final payment/refund on 31 January 2011.

# Tax credits

Despite the name, tax credits are state benefits (rather than anything to do with your tax bill). However, the amount you can get is based on your taxable income (with some adjustments). There are two types of tax credit – child tax credit for families with children and working tax credit for people on a low income – but they work together as an integrated system.

You can get a rough idea of the tax credits you can claim by using the calculator in Figure A.6. For a more precise check, use the online calculator

| INCOME ADJUSTMENTS | | £ a year |
|---|---|---|
| Your income for income tax purposes | A | |
| Income threshold<br>£6,420 if you are eligible for WTC in 2010–11<br>£16,190 if you are eligible for CTC only in 2010–11 | B | |
| Income in excess of threshold = A – B | C | |
| Taper rate 39% in 2010–11 | D | |
| ADJUSTMENT = C × D | E | |

| WORKING TAX CREDIT (WTC) EXCEPT CHILDCARE ELEMENT | | |
|---|---|---|
| WTC elements except childcare element from Table A.5 | | |
| Total WTC elements (except childcare) | F | |
| Lower of amounts E and F | G | |
| ADJUSTED WTC EXCEPT CHILDCARE ELEMENT = F – G | H | |
| Remaining adjustment = E – G | I | |

| WTC CHILDCARE ELEMENT | | |
|---|---|---|
| WTC childcare element<br>Weekly childcare costs up to limits in Table A.5 × 52 × 80% | J | |
| Lower of amounts I and J | K | |
| ADJUSTED WTC CHILDCARE ELEMENT = J – K | L | |
| Remaining adjustment = I – K | M | |

**Figure A.6**  Tax credits calculator

| CHILD TAX CREDIT (CTC) EXCEPT FAMILY ELEMENT | | |
| --- | --- | --- |
| Child elements from Table A.5 | | |
| Total child elements | N | |
| Lower of amounts M and N | O | |
| ADJUSTED CTC CHILDCARE ELEMENTS = N – O | P | |

| CTC FAMILY ELEMENT | | |
| --- | --- | --- |
| Your income for income tax purposes | A | |
| Income threshold £50,000 in 2010–11 | Q | |
| Income in excess of threshold = A – Q | R | |
| Taper rate 6.67% in 2010–11 | S | |
| Adjustment = R × S | T | |
| Family element from Table A.5 | U | |
| ADJUSTED FAMILY ELEMENT = U – T | V | |

| TOTAL TAX CREDITS | |
| --- | --- |
| TOTAL TAX CREDITS = H + L + P + V | |

**Figure A.6**  Tax credits calculator *continued*

on the HM Revenue & Customs website at www.hmrc.gov.uk/taxcredits/ questionnaires.htm. You claim by contacting the Tax Credits Helpline (see Appendix B). Credits are paid direct to your bank account.

## Families with children

You can qualify for child tax credit (CTC) if you have one or more children for whom you are claiming child benefit. Your initial entitlement is worked out by adding together the elements from Table A.5 that apply in your situation. This initial entitlement is then reduced if your income is above the relevant threshold. The family element only starts to be reduced if your income is more than £50,000 a year, so the vast majority of families are eligible for some CTC.

## Table A.5  Tax credits

| Element | Maximum in 2009–10 | Maximum in 2010–11 |
| --- | --- | --- |
| *Working tax credit (WTC)* | | |
| Basic element (everyone gets this) | £1,890 | £1,920 |
| Couple and lone parent element | £1,860 | £1,890 |
| 30-hour element (if claimant and/or partner work at least 30 hours a week) | £775 | £790 |
| Disabled worker element | £2,530 | £2,570 |
| Severe disability element | £1,075 | £1,095 |
| 50+ (working 16–29 hours) | £1,300 | £1,320 |
| 50+ (working 30 hours or more) | £1,935 | £1,965 |
| Childcare element – one child | 80% of up to £175 a week of eligible costs | 80% of up to £175 a week of eligible costs |
| Childcare element – two or more children | 80% of up to £300 a week of eligible costs | 80% of up to £300 a week of eligible costs |
| *Child tax credit (CTC)* | | |
| Family element | £545 | £545 |
| Family element, baby addition (for child under age one) | £545 | £545 |
| Child element (per child) | £2,235 | £2,300 |
| Disabled child element (per child) | £2,670 | £2,715 |
| Severely disabled child element (per child) | £1,075 | £1,095 |
| *Income thresholds and tapers* | | |
| WTC threshold | £6,420 | £6,420 |
| CTC-only threshold | £16,040 | £16,190 |
| Taper rate | 39% | 39% |
| CTC-family element threshold | £50,000 | £50,000 |
| Taper rate | 6.67% | 6.67% |

## Working tax credit

You can claim working tax credit (WTC) if you are:

- aged 25 or over and you or your partner work at least 30 hours a week;
- aged 16 or over with children (lone parent or couple) and you or your partner work at least 16 hours a week;
- aged 16 or over with a disability that puts you at a disadvantage getting a job and you or your partner work at least 16 hours a week;
- over 50 returning to work after a period of at least six months claiming specified state benefits and you now work at least 16 hours a week.

As with CTC, your initial entitlement is calculated by adding up all the elements in Table A.5 that apply to you.

If you have children, WTC can include a childcare element. This reimburses 80 per cent of your childcare costs up to set limits. To qualify for this element, you must either be a lone parent working at least 16 hours a week, or a couple and you both work at least 16 hours a week (unless one of you is unable to work because of illness or disability).

Your initial entitlement to WTC is reduced if your income is above a specified threshold. Tax credits are reduced in the following order of priority: first, any WTC other than the childcare element; next the WTC childcare element; and lastly CTC. The case study below shows how this works in practice.

## What income to use

Your entitlement to tax credits is based broadly on your income as defined for income-tax purposes. Essentially, your credits for this year are based on your income for this year, but there are some special rules that create exceptions.

- At the time you claim tax credits, usually you do not know what your income for the whole year will be. Therefore, initially your claim is based on your income for the previous tax year.
- After the end of the year, your income is known and so it is possible to correct your tax credit claim. If your income this year is lower than your income last year, you will have received too little and your tax credits will be increased. But, if your income this year is higher than it was last year, you will not necessarily have to pay back the excess credits you have received. This is because the first £25,000 of any increase in income is disregarded.

# Case study

Rob and Shivani have two children, aged three and six. Both parents work, Rob more than 30 hours a week. Between them, they earn £30,000 a year. They pay £200 a week in childcare costs for one of the children. In 2010–11, they qualify for £7,829 a year in tax credits – see Figure A.7.

| INCOME ADJUSTMENTS | | £ a year |
|---|---|---|
| Your income for income tax purposes | A | £30,000 |
| Income threshold<br>£6,420 if you are eligible for WTC in 2010–11<br>£16,190 if you are eligible for CTC only in 2010–11 | B | £6,420 |
| Income in excess of threshold = A – B | C | £23,580 |
| Taper rate 39% in 2010–11 | D | 39% |
| ADJUSTMENT = C × D | E | £9,196 |
| **WORKING TAX CREDIT (WTC) EXCEPT CHILDCARE ELEMENT** | | |
| WTC elements except childcare element<br>Basic<br>Couple<br>30 hour | | £1,920<br>£1,890<br>£790 |
| Total WTC elements (except childcare) | F | £4,600 |
| Lower of amounts E and F | G | £4,600 |
| ADJUSTED WTC EXCEPT CHILDCARE ELEMENT = F – G | H | £0 |
| Remaining adjustment = E – G | I | £4,596 |
| **WTC CHILDCARE ELEMENT** | | |
| WTC childcare element<br>Weekly childcare costs up to limits in Table A.5 × 52 × 80% | J | £175 × 52 × 80%<br>= £7,280 |
| Lower of amounts I and J | K | £4,596 |
| ADJUSTED WTC CHILDCARE ELEMENT = J – K | L | £2,684 |
| Remaining adjustment = I – K | M | £0 |

**Figure A.7**    **Example of a tax credits calculation**

| CHILD TAX CREDIT (CTC) EXCEPT FAMILY ELEMENT | | |
|---|---|---|
| Child elements from Table A.5 | | 2 × £2,300 |
| Total child elements | N | £4,600 |
| Lower of amounts M and N | O | £0 |
| ADJUSTED CTC CHILD ELEMENTS = N – O | P | £4,600 |

| CTC FAMILY ELEMENT | | |
|---|---|---|
| Your income for income tax purposes | A | £30,000 |
| Income threshold £50,000 in 2009–10 | Q | £50,000 |
| Income in excess of threshold = A – Q | R | £0 |
| Taper rate 6.67% in 2009–10 | S | 6.67% |
| Adjustment = R × S | T | £0 |
| Family element from Table A.5 | U | £545 |
| ADJUSTED FAMILY ELEMENT = U – T | V | £545 |

| TOTAL TAX CREDITS | |
|---|---|
| TOTAL TAX CREDITS = H + L + P + V | £0 + £2,684 + £4,600 + £545 = £7,829 |

**Figure A.7**  Example of a tax credits calculation *continued*

# Appendix B: Useful contacts and further information

*Accountant – to find one*

*Look in the Yellow Pages under 'Accountants' or contact the following profes-sional bodies for a list of their members in your area:*

Association of Chartered Certified Accountants
29 Lincoln's Inn Fields
London WC2A 3EE
Tel: 020 7059 5000
www.acca.co.uk

Institute of Chartered Accountants in England and Wales
Chartered Accountants' Hall (Moorgate Place)
PO Box 433
London EC2R 6EA
Tel: 020 7920 8100
www.icaew.co.uk

Institute of Chartered Accountants in Ireland
Burlington House
Burlington Road
Dublin 4
Tel: +353 1 637 7200
www.icai.ie

Institute of Chartered Accountants of Scotland
CA House
21 Haymarket Yards
Edinburgh EH12 5BH
Tel: 0131 347 0100
www.icas.org.uk

## ADVFN

www.advfn.co.uk

## Advice NI (Northern Ireland)

www.adviceni.net

## Affordable Art Fair Ltd

Tel: 020 7371 8787

## Age Concern–Help the Aged

(England) Freepost (SWB 30375), Ashburton, Devon TQ13 7ZZ
Tel: 0800 00 99 66 (freephone)
www.ageconcern.org.uk

(England) 207–221 Pentonville Road, London N1 9UZ
Tel: 020 7278 1114
www.helptheaged.org.uk

(Northern Ireland) 3 Lower Crescent, Belfast BT7 1NR
Tel: 028 9024 5729
www.ageconcernni.org

(Scotland) Causewayside House, 160 Causewayside, Edinburgh EH9 1PR
Helpline: 0845 833 0200
www.ageconcernandhelptheagedscotland.org.uk

(Wales) Units 13–14, Neptune Court, Vanguard Way, Cardiff CF24 5PJ
Tel: 029 2043 1555
www.accymru.org.uk

## Asset allocation tool

Iowa Public Employees Retirement System
www.ipers.org/calcs/AssetAllocator.html

## The Association of Art and Antique Dealers

Tel: 020 7823 3511
www.lapada.co.uk

## The Association of British Credit Unions (ABCUL)

Holyoake House
Hanover Street
Manchester M60 OAS
Tel: 0161 832 3694
www.abcul.org

## Association of British Insurers

51 Gresham Street
London EC2V 7HQ
Tel: 020 7600 3333
www.abi.org.uk

## Association of Consulting Actuaries

St Clement's House
27-28 Clement's Lane
London EC4N 7AE
Tel: 020 3207 9380
www.aca.org.uk

## Association of Investment Companies

9th floor, 24 Chiswell Street
London EC1Y 4YY
Tel: 020 7282 5555
www.theaic.co.uk

## Association of Private Client Investment Managers and Stockbrokers (APCIMS)

22 City Road
Finsbury Square
London EC1Y 2AJ
Tel: 020 7448 7100
www.apcims.co.uk

## Association of Residential Letting Agents (ARLA)

Arbon House
6 Tournament Court
Edgehill Drive
Warwick
CV34 6LG
Tel: 01926 496800
www.arla.co.uk

## Association of Tax Technicians

1st floor, Artillery House
11–19 Artillery Row
London SW1P 1RT
Tel: 0844 251 0830
www.att.org.uk

## Auction houses

Christie's
Tel: 020 7389 2820
www.christies.com

Sotheby's
Tel: 020 7293 6060
www.sothebys.com

## Bank of England – base rate

www.bankofengland.co.uk/monetarypolicy

## Banksafe Online

www.banksafeonline.org.uk

## Barclays Capital

5 The North Colonnade
Canary Wharf
London E14 4BB
United Kingdom
Tel: 020 7623 2323
www.barcap.com

## The British Antique Dealers' Association

Tel: 020 7589 4128
www.bada.org

## British Bankers' Association (BBA)

Tel: 020 7216 8800
www.bba.org.uk

## British Business Angels Association (BBAA)

Tel: 0207 089 2305
www.bbaa.org.uk

## British Insurance Brokers Association (BIBA)

8th Floor
John Stow House
18 Bevis Marks
London EC3A 7JB
Tel: 0870 950 1790
www.biba.org.uk

## Budget (annual)

www.hm-treasury.gov.uk
www.hmrc.gov.uk

## Building Societies Association (BSA)

6th Floor, York House
23 Kingsway
London
WC2B 6UJ
BSA consumer line: 020 7520 5900
www.bsa.org.uk

## Chartered Institute of Taxation

First floor
11–19 Artillery Row
London SW1P 1RT
Tel: 0844 579 6700 or 020 7340 0550
www.tax.org.uk

## Child Trust Funds

Child Trust Fund Office
Waterview Park
Mandarin Way
Washington NE38 8QG
Tel: 0845 302 1470
www.childtrustfund.gov.uk

## Citizens Advice

For local bureau, see phone book or www.citizensadvice.org.uk
For online information: www.adviceguide.org.uk

## Community Legal Advice

*For lawyers and advice centres in your area (England and Wales only) able to
help with, for example, debt problems and state benefits.*
Advice line: 0845 345 4345
www.communitylegaladvice.org.uk

## Competition Commission

Victoria House
Southampton Row
London WC1B 4AD
Tel: 020 7271 0100
www.competition-commission.org.uk

## Consumer Credit Counselling Service

Wade House
Merrion Centre
Leeds LS2 8NG
Tel: 0800 138 1111
www.cccs.co.uk

## Consumer Focus

4th Floor
Artillery House
Artillery Row
London SW1P 1RT
Tel: 020 7799 7900
www.consumerfocus.org.uk

## Co-operative Bank

www.co-operativebank.co.uk
www.smile.co.uk

## Council of Mortgage Lenders

Bush House
North West Wing
Aldwych
London WC2B 4PJ
Tel: 0845 373 6771
www.cml.org.uk

## Covered warrants

www.londonstockexchange.com/specialist-issuers/covered-warrants/
coveredwarrants.htm

## Credit unions

See separate entry for Association of British Credit Unions.

## Debt advice

Advice NI (Northern Ireland)
www.adviceni.net

Citizens Advice Bureau (England, Wales and Northern Ireland)
See phone book www.citizensadvice.org.uk (England and Wales)
www.citizensadvice.co.uk (Northern Ireland)

Citizens Advice Scotland
See phone book
www.cas.org.uk

Consumer Credit Counselling Service
Tel: 0800 138 1111
www.cccs.co.uk

Community Legal Advice (England and Wales)
Tel: 0845 345 4345
www.communitylegaladvice.org.uk

Debt Advice Network
Tel: 0300 011 2340
www.debtadvicenetwork.org

Debtline NI (Northern Ireland)
Tel: 0800 027 4990
www.debtlineni.org

Money Advice Scotland
Tel: 0141 572 0237
www.moneyadvicescotland.org.uk

National Debtline
Tel: 0800 808 4000
www.nationaldebtline.co.uk

PayPlan
Tel: 0800 716 239
www.payplan.com

## Debt Management Office

Eastcheap Court
11 Philpot Lane
London EC3M 8UD
Tel: 0845 357 6500
www.dmo.gov.uk

## Department of Health (Long-term care policy)

Big Care Debate
www.ournhs.nhs.uk/?p=1399

## Disability Benefits Centre

Warbreck House
Warbreck Hill
Blackpool FY2 0YE
Tel: 0845 712 3456
Benefit Enquiry Line (BEL): 0800 88 22 00
BEL textphone: 0800 24 33 55

## Direct.gov

*Information about all aspects of government and government services.*

www.direct.gov.uk

Redundancy calculator
www.direct.gov.uk/redundancy.dsb.

State pension age calculator
www.direct.gov.uk/en/Diol1/DoItOnline/DG_4017967

## Discount brokers

Chase de Vere
Tel: 0845 140 4014
www.awdchasedevere.co.uk/clients/cofunds/index.html

Hargreaves Lansdown
Tel: 0117 900 9000
www.h-l.co.uk

## Ecology Building Society

7 Belton Road
Silsden
Keighley
West Yorkshire
BD20 0EE
Tel: 0845 674 5566
www.ecology.co.uk

## Energy Saving Trust

Tel: 0800 512 012
www.energysavingtrust.co.uk

## Entitled to (state benefits calculator)

www.entitledto.org.uk
www.direct.gov.uk (Benefits adviser)

## Ethical Investment Research Society (EIRIS)

80–84 Bondway
London SW8 1SF
Tel: 020 7840 5700
www.eiris.org

## Ethical saving and investing

*See separate entries for:*
Co-operative Bank
Ecology Building Society
Ethical Investment Research Society (EIRIS)
Triodos

## European Health Insurance Card

EHIC Enquiries
PO Box 1114
Newcastle upon Tyne NE99 2TL
Tel: 0845 605 0707
www.dh.gov.uk/en/Policyandguidance/Healthadvicefortravellers/index.
htm

## Financial Ombudsman Service (FOS)

South Quay Plaza
183 Marsh Wall
London E14 9SR
Tel: 0845 080 1800 or 0300 123 9 123
www.financial-ombudsman.org.uk

## Financial Services Authority (FSA)

25 The North Colonnade London E14 5HS
Consumer helpline: 0300 500 5000
www.moneymadeclear.fsa.gov.uk

FSA Comparative Tables
Tel: 0300 500 5000
www.fsa.gov.uk/tables

FSA Register
Tel: 0300 500 5000
www.fsa.gov.uk/register/home.do

## Financial Services Compensation Scheme (FSCS)

7th Floor, Lloyds Chambers
Portsoken Street
London E1 8BN
Tel: 0800 678 1100 or 020 7892 7300
www.fscs.org.uk

## Financial Times

www.ft.com/home/uk

## Fund supermarkets

Chase de Vere
Tel: 0845 140 4014
www.awdchasedevere.co.uk/clients/cofunds/index.html

Funds Direct
www.fundsdirect.co.uk

Hargreaves Lansdown
Tel: 0117 900 9000
www.h-l.co.uk

Interactive Investor
www.iii.co.uk/funds

This is Money
www.sfsinvestdirect.co.uk/thisismoney/

## Funeral Planning Authority

Knellstone House
Udimore
Rye
East Sussex
TN31 6AR
Tel: 0845 601 9619
www.funeralplanningauthority.co.uk

## Government websites

Department for Communities and Local Government
www.communities.gov.uk

Department of Health
www.dh.gov.uk

Department for Work and Pensions (DWP)
www.dwp.gov.uk

HM Revenue & Customs
www.hmrc.gov.uk

www.direct.gov.uk

## Heyday

http://www.ageconcern.org.uk/heyday/

## HM Revenue & Customs (HMRC)

For local tax enquiry centres look in phone book under 'Inland Revenue'
For your own tax office, check your tax return or other correspondence or
ask your employer or the scheme paying your pension.
Orderline 0845 9000 404
www.hmrc.gov.uk.

Enterprise investment scheme
www.hmrc.gov.uk/eis

National Insurance married women's reduced rate contributions
www.hmrc.gov.uk/ni/reducedrate/marriedwomen.htm

National Insurance voluntary contributions
www.hmrc.gov.uk/ni/volcontr/basics.htm

Venture capital trusts
www.hmrc.gov.uk/guidance/vct.htm

## HMRC Inheritance Tax

(England and Wales) Ferrers House, PO Box 38, Nottingham NG2 1BB

(Northern Ireland) Level 5, Millennium House, 17–25 Great Victoria Street,
Belfast BT2 7BN

(Scotland) Meldrum House, 15 Drumsheugh Gardens, Edinburgh EH3 7UG

Probate and IHT Helpline: 0845 302 0900 (calls charged at local rates)
www.hmrc.gov.uk/inheritancetax

## HSBC Amanah Finance

www.hsbcamanah.com

## IFA Promotion

www.unbiased.co.uk

## Ifs ProShare

8th Floor
Peninsular House
36 Monument Street
London
EC3R 8LJ
Tel: 020 7444 7104
www.ifsproshare.org

## Independent financial adviser (IFA) – to find one

*For a list of IFAs in your area, contact:*

IFA Promotion
www.unbiased.co.uk

The Institute of Financial Planning
www.financialplanning.org.uk

Personal Finance Society
www.findanadviser.org/find_an_adviser.aspx

## Independent financial advisers who specialise in annuities

The Annuity Bureau
Tel: 0800 071 8111
www.annuity-bureau.co.uk

Annuity Direct
Tel: 0500 50 65 75
www.annuitydirect.co.uk

WBA Ltd
Tel: 0207 484 5366
www.williamburrows.com

## Insolvency Service

www.insolvency.gov.uk

## Institute of Financial Planning

Whitefriars Centre
Lewins Mead
Bristol BS1 2NT
Tel: 0117 945 2470
www.financialplanning.org.uk

## Insurance broker

Look in phone book under 'Insurance – Intermediaries'.

See entries for British Insurance Brokers Association.

To check an intermediary is authorised contact the FSA Register (see above).

## Internet comparison sites

www.fsa.gov.uk/tables
www.moneyfacts.co.uk
www.moneysupermarket.com
www.uswitch.com

## The Institute of Islamic Banking and Insurance

12–14 Barkat House
116–118 Finchley Road
London NW3 5HT
Tel: 020 7245 0404
www.islamic-banking.com

## Investment fund websites

www.abi.org.uk
www.citywire.co.uk
www.fsa.gov.uk/tables
www.fundsdirect.co.uk
www.fundsnetwork.co.uk
www.investmentuk.org

www.morningstar.co.uk
www.splitsonline.co.uk
www.theaic.co.uk
www.trustnet.co.uk

## Investment Management Association (IMA)

65 Kingsway
London WC2B 6TD
Information line: 020 7269 4639
www.investmentuk.org

## Iowa Public Employees Retirement System

www.ipers.org/calcs/AssetAllocator.html

## Islamic Bank of Britain

Islamic Bank of Britain plc
PO Box 12461
Birmingham
B16 6AQ
0121 452 7205
www.islamic-bank.com

## Jobcentre Plus

For local office, check website or see Phone Book.
www.jobcentreplus.gov.uk

## LIFFE

Cannon Bridge House
1 Cousin Lane
London
EC4R 3XX
Tel: 020 7623 0444
www.euronext.com

## Local authority

See phone book under the name of your local authority.

## London Stock Exchange

10 Paternoster Square
London EC4M 7LS
Tel: 020 7797 1000
www.londonstockexchange.com

## Lost accounts

To trace lost bank and building society accounts or NS&I investments
www.mylostaccount.org.uk

## Money Advice Scotland

*For contact details of local debt advisers:*
Tel: 0141 572 0237
www.moneyadvicescotland.org.uk

## Money Guidance

Tel: 0300 500 5000
www.moneymadeclear.fsa.gov.uk

## Moneyfacts

*Larger public reference libraries may have copies.*
Moneyfacts House
66–70 Thorpe Road
Norwich
NR1 1BJ
Subscriptions 0845 1689 600
www.moneyfacts.co.uk

## Moneymadeclear

Tel: 0300 500 5000
www.moneymadeclear.fsa.gov.uk

## Mortgage broker

www.unbiased.co.uk/find-a-mortgage-adviser/
To check an intermediary is authorised contact the FSA Register (see above).

## National Debtline

Tel: 0808 808 4000
www.nationaldebtline.co.uk

## National Friendly Society

Tel: 0800 195 9246
www.nationalfriendly.co.uk

## National Savings & Investments (NS&I)

Tel: 0845 964 5000
www.nsandi.com

## Newspaper money pages

Most Sunday papers
Saturday editions of the *Financial Times, Guardian* and *Independent*
Wednesday edition of *Daily Express* and *Daily Mail*

## NHS Choices (England only)

http://www.nhs.uk/Pages/HomePage.aspx

## NHS Direct (England only)

Tel: 0845 4647
www.nhsdirect.nhs.uk

## NYSE Euronext

See LIFFE

## Office for National Statistics

Personal inflation calculator tool: www.statistics.gov.uk/pic

## Payplan

Kempton House
Dysart Road
Grantham
Lincolnshire
NG31 7LE
Tel: 0800 716 239
www.payplan.com

## Pension Protection Fund/Fraud Compensation Fund

*Pension scheme members should first contact their scheme*
Knollys House
17 Addiscombe Road
Croydon CR0 6SR
Tel: 0845 600 2541
www.pensionprotectionfund.org.uk

## Pension scheme administrator (occupational pension scheme)

*Usually located in your Human Resources (Personnel) Department. Contact details will also be in any booklet and correspondence about the scheme and on any pensions noticeboard at work.*

## Pension scheme trustees

*Contact details will also be in any booklet and correspondence about the scheme and on any pensions noticeboard at work.*

## The Pension Service

*For local office, check website or see phone book.*

Tyneview Park, Whitely Road, Newcastle upon Tyne NE98 1BA
General enquiries: 0845 60 60 265
Textphone: 0845 60 60 285

International Pension Centre: +44 (0) 191 218 7777

Pension credit application line: 0800 99 1234

Pension tracing service: 0845 6002 537
www.direct.gov.uk

State pension forecast: 0845 3000 168

## The Pensions Advisory Service (TPAS)

11 Belgrave Road
London SW1V 1RB
Tel: 0845 601 2923
www.pensionsadvisoryservice.org.uk

## The Pensions Regulator

Napier House
Trafalgar Place
Brighton BN1 4DW
Tel: 0870 606 3636
www.thepensionsregulator.gov.uk

## Pension Tracing Service

Tyneview Park
Whitley Road
Newcastle upon Tyne NE98 1BA
Tel: 0845 6002 537
www.direct.gov.uk

## Personal finance magazines

*Investment Life and Pensions Moneyfacts* and *Moneyfacts* – subscriptions 0845
1689 600; www.moneyfacts.co.uk/subscribe

*Money Management* – subscriptions and back issues 0845 456151 – and
from newsagents

## The Personal Finance Society

www.findanadviser.org/find_an__adviser.aspx

## Personal finance websites

*There are many of these. Useful sites include:*

www.fool.co.uk
www.ft.com/personal-finance
www.moneyexpert.com
www.moneyextra.com
www.moneyfacts.co.uk
www.moneynet.co.uk
www.moneysavingexpert.com
www.moneysupermarket.com

## Primary Care Trust (England)

www.nhs.uk/servicedirectories/Pages/PrimaryCareTrustListing.aspx

## Rent-a-Room Relief

www.hmrc.gov.uk/manuals/pimmanual/pim4001.htm

## Safe Home Income Plans (SHIP)

83 Victoria Street
London SW1H 0HW
Tel: 0844 669 7085
www.ship-ltd.org

## Scottish Government

www.scotland.gov.uk

## Search engines (examples)

www.alltheweb.com
www.altavista.com
www.dogpile.com
www.google.com

## Simplyhealth

www.simplyhealth.co.uk

## Society of Pension Consultants

Tel: 020 7353 1688
www.spc.uk.com

## Society of Trust and Estate Practitioners

Artillery House (South)
11–19 Artillery Road
London
SW1P 1RT
Tel: 020 7340 0500
Answerphone for list of members: 020 7340 0506
www.step.org

## Solicitor – to find one

*Look in the Yellow Pages under 'Solicitors' or contact the following professional bodies for a list of their members in your area:*

Law Society
113 Chancery Lane
London WC2A 1PL
Tel: 0870 606 2555
www.lawsociety.org.uk

Law Society of Northern Ireland
96 Victoria Street
Belfast BT1 3GN
Tel: 028 9023 1614
www.lawsoc-ni.org

Law Society of Scotland
26 Drumsheugh Gardens
Edinburgh EH3 7YR
Tel: 0131 226 7411
www.lawscot.org.uk

## Spread betting firms (examples)

www.cityindex.co.uk
www.financial-spread-betting.com
www.igindex.co.uk

## Stockbroker – to find one

*See separate entries for:*

Association of Personal Client Investment Managers and Stockbrokers

London Stock Exchange

## Tax advice

*See separate entries for:*

Accountants

Chartered Institute of Taxation

Society of Trust and Estate Practitioners

Tax Aid

Tax Help for Older People

## Tax Aid

Room 304
Linton House
164–180 Union Street
London SE1 0LH
Tel: 0845 120 3779
www.taxaid.org.uk

## Tax Credits Office

Tel: 0845 300 3900
www.hmrc.gov.uk/taxcredits

## Tax Help for Older People

Helpline: 0845 601 3321
www.litrg.org.uk/about/activities/index.cfm

## Tax Office

See entry for HM Revenue and Customs.

## Triodos bank

www.triodos.co.uk

## Yahoo Finance

http://uk.finance.yahoo.com

# Index